THE FUN OF IT

THE FUN

OF IT

STORIES FROM
THE TALK OF THE TOWN

THE NEW YORKER

EDITED BY LILLIAN ROSS

INTRODUCTION BY DAVID REMNICK

THE MODERN LIBRARY
NEW YORK

All of the pieces in this collection were originally published in
The New Yorker. The publication date of
each piece is given at the end of the piece.

Library of Congress Cataloging-in-Publication Data

The fun of it: stories from "The talk of the town": The New
Yorker / edited by Lillian Ross;
introduction by David Remnick.
p.   cm.
ISBN 0-375-75649-3
I. Ross, Lillian. II. New Yorker (New York, N.Y.: 1925)

AC5 .F86   2001
00068237—dc21   00-068237

Modern Library website address: www.modernlibrary.com

Printed in the United States of America

4 6 8 9 7 5

ACKNOWLEDGMENTS

This book was created with the special help of Erin Overbey, and with the support of other talented people at *The New Yorker*, including Ann Goldstein, Dana Goodyear, Marshall Heyman, Ed Klaris, Pam McCarthy, Brenda Phipps, David Remnick, and Christopher Shay. Susan Morrison generously lent her particular touches—to be found weekly in *The New Yorker*'s The Talk of the Town—to this book as well. Modern Library's David Ebershoff, Christen Kidd, and Judy Sternlight shared their expertise with me. I thank them, one and all.

CONTENTS

1940s

INTRODUCTION

DAVID REMNICK

Fairly often, Lillian Ross will call the office to say, "I've got a good little story." She has been doing this for fifty years or so, and, in the particulars, it can mean anything. It can mean she's just paid a visit to Federico Fellini or Robin Williams; it can mean she's been listening in on the talk of private-school kids on the East Side; it can mean she's been hanging out on a movie set near the Cross Bronx Expressway. Anything. But what it always means, in the end, is that The Talk of the Town, one of the few features of *The New Yorker* that have been there from the very first issue, will bear her imprint that week.

Lillian Ross has been writing for The Talk of the Town since the last months of the Second World War, and she has never lost the taste for it—the fun of getting around the city, the immediacy and wit of the section at its best, the thrill of writing in a form that demands compression but allows for immense variety. Lillian is no cub reporter; she could easily stick with the more leisurely varieties of writing and labor, but she still likes a deadline. She's always ready to drop whatever she's doing, go off to report a Talk story, write it up that evening (she'll work all night to get it right), and hand it in the next morning. When the editors or fact checkers call to consult her on some change or other, they may well be told she is out—out taking a run around the Central Park reservoir.

From Thurber to Ross through Mark Singer and Nancy Franklin, Talk writers have shown a gift for telling a story in inventive ways. As a young Talk writer, John Updike could tell a story simply by quoting the overheard conversation at a bar or in a park; Philip Hamburger liked to go to Big Events, especially presidential inaugurals, and find his story within a story. It's never been much of a secret to the editors that readers of *The New Yorker* are most likely to read the short things first: above all, the cartoons and The Talk of the Town. And, like the cartoons, the best Talk pieces have a combustive power; they are miniatures that provide a burst of pleasure and a revelatory glimpse into some corner of life.

To read *The Fun of It* is to come across overlooked masterpieces by well-known writers (E. B. White's "Potter's Field" or James Thurber's "The Joyces"); to discover writers, such as Geoffrey Hellman, John McCarten, and Maeve Brennan, whose names have not persisted the way they should have; and to delight in some curiosities (a piece by Jacqueline Onassis—who knew?—and one by William Shawn, who edited the section himself for decades).

Nearly twenty years ago, I bought Lillian's book *Reporting,* a collection of longer pieces, mainly because her Profiles of Ernest Hemingway and the Brooklyn-born bullfighter Sidney Franklin were legendary, and I'd never read them. Her introduction was odd: seventeen numbered paragraphs of advice for young writers. Some of her points struck me as, well, arguable ("4. Do not write about anyone you do not like"), but many of them seemed right on and have stayed with me. I especially like the generosity of "14. Do not be afraid to acknowledge that you have learned from other writers." In *The Fun of It*, Lillian makes clear that she learned not only from her predecessors and her contemporaries but also from those who have come later: Ian Frazier, Mark Singer, Susan Lardner, Hendrik Hertzberg, Hilton Als, John Seabrook, Adam Gopnik, Anthony Lane, Susan Orlean, and Rebecca Mead among them. *The Fun of It* is true to its title, but it's also the selected reading course of a writer who helped to shape a form with her own gifts: reporting, storytelling, and clarity—the makings of a "good little story."

EDITOR'S PREFACE

LILLIAN ROSS

"TALK STORIES," as we at *The New Yorker* call the brief journalistic pieces in The Talk of the Town, have today evolved into the sharpest, funniest, and often timeliest short form writing in the history of the magazine. These little (a thousand words or less) gems now bear out the ultimate refinement of what Harold Ross told us, in his 1924 Prospectus, he wanted his magazine to be:

"It will assume a reasonable degree of enlightenment on the part of its readers. . . . It will hate bunk. . . . It will print facts that it will have to go behind the scenes to get. . . . It hopes to be so entertaining and informative as to be a necessity for the person who knows his way about or wants to. . . . *The New Yorker* will devote several pages a week to a covering of contemporary events and people of interest."

As a literary form, according to William Shawn, who succeeded Ross as editor in 1952, the Talk story was *sui generis*. It was not an abbreviated version of something else, and it imposed, he said, "certain demands on the writer, among them discipline, technical agility, swift movement, the power to make every word and every touch count, a feeling for facts, a warm response to people, and a sensitiveness to the particulars of place, situation, and event."

It took Ross, working with others, a couple of years of experimenting to find the way toward what he envisioned. The development is revealed in the chronological arrangement of the stories in this book. "Up the Dark Stairs—" —Robert Benchley's first piece for *The New Yorker* (December 19, 1925)— seemed to be the appropriate note to sound at the start here. Relevant to journalism, it might be regarded as a warning to writers who try to get fancy

and show off, instead of getting to the point of the story they're supposed
to tell.

Shawn, who edited the department himself for several decades, used to call
The Talk of the Town the "soul of the magazine." He was quick to recognize
its imperfections, especially when he made mistakes, including tolerance of occasional nonreporting reporters—wordy, would-be Tolstoys or misguided
would-be Gertrude Steins. Under Robert Gottlieb, who was the magazine's editor from 1987 to 1992, the department stayed more or less the same, with
some interesting new writers coming into the fold. When Tina Brown took over
as editor in 1992, she shook up the magazine as a whole, made bold artistic innovations, hired many talented and daring writers, artists, and editors, and directed attention to the need for freshness and immediacy. David Remnick, the
first reporter and writer to take on the job of editor, in 1998, made many additional innovations, including turning the focus of The Talk of the Town back to
the city—Ross's original intention—so that it would become again a "necessity
for the person who knows his way about or wants to." During the past eight
years, a host of brave newcomers have worked for The Talk of the Town and
have noticeably mastered the "discipline, technical agility, swift movement, the
power to make every word and every touch count." The department's current
editor, Susan Morrison, has unquestionably led the way.

The main progenitors of the seeds of today's Talk stories were E. B. White, who
arrived at the magazine in 1926, and James Thurber and Wolcott Gibbs, both of
whom came a year later. In the early years, Ross himself did some of the reporting, writing, and rewriting, but he had many advisers and helpers, among them
George S. Kaufman, Dorothy Parker, Alexander Woollcott, Robert M. Coates,
Ralph Ingersoll, Marc Connelly, and Robert Benchley. A Talk story, in Ross's view,
should include facts of interest, importance, and humor—indeed, these were his
priorities, and it took only a couple of years for his reporters, in both form and
content, to secure them. Although Ross shared many of the prejudices of his day,
and some of the early stories (and cartoons) display a certain snobbishness
toward blacks, immigrants, and the poor, his priorities were always clear.

It was exhilarating for me, as a reporter, to discover, in putting this book together, the journalistic development and accomplishment of so many writers,
especially Thurber. It was he who, in 1927, started the convention of using the
famous "we," as in "We were fortunate enough to be seated a few rows behind
Rachmaninoff the other night . . ." or "Having heard of great changes in store
for the Old Lady, as attachés affectionately call the Murray Hill Hotel, we went
half fearfully to dine there the other evening." Thurber, as his early stories here
demonstrate, pretty much was the inventor of the Talk story. (In addition,
Ross's first writers started the regular practice of beginning The Talk of the
Town section with short, light, funny, and some serious—especially during the
Second World War—essays of opinion, which ran under the slug "Notes and
Comment"—now simply called "Comment." Also included in the department

were Anecdotes, which finally disappeared in 1975.) The delightful—from a journalistic point of view—breakthrough stories from 1928 on by Thurber, White, and Gibbs are but a small sampling here of the giant talents of these writers. Through the following decades, other writers and editors took this short form on from there, and they have pushed it forward ever since.

In the first issue of the magazine, dated February 21, 1925, The Talk of the Town appeared on page 3, with an illustration over the title showing an owl tipping a top hat to a rooster against a backdrop of city buildings. Two weeks later, in the March 7, 1925, issue, Ross had relegated the department to page 13, the title still flanked by the owl and the rooster. A couple of issues later, The Talk of the Town was back in first place, now to stay, with a permanent logo as well, depicting Eustace Tilly, holding a quill pen, and a winking owl, flanking a skyline under the name of the magazine. In a recent redesign of the magazine, Remnick initiated, among other things, simple headings over the stories in red and black.

By the late twenties, the department usually featured a "fact" piece plus a "personality" piece plus a "visit" piece; the mix became traditional, but more and more loosely so in recent years. Ross had a ravenous and ingenious appetite for facts and regularly came up with scores of topics for reporters (and sometimes himself) to work on. The Talk of the Town in its first years became replete with mesmerizing facts of durable interest. Readers were treated to facts about such subjects as violins, town houses, chewing gum, cellophane, the Pulitzer Mansion, George Washington's 1789 Presidential Mansion at 3 Cherry Street, Panama hats, high hats, corsets, the availability of turtles for soup, the caviar shortage, Potter's Field, the impressive box-office receipts of Disney's cartoon film "The Three Little Pigs," who first thought of the idea for a newsreel theater, and Al Smith ("Mrs. Smith got him to the opera once this season, but after it was over he said he'd never go again. He won't go up in an airplane either; he never has been up in one. Swimming is his favorite pastime. Before a big banquet he always goes to the Biltmore and has a Turkish bath. He keeps in constant touch with Mr. Raskob but sees little of Governor Roosevelt. The latter has never requested Mr. Smith's advice on the conduct of the State's affairs. When they meet they talk about the weather.").

There were visit pieces about the bubble dancer Sally Rand ("The balloons stand her twenty-six dollars each. The night we saw her, her first balloon broke, anyway, when she bounced it on some pine needles left by a previous artist, and they handed her a second one from the wings."); about Eleanor Roosevelt going out to buy a new dress; about the scaffolding and stone placement at the building of the Cathedral of St. John the Divine; about Gertrude Stein signing her new book at Brentano's ("Miss Stein doesn't like people to be incoherent about names. . . . We just handed our book to her, and she glanced at us with her keen, humorous eyes and, seeing that we didn't have a name, simply put her own name on the flyleaf, and the date. She signs herself always Gtde Stein.").

There were personality pieces about the Astaires ("Adele is thirty and Fred is twenty-nine and they have been dancing together since she was six and he was five, professionally since they were nine and eight respectively. Their father's name was Fred Austerlitz and he was a Viennese and a brewer"); about Hank Greenberg ("the ablest Jew in baseball"); about Marian Anderson ("the young Negress whose contralto voice is, as you probably know, the latest sensation of the musical world. We . . . found her living in a Y.W.C.A. in Harlem"); about George Balanchine ("Quite a fellow, by all accounts. He lives simply in a one-room apartment at 400 East Fifty-seventh street, and is probably the only man in New York who keeps a grand piano in a one-room apartment . . . when he dines out, it's likely to be at a little Yiddish place in the East Nineties."); about Henri Matisse ("He is now sixty, handsome, and looks like a doctor. While here he spent most of his time walking up and down Park Avenue, or looking out of his window in the thirty-first floor of the Ritz Tower. He would like to be ten years younger so he could move to New York, which he describes as 'majestic' and whose skyscrapers surprise him because they compose well."); and about Isadora Duncan's brother Raymond ("He hasn't had on a pair of pants in nineteen years.").

Ross didn't like bylines. He wanted the stories in The Talk of the Town to sound as though they'd been written by a single person, and he wanted that person to have what he called "the male point of view." "We" was always supposed to be male. In the mid-forties, with many of the males relocated to the Armed Forces, four female reporters were hired—Andy Logan, Roseanne Smith, Frances "Scottie" Lanahan, and me. Their stories were called "notes," and they were rewritten by men, mainly Russell Maloney and Brendan Gill. Stories by men were called "originals." The four women were perceived as fine reporters, but their stories were nevertheless put through the motions of a rewrite. Shawn continued this practice, ending it only around 1961. From then on, stories by women were called "originals," along with those by men.

Harold Ross's penchant for anonymity for his staff and his writers extended to himself. He never permitted his own name to be used, even though he wrote and rewrote many of the magazine's stories, especially in The Talk of the Town. The only time his name appeared was in his obituary, which was written by E. B. White. This inhibition about accrediting bylines was continued carefully by William Shawn, whose own nature was ready-made for it; *his* name, similarly, never appeared in full until *his* obituary was published in the magazine. (A fictional piece by him about a meteor hitting New York City was signed only by the initials "W.S.")

Like Ross, however, Shawn also wrote and rewrote stories for The Talk of the Town, and every writer who worked with him had his own experience of benefiting from a Shawn piece of writing hidden in the writer's work. Shawn often shared his own knowledge, enthusiasm, and taste, for example, in matters of comedy and music. A 1967 Talk story of mine about the Beatles' thirteenth, and then newest, record, "Sgt. Pepper's Lonely Hearts Club Band," told about its unusual and mixed reception by people who couldn't understand what it was. Shawn accompanied me on a tour of record shops, where owners and customers talked about the record. In the story, I quoted them along with a "Lawrence Le Fevre" (aka William Shawn) who "gave us a little lecture." The Talk of the Town in the earliest issues of the magazine was signed by a "Van Bibber III," a pseudonym for a reporter named James Kevin McGuinness. After that, until 1934, the department was signed by "The New Yorkers." For about the next six decades, the department was unsigned until Tina Brown identified the individual authors of the Talk stories with credits at the end of the section; then she instituted bylines at the end of each piece.

For many years, the first-person plural was used comfortably by the writers, in line with Ross's idea that the department speak as a single entity. In 1961, however, a staff writer simply abandoned "we" and wrote a story as a scene in the third person. Shawn encouraged experimentation, so long as the story worked. From then on, writers used "we" or they didn't; no one cared particularly, if the story was a good one. For Tina Brown, the "we" became an extra word, and, without noticeable regrets, it finally was abandoned.

The anonymity of the old days was always OK with me. I felt at ease with it or without it. In recent years, I've been just as happy to have the credit. Like most of my colleagues, what mattered to me was that I always felt free to find whatever workable form was required for each new story. My enjoyment in the initial writing of a story has always been total. Although I have written hundreds of Talk stories, every time I go out as a Talk of the Town reporter today to do a story, I feel exactly as I did the first time. The singular challenge of creating these stories is pure fun for all of us who do them.

1920s

ROBERT BENCHLEY

"UP THE DARK STAIRS—"

A MONG the major menaces to American journalism today (and
there are so many that it hardly seems worth while even beginning
this little article) is the O. Henry–Irvin Cobb tradition. According to this pretty
belief, every reporter is potentially master of the short-story, and because of it
we find Human Interest raising its ugly head in seven out of every eight news
columns and a Human Document being turned out every time Henry H.
Mackle of 1356 Grand Boulevard finds a robin or Mrs. Rasher Feiman of 425
West Forty-ninth Street attacks the scissors grinder.

Copy readers in the old days used to insist that all the facts in the story be
bunched together in the opening paragraph. This never made for a very moving chronicle, but at least you got the idea of what was going on. Under the
new system, where every reporter has his eye on George Horace Lorimer, you
first establish your atmosphere, then shake a pair of doves out of the handkerchief, round off your lead with a couple of bars from a Chopin étude, and finally, in the next to last paragraph, divulge the names and addresses and what
it was that happened.

A story which, under the old canons of journalism, would have read as follows:

"Mary J. Markezan, of 1278 Ocean Parkway, was found early this morning
by Officer Charles Norbey of the Third Precinct in a fainting condition from
lack of gin, etc."

now appeals to our hearts and literary sensibilities as follows:

"Up the dark stairs in a shabby house on Ocean Parkway plodded a bent,
weary figure. An aroma of cooking cabbage filled the hall. Somebody's mother

was coming home. Somebody's mother was bringing in an arm-full of wood for the meagre fire at 1857 Ocean Parkway. Soon the tired form would be at the top of the shadowy stairs. But Fate, in the person of Officer Norbey, was present, etc."

A fine bit of imaginative writing, satisfying everybody except the reader who wants to know what happened at 1857 Ocean Parkway.

Most of the trouble began about ten years ago when the Columbia School of Journalism began unloading its graduates on what was then the *N. Y. Tribune* (retaining the best features of neither). Every one of the boys had the O. Henry light in his eyes, and before long the market report was the only thing in the paper that didn't lead off with "Up the dark stairs at—"

Fine writing in news stories was actually encouraged by the management and daily prizes were offered for the best concealed facts. The writer of this article (Robert Benchley) was a reporter at the time—"the worst reporter in New York City" the editors affectionately called him—and one day he won the prize with a couple of sticks on the funeral of Ada Rehan. This story consisted of two paragraphs of sentimental contemplation of old-time English comedy with a bitterly satirical comparison with modern movie comedy, and a short paragraph at the end saying that Ada Rehan was buried yesterday. Unfortunately the exigencies of make-up necessitated the cutting of the last paragraph; so the readers of the *Tribune* the next morning never did find out what had inspired this really beautiful tribute to somebody.

From the *Tribune* the scourge of fine news writing has spread to all the other papers with the exception of the *Times*. Your Monday morning copy of the *World* reads like something you find on the table by the guest room bed— "Twenty Tales of Danger and Daring" or "My Favorite Ghost Story: An Anthology". The news of the day is dished up like the *Comédie Humaine* with leads running from: "Up the dark stairs at—" to "This is the story of a little boy who lost his kitty." A picture of the City Room of the *World*, by one who has never been there, would disclose a dozen or so nervous word artists, each sitting in a cubicle furnished to represent an attic, sipping at black coffee, with now and then a dab of cocaine, writing and tearing up, writing and tearing up, pacing back and forth in what the French call (in French) *le travail du style*. There must be a little hidden music, too, to make the boys write as they do. One feels that back copies of the *World* should be bound and saved for perusal on rainy days when the volumes of "Harpers Round Table" have begun to pall.

Soon it will creep into the foreign dispatches, hitherto held somewhat in check by cable rates. From a debt conference in London we may have something like this:

"Up the dark stairs at 17 Downing Street trudged a tired figure in a silk hat. Under his arm he carried a brief case. Outside, the unheeding swirl of London swept by, but in the heart of the tired man there was peace. Austen Chamberlain had brought to a conclusion the negotiations for the day."

Or:

"The twilight falls quickly on the left bank of the Seine, and yesterday it fell even more quickly than usual. At a table on the sidewalk of a little café on Montparnasse, a pale man sat figuring on the back of an envelope. Not a man that you would look at a second time, perhaps, but, as Kipling says, that is another story. This man was Jules Delatour and he ran a little shop on the Boulevard Raspail. And Jules Delatour was sad last evening as the quick twilight fell over Montparnasse. For yesterday the franc dropped again, to twenty-six to the dollar."

When this has happened, we can have newstickers installed in our homes and let the newspapers give themselves over entirely to the *belles lettres.*

1 9 2 5

A MARQUISE AT HOME

GLORIA SWANSON is back with her titled husband, the Marquis de la Falaise de la Coudraie. A day or so after her arrival, she journeyed over to the Famous Players' Astoria studio, accompanied, of course, by the marquis. The reception was a touching one.

Attracted by advance announcements, a large crowd had gathered in front of the studio. The whole studio force was assembled on the steps and four policemen struggled to keep a lane open for Gloria's car.

Suddenly the cry went up, "Here she is!" The crowd surged forward, the quartet of police officers labored with might and main, and a smart foreign car slipped up to the steps.

Out stepped a dapper chap. "The marquis!" gasped the assembled stenographers in one breath. News cameras clicked. Cheers shook the studio. Bushels of confetti were tossed into midair.

When the air cleared it developed that the dapper chap was James R. Quirk, editor of *Photoplay.*

When Gloria and the marquis did appear a few seconds later, it was an anticlimax. Still, it was prettily done. The marquis looked pleasantly democratic, Gloria burst into tears and everyone cheered all over again.

The marquis is tall, smartly garbed and speaks excellent English.

There is, as was inevitable, a little story of the trip over from Paris. Gloria and the marquis had been pursued daily by curious passengers and finally the star decided to grace a ship's concert. Ranged alongside were some friends of the old lady in Dubuque. Gloria's nose tilted a bit in midair.

The marquis leaned close to his stellar wife. "Don't be a snob, Gloria," he said.

1925

THE KING'S PAJAMAS

THEY were pink and they positively set the exclusive social circles of Asheville and Biltmore, N.C., agog, for the pajamas in question belonged to King Babe Ruth himself.

In Asheville it was, as all the world knows now, that the King first swooned away. The fourth breakfast porterhouse and a rough train ride had upset His Majesty. Doctors were called. Consultations held. It was decided that the indisposed monarch must be sent home to New York. Then came the question of moving him from the hotel to the train. It was suggested that it might be better for His Majesty if he were carried out on a stretcher. The King was not adverse and, between pinochle hands, so expressed himself. A stretcher was ordered held until His Majesty should tire of cards.

But what of the royal raiment? The King had no pajamas. Being a democratic monarch he frowns on unwonted luxuries. A messenger was despatched to obtain the going out outfit, the King specifying that it must be pink. Search in every store in Asheville disclosed only one pair of pink pajamas in the city. They were size 42. The King measured a goodly 48. In the end the messenger had to take the small size. By discarding the trousers altogether and splitting the coat up the back, they were made to do, the King being cautioned to stay quiet on the stretcher.

1925

MIGHT HAVE BEEN—

"**A**BIE'S IRISH ROSE" is three years old today, and one wonders how Mr. and Mrs. Augustus Pitou are celebrating the event.

Mr. Pitou, it should be remembered, is one of the best known and most experienced of theatrical managers. He has not, to be sure, been as well represented along Broadway with productions as have others, but he has for many years operated profitably and extensively in the hinterland, where they also pay real money at box-offices.

A little over three years ago, then, "Abie's Irish Rose" was in great distress. Despite a lengthy run on the Pacific Coast, the New York production had been icily received and most of the critics had been openly contemptuous of it. The show was in a bad way and it seemed likely that it would have to close.

Miss Anne Nichols, its author and producer, had never for one second lost faith in it. But you can not, under the Equity rules, pay off your cast in faith, and theatre owners have a way of wanting to be paid for the use of their property. What to do?

Miss Nichols sought out Mr. Pitou and offered to sell him a twenty-five per cent interest in "Abie's Irish Rose" for $5,000. Five thousand dollars, she calculated, would be enough to keep the play operating until its public found it in remunerative numbers. She herself had parted with her jewels, with everything she had, to keep the play going.

Mr. Pitou promised to look into the matter, and the following Saturday he attended a matinee of her production with Mrs. Pitou. He instantly recognized the cheap quality of the play, but Mr. Pitou is too experienced a manager to let his personal reaction interfere with his judgment of a box-office attraction. The audience, he could not help noticing, was wildly enthusiastic about it and howled its head off with glee at the slightest provocation. The lobby, at intermission time, was filled with people who were announcing that they could hardly wait to see Cousin Minnie and Uncle Abe to advise them by all means not to miss this great human document, this gorgeously comic play.

And so Mr. Pitou ventured the opinion that he might buy the twenty-five per cent interest for $5,000. Mrs. Pitou for some minutes thereafter seemed to believe that Mr. Pitou had suddenly gone mad. The play, she announced, was horrible and had not the ghost of a chance for success. Mr. Pitou, in her opinion, could do better by just taking $5,000 and lighting cigars with them.

Mrs. Pitou's opinion was echoed by Louis Cohn, the ticket broker, who further informed Mr. Pitou that he had not sold a single ticket for "Abie's Irish Rose" in three weeks. . . . Mr. Pitou then told Miss Nichols that he could not accept her offer.

Miss Nichols, in some way or other, managed to keep the show going until it had hit its stride. That stride, by now, would have returned Mr. Pitou well over $1,000,000 for his investment of $5,000. And one somehow imagines that Mr. and Mrs. Pitou have a good deal to talk about on such an occasion as the third birthday of "Abie's Irish Rose."

1925

CAL AND BELLES LETTRES

MR. COOLIDGE is, beyond denial, a bachelor of arts and, as such, eligible to be stamped "inspected and passed as educated" whenever the Congress gets around to creating a bureaucracy to supervise learning. But, one reflects, governmental standards are likely to be low.

At any rate, Mr. Coolidge, looking upon his standing with his countrymen, was led to reflect that it would not pain him too deeply if the nation held for its president a warmer feeling, which reflection he put into words while talking lately with one of the Washington newspaper correspondents.

The correspondent, wise man that he is, knew the observation for a presidential hint that suggestions were in order.

"Why not recognize the arts, Mr. President?" he proposed. "You have had leaders of almost every other line of endeavor for breakfast in the White House; why not invite some of the leaders in one of the arts—some poets, perhaps?"

"Who are the leading poets?" came from Calvin, after the customary silent interval.

"Oh, Edward Arlington Robinson, Carl Sandburg, Robert Frost, Edna St. Vincent Millay, Edgar Lee Masters, Elinor Wylie," Mr. Sullivan tossed off.

The President considered this.

"When I was in College," he observed, presently, "there was a man named Smith—who wrote verse."

1925

MODEST MR. SHAW

BERNARD SHAW as a short story writer would be new to most people, and even those who, as far as they know, read everything he writes, have met with him in that field just once, if ever. But on his own statement he is thinking and has been these four years of presenting himself in it—and, morbidly modest though he is about his plays, he doesn't think his short stories are so worthless.

In 1908 the short story referred to, a very Shavian and very good one, called "Aerial Football," appeared in *Collier's*. It attracted even wider attention than its merit deserved, for *Collier's*, then edited by Norman Hapgood, was awarding every three months a $1,000 prize to the author of the best story it had published in that period, and was rash enough to make such award to Mr. Shaw. He returned the draft with a rebuke—he had been duly paid for the story, and giving him a prize was insulting—all of which *Collier's* imperturbably printed.

In 1921, when the *Evening Post* was reprinting short stories, somebody in its office bethought him of that one and made the best possible offer for the use of it. Mr. Shaw replied that he was much obliged, but expected to bring out a book of his short stories and would rather not have "Aerial Football" reprinted in the meantime.

There has been no further word of the book, and this Spring a prosperous magazine which knew of the *Evening Post*'s offer mentioned it in making another, of as much money as prosperous magazines, even in these author's-bonanza days, are paying for some of their stories, brand new.

In reply, Mr. Shaw's secretary was bidden to state that "the situation with regard to 'Aerial Football' is unchanged, and that anyhow, three hundred dollars is not up to his rates." The magazine is far from blaming G. B. S. for wanting all the traffic will bear, but if he can get more than that for "second serial rights" in one short story anywhere on earth, its admiration of him will rise to reverence; and the Author's League will build a statue to his memory.

The book still is unannounced. Indeed, this is a sizzling news "beat," which may affect the stock market, on the fact that such a book may be impending.

1 9 2 5

VACHEL LINDSAY

A REAL character recently passed through New York, flaring a large head, partly gray, partly red, wholly unkempt. This was Vachel Lindsay, the author of "The Golden Whales of California" and sundry other books of poetry.

Whether or not he is the best of the New Poets, may be a moot point with some, but not with him. He admits he is a conceited man and that his egotism is so enormous that he can't get on with anyone. He has little use for New York; the provinces are solid, he says, "and I can understand them."

We saw him slopping by several times. He has always lived carelessly. Years ago with Stephen Graham, who now visits various countries and writes books on them, he tramped about America giving a little book of his poems to whoever would trade a square meal for it. He started in Springfield, Illinois, thence went for a little education to Hiram College, then about the middle West, then far west and south; doing a little teaching, reading very little, shouting Walt Whitman's poetry. And now he is about to embark on a tour of lectures to read his poems. "I will teach America six poems," he says. "That's enough to do in one lifetime."

He is indifferent to comfort and the mellow surroundings so many writers love. He can do his best work in a hotel writing room if that is where he happens to be. He also does queerer things than write poetry. For example, he studies Egyptian hieroglyphics, still clings to an anti-liquor prejudice, which, they say, he inherited from his mother, loves the Woolworth Building, and is inclined to speak of his wife as the little woman.

As he sits in the Hotel Commodore, he is for all the world like an obviously inspired ex-cowboy with red hair. His is a startling personality that is always shouting, but he has plenty of humor. They are still telling a story about him in a town in southern Texas. He had read some of his poems in the meeting hall and was asked if he would autograph some of his books. He agreed, but it was found that there weren't any of his books in town. Two old ladies, however, had Bibles with them and brought them up to the platform.

"Certainly I'll autograph them," he said, sitting down.

In one Bible he wrote, "Now is the time for every good man to come to the aid of his party"; in the other, "I did not write this book. Vachel Lindsay."

1 9 2 6

FENCE BUSTER

SOME facts about Gehrig, the baseball player who is rivalling Ruth as a home-run hitter, seem to be worth recording. To begin with, he is one of the few native New Yorkers on our local nines, and a former student at Columbia University. He is twenty-four, and of German descent. His father, we are told, was a janitor and grass-cutter at Columbia, and the son decided to attend college there, not so much because of the classical opportunities but because he had heard the plaudits for the university baseball stars and he knew he could play as well as they. He remained only two years, but during that time he made such progress as a hitter and a pitcher that the New York Yankees signed him. That was five years ago. After a year with a minor league club he was recalled here and has been on the local roster ever since. Last year he played regularly, but it was not until the present season that he began to puncture fences and figure as a home-run king.

Gehrig is no intellectual giant on the diamond, but he is determined. When he was at Columbia he would practice hitting balls until it was too dark to see and mothers called home to bed the boys who chased them for him. Even now, during the training season, he is the first man on the field and the last off. He practices and studies and he seldom takes his eyes off Ruth. He idolizes that gentleman, and they say Ruth has shown no jealousy, but has helped Gehrig considerably.

He is of middle size and quite squarely built, with great, stocky legs. Naturally clumsy, he has overcome much of his ineptness. He is so hardy that he never wears an overcoat, and on the bitter January day he signed with the Yanks one of the officials felt so sorry for him he offered to lend him money to buy one. He makes about $10,000 a year, but next season it will be much more.

Gehrig does not drink, smoke or gamble. He has never had a girl. His hobby is fishing for eels. There is a mystery about this. No one knows where he catches them, except that it is somewhere in the vicinity of Harlem, but he never fails in his quest. He likes his eels pickled, and his mother does the pickling. Pickled eels, in fact, have become a Yankee superstition. The players have come to believe that they produce hitting power, and whenever the team is in a slump the boys urge Gehrig to go fishing, and then they join in the feast.

1 9 2 7

THE SIN OF ADAMS

NOT long since, in these columns, we recounted the story of the origin of ice-cream soda in Manhattan. We now feel it our duty to fix the responsibility for chewing gum on the Borough of Richmond, for it was on Staten Island, in the otherwise uneventful year of 1866, we are told by the scion of one of the oldest and most reliable families of those parts, that the possibilities of chicle came to light. It appears that in June of that year the Mexican general, Santa Ana, having found it necessary to absent himself from his native land, put into Snug Harbor. He hobnobbed frequently with the islanders, and one of his acquaintances was a young photographer named Thomas Adams, an ambitious young gentleman and something of an experimenter.

During one of his chats the general produced a lump of rubbery substance which he said was the gum of the zapote tree and which he liked to chew. He gave Adams a piece. The photographer saw possibilities in it. He believed that, with proper treatment, it could be made—of all things—a substitute for the rubber used in plates for false teeth.

Adams is said to have experimented for weeks with this in mind. It was only after a final test, when, disgusted by failure, he slammed the mass on a table, that he tried the general's plan. He picked up one of the pieces and absently put it in his mouth. He found that it did not dissolve and that crunching away at it was somehow diverting. Eventually he and his father, after obtaining additional chicle, set up a workroom in which they boiled the product, cooled it in water, cut it into long strips and packed it in boxes. These they peddled. The idea of sweetening it and flavoring it came later. Then they moved to Jersey City. It is said that gum was not well received at first. The makers, however, hit upon the idea of giving away chewing gum with candy and thus developed a taste for the product. Eventually they became a great corporation and sold out for millions. We hear that fifty million dollars' worth of the stuff is produced annually now and that all the department stores in New York have squads of men detailed to scrape it off the floors every night.

1 9 2 7

DIME NOVEL

U PON requesting, the other day, to view some of the works of the Beadle Collection of Dime Novels which is kept in the Reserve Room of the Public Library, we were asked if we had any connection with the movies. "Dr. O'Brien, the donor," we were informed, "has reserved the right to withhold the books from motion picture people."

This deepened our interest to such a degree that we paid a visit to the author of this discrimination, who is a New York dentist and whose name is Dr. Frank P. O'Brien. He confessed having made the reservation we have mentioned and went on to exhibit to us an even larger collection of dime novels than the one of fifteen hundred volumes which now rests aristocratically in the library. There are nearly three thousand in this second collection. They are kept in two huge safes.

Dr. O'Brien permitted us to take a handful of them to hold and let us turn the pages of "Malaeska, or, the Indian Wife of the White Hunter," the first dime novel published in America. It is by Mrs. Ann S. Stephens, and was published May 15, 1860, and shortly was translated into five different languages.

For many years, between times of dabbling in teeth and Wall Street, Dr. O'Brien has spent his leisure in travelling about the country seeking out these old books. He obtained a few of them from Mrs. Sophie B. Raymond, Erastus Beadle's only daughter, now living in Cooperstown, New York.

Erastus Beadle, the man who made "The Pioneer Books," was born in Pierstown, Otsego County, New York, in 1821. As a miller's apprentice he laid the foundation of his career as a publisher. Need arose in the mill one day for some letters to be used in labelling the bags of grain. Erastus cut the letters from blocks of hard wood, just as the old block letters had been made in the days be-fore Gutenberg. He later left the mill with his equipment and travelled about the country, stamping bags and marking lap-robes, wagons and other things.

In Cooperstown, Elihu Phinney, a pioneer printer, offered him work and Bea-dle there learned printing. By 1852 he had a shop of his own in Buffalo and in that year issued his first publication, "The Youth's Casket." This was not a dime novel, but nearly three thousand of them followed later, among which are such alliterative titles as "Alkali Abe," "Border Bessie," "Bowery Ben," "Corduroy Charlie," "Daisy Dare," "Dandy Darke," and "Roaring Ralph Rockwood." In the fall of 1859 he came to New York, where he set up shop at 141 William Street. According to Dr. O'Brien, Erastus Beadle was not a sensational publisher, even though his successes were of this nature. He had no thought of bringing out "dime novels" in the sense that we think of them; rather, he published the tales and records of early pioneer struggles and adventure to preserve them for fu-ture generations.

1927

THE OLD LADY

HAVING heard of great changes in store for the Old Lady, as attachés affectionately call the Murray Hill Hotel, we went half fearfully to dine there the other evening. We were reassured, however, when we found the old street lamps before the Park Avenue doors still blinking, even as they did at the turn of the century. Walking around to the Fortieth Street doorway we were happy to see the doormat marked "Ladies' Entrance" just where it was when Mark Twain in his white suit played billiards below stairs. When later we went into the billiard room, it was charming to see two old cronies pottering about a table and chuckling over each other's wobbly shots. The gilt-pillared lobby gave us the impression it always does—that in this building time has stopped. An elderly gentleman drowsed over his Springfield *Republican* and a long-ashed cigar. Gray-haired couples shared the deep lounges. It might have been an evening in the nineties except for a radio, which, however, was silent. It is always, we were told later, turned on for Mr. Coolidge's speeches.

For years we have heard whispers that time has stopped more in truth than in fancy at the Murray Hill. It has been true: the clocks of the old hotel have, figuratively speaking, just been rewound. Almost fifteen years ago a chronic illness from septic poisoning sent the hotel's venerable owner-manager to his room and kept him there. Just a month or two ago he came downstairs for the first time, to find dusty tapestries, outworn equipment and servants who had grown gray-haired since he had last given them instructions in person. With fine devotion they had gone on, working longer hours and accepting pre-war pay. The guardian of the Old Lady's tranquillity is Mr. B. L. M. Bates, an innkeeper of the old tradition. All he intends to do, he says, is to redecorate the hotel gently and tastefully; gold doorknobs and newfangled elevators may come to other hotels but the Murray Hill will go on unchanged in spirit. One of Mr. Bates' first acts upon resuming active responsibility was to retire an aged cook on pension, who died a few weeks later. Now the rest of the old servants can stay on until they are happily a hundred. There are four of these ancients in the dining-room. One serves the same group of tables that he presided over forty-three years ago when the hotel opened. Two-thirds of the diners are gray-haired too, and many have lived here for a quarter of a century. There is a soft tone of an old Continental hotel about the dining-room. A *dame du comptoir* sits behind an oak counter and keeps track of things. A trio of violin, piano and cello playing nineteenth-century music broke softly into "Lady Be Good" and seemed almost skittish.

Mr. Bates was the first proprietor of the Everett House, one of the city's oldest residential hotels. Later he managed the Belmont and then leased and finally purchased the Murray Hill. He says he does not fear that the younger set will invade the hotel, except "now and again to rest their nerves."

1 9 2 7

MUSIC MAKERS

WE were fortunate enough to be seated a few rows behind Rachmaninoff the other night in the Plaza ballroom when Theremin, the young Russian scientist, produced strange sounds, then tunes, and finally played Scriabin and Saint-Saëns by waving his hands gently at antennae on a box. Rachmaninoff was in his seat, an uncomfortable chair about fifteen rows back, many minutes before the strange concert began. As the curtains parted and revealed a lot of curious electrical apparatus, the pianist sat up straight and put on a pair of horn-rimmed spectacles.

But when an assistant immediately began to read an explanation of what was going to happen, Rachmaninoff took off his glasses and lapsed into reading several pieces of literature on the subject. These were spread out on his lap. He put on his glasses and took them off again every few minutes during the evening.

His interest was casual until Theremin produced the first semblance of a melody. Then Rachmaninoff turned around and smiled and lifted his eyebrows at some friends behind him. He applauded but twice, once after the playing of Rubinstein's "Night" and once when the concert was finished. His applause was brief, soft-handed and unemotional. Although the long program and its final monotony caused about half the audience to depart before it was over, Rachmaninoff stayed till the last and did not appear restive. At the beginning he had crossed his left leg over his right and he did not shift this position. When, as often happened, something went wrong musically, he showed no annoyance. His intervals of intense interest were comparatively few, but one of them was when Theremin and his pupil, Mr. Goldberg, played together Glinka's

"Elegy." On one occasion he raised his right hand and imitated the motions Theremin was making with his left. These were the open-fingered motions of a hand playing the piano. During one composition, however, he read apparently all the way through a sketch of Theremin's life. When at one point the scientist caused the music to sound from the rear of the hall, Rachmaninoff was one of the few who did not turn around and stare.

The concert over, Rachmaninoff was surrounded. More people seemed in fact to know him than anyone else there. As one excited woman who, speaking in Russian, apparently attempted to fire his enthusiasm for the concert with her own, he shook his head two or three times unsmilingly. He did smile when a very young lady at his side began shouting "Bravo!" and "Magnifique!" to the bowing scientist. He patted her gently on the shoulder, and said "Sh-h." Then finally, still smiling, he said in French, "You exaggerate."

1 9 2 8

POTTER'S FIELD

NEW YORK'S pauper dead are buried in a sandy hill on the north end of Hart's Island in Long Island Sound, a mile from Execution Light. They lie in big graves, tier on tier, unclaimed. It was blowy the day we went out there to see the field, and the low storm-swept island looked particularly weather-beaten. Michael Breen, warden of the island prison, met us, smiling broadly, glad of a visitor.

Twice a week the boat comes up from Bellevue. The prisoners bury the dead, solemnly and without ceremony, one hundred and fifty to a grave, one white headstone for the lot. It is a beautiful spot—the sweep of the Sound, the restless clang of the bell buoy at the point. An incongruous spot, too, for directly across the water are the homes of the millionaires, Hearst's place on Sands Point, the broad lawns and grandeur of Great Neck.

On the cemetery hill are the frame houses which served as barracks in the Civil War. Now they house ancient prisoners who are too feeble to require iron bars for their detention: old beggars, cripples, panhandlers, old men who hang magazine pictures of beautiful girls above their iron cots. In the centre of the is-land are the dog-eared brick buildings where the regular prisoners live and work, making clothes, making brooms and shoes, snatching a little sleep on the sea-wall, in the sun, between jobs. At the extreme southern end is a house formerly owned by a negro, who ran a negro resort there until a year ago when the City acquired the property.

But nothing much interested us except the field for the dead. Even the statis-tics seemed important—two hundred and sixty-six thousand persons in that small hill. Mr. Breen allowed us to look at the record books, and we glanced at a few entries: a baby found in the parcel room of the Penn Station, a man picked up in the Fifth Avenue sewer, page after page, six thousand a year. There is a single monument to honor them—a small cross bearing the inscription: "And He shall call His own by name."

As we stood there a gull wheeled and circled above our head. From the far side of the island the wind brought the smell of tide flats, the incessant sounding of the bell. And rather vaguely we heard the fine Irish voice of Michael Breen: "Thim horsechissnut trees will be all full o' blossoms soon—pretty as a picture!"

1 9 2 8

HARRIETT

OF all the orchids at the Orchid Show, we liked Harriett—she was so rare. Other orchids had exotic backgrounds, but only Harriett had a gold case lined with black, in front of which her lover, Mr. Louis Burk, paced up and down. We talked to Mr. Burk about Harriett and she is indeed his passion. He brought her here from Philadelphia in his private car, and every night during the show Harriett went home with Mr. Burk's gardener to his hotel room.

In color and size, she is not such an orchid. But she is the only one of her kind in the world, and she is thirty-eight years old, with a strange waxen beauty. Two white, star-shaped blossoms, pink in the centre, are her present charm, and a third bud is coming, which Mr. Burk is not going to allow to mature—it would weaken Harriett. Even the existing two flowers weaken her and will be removed before they wither. She is not for sale, and although there are no other orchids like her, there will be!

"Due to a certain accident," said Mr. Burk, "I have another plant coming along."

"What certain accident?" we asked. And then Mr. Burk told us Harriett's story. She used to belong to Mrs. George B. Wilson, the orchid queen of Philadelphia. That was fifteen years ago when Harriett was young. When the war came, coal became scarce, Harriett grew cold and seemed about to die. In desperation Mrs. Wilson let Mr. Burk take her, and he nursed her back to health. It was the custom, in the Burk greenhouse, to place her over a water mote so that no insects could attack her. But one night this precaution was neglected, a slug invaded the pot and a certain accident happened—the slug ate Harriett's new growth of roots, all round and about. Mr. Burk's heart bled, but when he found that Harriett—instead of dying—was putting out a side-shoot, a surgical operation was performed, and now Harriett has a child (for which somebody offered a thousand dollars the other day and received from Mr. Burk only a smile).

That was how it was. At home, Mr. Burk keeps his love in a certain place in his greenhouse, right where he can see her whenever he comes in. He says he moved her once to a place that seemed more favorable, but that she began to fail and had to be returned immediately to the old location. Her complete name, Mr. Burk says, is Phalaenopsis Harriettae, but we won't go into that. She will live forever, God willing.

OTHER things we learned at the Orchid Show were that most of the orchids for New York City consumption are grown in Westchester, Jersey, and Long Island; that an orchid seed-pod contains one hundred million seeds; and that if you are not scared to try, it is really possible to grow a common orchid plant in a window, as one does a geranium.

1928

DANCING COUPLE

T HE career of the Astaires, as it has been told to us, is worth making some record of. Particularly since, April rumor has it, this year may be their last together. They are of course really brother and sister. They were born in Omaha. Adele is thirty and Fred is twenty-nine and they have been dancing together since she was six and he was five, professionally since they were nine and eight respectively. Their father's name was Fred Austerlitz and he was a Viennese and a brewer. Being from Vienna he didn't scoff when an excited lady who wrote pieces for a paper in Omaha announced in her columns that the two children—whom she had seen perform at an ice cream social or something— were clever and would surely go on the stage. Mr. Austerlitz looked his children over himself the next time they did their little dance together and decided the lady was right.

The reason this season may be their last together, after twenty-two years in which they have never appeared separately, is because Adele expects to be married and will live in England and raise Scotch terriers. Fred also yearns to get away from the amber spot and out in the open. His ambition is to produce, but he also wants to own a great stable of horses some day. Knowing this, the management of "Funny Face," in which the pair are now appearing, presented Mr. Astaire (and probably sighed as they did so) with a Copenhagen China horse and jockey the night the show opened. He keeps it on his dressing-room table.

Their first appearance in this city was in 1907. They did a clog dance in a vaudeville house until the Gerry Society objected. In those years they were forced to play in Shamokin and Passaic and places like that in order not to be molested by societies who knew that dancing was terrible for children.

Their first real chance in New York, after they got old enough to be let alone, came at the old Fifth Avenue Theatre and their hearts were high with hope. On the same bill was Douglas Fairbanks. He got over very well but after the first show the Astaires sadly noted that their names had been scratched from the call-board, which meant the management had given them, as Mr. James Gleason would say, the works. You couldn't daunt the children, however, and they made their first big success not long afterwards in the revue "Over the Top." Since then they have snapped their fingers at call-boards.

One of their earliest friendships was with George Gershwin, then a piano player for Remick. He used to say he hoped some day to write a score which the brother and sister could dance to. That happened first in the production of "Lady Be Good." Then came "Funny Face." We were interested to learn that dancing shoes rarely last the Astaires more than three weeks, which, to coin a statistic, means that each of them has used about four hundred pairs since they began to dance together. Fred is superstitious and on opening nights always brings to his dressing-room and wears a funny looking red and green bathrobe he bought in Bridgeport thirteen years ago. It hasn't always brought him luck though. For instance, he was selected, not long ago, by a Columbia professor and a cigarette manufacturing company, to be blindfolded and to pick out, as the best of four cigarettes offered him, the kind manufactured by the company in question. He picked the wrong one.

1928

BIG BOY

THE tall, somewhat paunchy, but still erect figure of Jack Johnson may be seen about Broadway these days. He walks proudly. He never forgets his gloves. His step is a little less springy and his face no longer gleams in the ebony and gold splendor which admiring Londoners compared to a "starry night" almost twenty years ago when he was the rage over there. He might pass for thirty-five. He is fifty-one. People along Broadway recognize him, and wonder why and when he came to town. It is different from the day in 1911 when he sailed in on the *Kronprinzessin Cecilie* with a white valet, a white secretary, a limousine, a touring car, and two racers, boasting of the prodigious amounts of his weekly hotel bills abroad. The once famous champion and notorious bon vivant has fallen on less glamorous days. He is not broke, but he is not affluent. Wealth he never hoarded. The fifty-one hundred dollars he got for boxing Philadelphia Jack O'Brien before the war, for instance, he spent in four days, on dinners, a ring, and an automobile. Now he is eager to sell stories of his life for money. He holds off on his real biography, for which he hopes to get a hundred thousand dollars. "Ah am a deep and colorful personality," he says. He lives in Harlem, gets around to the prizefights, takes in the shows. His plans are uncertain, but he may go into a vaudeville act, as he did some years back, or he may fight some more obscure fights as he has been doing off and on for several years, for small profits, in the West and Southwest. He won a match in 1926, but was knocked out the following year by an unknown named Bearcat Wright (colored) of Omaha, tasting the bitter cup that he himself handed to Fitzsimmons in 1907 and the groggy Jeffries in 1910. He still thinks he could lick Dempsey and that Tunney would be easy.

Some people have the notion that Johnson is still legally banned from America. He gave himself up in 1920, however, and served ten months in Leavenworth for violation of the Mann Act, after evading sentence for seven years, living abroad. He is free to come and go. The churches and the women's clubs, which made his heyday miserable, have forgotten. The suicide of his first white wife and his subsequent marriage to another white woman, chief witness for the state in his trial and conviction, are vague memories. Proof of this was given not long ago, when Johnson was cheered by the clergy at a general conference of the Methodist Church in Kansas City at which he denounced liquor, saying, "To serve God, you must train the mind as well as the soul." His Café de Champion in Chicago was padlocked some years ago.

Johnson enjoys recalling the old times. He loves to talk of his favorite city, Budapest, and of the time at the start of the war when the Germans did not molest several trunks containing his wife's sables. During the war he says he did secret-service work in Spain, at the request of a Major Lang, U. S. A., paying half his expenses. Of his "deeper life" he is proud and sensitive. "Ah am," he says, "a very tendah man." He likes to display his hands and face to show how unscarred they are by battle. There is no mark on his head. His skull was X-rayed in San Francisco eighteen years ago. It took five and a half minutes to get the rays through, as against the customary five to fifteen seconds. The bone was found to be from a half to three-quarters of an inch thick, which is thicker than the skull of an ox. Surgeons said that a blow which would fell a steer would simply jar Mr. Johnson. He doesn't admire Tunney as a man. He enjoys the books of Richard Harding Davis. He has never met Paul Robeson. He is stopping now at 148th Street. Once he lived here in an apartment which was approached by stairs spread with a crimson plush carpet. On rainy days crash towels were put down to protect the plush.

1929

NEWSREEL

THE big question now about the newsreel theatre is, who thought of it first? Probably everybody has had the idea at one time or another. It is on record that five years ago an enterprising Frenchman actually tried it out in Paris, in a theatre so small it didn't even have seats. His idea was that people would drop in for a few minutes between appointments, glance at the newsreel as they would at the headlines of a newspaper, and saunter out again. He failed. The present venture at the Embassy Theatre is done with much more elegance. They have snappy usherettes, a gleaming doorman, and a sign in the lobby which says: "The thirst for news may now be quenched, so drink thy fill of Knowledge." So far about fifty thousand people have attended the theatre weekly. Such a success is it, that they are talking of a country-wide string of newsreel theatres.

Everybody concerned is pretty much up in the air about the idea, rushing cameras here and there, and talking about revolutionizing the movies. When that unfortunate flier crashed into the side of the Y.M.C.A. building they had a cameraman on the spot within twenty minutes. Four hours later they were showing the film together with a short talk by Mr. Robert Baillie, the passenger who jumped by parachute and survived. That evening Mr. Baillie dropped into the theatre to see and hear himself.

The actual news part of the program—news, as distinct from human-interest stuff—is made up from the four regular weekly newsreels the Fox people put out. It represents a culling from one hundred and fifty thousand feet of film sent in every week from all over. Two projecting-rooms are going almost constantly, running off the film, while editors, caption-writers, sound experts, etc., sit at a row of desks in the back of the room, making notes. The staff also thinks up the human-interest features. It has been found that audiences like to see and hear other people talking—Mrs. Byrd telling Commander Byrd, by radio, that she drives her own car now; Miss Shilling, of Baltimore, explaining why she offered to marry any man who would give her five thousand dollars. The audience wept when Mrs. Fall said that she still believed Albert Fall innocent. It hissed at Senator Sheppard boosting prohibition. Animal pictures go well. They are the hardest to get. Last year somebody in the Fox company got the idea of making a picture of two cats fighting on a fence, with sound. Cameramen worked three months on it, using over two hundred thousand feet of film. Finally, when they got the picture, it ran a minute and a half.

1929

ROBERT M. COATES
AND JAMES THURBER

CALDER'S CIRCUS

ONVERSATION lagging one night at a dinner party in Paris some three years ago, Mr. Alexander Calder amused his table companion by making a chicken out of a piece of bread and a hairpin. A success story has grown from that idle bit of modelling. Mr. Calder's kangaroo is now one of the heaviest-selling gadgets in the Christmas toy lists; his bear, bull, and dog are also popular numbers. He has also had an enormous *succès d'estime* with a wire, felt, and beaver-board circus. These raw materials he took up when he abandoned bread and hairpins. The Calder circus is in town now. You can't buy tickets to it, but people who have seen it say it is worth getting a bid to a private showing. The circus is held in the drawing-room, or kitchen, of some friend. Mr. Calder sits on the floor, beside a miniature tanbark ring, and is very busy. He keeps seventy performers doing incredible things with their wire joints and felt bodies—trapeze artists, high-divers, bareback riders, clowns, lions, horses, and dogs. The tricks are often ingeniously contrived. For example, the horses are mounted on a disc which Mr. Calder can whirl madly, by turning the handle of an old eggbeater. At the proper moment, a spring or something is released, a bareback rider in ballet skirts flies through the air, bursts through a hoop, and lands astride a horse. People scream. Calder seldom misses. For faint hearts, a net is spread beneath the trapeze performers. Clowns tumble about the ring, poodles sit up, a hoochie-coochie dancer brings down the house. It all lasts about two hours, and nobody ever walks out or even gets restive. Jean Cocteau, who is easily bored, saw the show in Paris at the studio of Foujita, the Japanese painter, and was enthusiastic. He wants to put it on the stage somehow.

. . .

MR. CALDER does this sort of thing on the side. He is a serious sculptor, the son of a serious sculptor, A. Stirling Calder, who most recently did the I. Miller marbles, Mary Pickford, Marilyn Miller, and so on. That shows how serious he is. The son can even do serious things with his beloved medium, wire. Two seasons ago he had a one-man show of caricatures and portraits in wire at Weyhe's gallery. His penetrating portrait of Calvin Coolidge shocked onlookers and gained considerable renown. His ballet-dancers (the serious ones, not the common circus women) are miracles of lightness and grace. For these he uses nothing but wire, which he bends with pincers and nippers. It was hard at first to interest toy-manufacturers in his lions, bears, etc. As a matter of fact he couldn't interest any of the old-line, suspicious toy-makers. It was a manufacturing concern of another sort, out in Oshkosh, which finally took a chance and made up some of the animals from the Calder pattern. As we said, they are selling heavily.

1 9 2 9

ISADORA'S BROTHER

RAYMOND DUNCAN is in town with the idea of starting a branch of his academy here. He serves tea every afternoon in his studio in West Seventy-fifth Street, surrounded by his fabrics, his poems, his shepherdess, and his disciples. Reclining on a couch, he talks with you about the future, which he believes must be prepared for by throwing off the past and learning to perform the simple motions of life, such as digging and making sandals. His poems are five dollars, his "Eternal Beauty" is two dollars, and his fabrics run from four dollars on up. The couch is very hard.

The little brother of Isadora is getting on in years, and looks more like a witch than a shepherd. His long gray locks are held back by a ribbon, his tunic flows classically from his shoulders, and his chubby little arms that have woven so many yards of piece goods look rather flabby and old. After years of tending donkeys and goats on the Acropolis with Penelope, organizing refugees, rebuilding a city in Albania, weaving rugs, digging holes, dyeing linen, writing poems, and administering academies and temples of arts, always clinging tight to the immortal and somewhat elusive spirit of his inspired sister, he is still hopeful. He hasn't had on a pair of pants in nineteen years, man and boy.

While we were reclining with him, doing our best to look like a goatherd despite our sack suit, a lady entered the room and asked him "if it would brutalize him if she suggested a cup of tea." "My dear Julia," he replied, "the whole world is trying to brutalize me."

Brute that we were, we drank the tea, bought a small doily, and departed, our sandals clinking merrily along the pave.

1929

1930s

ROBERT M. COATES AND
GEOFFREY HELLMAN

SOUP OF THE EVENING

WHEN the late August Belmont felt particularly expansive, he would drop in at Walter T. Smith's turtle shop in Front Street near the Fulton Market, pick out a few hundred terrapin from the tanks, and send them to his friends, the Rothschilds. That was in the turtle's heyday. Every hotel featured green-turtle soup; no banquet was complete without terrapin. Mr. Smith supplied them all—the famous Bradley Martin ball, the Waldorf opening, Delmonico's, Sherry's. Nowadays, Mr. Smith feels, much of the old epicurean gusto has departed; though he still handles more than half a million pounds of turtles a year, he thinks it is nowhere near enough for a city the size of this. In proportion to population, it is far less than when he started business, fifty-two years ago.

Prohibition is largely responsible. Both terrapin and green turtle must be cooked in sherry, and this has wiped them off most menus. They are still, however, much in demand for banquets, and he sells a good deal to clubs: the Metropolitan, the University, the Racquet and Tennis, as well as the Brook, which makes a specialty of terrapin, and the Union Club, to which he has furnished turtles for forty years. He still has a few private customers, gourmets all, who come down to the shop and pick out their turtles themselves. The terrapin are caught in the marshes along the coast from Long Island to Georgia, shipped in water, and kept in tanks in the shop. Green turtles come from the Caribbean and the Gulf of Mexico. They are caught along the shore when they come in to lay their eggs in the sand, or in nets anchored over their feeding beds. They can live a long time out of water, however. In the shop, they are laid in rows, on their backs, in a large room where the dealers can inspect them. The best ones range from seventy-five to two hundred and fifty pounds. Really big ones he sends to the Aquarium. Once he got a rare albino terrapin from Louisiana, with pink eyes and a gleaming white shell. He sent it to the Zoölogical Garden in San Diego. He enjoys his business, and, though now he no longer follows it actively, he often comes in from Long Island to look things over and finger a turtle's flipper. He loves a good terrapin stew, and considers green-turtle soup, properly prepared, the king of all soups. You can feed it to a three-months-old baby, he says.

Chinese customers are numerous at Mr. Smith's, buying diamond-back terrapin which, it seems, the Chinese pharmacopoeia has down as a cure for all ailments from sore tooth to lung trouble. Before the shop a sign dangles incongruously, advertising terrapin in Chinese characters—pronounced "gim ten guoy."

1 9 3 0

CORSETS DE LUXE

WHENEVER Mae West needs a new corset for something like "Diamond Lil" she goes to Mme. Binner's in Fifth Avenue at Fifty-eighth Street. Many, many people needing corsets go to Mme. Binner. She started on her career in Vienna. At the age of eleven she took to making corsets, to pass the time away. After coming to this country, in the early eighties, she was a lone—but a loud—voice in the wilderness, pointing out the horrors of the hourglass corset. Women clients who insisted on having them she sent to doctors for X-rays, to show them what a mess tight corsets made of their ribs. The grateful doctors sent clients to Mme. Binner, who made them light sensible corsets. At present, they say, she has two thousand customers, including such women as Mrs. Charles Steele, Mrs. Seth Thomas, Mrs. John D. Rockefeller, Jr., Mrs. Elbridge Gerry, and Mrs. Thomas Lamont. Some ladies buy ten or a dozen corsets at a time. Mme. Binner also has a few men customers who have curvature of the spine or who need artificial support while recovering from an operation. For them she designs special corsets. She is also the inventor of the detached brassière and—probably more important—she was the first person to think of attaching garters to corsets. Before that garters had just wandered around with no real home.

The first gartered corset was made for Lillian Russell, who was so enchanted with it she became a regular customer, later ordering from Mme. Binner the most expensive corset ever made. It cost thirty-nine hundred dollars—fourteen hundred dollars for the corset proper and twenty-five hundred dollars for the garters, which had diamond buckles. Once, when her house in Long Island burned down, Miss Russell's first cry after her escape was, "My support! My support!" "Your what?" demanded a fireman. "My corset!" shrieked Miss Russell. It was at about this time that Anna Held came to Mme. Binner with an offer of one hundred dollars for every inch taken off her waist. It cost her quite a bit. Mme. Binner fixes up any number of opera stars. This is the devil of a job, because of the sisterhood's inclination toward rotundity.

Mme. Binner is short, dark, and vivacious. She lives in town with her twenty-three-year-old son, who is an art director in the movies. He designed his mother's present establishment, a modern affair of silver, orchid, and green. Summers Mme. Binner goes to Carlsbad and takes mud baths with Frieda Hempel and Ganna Walska. She is very psychic. She once went to Evangeline Adams to learn if she should sell some real estate, and as soon as she came in, Miss Adams said, "Are you in this business also?" The corset-maker and her late husband, a Neapolitan, were among Caruso's best friends. Often he would come to dinner and they would cook spaghetti together in the kitchen. When Caruso sang Mme. Binner always went to the opera and applauded longer than anybody else, which was no mean feat.

Mme. Binner thinks the long dresses will tend to dignify conversation, that women won't say the things they used to say in short dresses.

1 9 3 0

PAINTER IN TOWN

FOR a few days last week, Henri Matisse was in town, but nobody much knew it. He is now sixty, handsome, and looks like a doctor. While here he spent most of his time walking up and down Park Avenue, or looking out of his window in the thirty-first floor of the Ritz Tower. He would like to be ten years younger so he could move to New York, which he describes as "majestic" and whose skyscrapers surprise him because they compose well. He dined at Childs, saw a show or two, sleeping through them, and was taken to the Paramount—that being the one thing in New York he asked to see. There, too, he slept. Once he awoke to see two terrible organs emerging out of the depths. "My God, what's that?" he asked. The Jesse Crawford family was explained to him, and he went quietly back to sleep.

Mostly, Matisse had a very grand time out of his visit, eating chicken and drinking cocktails, a pleasant relief from his home-life in Nice, where his wife makes him eat only vegetables, no drinks. He went to the Zoo, the Aquarium, and Wall Street, and was let into the Havemeyer collection before the public saw it. He liked the early Corots. He knows little of American artists; at any rate knows by name only two or three who called on him in Paris, but predicts that the great art of the future will be produced in this country, because we've got energy and great order.

Matisse came from the north of France, studied to be a lawyer, was admitted to the practice, and then got sick of it. Not having anything better to do for the moment, he bought some brushes and paint and started fooling around with color. His first picture was a study of law books. It was shown in New York last year, a perfectly staid academic thing. His early pictures were all signed Essitam (his name backwards) and soon began to bring eighty dollars each. He says the turning point in his career was the day he put his foot through a canvas instead of selling it for the four hundred francs he knew he could get, to feed the three children he knew he had. After that experience he took more pains with his work and never sent out a canvas that did not entirely please him. Lay people call him "sloppy," but one picture of his shown recently in the Valentine Gallery was the result of some twelve hundred preliminary sketches. A picture of his now would cost you about sixteen thousand dollars if you could buy it, which you can't, because he likes to have his pictures around. He is now the acknowledged leader of the French moderns, credited by artists generally as having the best color eye that has glanced at life these many, many years.

Matisse is on his way to the South Seas. He may paint a bit in California and elsewhere on the way. When put on the train for Chicago his friends explained to the porter that he could speak no English. Matisse said he would make out all right, that whenever he got into language difficulties anywhere he would take out his sketch pad and begin drawing. In a very few minutes some woman was certain to come up and speak to him in French.

1 9 3 0

SEVEREST CRITIC

M R. LOUIS N. FEIPEL, a hazel-eyed scholar, has a job at the Brooklyn Public Library. He is director of publications. Nights, however, he goes home and sits down to a popular novel, slyly taking notes as he reads. When he has finished a book he gathers up his notes and addresses a letter to the author, beginning: "Dear Mr. Lewis, I enjoyed reading your book 'Dodsworth.' While doing so I made note of certain points about its editing, typesetting, and proof-reading, which may possibly interest you. . . ." Then follow about two closely spaced pages beginning "Misprints or Editorial Lapses," going on through "Orthographic Inconsistencies," and ending with "Miscellaneous," covering everything from fuzzy pronouns to misplaced subjunctives. The author, on receipt of the letter showing up anywhere from two hundred to four hundred mistakes in his book, usually has to go to bed for a couple of days.

Eventually the author recovers sufficiently to reply. Mr. Feipel has received, in ten years of gratuitous proof-reading, more than three hundred replies—from Arnold Bennett, Galsworthy, Shaw, D. H. Lawrence, Cabell, Norman Douglas, Sherwood Anderson, Max Beerbohm, Ellen Glasgow, William McFee, Santayana, Havelock Ellis, Bertrand Russell, every writing person you can think of. Everybody but Conrad. Conrad maintained an eloquent silence, although Feipel managed to itemize a couple of hundred blobs in "The Nigger of the Narcissus" and "The Rescue." Shaw called him "the prince of proofreaders," and Galsworthy humbly promised to mend his ways in the future.

The bald, unconcerned manner in which Mr. Feipel lists the mistakes must be very galling. His letters (he types them himself and makes no mistakes in typing) merely list the inconsistencies, without comment. Like this:

apple-tree (195)   apple tree (7)
well-known (80)   well kept (158)

Where a point of English usage is involved, he uses a question mark, to show he's open to reason:

adam's apple ? should be Adam's apple

And he concludes with a long list of words and phrases headed: "Are the following as you intended them, or should we emend them as indicated?"

Lady authors, we have heard, are the most deeply stricken by the receipt of a Feipel letter. Many authors have offered him large sums to go over manuscripts of forthcoming books, but he likes his job in the Brooklyn Library. In a few cases he has acceded—he has read scripts for Fannie Hurst, Llewelyn and John Powys, and Francis Hackett. He is deadly serious about his hobby—hopes to clear things up generally. He thinks books are better than they used to be but now even the average well-printed book has one hundred and fifty mistakes.

We expect a letter from him ourself, about this little story.

1 9 3 0

ANGEL

HOWARD HUGHES, who spent four million dollars, his own money, making "Hell's Angels," sat alone in the balcony during the première at the Criterion. He didn't come downstairs for the hoopla during the intermission. His name is up in big red lights on Broadway, but he is shy about meeting people. He wouldn't be interviewed or photographed when he arrived here—he has sat for only one picture since he hit the movie world like a comet three or four years ago.

In appearance the young millionaire, not yet twenty-six, reminds people of Lindbergh, being six feet three, lanky, and gifted with a becoming uneasiness in the limelight. He is reputed to be shrewd and commanding in business conferences. He spends most of his time in planes and laboratories, however. He is an eminent sound engineer, and an expert with the camera. In a private laboratory in Hollywood he monkeys with devices for improving lenses, lighting, noises, etc., and also tinkers with an idea for a new steam automobile.

Hughes perhaps inherited his mechanical bent. His father was a big tool manufacturer in Texas who also made a lot in oil. He died when Howard was twenty and left him the works. The restless young man promptly turned the industry over to associates and took a flyer in the movies, financing a picture which returned big profits. Following this he went into the movies in earnest, spending money lavishly. His pictures were not only profitable but good. "The Racket" was one of them. He'd always had a dream of glorifying the World War aviators in such a spectacle as had never been seen before, and he worked it out on a scale that appalled producers of the old, one-million-dollar school.

You've read about how he leased counties, rounded up authentic wartime planes in Europe, hired and organized a staff of approximately two hundred fliers, built on the lot a dirigible half the size of the Los Angeles. It took a year and cost a million to make the Zeppelin shots alone. No miniatures were used; tricks were employed to get only a comparatively few effects, such as the clouds into which the Zeppelin rides. Bewildered by the task of commanding nearly a hundred airplanes in maneuvers as dangerous as those of actual warfare, the director Hughes had hired gave up. Hughes took over the job himself. He piloted his own plane to direct the scenes in the air. It took eighteen months to complete them. Hughes has been a licensed pilot since he was twenty-one.

Three men—perhaps we should say *only* three men—were killed during the making of the picture. They say that if you look close enough during the shots of the thrilling "dogfight" between fifty or more planes, you can see one of them, a small trailing thread of smoke in the background, plunging ten thousand feet. Another man was killed in a collision between two planes. He was equipped with a parachute, as were all the fliers, but didn't get loose in time to jump. The man in the other plane made it. The third fatality was due to the failure of one of the German Fokkers attacking the big bomber.

The picture was started in pre-talkie days and the on-the-ground part of it, including a plot which doesn't amount to much, had to be retaken. The air scenes, however, were made later, with sound, and didn't have to be redone.

Hughes next plans to do some all-color pictures. He has bought the rights to "The Front Page" and to "Queer People," a novel satirizing Hollywood life. Nobody reads or buys stories for him. He does it himself. He rarely writes letters, using the long-distance telephone instead. He has put in as many as twenty calls to Los Angeles in one afternoon during his stay here.

1930

THE HIGH PLACE

ONE minute we are comfortably reading the "Idylls of the King" and the next thing we know we are climbing up scaffolding. Last week it was the Empire State Building, to which we were lured from our Tennyson, out of a preposterous desire to climb to a point where we could kiss the Chrysler Building goodbye and report the sensation to our earthbound readers.

It was a pleasant day and the outside of the building was shining in the sun. You've noticed that gleam. It is obtained by the use of "Allegheny metal," an alloy of iron and chrome-nickel tougher than aluminum, lighter than steel, and calculated to glitter seven years without cleaning. Just now it represents the bright face of danger. Inside the building, seven thousand workmen chevy you about. High-voltage coils have to be stepped around. Elevators take you by fits and starts as high as the seventy-eighth floor; from there you have to walk. (These elevators, by the way, will go at a speed of a thousand feet a minute in the completed building, this by special dispensation of the building commission, which has never permitted elevators to go that fast before.)

If we counted right we got to the eighty-first floor, from which point the apple-vendors looked like midgets selling red peppermint hearts. Al Smith recently went that high, looked down, and decided he was high enough. He likes to have walls around him. It had been planned to have Mr. Smith go up to the tiptop of the steelwork, when it is completed around Thanksgiving Day, and put a golden bolt in the last beam, but chances are he won't. Even the steelworkers themselves felt a bit jittery when they got to the eighty-fifth floor, and asked for a bonus. They got it. There have been few accidents on the job. Steel was hoisted up on the inside, a new idea to avoid endangering passersby. The schedule was so carefully timed that a minute or two after a steel beam arrived from Pittsburgh by way of Weehawken, it was on its way up to its appointed place. It represents the fastest job of steel construction on record. The men wanted to celebrate this and asked Al Smith, when he was there, if they could build a hundred-and-twenty-foot brown derby and stick it on top of the mooring mast for a while. He was too modest to allow this.

The mooring mast, the builders say, is no publicity stunt, no ornament to be set on top of the building for beauty's sake. So they say. It will cost a hundred and twenty thousand dollars. The topmost room in the building will be in the mooring mast and will hold fifty people easily and staunchly. The roof of it will also hold fifty people and sometime next spring these fifty will be balloon-moorers, for plans are being made to anchor a Zeppelin to the mast next May or June—the ZRS-4, a thousand-footer, now being built by Goodyear. The dirigible will drop a grappling hook to the roof, draw up a mooring line, and then (if all goes well) the moorers will drag the ship down by a winch on the roof. Passengers will exit into the tower through a door in the airship's nose. Anyway, that's the plan. Sightseers can't use the mast; there'll be a glassed-in observation-room for them on the roof of the eighty-fifth floor. The last office floor will be the eightieth—and will be occupied by the Messrs. Smith, Raskob, Pierre du Pont, and Louis G. Kaufman.

The Empire State is sunk in solid rock; three hundred thousand tons were removed and the building will weigh only half of that. Safe, you see. As for the old Waldorf, most of it rests today at the bottom of the ocean. The building was so toughly constructed that it cost nine hundred thousand dollars to tear it down. Usually wreckers pay for the privilege and make money on what they salvage, but much of the Waldorf had to be ruined to knock it loose, and the ruins were towed to sea in barges and dumped.

1930

TRIVIA

CHAPLIN took cover as soon as he got to town and didn't go many places while he was here. He didn't have an automobile; rode mostly in cabs. He would have gone to the opening of his picture in a cab if someone had not hired a livery car for him. He was gleeful at the success of the film, to the first showing of which he took Constance Collier, the actress, his old friend. She invited him to the première of "Peter Ibbetson," the opera, of which she was co-librettist, next day but he didn't go. He doesn't like opera. He went out to Mrs. Hearst's on Long Island for the weekend instead. He didn't talk about anything much but his movie while here, although he did talk about the soldiers' bonus once: got into a hot argument with C. E. Mitchell, the banker, about it at a dinner party. Chaplin said the bonus ought to be paid, Mitchell said it would just aggravate conditions. Chaplin is still pretty much of a radical. He's still English, too, in citizenship, and pretty much in spirit. Quite a few hours here were spent fixing up his papers so he could get back into the country again. He wouldn't sail on anything but an English boat. When he learned that Major Campbell, the racing driver, had booked passage on the same ship he offered to defer his departure so as not to divide Campbell's welcome in England. He finally went on the same boat when he learned Campbell was disembarking at Southampton instead of Plymouth.

He has thousands of feet of film left over from "City Lights," much of which he thinks he can work into future pictures. He works that way, builds things up gradually. The suicide gag in the present picture had been in his mind ten years. The rap he took at "sound" and speech-making was the first time he had ever gone seriously satirical. He makes a new mustache out of hair crêpe every time he acts. His property shoes are the largest he can buy in a shoestore, run over several times by an automobile. That's all there is to these. He saw but one show here, the Noël Coward one. After the performance he decided to go with Coward and others to a party at Katharine Cornell's. He's always casual in his social activities; is miserable if he has two or three engagements ahead. In California he lives casually, associating almost exclusively with a small number of picture people. He has given up smoking entirely and drinking almost entirely. Thinks one ought to around forty. In general he's apprehensive of people and everything; keeps his money in half a dozen banks scattered around the world—Toronto, Berlin, Paris, New York. His wealth, all other things are secondary to his picture-making. His expenditures are modest. Fifty thousand a year would easily cover his cost of living. The scene in which the sidewalk elevator rose and descended wasn't as difficult in the taking as it may have seemed. He had an indicator behind the camera which went up and down with the platform and he knew where the elevator was all the time.

1931

TEX AND ELLA

ONLY one of the Wendel sisters is left: Miss Ella, who is eighty-one years old. She owns about a hundred million dollars' worth of New York real estate and lives alone in that silent, mournful old residence at Thirty-ninth and Fifth Avenue—the Wendel house. For years the three Wendel sisters lived there, mice-like, working a miracle of solitude in the heart of the city's traffic and trade. The death of Miss Georgiana in 1929 left Miss Ella all alone. One supposed the old house would be more mysterious than ever, that the world would never see the one old lady stirring outside it. Certainly nobody would have dreamed that Miss Ella would one night step out and visit, of all places, Texas Guinan's night club. Take a firm grip on your chair arm while we tell you that this, however, is exactly what, one night, she did. Here's how the strange visit came to pass:

Miss Guinan writes a column for the *Graphic* and a few weeks ago she printed in it an open letter addressed to Miss Ella Wendel, addressed, indeed, informally, just to "Dear Ella." It was a cheerful, impudent, teasing letter. Miss Guinan asked Ella why she didn't have a telephone put in, why she didn't try out the new invention, the electric light, why she didn't come on up to her night club some night and have a good time—chatter like that. A day or two after the column was printed an old gentleman who looked as if he had stepped out of the eighteen-eighties, as indeed he probably had, appeared at the night club. He announced himself as Miss Wendel's attorney. At this point you could, of course, have knocked Miss Guinan down with a quill pen, she was so astonished—and frightened. She thought she was going to be sued for libel. The old gentleman from out of the past explained that Miss Wendel had read the open letter and had decided to accept the invitation. Personally he deprecated the whole affair, had tried to dissuade her, but she had made up her mind and that was that. He felt it incumbent upon him to convey to Miss—ah—Guinan her acceptance. Miss Guinan managed to keep ahold of herself and said she was very happy. A date for Miss Wendel's appearance was then set.

On the great night Miss Wendel appeared, accompanied by her emissary, another old gentleman, and another old lady. All were over eighty. Miss Wendel wore a sable coat and a diamond hair ornament. They arrived at nine-thirty but Miss Guinan and her troupe happened to be on hand then as they were making a radio broadcast. The four old people sat through this, deeply interested, and they remained on for the regular show later. It was two A.M. before they bowed their way out of the uproar.

Miss Wendel was interested in everything that went on. Miss Guinan sat at her table for half an hour. The ladies called each other "Tex" and "Ella." They had a nice chat. In the course of this, Miss Guinan mentioned that she was upset because earlier in the day she had lost a valuable handbag, a present from Larry Fay—whom, we must suppose, Miss Wendel could not place. Ella listened sympathetically, however, and asked what sort of a bag it was. Tex told her in detail. About a week later Miss Guinan received a package—from Ella—containing a little gift. It was a handbag as nearly like the lost one as Miss Wendel had been able to describe it to the bagmaker. It cost around forty-five hundred dollars.

Both the night club and the old house at Thirty-ninth Street have now resumed their usual humdrum existence.

1931

AL

WE haven't reported on Al Smith for quite a while, and you may wonder what he does with his time now. He spends a lot of it in the solarium of his penthouse in lower Fifth Avenue, smoking. He never lies late, but is always up by eight o'clock. He takes a cold shower, and always sings. Most every morning he phones long distance to Miss Mary Adams Warner, his granddaughter, aged four, in Albany, and they talk over the situation. Now and again she visits the Smith apartment, in which there are always kept, ready and waiting for such small visitors, a crib, toys, and all the other paraphernalia demanded by weekend guests of her age.

Mr. Smith gets to his office at ten o'clock, and the first thing he does is to empty his pockets—coat, trousers, and waistcoat—on top of his desk. He has the habit of making memoranda on small slips of paper all the time, which he tucks away in his pockets. He puts them in a drawer of his desk and later a secretary goes over them with him. He throws the silly ones away, and she files the others.

The former governor gets an average of sixty letters a day, many of them freakish ones—that is, they are addressed simply to "Al, New York," or to "Smith" (no address at all), or they bear nothing on the envelope except a photograph of Mr. Smith or maybe some famous saying of his. The sender usually incloses a little note in which he merely wonders whether Mr. Smith will receive the letter. Smith spends several hours a day, sometimes, talking things over with the various technicians who are still puttering around the Empire State Building.

His social life is unexciting: mostly he stays home of an evening playing double solitaire with Mrs. S. He goes to musical shows quite often (Joe Cook is his favorite comedian), and is always recognized. Very often some woman or other runs up to him in the lobby and hugs and kisses him, in the name of Democracy. Mr. Smith blushes furiously but is always kind to these women and never knocks them down or anything. Mrs. Smith got him to the opera once this season, but after it was over he said he'd never go again. He won't go up in an airplane either; he never has been up in one. Swimming is his favorite pastime. Before a big banquet he always goes to the Biltmore and has a Turkish bath. He keeps in constant touch with Mr. Raskob but sees little of Governor Roosevelt. The latter has never requested Mr. Smith's advice on the conduct of the State's affairs. When they meet they talk about the weather.

1931

THE FLYING SPOT

THE Jenkins Television Corporation, which makes television sets, has sold about twenty-five hundred of them in the past year and a half. People have them in their homes—engineers, dabblers, optimists, believers in the future of television. A set, as you may know, is like a radio cabinet, dials and all, except that in place of a sound-emitter it has a lens the size of a pie pan. You sit in a chair, twirl the dials, look through the lens, and if all goes well images appear on a screen about eight inches square on the other side of the lens. Sets can be bought at several of the department stores.

The National Broadcasting Company just broadcasts its television signature, WXZ or W4Y, or whatever it is, and sometimes the figure of a cat going round and round in a circle. It keeps using the wave length merely to hold its franchise. Columbia, on the other hand, broadcasts singers and speakers and piano-players every evening. The images are synchronized with sound: you see a tenor's lips move and hear his voice. That is, if you've tuned in properly. Columbia gets five or six fan letters a day. One man in Toronto and another in Chicago wrote that they got New York programs on their sets.

One night last week Columbia broadcast two prizefighters in action, to give its public some idea of what it will be seeing in a few years. With a dozen other people we watched the shadowy images of Benny Leonard and another boxer on the small screen of a receiving set. Only about two people can really see comfortably into the present set; the others have to bend and duck and crane their necks over the lucky ones' shoulders.

The fight wasn't very good. The boxers had to stay inside a space about five feet square and you could see them only from their waists up. Now and then there'd be a clear picture; then the pugilists would appear to be groping in a fog or chasing each other in a tank of milk. Faces and arms dilate and contract and look crazy, like images in those trick mirrors at amusement parks.

Lighting is a major difficulty. For the last round, we went up into the room where the fight was going on. It was about the size of a bathroom and dark. Out of a small glass-enclosed control-room a finger of light plays upon the figures of the performers. If it were allowed to come to a full stop, it would be just a spot as big as a thumbnail, but a disc with sixty holes in it whirls in front of the line of light, scattering it. This light, reflected back from the body of whoever is being televised, is registered, after a lot of little miracles, on the screen of a receiving set. Right now it's hard to get more than two persons in a picture. Four or five would have to stand back so far that they wouldn't reflect the light strongly enough. Performers have to be made up like movie actors, with grease paint and lipstick.

1 9 3 1

OXFORD MAN

WILLIAM FAULKNER, whose violent novels about the darker reaches of the soul have been attracting increasing interest latterly, is now occupying an apartment in Tudor City and will be there until the middle of December. He spends most of his days alone, working on his next novel, which is to be called "Light in August." It's about a quarter done. Invitations have poured in on him, but he's been to only one literary party, one given by his publishers. The usual crowd was there.

Faulkner is very Southern, his "a"s very broad. This is his second visit. He was here four years ago while still obscure. He was born in Oxford, Mississippi, thirty-four years ago and that has been his home ever since. He owns a small cotton plantation and lives on it, with his wife and two children, in a fine old house built in 1818. In 1915 he enlisted in the Canadian air force and went to France. He crashed behind his own lines. He was hanging upside down in his plane with both legs broken when an ambulance got to him. He heard one of the men say: "He's dead all right," but had strength enough to deny this. After he recovered he transferred to the American air force. He has a pilot's license now and sometimes flies a rather wobbly plane owned by a friend in Oxford. After the war he studied about five months in the University of Mississippi, which is at Oxford, and of which his father is secretary. That is the extent of his higher education. In Oxford he spends much time writing. "Ah write when the spirit moves me," he says, "and the spirit moves me every day." For relief he fishes, hunts, and bosses the plantation. Only a few of the townspeople know he writes at all; most of them think he's lazy. The local drugstore ordered several copies of his last novel but didn't do very well with them. His mother reads every line he writes, but his father doesn't bother and suspects his son is wasting his time.

1931

THE FRESCOER

DIEGO RIVERA painted his frescoes in a bare and cold room on the sixth floor of the Heckscher Building. We got there at four o'clock one afternoon to see him work. We stayed until six and he hadn't started in, was still sauntering around. The night before he had got up on his scaffold at seven o'clock and worked until nine in the morning, which is fourteen hours—mostly to get a little detail right. It was a terrifying picture he was working on then, one showing a Mexican Indian dressed in the skin of a jaguar or some such animal, head and all, killing a Spaniard in armor with a stone knife.

Around the walls were larger frescoes, completed on previous nights, all of them scenes from the violent history of Mexico. We were studying one when Rivera walked up and pointed to a spot where a brown he had been using came out thin. "It's not very good," he said, amiably. They say he never loses his grinning calm, no matter what goes wrong. He had slept only five hours that day and was just about to put in another night painting on the damp plaster, which was made up of marble dust, lime, and water. The steam heat in the room had to be turned off, as otherwise the compound would have solidified too fast. Painting frescoes is a race against drying, with mistakes and disappointments beyond repair. Rivera's frescoes, when dry, are as hard as concrete and as heavy. It took six men, while we were there, an hour to move one about seven feet square and three inches thick out of the room and up to the Museum of Modern Art galleries on the twelfth floor. The thing weighed more than a thousand pounds. The bottom of the fresco was slightly chipped in the moving, and the foreman of the haulers was distraught. Not so Rivera. "It's all right," he said.

Rivera seldom has a photograph or a sketch of anything to go by, painting even steam shovels, disc harrows, etc., from memory. "Some of them wouldn't work," a follower of his told us, "but machinery in a painting doesn't have to work." Occasionally, however, the painter makes a miniature sketch of a fresco he is about to begin; sometimes, even, he uses one exactly the size of the projected fresco, pinning it to a wall where he can look at it. We saw one of these, an idea he got from a visit to No. 1 Wall Street. Rivera was much impressed by the great money vaults down there. This sketch, a completed fresco now, we suppose, showed the vaults, with all their gold, at the bottom of the drawing. On the street level, just above, were hundreds of unemployed, lying asleep, or worrying. Above them towered the skyscrapers of the financial region.

The exhibition, planned for a month, may last two. Thirty-five thousand people saw the Matisse show and more are expected for Rivera's. When it's over, the frescoes will be sold. It'll cost plenty to move them, if you live far.

When he is working at night, Diego sometimes varies his milk diet with a spot of coffee. He doesn't smoke, because ashes might get into the plaster, and besides you can't smoke and keep both hands busy with paints and brushes. Enthusiasts usually stayed until four o'clock in the cold room, watching their idol. After they left he sometimes slept for fifteen minutes, sitting in a chair, then got up and went to work again. We met a lady who, a year or so ago, sat with Rivera on a scaffold in Mexico City for nineteen hours. At the end of that time, night having given way to morning and morning to afternoon, she got up and started down the ladder. Rivera looked surprised and injured, and remarked sadly: "I have begun to bore you."

1931

INAUGURAL BLUES

AN early robin that accompanied Mrs. Roosevelt on her dress-buying tour last week tells us some of the things that happened. At Milgrim's, a cop was waiting when the First Lady–elect arrived. He hadn't been sent for; the doorman had told him of the expected visit and he thought he had better stick around.

Mrs. Roosevelt, accompanied by her secretary, Miss Helen Johnson, met her daughter, Mrs. Dall; a friend, Mrs. Rosenman, wife of a Supreme Court justice; and Mr. Milgrim in a private room on the third floor. Half a dozen models showed off evening gowns. Mrs. Roosevelt and Mrs. Dall each bought one. Then a black-lace-and-chiffon dress was brought in, occasioning "oh"s and "ah"s. Mrs. Roosevelt and her daughter both wanted it. They both called chiffon "cheefong." "Now Mummy, don't forget that I get first chance at this," said Mrs. Dall. Mrs. Roosevelt said, "Why don't you get it in some other color, Sis, and I could have it in black." Sis said, "But Mummy, I need an all-round black dress. My all-round black dress is all gone." The subject was dropped for a while, but later settled quite simply. "I'll take it in black," Mrs. Roosevelt said quietly. Mr. Milgrim held up a black-wool dress with piqué collars and cuffs. "For you, Mrs. Dall?" he asked. She said, "Ugh, no! That's for Mother. I hate those cuffs and collars." Next, everyone moiled over a tan-and-gold brocade evening dress proposed for Mrs. Roosevelt. Mrs. Dall said tan would never do, and asked if they had the dress in blue and gold. While this was being hunted up, the same thing was shown in red and gold. Mrs. Roosevelt liked it but the others were against it. The blue and gold arrived and the others all liked it but

Mrs. Roosevelt didn't. Well, in the end they let the whole thing go. They're probably still talking about it, though.

Mrs. Dall now started to buy a flock of gowns for herself, and at this point Mrs. Roosevelt brought up the question of price. It was all whispery and embarrassing. Finally, Mrs. Roosevelt called a figure to Mrs. Dall in French. There was some conversation between the two in French—although the others in the room looked as if they might know French—and the matter was settled.

That same afternoon, Mrs. Roosevelt bought her afternoon inaugural outfit at Arnold Constable. Velvety-finish stuff, girls, of Eleanor blue, which used to be Periwinkle blue but was renamed in honor of Mrs. Roosevelt. The collar of the dress comes high in back with crisscross drapery in front of the blouse. The coat, made of the same material in navy blue, is three-quarters length and hangs loose from the neck; it has a soft, fluffy collar and a tie. The hat, also navy blue, is to have a brim, although Mrs. Roosevelt usually wears turbans.

Next, Mrs. Roosevelt went to Le Mouchoir, a shop on Madison Avenue around the corner from her home on Sixty-fifth Street, and picked out five dresses, all of various shades of blue. One, an afternoon dress, was of powder-blue silk. Mrs. Roosevelt referred to it as her "hand-shaking dress."

1933

LONG RANGE

THE Tippenhauer Weather Service, 2–4 Stone Street, will forecast the weather for you three years in advance, making a sucker out of the government, which refuses to guess more than forty-eight hours ahead, and keeps hedging on that. The government is inclined to treat the Tippenhauer brothers (there are two, Louis and Henry) with a certain amount of detachment, calling them visionary, but at the moment they have more than two hundred clients around New York who take them seriously. The biggest customer is the Metropolitan Golf Association, which signed up a few weeks ago for one hundred and fifty affiliated clubs. They paid $360 for six months, getting one-month-in-the-future predictions. Consolidated Gas pays $125 a year for forecasts of the metropolitan weather six months ahead; the North German Lloyd pays $25 a year for predictions one month ahead; the University Club takes it on the same basis; Percy Rockefeller has been a subscriber since 1929 (six-months-in-the-future service). Weber & Heilbroner are another. Obviously, the gas company is interested because heat and cold affect gas consumption, Weber & Heilbroner because the weather influences the sale of Palm Beach suits, and so on. It's hard to tell why Mr. Rockefeller or the University Club cares. Just want to be on the inside of things, probably.

The service consists mostly of a big chart full of enough graphs to floor Einstein. We didn't bother to try to make sense out of it, although Henry Tippenhauer, whom we went to see, says it's simple enough. In a nutshell, he says, the weather on earth varies with the movement of neighboring planets, so all you have to do is watch things up there and you'll know what to expect in New

York, or anywhere else on earth. It's not quite as easy as that, really, because comets are likely to show up in the solar system, monkeying up calculations.

The Tippenhauer system was perfected in Haiti during the war, which Louis spent as an interned enemy alien. He was imprisoned until seven months after the Armistice, which ruined him financially but enabled him to work out his theory. When he was liberated, he announced he was prepared to forecast weather for any point on the earth's surface as far as three years in the future. He began issuing forecasts a month ahead and worked up a nice little business, Haitians feeling strongly about the weather. In 1925, his brother Henry came here from Germany and established a Tippenhauer office. Louis stayed in Haiti and still does, using the astronomical equipment of the Observatory of Jesuit Priests in Port-au-Prince. He mails his findings to Henry here each week, and Henry has them printed and mailed to clients. There has been no profit yet from this office, but Henry says there will be.

The Tippenhauers estimate their present accuracy to be between seventy-five and eighty-five percent, and hope to pull it up to ninety before long. They haven't had any commercial inquiries yet for a prediction three years in advance. People aren't interested in the weather more than a year ahead, Henry says, a little sadly.

1933

HIGH HATS

FORTY years ago, when Max Fluegelman was an apprentice of fourteen, there were more than five hundred silk-hat makers in New York. Now there are only about twenty in the entire country; and fifteen of these work for Mr. Fluegelman, who is head man of the silk-hat world. I. S. Wyatt, one of the hatters in his shop, at 848 Sixth Avenue, is eighty and still turns out a mighty nice hat.

Ever since the nineties, the top-hat business has been going down. Even by present-day standards, business has been dullish for years, except for a brief spurt a few seasons back when college boys went in for them. Last year, Mr. Fluegelman, to stir up trade, went down to City Hall and gave a topper to the first June groom. He got a modest mention for it, but was annoyed the rest of the summer by Tammany men who came in wanting free hats. He offered them hats at cost, but they just went off grumbling. This June, he tried again. The groom (Alex Freirich, 7⅛) got his picture in the papers, but Mr. Fluegelman wasn't mentioned. So he'll never do *that* again.

Nothing, however, can take away from Mr. Fluegelman his claim to fame and source of great satisfaction: he has made a silk hat for every President since Theodore Roosevelt. The hatter had met Roosevelt when he was Police Commissioner, and when he was elected President, Fluegelman made the inaugural hat. When the current Roosevelt was elected, Fluegelman went up to his New York house and fitted him personally. It was kind of funny. Fluegelman uses a "conform-measurer," a hellish-looking device with movable wooden flanges. It is placed on the head and the flanges stretch until they take the shape of the skull; then a cork-lined flap on top of the device is snapped down and a lot of spikes mark the shape of the head on a piece of paper. Roosevelt took one look at this thing and told Fluegelman he thought he would wear a soft hat—for the inauguration! Fluegelman was firm. He put the conform-measurer on Roosevelt's head, set the flanges, pressed the flap, and said sternly, "I have made silk hats for every President since Theodore Roosevelt and you're going to wear one, too." "But I really think I'll wear a soft one," insisted the President. "I'll make you one of each," said the hatter, and he did, but the soft one was of such a frivolous shade of pearl gray that Roosevelt didn't dare sport it on that dour day when he took the oath.

The two Roosevelts are the only Presidents Fluegelman saw personally. He got the others' sizes from secretaries, and skull shapes from photographs. The secretaries of all the Presidents except one wrote thank-you notes to Fluegelman for the hats. The exception was Coolidge. He wrote his own letter. The biggest head was Taft's, 7¾ oversize, and the smallest Coolidge's, 7⅛. The other head sizes were: Wilson, 7¼; Hoover, 7½; and Harding and the two Roosevelts, 7⅜. Theodore Roosevelt's head was what the trade calls pear-shaped, as is Franklin's. All the other Presidents had ovals, except maybe Wilson, who leaned toward pear-shaped. Wilson's hat, second smallest of the bunch, was too big when he got it and had to be altered. It was this hat, Mr. Fluegelman says, which caused Wilson to remark that Presidents' heads got smaller after election, not bigger.

Fluegelman used to make a lot of silk hats of the old stovepipe style for Oscar Hammerstein, who started a vogue for this style among actors. David Warfield used to drop in twice a year for a hat—felt, though, not high silk. "He talked to me in the same soft woice as he was on the stage," says Mr. Fluegelman, who was born in Roumania. The great silk-hatter has a theory about the falling-off of toppers. He thinks the automobiles did it. Men liked to wear high hats in carriages, but somehow the automobile is no place for them.

1933

GREAT MEN

PROBABLY nobody who has written to Lindbergh asking for his autograph has got one except Mr. Seymour Halpern, age nineteen, of 120-06 Ninety-seventh Avenue, Richmond Hill, Queens. Halp seems to be top autograph-hunter of the Americas. He's got everybody you ever heard of except King George, the Prince of Wales, and Stalin. "I've only written them six times," he says. He wrote Lindbergh sixteen times, always enclosing a photo of the Colonel to be signed; several were group photos on which everybody shown, except Lindbergh, had put his name. Halpern never got one of them back. Finally, he wrote to the late Senator Morrow and put his problem up to him; Morrow wrote back that Halpern might use his name in writing his son-in-law. The young man did, and the seventeenth photo came back, signed.

Morrow's letter was written a week before he died. Young Halpern has had strange experiences that way. Taft signed a group photograph of his Supreme Court only a few days before his last illness; Coolidge, who had already sent the Brooklyn youth various signatures, autographed the week before his death a pen sketch of himself by the young man. Nansen, the explorer, Schnitzler, the author, and Edward T. Sanford, a justice of the Supreme Court under Hughes, all died the day they wrote autographs for Halpern. Clemenceau's signature was the last thing he ever wrote—Seymour has a note from the Tiger's secretary saying so. In addition, these other men died within a day or two of writing their names for the young hunter: Joffre, Belasco, Vachel Lindsay, Nicholas Longworth, Nathan Straus, and Knute Rockne. Of course, they represent a small percentage of the notables Halpern has landed—four thousand and some odd—but they were enough to scare Eddie Cantor when, in calling on him, Halpern told about the deaths. Cantor paled for a moment, and then brightened. "Quick," he said, "here's George Jessel's address!"

Halpern's biggest thrill came when he got the Pope, who wrote a small message of greeting on his photo. The young man sat right down and wrote Mussolini, who had ignored six or eight previous requests. He told Il Duce he had landed His Holiness, so what? A few weeks later, an attaché of the Italian consulate here called on Halpern (whose home is about an hour's ride from Manhattan) and asked if he might see the Pope's autograph. Halpern showed it to him—he keeps his prizes in his bedroom, on the walls, in files, on tables. The visitor scrutinized it closely, and nodded, with a touch of admiration. A few weeks later, Mussolini came across.

One of Halpern's stunts is to make sketches of great men from their photographs and send them to be signed. Queen Helen kept one of young Michael, the boy King, and the Kaiser kept the one of himself, each sending an autographed photo instead. This sketch trick also landed Einstein, Shaw (who wrote under the drawing, "Have I deserved this?"), and Franklin Roosevelt. Halpern called on Roosevelt when the latter was Governor. Roosevelt was tickled with the likeness of himself, and showed it to Mrs. R. and to the butler, both of whom were pleasant about it. Then he started to write "To my young friend" on the drawing, but couldn't remember whether "friend" was spelled "ie" or "ei." He asked Halpern, who didn't know either, so then he wrote it "ie" and looked it up in a dictionary to make sure. He was right.

Once when Greta Garbo was here, Halpern barged into her hotel and somehow or other got to see her. She wasn't seeing young men then, being afraid they were noosepapermen, but she talked to Halpern for half an hour. He was so flustered he left without getting her autograph. He had, however, an interview he could have sold anywhere, but he didn't think of that. To trap the intellectuals, the canny Halpern usually writes them asking how they account for their success. This system fetched Professor John Dewey and Dr. George Santayana; they both wrote conscientious pieces for him on success. All authors are pushovers, anyway. Halpern has never failed to land an author yet.

Halpern even got a dog, the late Rin Tin Tin. The animal's owner dipped the right front paw into some ink and pressed the paw on one of Rin's photographs.

1 9 3 3

THE BLUES MAN

O UR mention of Ferde Grofé reminded us that we should look up W. C. Handy, who, as everybody is supposed to know, wrote the "St. Louis Blues." He is playing around vaudeville theatres in the East now, in an act composed of old-timers. In his late fifties, he is a tall, sturdy, nearly bald Negro. He plays in the act for fun, as he doesn't need the money, having done very well.

In his teens, Handy was water boy for a gang of laborers building a dam at Muscle Shoals. On the side he played a trumpet in a band, and before he was twenty he got up a Negro quartet and they started out to sing their way to the World's Fair in Chicago. When they got there, they found the Fair had been postponed for a year, so they sang their way to St. Louis and disbanded. Handy walked the streets for two weeks looking for work, and then wandered down to Alabama and got a real position, musical director of the State Agricultural and Mechanical College, at Huntsville. "It bored me," he says. Finally he joined up with a minstrel company for six dollars a week, played the cornet in the parades, the bass viol in the pit, and led a quartet on the stage. In 1903, he had a nine-piece band of his own down in Mississippi. It was there that he first took down the notes of one of those mournful songs which Negroes had been singing all over the deep South for decades. "Gwine take morphine an' die, gwine take morphine an' die, gwine take morphine an' die," one of the most familiar of them ran. It was Handy who first called these songs "blues." They differed from spirituals in that they were not for group singing and they were based on some murder or scandal, or simply the singer's personal misery.

In 1906, the restless Mr. Handy was in Memphis, where he organized a fifty-five-piece band. When a man named Crump ran for mayor of the city, he hired

Handy's band to play on street corners for him. Handy wrote a song for the campaign called "Mr. Crump." It wasn't flattering—the last line 'lowed that Mr. Crump could go ketch hisself some air—but Mr. Crump was elected. The song caught on in Memphis, and in 1912 Handy brought out a thousand copies, with the title "The Memphis Blues" and no words. He tried to sell it to New York publishers, but couldn't until a daring man gave him a hundred dollars for all rights to it. The republication of this song, with new words, marked the beginning of the great blues phase the country has gone through. In 1914, Handy wrote his masterpiece, "St. Louis Blues." More records of this song have been sold than of any other, and Handy's own music company, on Broadway, sells fifty thousand copies of it a year in sheet music. In 1919, his "Yellow Dog Blues," written four years before, sold more than a million when Victor brought it out on a record. In all, he's written around sixty blues songs, his latest last year: "Way Down South Where the Blues Begin." Royalties keep coming to him from the radio, talkies, and vaudeville. When his vaudeville act played the Paradise Theatre in the Bronx a few weeks ago, a singer in another act did "St. Louis Blues," and in the movie running on the same bill an actress sang the opening line of it: "I hate to see de evenin' sun go down."

Handy has lived on Seventh Avenue near 112th Street since 1917. He has a lot of children and grandchildren. Two years ago, he went down to Memphis for a hullabaloo in his honor. A market place on Beale Street was made into a park and called Handy Square ("Beale Street Blues" was another of his compositions). Handy is just now arranging "Steal Away to Jesus" as a funeral march for brass band. His hobby is politics: municipal, national, and international. He says he predicted the World War twenty years before it came. He won't venture a prediction about the coming mayoralty election.

1 9 3 3

HELEN COOKE, CHARLES COOKE,
CLIFFORD ORR, AND HAROLD ROSS

AS MILLIONS CHEER

EVEN as you read this, the first large post-prohibition cargo of liquors, cleared frankly and legitimately for this repentant land, probably will be at sea, churning westward. Reports from Liverpool were that the loading had been completed early this week and that the ship was expected to sail Thursday, the nineteenth. It's an eight-thousand-ton freighter, chartered by Park & Tilford, and bound for San Francisco. It is expected off that port about December 1, and the captain is instructed to lie twelve miles offshore until he gets a certain signal and then to rush right in as fast as his little propellers will carry him. A second ship, of twelve thousand tons, will shortly start loading 150,000 cases of potables for New York; and a third, and others, probably. The two boats mentioned by tonnage are chartered by Park & Tilford, our enterprising sellers of liquors, who have been doing all the full-page newspaper advertising lately. They are American boats, and the owners were so happy when they were hired that they exuberantly offered to repaint both ships any color Park & Tilford wanted. The San Francisco ship wasn't redone, because there wasn't time for the paint to dry, but the New York boat will be repainted in some appropriate color not yet decided upon and, to boot, will probably be renamed the Park & Tilford. It will be off New York by December 1 and P. & T. hope it will be the first liquor boat to land here, but expect a race, for at least one other importing company is known to have chartered a special ship for the deadline, and probably others have, too. There's quite a bit of mystery about the business.

We learned the foregoing when we called at Park & Tilford's central office to inquire about prospects in the liquor business and the results of their big advertising campaign. They wouldn't give us the figures on the advance orders they have received as a result of their advertising, but they did tell us that they considered it a terrific success and that they now intend to continue it right up to December 6, the date upon which they hope to land their first liquid imports. And it would have done your heart good to see the activity about the place—a dozen customers in the reception-room waiting to place their orders and make their deposits of ten dollars a case, and scores of clerks in the order-room with mail-openers, typewriters, adding machines, etc., receiving orders and lovingly filing memos for future deliveries. Orders and inquiries have kept a hundred clerks busy since October 5, we were told, twenty extra office workers being hired that day. October 5 was the day P. & T. ran full-page ads in six newspapers. Since then they've been running a page a day, rotating it among the papers.

The firm wouldn't tell us the names of any big orderers but said that the largest order received came from a very big political bug right here in New York: sixty-five cases of assorted Scotch, brandies, champagnes, and gins. The second largest came from a man in Denver (richest man in Colorado, they had heard): twenty-five cases of gin, twenty-five of sherry, and two of vermouth. The average order is for two or three cases. Scotch is the biggest seller, half the total. Orders have been received from every state in the Union, and the ads, although they appeared only in New York papers, have brought in five thousand inquiries about wholesale prices.

1 9 3 3

HOUSE OF BRICK

WALT DISNEY raised his own salary from $150 a week to $200 a week, as a reward for having produced "Three Little Pigs." We got that from his brother, Roy Disney, who was in town last week. Roy manages the Walt Disney interests, and is full of figures about the pigs. They, the pigs, have been shown at 400 theatres in New York City alone, for a total run of 1,200 weeks. They ran for eight weeks at the Trans-Lux Broadway theatre, the only picture that was ever shown there for more than one week. It, or they, flashed on the screen one hundred times a week, and about 250,000 people cheered the opus at that one theatre alone. Out of town, the pigs were just as much of a smash, and Walt has received countless requests for further adventures. He doesn't think he'll make a series, though: thinks the chances are against his being able to repeat.

The Music Hall gets the credit for having first shown "Three Little Pigs" here, the week of May 25th to 31st, 1933. Pinto Colvieg, a former newspaperman now working for Disney, gets the credit for the line "Who's afraid of the big bad wolf?" The song was published in September by Irving Berlin and in two weeks had become the second national best-seller, being topped only by "The Last Round-Up." The Disney staff are just a bit sheep-faced about the pigs, because when Walt suggested the idea, in September, 1932, none of the directors reacted. It seems that the Disney procedure is, Walt proposes but a director disposes. Not getting any reaction, Walt shelved the pigs. They kept coming up in his mind, though, and he suggested them a second time. Again no reaction. The third time, the reaction came and the pigs went into production.

A Mr. Frank Churchill, one of Disney's 140 employees, took five minutes off

and wrote the chorus of the wolf song. It is the first song hit ever to come out
of an animated-cartoon studio (and incidentally it always seemed to us to
come out of "Die Fledermaus"). Originally the words appeared like this: "Who's
afraid of the big bad wolf, big bad wolf, big bad wolf? Who's afraid of the big bad
wolf? He don't know from nothin'." The last line didn't seem to fit, somehow,
and the staff men convened and tried to find a word that rhymed with "wolf."
They huffed and they puffed, but they finally gave up and had the two pigs who
sing the song play the last line on their flute and violin.

Colvieg was called upon to speak the part of the wolf, and he also did the pig
in overalls. Girls from a trio called the Rhythmettes, Hollywood talent, sang for
the two jerry-builders. The cost of making a Silly Symphony runs from
$18,000 to $30,000; and the pigs were by no means the most expensive to
make. Most Sillies gross between $80,000 and $100,000 over a three-year period; "Three Little Pigs," Roy told us, would probably triple that amount. Walt
makes thirteen Mickeys and thirteen Sillies a year. All the profits go back into
the business. Two new Sillies are all ready to be sprung: "The China Shop," to
be released in the next couple of weeks, and "The Night Before Christmas," at
Yuletide. The pigs are soon going into the French and the Spanish. We'll try
and get you the words.

1933

LENOX 1734

T HE mansion where Joseph Pulitzer lived is as cold as the moon. We shivered for an hour up and down its tremendous sprawl of rooms and halls one afternoon last week; they are littered with débris and have been deserted for twenty years. The estate is turning the famous residence over to real-estate men to be made into apartments, and we wanted to see it as it was, back before the war, when the nervous genius of the *World* gloomed like a spider in his far, quiet corner of the rambling palace of sixty rooms.

Most people had forgotten the abandoned masterpiece of Stanford White on Seventy-third Street just east of Fifth Avenue until the new plans brought it into prominence again. It was completed in 1902 and for ten years vibrated to the power of the eccentric man who lived in curious soundproof rooms at one end of it. Then he died and the life went out of the place. Nobody has lived in it for two decades. None of the bells in the elaborate system of bells rings now, none of the myriad lights will light. Cold, lonely, and sad, but still magnificent, and a touch mysterious, the mansion is like a grand duchess gone blind and deaf in her old age.

Pigeons flutter disconsolately outside the windows beyond the organ loft. The organ console stands at the head of the central marble staircase, covered with dust. The gold-and-white woodwork of the impressive main salon on the second floor, fifty feet long, with a ceiling twenty feet high, is tawdry under its dust; the two large crystal chandeliers, one at each end, are gray and dismal. Dirty windows keep out the light and give the baronial dignity of the mansion a deep, melancholy gloom. Before long it will be altered, polished, and brightened up, elegant doormen and lively attendants will move about, people will live there again, but it will be a different kind of life.

Joseph Pulitzer probably was never inside of three-fourths of the rooms. He lived in a few padded rooms of his own to the west. The old doors of his hideaway, soft as leather chairs, are torn and ripped now, but the thick walls and the triple-sashed windows still shut out most of the street sounds that tore at the nerves of the publisher, whose hearing was sharpened by blindness. He had lost his sight when he moved into No. 7 and never saw the palace he had built around his isolation.

The marble façade, pierced by windows twenty feet high, is Stanford White's reworking of the front of an Italian Renaissance palace. It is still white and unmarred except for a few names scrawled by children in chalk on the entrance pillars. Graceful marble cherubs smile in languid peace above the windows, as if time and the hour had not moved in thirty years. The heavy front doors of glass and scrolled iron are locked, and propped up with strong timbers inside. We went in by a side door, whose lock protested against the unfamiliar key.

The library is filled with axes, wheelbarrows, and red lanterns belonging to the firm that will reconstruct the interior. High ceilings, wide, deep fireplaces, and elaborately carved mantels are characteristic of the house. There are many strange and unique rooms: a tall, circular breakfast room, an enormous dining-room whose six pairs of windows to the west are made of curved glass in panes more than four feet square, a squash court with a gallery in which we had to light matches to see anything at all. There are three floors in front and eight in back, counting mezzanines. The bathtubs are the high, clumsy monstrosities of their day, except for the master's own, which is sunk into the floor. He had a washbasin two feet higher than any we ever saw and a specially made combined toilet seat and magazine rack.

On one faded wall a card gave the telephone number of the Pulitzer residence when it was alive: Lenox 1734. There isn't even any such exchange any more.

1934

JEANN AND JIMMY

IT'S been five years since we checked up on Jimmy Walker through his tailor, so we called on Mr. Friedman a few days ago to see if they're still friends. We should say they are. Mr. Friedman still thinks that Mr. Walker is the greatest fellow who ever lived, bar nobody, and he showed us a letter he had from him not long ago in which Jimmy spoke of Jeann as "the world's greatest tailor and the best friend anybody in the world ever had."

The last time we called at Friedman's shop on East Forty-sixth Street, he had just won a blue ribbon at the Custom Cutters' Club show for a one-button dress topcoat designed for Walker. He has won other ribbons since then, and even made Walker another dress topcoat that would knock your eye out: a double-breasted, six-button, one-button-to-button model, with silk collar, lapels, and cuffs, which Walker took with him into exile. But the place has changed. It's become a kind of Walker Memorial or Museum.

At the left, as you enter, are two photographs of the Great Pal, each about two feet by two and a half. At the right, on a table, are two more pictures—of two Walker jackets photographed on Walker's personal dummy. Standing in the middle of the shop is the dummy itself, draped in a dark coat. And running around the shop, looking as if he were struggling to remember something, is Togo, Walker's Japanese spaniel, which he left with Friedman when he went away. On the wall is an old motto, read by Mr. Walker many times in good faith and high hope; it says "Don't worry . . . it won't happen."

The former Mayor used to have about seventy suits, and he always kept ten or twelve of them in Friedman's shop, as spares. That was in the days when he was spending about three thousand a year on clothes. Now he has only about fifty-five suits and Friedman has shipped him the last of the reserves. And it's been a full year since he bought a new suit; that is, a regular suit. Last fall Friedman made and sent to him an English walking coat and a dress suit—"with the most outstanding dress coat in the country," says Jeann, proudly. The unusual feature of the coat, he explains, is a silk binding which goes five-eighths of the way around the edge; the fabric is a diamond weave and dark blue, not black. Friedman says Walker has always preferred blue to black in evening clothes, because blue looks blacker than black at night. The only change in Jimmy since he went away, Friedman says, is that his waist is down from 29½ to 29.

Friedman is Governor Lehman's tailor, too. He is making him two blue spring suits. Mr. Lehman wears only dark blues and dark browns, never grays, and he doesn't go in for any fancy business, but nevertheless Friedman thinks he is probably the best-dressed governor in the United States. The Governor always whistles and sings while he is being fitted. Friedman likes him immensely, but nobody can ever take Jimmy Walker's place.

1934

BRONX TIGER

HENRY BENJAMIN GREENBERG, home-run hitter of the Detroit baseball team, which has just won its first pennant in twenty-five years partly on account of him, was born in Greenwich Village. A lot of the young men down there can point out the house: on the corner of Fourth and Barrow. The kids used to call him Bruggy when he played ball in the downtown streets with a broom handle for a bat; now he's Hank, and the ablest Jew in baseball. He'll be twenty-four on January 1st (his mother used to tell him that all the noise on New Year's Eve was in celebration of his birth), and he's lived most of his life in New York. When he was seven, the Greenbergs moved to the Bronx and he went to P.S. 44, at 176th Street and Prospect Avenue.

The year—1928—that the late McGraw found a Jew named Andy Cohen who could play well enough for the big leagues, Hank Greenberg was first baseman for the James Monroe High School. His team won the city championship in his last year there and major-league scouts began to take an interest in him. McGraw apparently overlooked him, but the Yankees were after him and offered him a big bonus to sign up—that was in 1930, when he was playing semi-professional baseball with the Bay Parkways of Brooklyn. Hank was too smart to go with the Yankees, however; he knew he was too big to play anything but first base (he's six feet four, and weighs two hundred and twenty), and the Yankees' great first baseman, Lou Gehrig, hadn't missed a game since 1925.

Greenberg finally took the offer of the Detroit Tigers, which was six thousand dollars for signing a contract, and three thousand more for reporting for work. He quit N.Y.U. at the end of his first semester to join the Tigers at their training camp. The first year he got in only one game—as a pinch hitter—and then was sent to Hartford. He wasn't very good there, so the Tigers took him back and sent him to Raleigh; later he played with Evansville, and finally with Beaumont in the Texas League. There, in 1932, he hit thirty-nine home runs and was a favorite with the fans. They liked him from the day he started a fight that finally involved all the players and substitute players of both teams that were playing. The genial Jewish boy had been taking a lot of "riding" and suddenly turned on his tormentors.

Last year Detroit took him back and he did well, but this past season was his best yet. When he stayed out of the game on Yom Kippur, his team lost. The week before, he had played on Rosh Hashana because the Yankees were pushing the Tigers hard and he was needed. He hit two home runs and his team won, 2 to 1. Detroit, of course, is crazy about Greenberg, and Greenberg likes Detroit well enough, but the New York Giants have always been his favorite team. He used to go to see them play whenever he had a chance as a boy. Cohen, by the way, lasted only a year with the Giants and is now playing with Minneapolis. He was somewhat carried off his feet by the fuss made about him, but Greenberg takes it more easily. He recently refused a testimonial dinner in Detroit that was to have been given by fifteen hundred Jews and at which he was to receive a fifteen-hundred-dollar purse. His salary is seven thousand dollars a year.

Greenberg's father is president of the Acme & Textile Shrinking Works on West Twentieth Street and came here from Roumania. He frequently goes to Detroit with his wife to watch Hank play and has bought four hundred and eighty dollars' worth of World Series tickets—intends to take the family and a lot of friends and business acquaintances. There are three other children, including Joe, nineteen, who is a sophomore at N.Y.U. and shortstop on the baseball team there. Joe thinks he is a better player than Hank. Maybe that's because Hank never plays very well in New York; he gets kind of intense and strikes out often.

1934

THE DAKOTA

OUR landmark reporter came in, insisting that we run a little article on the Dakota apartment house on Central Park West at Seventy-second Street, and as he had all the facts in a convenient form, we said all right. It's fifty years old this month. It was the first apartment house to be built on the edge of the Park, and the neighborhood then was a shanty town with goats and pigs running around. There's a legend that it got its name because of its absurd location far to the northwest of things. Edward Clark, organizer of the Singer Sewing Machine Company, began it, but died during the four years it took to build and left it to his grandson, Edward Severin Clark, who owned it until his death last year, when it passed to his brother, Stephen C. Clark. During its whole existence, it has never advertised or hung out a sign. It has never given more than a one-year lease, yet has an amazing record of continued tenancy. Ninety per cent of the original tenants lived there until they died. Two of them still live there, Miss Cordelia Deal, in a four-room apartment, and Mr. Maxwell D. Howell, nine rooms. Frederick T. Steinway (pianos) and A. J. Cammeyer (shoes) lived there for years, and Sir Douglas Alexander, president of Singer now, and Charles J. Hardy, president of the American Car & Foundry Company, still do. In all, five or six hundred people live in the house, and there are a hundred employees, who on an average have been there as long as the tenants. The head painter's incumbency totals forty-eight years, and the head carpenter's forty. The elevator operators are all middle-aged women, every one of whom has held her job since she was first hired. That was during the war, when men were scarce.

Tenants of the Dakota come and go through the Seventy-second Street gate,

which is guarded by a new sentry box (only fifteen years old). After midnight,
the gates are closed and visitors are challenged. This entrance leads into a
court with two fountains, each containing twelve iron lilies. The dining-room
of the Dakota is all marble, carved oak, and brown tile embossed with Indian
heads, arrowheads, and ears of corn (for the Dakota region). The eight elevators are originals, Otis hydraulics run by steam pumps in the basement. Some
years ago the pull ropes were replaced by levers, but otherwise the elevators
haven't been touched. All the gable rooms on the ninth floor, with first-class
Park views, are occupied by resident employees. That shows how quaint a place
can be.

Only one tenant moved out of the Dakota last moving day; six moved in.
There are vacancies now, but from 1884 to 1929 there wasn't a single one.
Our landscape man saw a nine-room apartment being done over—it takes up
to six months for the Dakota to remodel. All the doors, he says, were of hand-
carved mahogany with brass knobs, and there were five fireplaces. That's what
he noticed most. The electrical and bathroom fixtures are modern, though,
throughout the building, with the exception of one zinc bathtub an old tenant
won't give up. There's a second gated entrance to the Dakota on Seventy-third
Street, which few people ever see open. It was originally the servants' entrance,
but Mr. Edward Severin Clark locked it when he took the building over and de-
creed that it should never be used except for funerals, and it never has been. It's
used about once a year.

1934

GTDE

MISS STEIN was seven or eight minutes late for her autographing at Brentano's last week and about fifty people were waiting restlessly for her when she solidly arrived with Alice B. Toklas pertly in tow. On a table were arranged solid stacks of Miss Stein's books and next to the table was a big desk at which she sat solidly down. She was calm, quick, and smiling throughout the ordeal. Of course, it wasn't as exciting as the immortal Hugh Walpole–Gene Tunney autographing, but it had its moments. As soon as she sat down, Miss Stein looked up expectantly and people began pushing toward the desk, carrying books. Clerks fluttered about selling the pushers whatever book of Miss Stein's they might want: the books ran in price from ninety-five cents (the Modern Library edition of "Three Lives") to $3.50. At an autographing, you are supposed to write down on a card your name, or Aunt Lisbeth's name, or the name of whomever you are buying the book for, and hand the book and the card to the autographer. This speeds things up, because people standing in front of an author and meeting the author's eyes are likely to get timid and dry-throated and say "Zassfrank Dooselinch" or what sounds like "Zassfrank Dooselinch" to the author. Miss Stein doesn't like people to be incoherent about names.

She signed two hundred and seventy-five books in all, and her signing time was a little under an hour and a half. She wrote with a big pen, vigorously. We bought one of her books and got in line behind a man named Twifflefinks, Moited Twifflefinks (he hadn't written his name on a card). That was straightened out after a while—Miss Stein is always gracious and patient. We just handed our book to her, and she glanced at us with her keen, humorous eyes and, seeing that we didn't have a name, simply put her own name on the fly-leaf, and the date. She signs herself always Gtde Stein. Now and again some-body (once it was a girl of twelve) would slip her an autograph book or a blank sheet of paper, but she would push these away and say "No," and these auto-graph-hunters would retreat in humiliation. There are ethics in autographing: you can't just walk into a bookstore out of the street and get an author to sign his name for you. You have to buy or bring one of the author's books.

One confused man somehow found himself standing in front of Miss Stein without a book, so he shouted at a clerk, " 'Three Saints'! 'Three Saints'!" he said. "Give me a 'Three Saints'!" The right title is "Four Saints." A clerk cor-rected the gentleman coldly. Miss Stein just laughed. She doesn't get peeved about things like that. Behind us was a lady named Mielziner. Miss Stein, hear-ing the name, looked up and asked about Leo Mielziner, Jr. "Leo Mielziner is Kenneth MacKenna," said the lady. Miss Stein took that in her stride. Now and again someone would ask the hovering Toklas to sign a book, and she always did. Somebody asked Miss Stein what had been her greatest thrill in America. She said her airplane trip to Chicago.

A friend of ours who heard the great lady lecture a few days after the auto-graphing said it was very interesting and seemed to make sense. Our friend, however, copied down a few sentences that Miss Stein said and showed them to us. Our favorite was "When the inside had become so solidly inside that all the outside could be outside and the inside inside." The lady who listened said that when you hear Gtde talk that way, you can see what she means, or think you can. People who hear her always like her as a person. After her lectures she will answer any questions—if they are sensible. Once she waved her hand and said pooh at a woman who asked her what she thought of the effect of psychology on literature. She then said that psychology hasn't any effect on literature. She told some other questioner that she doesn't believe much in the subconscious. "It's subconscious because it's inarticulate," she said.

This is probably all we're going to tell you about Miss Stein.

1934

MISS RAND

WHEN Dr. Dafoe of the quintuplets came to town and said one of the things he wanted to see was Sally Rand's bubble dance, we thought it was time we were seeing her, too, and we arranged to do so, and also to interview her. Like the adagio dance, mentioned here recently, the bubble dance, which Miss Rand is now performing at the Paradise Restaurant on Broadway for an admission fee of a dollar and a half, dinner included, was inspired by Pavlova. Indirectly, that is. Miss Rand invented the fan dance because she caught the sacred fire of the great Russian, and she wouldn't have invented the bubble dance for the 1934 Chicago Fair if the fan dance hadn't been such a success at the Fair in 1933. Miss Rand was only six when she caught the sacred fire. She saw Pavlova in the "Dying Swan" number. "A white bird flying in the moonlight," Miss Rand told us, "was the emotional effect I always wanted to convey. I dreamed of it all my life." She didn't get a chance to try it out until the Fair. Her present dance is also symbolical. "The bubble" (it's of rubber and five feet in diameter), Miss Rand explained, "represents man's dreams, which ultimately become material progress. No ship ever sailed, no spire ever rose, without a dream. The dream shimmers and floats away from you, returns. Finally, in all its movements and through the Dance of Life, it becomes part of you, of your material progress. After my dance, when I put the bubble aside, you do not, I am sure, look at me as, let's say, a personality, a human being, but rather as some sweet, some marble abstraction."

Miss Rand is five feet one-half inch tall, blonde, eupeptic, and weighs a hundred and eleven pounds. Her dancing costume is white adhesive tape and a coating of a white cosmetic of her own composition. She does not hide behind

the bubble that represents man's dreams, but hoists it high over her head and
lets it float away from her several times before she puts it aside at the end of her
dance, to the loud applause of Paradise patrons, who can appreciate a sweet
marble abstraction as well as the next ones. A black-net curtain is lowered
around the stage for Miss Rand's dance, to accentuate the whiteness of her
body and to protect the balloon against patrons with lighted cigarettes. The
balloons stand her twenty-six dollars each. The night we saw her, her first balloon broke, anyway, when she bounced it on some pine needles left by a previous artist, and they handed her a second one from the wings. She always has
three or four in reserve backstage.

Miss Rand was a Wampas Baby Star in the films in 1927, and afterward
toured in vaudeville with her own company of twelve dancing boys. Originally,
her name was Helen Gould Beck. The first part is for Helen Gould, the "angel of
the Spanish War," she explained. She is a native of Hickory County, Missouri.
She told us that in 1929 she fell on lean days and danced in the chorus at the
Capitol Theatre. She lost that job and made hats in a wholesale house, and later
waited on table at the Alps Restaurant on Fifty-eighth Street. She went to the
Fair with the fan-dance idea and started at a hundred and twenty-five dollars a
week. Since then she has received as much as a thousand dollars a day (at the
Steel Pier, Atlantic City, for two days), a vaudeville salary equalled only by one
other woman stage performer, Sarah Bernhardt. "And Bernhardt had a company with her," Miss Rand commented modestly. Miss Rand's average salary
since the first year at the Fair has been around three thousand dollars a week,
but she's taking twenty-five hundred at the Paradise because it's a small place.
(Seats only eight hundred and fifty.)

1934

THE JOYCES

THE Giorgio Joyces have been living quietly in and around town since they arrived with their small son on the Bremen last May. Giorgio is the son of the famous James Joyce, but he has no prose work in progress himself. He's a bass singer. He made his radio début in November as George Joyce, because he doesn't like the name Giorgio—it was given to him because Italian was the language spoken in Trieste, where he was born in 1905. He has sung twice on the radio so far—a Mozart aria, a Tschaikowsky song, two old Irish ballads. His father sent him radiograms wishing him luck. James, who started out to be a singer himself, is proud of Giorgio's voice and hopes he will be a great concert singer some day.

Giorgio won't talk about his father's work, but he told us some interesting things about the author's way of life, speaking with a slight accent. (He lived in Trieste till he was nine, in Switzerland during the war, and has been in Paris since 1919. He and his father always converse in Italian.) James Joyce's eyesight, his son says, is much better than it used to be, but he can see only with his left eye, the right being entirely blind. A few years ago he had to write with blue crayon on huge sheets of white paper, but now he uses pen or pencil on any paper that is handy. He can typewrite, using one finger on each hand, but uses a typewriter only for his infrequent correspondence, never for manuscripts. His friends drop in and type his manuscripts—he hates professional secretaries and has never hired one. His friends also read to him, out of dictionaries, encyclopedias, and other reference books. When he wants something read to him for relaxation, he usually asks for Ibsen. He has never had a line of Gertrude Stein read to him and seems to have no interest in her work.

The two have met, but that's all. The only thing Joyce reads for himself is his "Work in Progress." He reads parts of it aloud to his friends, chuckling now and then, going back and rereading sometimes passages he especially likes. He never reads from "Ulysses" or any other of his old works, being bored with them after they are written and published.

Joyce sees very few people. He never goes to literary teas or other parties, but gives three a year himself—at Christmas, New Year's, and on his birthday, February 2nd. Only his small circle of intimates are invited to these parties. Joyce always sings Irish songs for them, playing his own accompaniment. His voice is tenor and his favorite song is "Molly Brannigan." (His son, incidentally, doesn't play the piano.) Joyce gets up around nine, writes a little, but spends most of the morning telephoning. He actually likes talking on the phone, and chins with his friends by the hour. Before lunch he plays and sings, and afterward works until five o'clock. He has been at his new book for years; nobody knows when it will be finished, but Giorgio thinks it's about half done. After five, Joyce takes a walk, alone. He detests dogs and wouldn't walk with one. There are no pets at all in his household, which consists of himself, his wife (who was Nora Barnacle), and his other child, Lucia.

Joyce's favorite restaurant in Paris is Fouquet's. He likes the opera, the theatre (never misses a Thursday matinée), song recitals, and even the movies. His favorite opera is "William Tell," which he has heard dozens of times. The only thing he drinks is white wine. At present he is in Zurich. Giorgio had a letter from him recently. It began "Dear Oigroig and Neleh." That's backward for Giorgio and Helen, the latter being Mrs. Oigroig. It ended "With much love, Obbab." Obbab is backward for Babbo, which means Daddy in Italian. Babbo has been James Joyce's family nickname for thirty years.

1935

CHARLES COOKE
AND RUSSELL MALONEY

MET'S MAÎTRE

S OME of our friends with musical and operatic connections have been
telling us about young George Balanchine, the Met's new *maître de ballet.*
Quite a fellow, by all accounts. He lives simply in a one-room apartment at 400
East Fifty-seventh Street, and is probably the only man in New York who keeps
a grand piano in a one-room apartment. Plays for relaxation: Bach, Stravinsky,
and opera and ballet scores. He is an open-mouthed admirer of Fred Astaire
and Ginger Rogers. He reads Goethe for fun, does Russian acrostics, and cooks
Russian food excellently. The White Russian set here have tried to lionize him,
but he usually turns down their invitations; when he dines out, it's likely to be
at a little Yiddish place in the East Nineties. He's unmarried, and has been since
1927, when he and Tamara Geva, the dancer, were divorced. His aquiline pro-
file, earnest poker face, and shiny black hair give him an Indian look; he's far
from showing his thirty-one years. He speaks English without conspicuous
success, gesturing wildly with both hands and interjecting phrases of French
and Russian.

Right now he's busy conducting rehearsals in the big ballet-room on the fifth
floor of the Opera House. His *corps* is composed of five youngsters from the old
Met ballet, twenty pupils of his from the School of the American Ballet, and five
outsiders whom he picked at tryouts. He was startled at the ineptitude of most
of the candidates. "Zey say, 'I loff so much ze dance, I want so much dance wiz
you,' zen zay pirouette and fall on zair face." Very discouraging. At rehearsals
he wears sneakers, gray trousers, and a blue plaid shirt open at the neck. Never
loses his temper, never praises, never reproves. When a dancer is doing badly,
Balanchine says politely, "You're tired, aren't you?" He has been through all

this before, twice—at Copenhagen in 1930, and at Monte Carlo in 1931. He
studied dancing for seven years at the Russian Imperial Dancing School (it had
become the State Dancing School by the time he left). He joined Diaghileff's
troupe during a tour in England, and was the great man's *maître de ballet* until
Diaghileff's death in 1929. Then followed the training of dancers in Copenhagen and Monte Carlo, and in 1933 he came here to be director of the School
of the American Ballet. He knows all the great ballets, and has composed almost thirty of his own. There are plans afoot for him to do "serious" dances for
two musical shows this fall; if anybody asks him how he reconciles this hotcha
stuff with the Met work, he says cagily, "Each is for different pooblic." Besides,
he considers that tap-dancing can be used in a serious ballet, and has vague
plans in the back of his head involving Fred Astaire.

Balanchine wants to compose some American ballets, and this summer
made a coast-to-coast automobile trip with two of his friends, in search of
material. In Texas, they were marooned by a cloudburst, and dashed into a
place that displayed a cafeteria sign, in search of coffee and sandwiches; didn't
get any, though, because the restaurant had been turned into a temporary
drought-relief headquarters. In Arizona, Balanchine knotted a red handkerchief around his head, talked Russian to the Indians, and gave them the idea
that he was a brave from a distant tribe. It all ought to make a fine ballet.

1935

DARK CONTRALTO

YOU'D have to go far to find a person more quiet and modest than Marian Anderson, the young Negress whose contralto voice is, as you probably know, the latest sensation of the musical world. We called on her while she was here for her Town Hall recital of December 30th, and found her living in a Y.W.C.A. in Harlem; it's not improbable that she will make use of the same unpretentious diggings when she comes to town for her next recital—Carnegie Hall, on the twentieth. She hasn't even bought herself a car. She plans to live, between concerts, with her mother and her two young sisters in a little brick house she bought in Philadelphia's colored section. She has been in Europe since 1931, and is still startled by her success there. "Why," she says, "we gave a hundred and fifty concerts in Scandinavia alone last year." "We" includes Kosti Vehanen, who has been her accompanist for the past five years. He's white—Finnish.

When we saw Miss Anderson, she had her foot in a cast and walked with crutches, recovering from a broken ankle; it will be all right by January 20th, she said. She wore an inexpensive-looking gray fur coat and a plain green dress. She has coffee-colored skin, black hair, wide-set eyes, a large and mobile mouth. There's no trace of a Southern Negro accent in her voice. When she's talking to you, Miss Anderson frowns a lot, amiably, and once in a while gives you a broad wink. She told us she was born in a Negro neighborhood in South Philadelphia. Her father sold ice and coal, and her mother took in washing; the family lived in a single rented room. They all used to sing spirituals on rainy Sundays, to keep cheerful. When Marian was six years old, she made her first concert appearance; sang a duet, "The Lord Is My Shepherd," with another pickaninny at a service in a neighborhood Baptist church. When she was eight, she received her first money for singing in public—half a dollar; she was billed as a "baby contralto." Her father died soon after this, and several Negro organizations advanced money for her to study seriously. In the summer of 1925 she beat three hundred other aspirants in a contest here, and sang at Lewisohn Stadium, accompanied by the Philharmonic. Then she went to Europe to study further, returning in 1931 to give a recital, which won her good notices and enabled her to move her mother and sisters into a better neighborhood. Then her next European tour, from which she has only just returned.

Her repertoire at present includes some hundred and twenty-five songs. She practices when she feels like it—perhaps ten hours one day and not at all the next. She plays tennis, and swims a little, for relaxation. She told us (with a broad wink) that she had followed the career of Joe Louis with great interest, and would like to meet him some time. We sounded her out about superstitions; she said she had none of her own, but once a woman told her it would bring her luck if she always sang with a certain little handkerchief in her hand. Marian, the soul of amiability, tried it, but it didn't seem to make much difference, and she gave it up.

You might call her cautious as well as amiable. "Who is your favorite composer?" we asked. "I haven't one," she said, "but if I had one, it would be Schubert." "What is your favorite song?" we pursued. "I have no favorite song," she told us, "but if I *did* have one, it would be Schubert's 'Ave Maria.' "

1 9 3 6

WALTER'S BANKS

WE happen to be the only journalist ever permitted to see Walter Chrysler's collection of penny banks, and we're going to tell you all about them. The hell with whether or not you're interested. Mr. Chrysler, it seems, has been collecting banks for three years but keeping it pretty much of a secret, because he was afraid too much publicity might interfere with his negotiations with dealers. Now he has almost a thousand banks, and he doesn't care who knows it. He received us last week in his office on the fifty-sixth floor of the Chrysler Building, and he and his secretary, a Mr. Morrison, told us the whole story. You probably didn't know about it, but penny banks are now popular as a collector's item.

The great penny-bank period was from 1870 to the end of the century, and collectors will tell you that the banks, like Currier & Ives prints, reflect their period, ranging in subject from representations of Civil War soldiers in forts to Teddy Roosevelt shooting a bear. There are two sorts of banks, stationary and mechanical: the stationary kind are just more or less elaborately sculptured affairs of cast iron or pottery, with slots for pennies; the mechanical banks all do things when you drop in a penny—a clown does a little dance, Buster Brown and his dog Tige go down a chute-the-chutes, an American gunboat sinks a Spanish ship, and God only knows what else. Mr. Chrysler tries to keep all the banks working perfectly, and when he acquires a bank with a missing part he has a new one made. One of his favorites is the Snapping Bulldog, which snatches a penny out of a man's hand and gobbles it up. "Watch this," he said to us, putting a penny in the man's hand. Nothing happened. "Somebody's been playing with this," said Mr. Chrysler sternly. "People sneak in and play with them all the time." He wound up the bank, and this time it worked O.K.; the bulldog engulfed the penny in a series of well-cadenced gobbles. Mr. Chrysler moved about his office, operating all his favorite mechanical banks. (He keeps them right where he works, on shelves. The stationary banks are in a little side room.) There was Prof. Pugfrog on the Bicycle, Darktown Baseball Battery, Dentist Pulling Tooth from Colored Man's Mouth, Owl Blinking His Eyes, and a figure called Young Tammany, made in the seventies, who dropped a penny into his poke and waved his hand at you in thanks. Mr. Chrysler keeps a little tin can full of pennies on hand, to work the banks, and never tries to get them back, for fear of breaking something. That's what wealth does for you.

The Chrysler collection at present lacks only thirty-nine of the rare collector's items that Mr. Chrysler set out to gather, and he doesn't expect to have much difficulty with those. For one thing, Chrysler dealers all over the country know that he is interested in banks, and are keeping their eyes open. He is scrupulous about never paying more than he thinks a bank is worth, and has often knocked fifty cents off a dealer's asking price. Whenever he gets hold of duplicate banks, he trades with other collectors, like a stamp-collector.

There are a couple of famous penny-bank collections in town in addition to the Chrysler collection. One belongs to a Dr. Arthur Corby, a dentist, and the other to the Seamen's Bank, at 74 Wall Street. The Seamen's Bank collection is public.

1 9 3 6

KNOCK OF OPPORTUNITY

WILL ROGERS, in case there's doubt about it, was started on his literary career by Kermit Roosevelt, the late Frank Munsey, and the late Louis Wiley. Kermit Roosevelt induced Rogers to make a speech in Town Hall on the evening of October 26th, 1922, in favor of Ogden Mills, who was running for Congress from the Silk Stocking District. The speech accidentally caused some journalistic disturbance, and this resulted in a sudden increase in the cowboy's fame.

The Mills rally was an evening-dress affair. Formal clothes would have been obligatory at a riot in the Silk Stocking District in those days. The decorous patting of kid gloves had rewarded a series of dull speakers who preceded Rogers. When he started, he stunned his audience immediately by saying that Ogden Mills was the brother of Eleanor Mills of the celebrated Hall-Mills double-murder case, which was then in the height of its glory. After dragging Ogden Mills through this scandal for a while, Rogers informed his audience that Mills had been wealthy before getting into politics, but that he had grown vastly more wealthy in office. "I don't know the man," added Rogers, "and that is why they have asked me to come here to speak." After some other insults, he continued, "We need Mills. This country needs a man in Congress that owns his own dress suit. Our candidate," he added, "is the only man we could send to Congress who could go into a Fifth Avenue home without delivering something."

Rogers explained that he had consented to make a speech for Mills because Kermit Roosevelt had asked him. "I would make a speech for Harding, if a Roosevelt asked me," he said. At first the audience was mortified and silent. Finally, somebody thought it was funny and laughed. Soon everybody was laughing. Ogden Mills was the last to break down.

The newspaper reporters who covered the meeting dismissed Rogers with a line or two. It was a law of journalism not to give any free advertising to professional comedians, and Rogers was then doing his rope act in the Ziegfeld "Follies." The law was broken by the *Times* because Louis Wiley, then business manager, hurried to the editorial offices after the meeting and told them the speech was the funniest thing he had ever heard. He sat down and tried to give a reporter an account of it, but was so overcome with laughter that he could remember little of what Rogers had said. Between the acts at the "Follies," Rogers, who had spoken from notes, dictated his speech to the reporter and the *Times* printed it in full.

Frank Munsey was then owner of the *Herald.* He was in a towering rage because his paper had not printed the speech. He was still more enraged when he was told that it was not the custom to print the speeches of comedians. Finally, he learned that a woman reporter had represented the *Herald* at the meeting. He had specifically requested a week before that a good man be assigned to cover the Mills campaign. The explanation that the woman was one of the best reporters in town did not mollify him. He had asked for a good man and he would not let anybody palm off a good woman on him. He then ordered that stenographers be hired to attend every meeting where Rogers spoke and to take down his utterances in full. The *Herald* would come out every few days with two- or three-column speeches of Rogers. The McNaught Syndicate soon became excited and sent Rube Goldberg around to persuade Rogers to become a writer. The cowboy signed up to do a series of Sunday stories. The McNaught Syndicate sold the New York rights to these to the *Times,* without offering them to the *Herald.* Word was shortly circulated through the *Herald* offices that Mr. Munsey would prefer never to see the name of Will Rogers in the *Herald* again.

1 9 3 5

DÉSHABILLEUSE

WHEN Ann Corio opened at the Apollo last week, we went over and interviewed her, considering it no more than our plain duty to be able to tell you something about the greatest strip woman in burlesque. (A strip woman, in case you've led a sheltered life, is a beautiful creature with vague talents as a singer or dancer, who climaxes her act by removing, piece by piece, as much of her clothing as the local censors permit.) La Corio, during the forty-odd weeks of her working year, earns a bit over a thousand dollars a week, while run-of-the-mill strip women are lucky to get a hundred. The reason for this disparity had been a mystery to us ever since we'd heard about it, because offhand it would seem that every *déshabilleuse* has the same stock in trade, but Miss Corio cleared that up right away. "It isn't what they see that counts," she told us, with an angelic smile. "It's what they don't see. If I ever stripped completely, there would be no curiosity left. Besides, it wouldn't be modest. So I always wear little panties with embroidery. Like that, a girl has something to follow up with. Only I never do." She has a sort of Madonna face, oval, with round, deep brown eyes and excellent teeth, and is tall and slim. Talking with her, one understands why the late Justice Holmes never missed a single one of her visits to the Capital.

Miss Corio's parents were natives of Italy who wound up in Hartford, Connecticut. She broke into show business when she was a senior in a Hartford high school, by winning a Charleston contest. That would have been in 1926. She immediately came to New York to be a musical-comedy star, and within a month was dancing in a Minsky chorus at the National Winter Garden on Houston Street. Before her family discovered that this wasn't the uptown Winter Garden, Ann was making so much money that it would have been foolish to object. Although most ladies were streamlined back in 1927, the billowy tradition persisted with burlesque dancers. Ann was too slim for effective Oriental dancing, so she began stripping, waiting for applause after each discard. Other ladies have claimed the honor of being the first stripper, but Ann says they were just cootch dancers who took off their clothes. "I make no suggestive motions," she informed us with calm pride. "No grinding, no bumping, no tassel-tossing." She's meticulous about her costumes, because, as she says, "It's like a box of candy. The package has to be nice or they won't want to know what's inside." Sometimes she sings a song—if possible, to some bald-headed gent in one of the boxes. If he is accompanied by his wife, she always asks her permission. "I always say, 'Do you mind?' and they never say they do."

In private life Miss Corio is the wife of a Mr. Emmett Callahan, manager of the Apollo Theatre. They have a summer place on Cape Cod, and when they are in town live in a hotel on Forty-ninth Street, attending Mass at St. Malachy's. She has made motion-picture tests and received attractive offers, but nothing as high as she makes in burlesque. "Seventeen hundred dollars for one week in Cleveland," Mr. Callahan said to us. "That is not hay." Locally, Miss Corio may not be as well known a strip artist as Gypsy Rose Lee, but she certainly has more of a national reputation, with such solid followings in several large cities that she works on a percentage basis. We mentioned Sally Rand to Miss Corio. "I was introduced to her in Boston," she said coldly. "She couldn't get away with that in burlesque for a minute—hiding behind a bubble or a couple of fans. In burlesque they want a good look at you, and that grease she wears all over herself practically amounts to a suit of heavy underclothes."

1936

FRED WITTNER

DEAD PAN JOE

ALL we know about big-league baseball is what our office boy finds
time to tell us. He says that the Yankees' centre fielder, Joe Di Maggio,
is likely to be the batting sensation of the World Series. This is Di Maggio's first
year with the Yankees, and he cost them $25,000 and four players. The Yan-
kees needed a colorful hitter to replace the retired Babe Ruth in the hearts of
New York baseball aficionados, and he seems to have succeeded: his fan mail
weighs about as much as Ruth's used to, and he has charmed the entire Italian
population of the city, bringing a goodly number of them out to see their first
baseball game, carrying little Italian flags. In person he is a tall, well-made,
rather lazy-looking youth, with none of the off-diamond characteristics of the
average ballplayer: he hangs up his clothes and keeps his hotel room neat,
dresses quietly, doesn't drink, answers his mail promptly, and always tries to
remember your name (the Babe used to call you Charlie, whatever your name
was).

Joe pronounces his name "Dih-mah-jio," and says it means, in Italian, "of
the month of May." He comes of a biggish tribe of Di Maggios on the coast of
California, most of whom follow the trade of crab fishermen. Joe never intended to be either a crab fisherman or a centre fielder. As a boy he played the
usual amount of sandlot baseball, but gave it up when he was fourteen. During
the next four years he worked as an office boy, and played tennis for fun. His
brother Vincent, who was playing with San Francisco in the Coast League,
wasn't satisfied to let well enough alone, however, and one day in 1932, when
Joe was eighteen, urged him to come around to the ball park for a tryout. That
was Vincent's mistake, because Joe immediately made the club, and the follow-

ing year took away his brother's job in the outfield. He played for two years with San Francisco, batting .399 in 1935; the Yankees were ready to buy him for the 1935 season, but he wrenched his knee just before the deal went through, and they made him play another year with San Francisco to prove that it was all right. One of his brothers stepped in to manage Joe when he was sold, and succeeded in getting for him $6,500 of his purchase price. Joe gave it to his family to buy a fishing boat.

Joe isn't such a spectacular batter of home runs as Babe Ruth was, but baseball managers say he's a better all-round batter, showing up especially well in the "runs batted in" column of his record, which is a pretty good indication of a batter's value. Pitchers haven't been able to find any predictable weakness in his batting, although, like every other player, he has his good and his bad days. One of his worst days came in July, when he was chosen to play in the all-star interleague game in Boston. He fumbled one hit, missed a fly completely, and came up to bat five times without getting a hit. His fielding is generally phenomenal, though, and he can make throws of three hundred and fifty feet, from deep centre to the plate. (Most players are well satisfied with an accurate throw of two hundred and fifty feet.) In his Coast League days he established a record of hitting safely in sixty-two straight games.

Joe is now getting $8,000 a year, most of which he sends home to his family. Next year he ought to get double that, and it is to be supplemented by the proceeds of a vaudeville tour he plans to make with Vincent. Vincent will furnish the patter, and Joe will bat balls into the gallery—tennis balls, according to his present plans. That's all we know about Joe Di Maggio, except that Winchell says he's stuck on a bubble dancer down in the Village, that his friends call him Dead Pan Joe, and that he likes to sit through movies twice—likes to get a thorough understanding of them.

1936

ET TU, SHADOW?

MOILING through the Sunday paper last weekend, we came upon a notice of a radio program scheduled for 5:30 by WOR: "The Shadow, with Orson Welles." "Orson Welles!" we murmured, astonished. "The same Orson Welles whose modern-dress production of 'Julius Caesar' is now playing to packed houses?" Deciding that it must indeed be he, we tuned in on WOR at 5:30. What we heard was a fiendish laugh, the words "The Shadow knows," in a quavery, gloating voice, then more fiendish laughter. Followed a chilling half-hour (sponsored by a product called Blue Coal) in which a masked maniac named Anton Spivak, who was plotting to blow up people with dynamite, was frustrated by The Shadow. And this Shadow, played to the hilt by Mr. Welles, was a rich playboy named La Monte Cranston who, by night, became invisible and foiled evildoers. You can believe us or not.

The next evening we went backstage at the Mercury Theatre, after the final curtain, to interview Mr. Welles and find out how La Monte Cranston jibed with Brutus. "Did you *have* to listen to that?" said Mr. Welles. He had just come from the stage and was still in costume, a blue serge business suit. Offstage, he's still a tall, moon-faced youngster with a baby's complexion and a mop of brown hair. The only new characteristic we discovered was a sudden giggle. If you read the dramatic pages, you already know that, at the surprising age of twenty-two, he had created history with his productions of "Macbeth" and "Doctor Faustus" even before "Julius Caesar." Probably you also know the story of how, when sixteen, he left his native Kenosha—"a nasty little Middle Western city," he calls it—to go to Ireland and paint. Running out of money, he introduced himself at the Gate Theatre as a Guild star on vacation and was immediately presented by the trusting Dubliners with a series of leading rôles. He even made guest appearances at the Abbey Theatre. "I don't want to sound jaded," he told us, "but this success here, grateful though I am for it, isn't a patch on my Dublin success."

Back in New York (after a sojourn in Africa during which he wrote "Everybody's Shakespeare"—90,000 copies sold so far), he married and cast about for something to work at. Radio turned out to be his first dish; three months after he was first inside a studio, he had a finger in the production of about twenty big-time programs and some weeks was making as much as $800. Then, last season, he tied up with the WPA and started doing Shakespeare. He now won't let his name be announced on the air, but can't prevent the newspaper billing. "Honestly," we said, "what do you think about the radio?" "I think it's a lovely medium," he said. It has been a lovely enough medium to buy him a house at Sneden Landing, where he maintains his wife, a chauffeur, a cook, a gardener, a cocker spaniel, and a Lincoln limousine.

The success of "Julius Caesar" came as pretty much of a surprise, Mr. Welles says. "When I took the Mercury on a five-year lease, it was the most presumptuous act in modern theatrical history. I still go into a cold sweat when I think what might have happened." What *did* happen was bad enough; Mr. Welles, director and star of the production, fell through a trapdoor the night of the dress rehearsal and almost killed himself. (The Shadow knows . . . hahahahaaa!)

1937

LEFTIST REVUE

"**P**INS AND NEEDLES,**"** that lighthearted revue produced and acted by members of the International Ladies' Garment Workers' Union, being practically an obligatory topic of conversation these days, we dropped in at the Labor Stage (né Princess Theatre) last week to see what we could find out about it. The stage was filled with ladies' garment workers in rehearsal—a last-minute brushing-up before the revue opened on a full-time basis. (They started out, as you undoubtedly know, by giving only weekend performances.) Charles Friedman, a professional director, was badgering them. "That 'Hell' wasn't focussed! It quavered!" he shouted. "Paul, *relax* when you walk into that wall!" he screamed. Young Harold Rome (words and music) was patiently giving out the piano accompaniment. We crept up behind him and whispered, "Are you a Leftist?" He didn't miss a note. "It's not a question of being a Leftist," he whispered back. "It's a question of keeping your eyes open."

Louis Schaffer, labor editor of the *Jewish Daily Forward* and manager of Labor Stage, Inc., the "Pins and Needles" producing company, took us around and introduced us to some of the thirty-nine members of the cast. There are, he told us, absolutely no ringers—everybody's a paid-up member of the I.L.G.W.U. Ten of the thirty-eight locals in the metropolitan area are represented. Ruth Rubinstein, the comedienne, belongs to the Corset and Brassière Workers' Local, and works for the Belle-Mode Brassière Company, or did until the present eventuation. It's her boast that she can turn out forty-five dozen brassières a day. Al Levy, who has one of the show's hit songs, "One Big Union for Two," belongs to the Dressmakers' Local, but has never worked at his trade; graduated two years ago from the Central Needles Trades School but couldn't get a job. He'd be just as happy, he told us, if the Labor Stage went on permanently, so that he'd *never* have to work with a needle. The somewhat esoteric Bonnaz Embroiderers' Local is represented by Paul Seymour, who has been working as a pleater of women's skirts with the Star Stitching Manufacturing Corporation. "How many skirts can you pleat in a day?" we asked. "Ask rather how well I pleat," he said coldly. Hyman Kaplan, a cutter with Wellesley Modes, who plays a policeman in one of the skits, is bored, utterly bored, with being ribbed about H*Y*M*A*N K*A*P*L*A*N.

With the exception of two or three players with minor parts, the entire cast will take a leave of absence from their jobs during the run of "Pins and Needles." The I.L.G.W.U. will pay them strictly according to garment union scales. This being a slack season in the garment industry, the girls are receiving $23 a week, the men $45. If the run extends to February, when business always picks up, the pay will be raised to $45 and $80 respectively. The production, which cost $10,000, will be out of the red if it runs until March. Any profits will be turned back to the union for future productions.

1937

E . J . K A H N

EXILES IN PRINCETON

WITH both Thomas Mann and Einstein settled in Princeton, that community could easily advertise itself as a centre of German intellectualism. Dr. Mann has rented a large red-brick house at 65 Stockton Street, a short distance from the campus, and lives there with Mrs. Mann and whichever of his six children are at home. Ever since he left Germany, the author told us in his library the other afternoon, he has wanted to live in a university town. Princeton opened the way by appointing him Lecturer in the Humanities. He is giving six lectures, four in English to the public and two in German to advanced students, on four subjects: Goethe, Wagner, Freud, and his own book, "The Magic Mountain." He writes his lectures in German and his wife translates them into English. He will continue to write in German no matter what Hitler does. His only composition in English to date, aside from a few letters, has been his speech at a pro-Czechoslovakian meeting in Madison Square Garden a couple of months ago. At the moment he is at work on a novel based on the life of Goethe. Dr. Mann says this will be a "tragi-comic little thing." He writes about three hours every morning, starting directly after breakfast. His afternoons are devoted to reading and answering correspondence. His wife serves as his secretary.

The Manns took out their first citizenship papers last May, about the time the author was completing a lecture tour. On this trip so many people wanted to hear him that frequently the police had to be called out. In Cleveland the excitement was so great that Dr. Mann thought the cops were present to shield him from enemies. He had scarcely regained his calm when two days later, in Toronto, he and Mrs. Mann awoke to find a note under their door reading,

"We've got you now," or words to that effect. The Manns ran next door to the room of their lecture agent. It was ultimately revealed that the note had been left for the agent by some ribald friends of his who had made a mistake in doors. We found Dr. Mann troubled not only about the Nazis but about a Christmas tree, which he didn't realize could be purchased in Princeton. The library is his favorite room. He writes there at a large desk which he sneaked away from Hitler by a ruse, sending it to a friend in France, near the border. On the desk are the bronze head of a Siamese warrior, a wooden figure of a servant taken from an Egyptian tomb, and half a dozen medals, one of which was presented to him by President Hindenburg in the old days for his services to German culture. He took another from a case and handed it to us with the remark that it was heavy—"and solid gold, too." We admired the sculptured figures on one side and the bas-relief of a head on the other, and the inscription, "Nobel."

Before he moved to Princeton, Dr. Mann had frequently visited Einstein there. The two men were friends in Germany. Now they meet for lunch or dinner at each other's homes or at the home of Dr. Mann's other translator, Mrs. Lowe-Porter. Einstein is no longer regarded as a campus novelty in Princeton. There is a story to the effect that one time none of his neighbors' radios would work and a repairman who was called attributed this to the presence of a certain type of electric heating pad in the vicinity. They eliminated every house but Einstein's, and then sent a timid delegation there. Einstein readily admitted he had such a device but insisted on illustrating, by a bewildering series of mathematical calculations, that his heater couldn't possibly cause trouble. The neighbors nodded politely but, nudged by the repairman, asked if he would mind if they bought him a different kind of heater. Einstein agreed, and after they got him a new pad all the radios worked.

1938

1940s

INTERNE

DAVID ROCKEFELLER, the youngest of the sons of John D. Rockefeller, Jr., has now been working at City Hall as an unpaid secretary to Mayor La Guardia for six months, with little or no fanfare. He has stayed, in fact, well under cover, being seldom photographed and never interviewed. The Mayor speaks of him as an "interne," a term used at City Hall to describe a student who performs municipal chores without pay, in return for the experience and whatever academic credits he can arrange to get from his college. This doesn't seem quite accurate as applied to David Rockefeller, who is already up to his waist in academic credits: he graduated from Harvard when he was twenty, stayed on for a year of postgraduate work, put in another year at the London School of Economics, and last summer took his Ph.D. at the University of Chicago. His doctoral thesis, incidentally, dealt with "the theory of unused capital resources," and is said to agree with the New Deal theory of deficit financing during depressions. At any rate, young Rockefeller sits at the desk formerly occupied by the Mayor's press secretary, who drew a weekly salary of $125.

When Rockefeller reported for work, La Guardia warned him to "stay away from those fellows in Room 9" (the City Hall press room), and also warned the photographers that if they took any pictures of Rockefeller not authorized by the Mayor, Rockefeller would be fired. The striking injustice of this dictum paralyzed the photographers' trigger fingers, and the young man gets on well, in a noncommittal way, with the fellows in Room 9. "He's a swell guy," one of them told us. Also, he added, he is certainly the best-dressed man in City Hall. Usually he wears modest gray or brown suits, with white, soft-collared shirts and a Homburg. He drives down to work in a Lincoln Zephyr, arriving at nine and staying, like most of LaGuardia's staff, until six or seven in the evening. The Mayor's secretaries—there are seven of them—must answer the bulk of the thousand-odd letters that come in every day from citizens, asking favors, complaining about the insolence of police officers, etc.; Rockefeller handles his share of these, and also talks on the telephone to impetuous people who want the Mayor's ear. You can't telephone the Mayor; he hasn't got a telephone. Occasionally, Rockefeller welcomes moderately famous people to City Hall, a chore once performed by Chief Magistrate Curran when he was Deputy Mayor.

Rockefeller shares with Byrnes MacDonald, another of La Guardia's secretaries, the job of accompanying the Mayor at his various public appearances—a tree-planting on Sixth Avenue, a ladies'-club luncheon in Brooklyn, or whatever. At first he seemed surprised and amused by these modest ceremonies; now, apparently, he accepts them as part of the necessary technique of politics. The only time Rockefeller has really caused any talk at City Hall was last September, when he got married and announced the fact to some of his colleagues. The announcements bore a crest, and this floored some of the earthier councilmen.

1940

EUGENE KINKEAD

THE ADMIRAL'S CHAIR

NOW, here is an item about a distinguished naval man who, among many other things, is, in both senses of the word, the Waldorf-Astoria's oldest resident—Rear Admiral Bradley Allen Fiske, U.S.N., retired, who is close to eighty-eight years of age and has lived in the present Waldorf ever since it was opened for business. Matter of fact, that isn't all the story. Admiral Fiske checked into the *old* Waldorf ten years after his retirement from active service in 1916; he lived there until it closed down and then waited fretfully in the Commodore for the new one to open up. These days Admiral Fiske doesn't venture out of the hotel at all. He comes down to Peacock Alley every morning after breakfast and sits there until toward dinnertime, leaving it only to go to lunch in one of the restaurants, where a table is reserved for him. His Peacock Alley armchair is reserved for him, too, and bears a sign to that effect.

We called on Admiral Fiske one afternoon last week, but before doing so we read up briefly on his career, which marks him as one of the notable naval inventors of all time. He was born in Lyons, New York, the son of an Episcopal clergyman, graduated from the Naval Academy in 1874, second in his class, and first smelled powder at Manila Bay as a lieutenant on the gunboat Petrel. Dewey cited him for gallantry. In addition to putting in a full term of active service, he found time to invent a hundred and thirty-odd improvements to naval equipment, the most far-reaching being the telescopic sight for ships' guns, which, we gathered, is now used on every warship in the world, and the torpedo-plane.

When we found Admiral Fiske in Peacock Alley he was occupying his armchair, reading P. G. Wodehouse's "My Man Jeeves," and smoking a cork-tipped cigarette. He was sprucely dressed in a blue suit, white shirt, and bow tie, and we couldn't help remarking that he didn't look his age. "It's my complexion," he said. "I got it from my father." Wodehouse, he explained to us, was by way of change from his customary literary fare, the works of Charles Dickens. "The language's greatest writer," he observed, with naval decisiveness. He added that he has read "The Pickwick Papers" fourteen times.

Marking his place in "Jeeves" with a picture postcard, Admiral Fiske told us that the idea for the telescopic sight came to him more than fifty years ago, when he was a lieutenant. His ship, which had the old open sights of that day, was returning from gunnery practice when he happened to raise his telescope to his eye and picked up several fishing schooners. He had the sudden impish thought that it would be easy to sink them all if the guns of his ship were sighted through a telescope. Not long after, in 1890, he took out the first of several patents on telescopic sights. It was a great joke among his messmates and for a time he thought he was crazy, or at least misguided. The first test of his invention was a failure, but the second, six months later, was a convincing success. Admiral Fiske first thought of the possibilities of the torpedoplane in 1910 while brooding over the problem of defending the Philippines. He reasoned that if airplanes got bigger, a group of them, based on one or more of the many Philippine Islands, could be fitted out to carry torpedoes and attack any invading fleet. In 1912 he noticed that planes *were* getting bigger and worked out a device to accomplish his purpose. He recalls that he remarked sweepingly at the time that he had invented not only a new weapon but a new method of warfare. In the cold light of 1942, he seems to have made no overstatement. We asked the Admiral if his theory was that of the British at Taranto and, more recently, of the Japanese at Pearl Harbor, and he said yes, that was his theory exactly. As we left the Admiral, we asked him the inevitable question, "How long do you think the war will last?" "How the hell would I know?" said he, reasonably, returning to Jeeves.

1 9 4 2

COOKLESS CONGRESSMAN

CONGRESSMAN CLARE LUCE is living in an apartment—two bedrooms, living room, dining room, and kitchenette—in the annex of the Wardman Park Hotel in Washington, where she percolates her own coffee every morning and reads herself to sleep with the *Congressional Record* every night. She hopes to have people for dinner someday but has had a hell of a time trying to get a cook-maid. For a few days she had a girl who mixed everything up—chicken on the butter plate, butter on the chicken plate, and so on. Representative Luce, well aware of the servant scarcity in the nation's capital, kept her mouth buttoned up during these goings-on, but a glance must have betrayed her, for soon the lass said, "I've worked for some mighty fine people and I ain't ever had a complaint yet," and left. Mrs. Luce, hoping that her well-publicized championing of the Chinese might stand her in good stead, telephoned a prominent Chinese friend in Washington and asked her if she could recommend a Chinese cook. The lady replied that she hadn't been able to find a Chinese cook for her own household, although anxious to do so, and as we go to press Mrs. Luce is still cookless. Because of the manpower shortage, Wardman Park waiters are permitted only to leave meals in rooms; they may not serve them. Mrs. Luce eats in the hotel dining room when she is home of an evening. Weekends her husband generally joins her.

We obtained these items, and one or two others, from our non-military attaché in Washington, who, shortly before Mrs. Luce made her splash, sought her out in her congressional office—a couple of rooms equipped with global maps; an electrical teapot on which the Representative, who stays around till six-thirty or seven, makes tea at five-thirty every afternoon; a perfume atomizer which a thoughtful friend sent her to squirt around after the departure of cigar-smoking visitors; and a small, carved figure of a Chinese god of luck, the belly of which she scratches every morning for luck. When our man arrived she was wearing a dark-red dress, two black bows in her hair, and a black kerchief with "Clare" printed on it in scarlet.

"Congressmen are a more patriotic lot of people than people give them credit for," Congressman Luce told our man. "They understand the people a great deal better than the people understand Congress. They have been forced to abdicate so many of their powers that they feel completely frustrated. People are demanding that Congress behave in a way it can't possibly behave because it no longer has the power. Freshmen congressmen come here half persuaded that their constituents' impression of them is true, that they are going to save the country, only to find out that the mechanics don't exist for saving the country through Congress." Mrs. Luce herself is not disillusioned, having read a lot of books about Congress before taking office. "Just as, when I went to China, I read a lot of books about China first," she said. "Far from being disillusioned, I was agreeably surprised about the personnel of Congress. The trouble is most of them live in the shadow of reëlection, and the pressures get to work on them. Gertrude Stein should have written a poem called 'The Congressman'—'A pressure is a pressure is a pressure is a pressure.' " Mrs. Luce's main pressures, as indicated in her mail, come from Connecticut hatters, plumping for women's hats; from householders, plumping for more fuel oil; from businessmen, plumping for the Ruml tax plan; and from members of the armed forces, plumping against strikes. She received two letters opposing Errol Flynn's nomination for Ambassador to Australia, and almost every day some sheet music arrives, accompanied by a request from the composer to promote it. She showed our attaché a sample entitled "Do God's Work and Smile," along with a note from its creator asking her to introduce a bill to have it sung on the floor of Congress. "Fairfield County is just a cross-section of the country," she said.

Mrs. Luce brought a car and chauffeur to Washington but uses them only to go to work and back. She is sure that hostile snoopers are on the job, hoping to catch her using her car while pleasure bent, and is so wary of them that she taxies to business dinners. Her chauffeur has threatened to quit, saying he is tired of seeing her into cabs. This, and her cook problem, and the dwindling power of Congress have made her a less carefree girl than she used to be. "What I need is a wife, to get me a cook," she said. "A congressman's life is not a happy one."

1943

MARY WEBB AND
BERTON ROUECHÉ

PREPARED PIANIST

THE subject of this short article is a young composer named John Cage, who has invented several hundred brand-new sounds. With the assistance of five so-called prepared pianos (we'll discuss them in just a minute), he demonstrated his achievement a couple of Sundays ago at a concert at the New School for Social Research, but since you probably weren't there we will start from scratch. As our more attentive readers should know by now, there are a number of composers who suffer from claustrophobia in the presence of the conventional twelve-tone scale. Well, Mr. Cage can't stand tones at all. "I have developed a way of composing by means of rhythm," he informed us when we looked him up at his apartment the other day. "That is, by organizing sounds through their time or rhythmic relationships, I have a profound lack of interest in harmony."

Mr. Cage, who was wearing a black corduroy jacket, green corduroy trousers, a blue shirt, a rose sweater, and red socks, told us that he was teaching piano and composition in Seattle, his native town, eight years ago when the pioneering impulse seized him. "I wanted to explore the possibilities of rhythm," he said. "But naturally I had to develop a new set of sounds first. I had to have sounds that people had never heard before in music, so that the *sound* would call attention to the rhythm. Do you follow me?" We signalled to him to go on. His first move, he said, was to forget about his piano and organize a percussion orchestra composed of such inharmonious instruments as tom-toms, wooden blocks, bells, gongs, cymbals, anvils, and automobile-brake drums. The orchestra, while it lasted, occupied itself exclusively with rhythmic items composed by Mr. Cage. "However," Mr. Cage told us, "it was too unwieldy.

I'd collected about three hundred different things that would make the kind of sounds I needed. You can see what a personnel problem I had on my hands." He solved this problem by going back to his piano. "I remembered," he said, "that hot jazz pianists used to get new effects by placing sheets of paper between the piano strings. I started monkeying around with my piano strings." Mr. Cage ended up with what he named the prepared piano and an itch to come to New York, which he did two or three years ago. "People are more receptive to new ideas here than in Seattle," he said. "The New Music Society was very receptive to me."

Mr. Cage prepares his piano by inserting between its strings various objects—screws, pennies, splinters of wood, bits of felt or rubber, and practically any other small objects you can think of. This, as you might imagine, changes the sound of the strings. Mr. Cage gets the particular sounds he requires by paying close attention not only to the kind of object but also to its size, weight, and longitudinal position on the strings. The possibilities are limitless and bloodcurdling. There are about two hundred and twenty-five strings on a piano, and each key, depending on the register, strikes from one to three strings. Nothing but prepared strings are played in Mr. Cage's compositions, and he prepares only a fraction of the strings. The most elaborate piano he has worked out so far has seventy-five prepared strings. No two of Mr. Cage's compositions (he has a repertoire of fifty) have the same preparation; his recent concert consisted of three compositions and required five different prepared pianos. "It's kind of a bother," he said. "Sometimes it takes me three hours to prepare a piano for a complicated number—my 'The Perilous Night,' for instance." Mr. Cage is holding back some of his most effective sounds until after the war. "They're too frightening," he told us. "They sound too much like the scream of bombs, and planes, and rifle shots. It wouldn't be good taste to use them now. One of them even shocks me sometimes."

At our suggestion, Mr. Cage ran through one of his shorter compositions. We listened closely and without flinching. When the echo of the last guttural thump had died away, he asked us what we thought of it. It was fine, we said, but it was certainly different. "Really?" he said. "*Really?* Some people," he said with disgust, "say it sounds Oriental."

1945

MASTERPIECE

THE Associated Press picture of the raising of the American flag on Mount Suribachi will soon, without question, be as inescapable as "The Spirit of '76" and "Washington Crossing the Delaware." It has already been made into a poster for the next bond drive and will be seen everywhere on billboards and car cards, and in delicatessen stores, movie-house lobbies, bars, and so on. It has been generally called the most inspiring photograph to come out of this war—or out of *any* war, for that matter. Any day now it will be reproduced on a new postage stamp. Plans are afoot to install a two-hundred-foot reproduction of the scene in Times Square, and it will inevitably become the theme of uncountable tableaux in the Victory parades. All this has been very pleasant for the A.P., and last week it brought to town Joe Rosenthal, the man who took the picture. We got hold of him at the New Weston the day after he arrived, and he was already wobbling under the strain of the program the A.P. had laid out for him. He had been interviewed by the papers, dined with Kent Cooper, president of the A.P. (whom he'd never seen before), looked over the bond posters, arranged to broadcast on "We, the People," selected a series of his photographs for publication in *U.S. Camera*, lunched with the Dutch Treat Club, and been fêted at Hamburger Mary's by several high ranking A.P. colleagues. Rosenthal had hoped to visit the Statue of Liberty, but when we talked to him it didn't look as if he would be able to make it before leaving for Washington to do something further about the posters. He was born in Washington, but when he was a boy the family moved to San Francisco, and he had been on Manhattan Jima only once before. That was a year ago, and he was too rushed then to see the Statue of Liberty, which he has never seen and has always wanted to see.

Joe—nobody ever calls him Joseph—freely admitted that all the hoopla about the picture had come as a surprise to him. "I wasn't around when they raised the first flag on Iwo—the little one," he said. "My shot was taken about three-quarters of an hour later. I went up the mountain with the detail that was sent up with the big flag and the flagpole, along with a Marine Corps movie man and a Marine Corps still man. I took one picture when the staff was halfway up, another when it was all the way up, and then I got a lot of Marines to stand around cheering to make my last one. When they wired from Guam that my flag picture was very good, I thought they meant the last one. All my stuff from Iwo was shipped out in negative, and I never had any idea how the picture looked till I got back to Guam and saw how it developed." When Joe's picture was published, a commentator on the Blue Network said that the picture had been carefully posed by Joe. Later, he retracted the canard. "It wouldn't have been any disgrace at all," Joe told us, "to figure out a composition like that. But it just so happened I didn't. Good luck was with me, that's all—the wind rippling the flag right, the men in fine positions, and the day clear enough to bring everything into sharp focus."

Joe has been taking pictures in the Pacific since January, 1944, when he got out of the Maritime Service, in which he had served as a photographer. Because of weak vision, he'd been turned down by the Army, Navy, and Marines before the Maritime Service took him in. Since he took his flag-raising picture, his draft board in San Francisco has honored him by stepping him up from 4-F to 2A-F. He worked around San Francisco as a photographer for fifteen years before the war, and joined up with the A.P. when it absorbed another news agency he was working for, in 1938. A serious character, Joe gave us a few technical details about his masterwork that we pass along to any camera sharps among our readers. The shot was taken with a Speed Graphic, between f/8 and f/11 at 1/400th of a second, on an Agfa Ansco Superpan Press film-pack, against an overcast sky, with camera visibility about five miles. Joe got his composition in line by standing on a sandbag on top of some stones he piled up on the rim of Suribachi's crater. Joe said that the raising had no perceptible effect on the Marines fighting at the foot of the mountain because they were too exhausted to rejoice. Incidentally, there are six Marines in the picture, although everybody thinks there are four or five. We asked Joe if he had any other flag pictures to his credit. "I am," said Joe, "the man who took the pictures of the two kids on Guam with homemade flags that had seven and nine stripes and thirteen and forty-three stars. I am also the man who was attached to General MacArthur's headquarters for a month without taking a picture of the General."

1 9 4 5

THE CELLULOID BRASSIÈRE

FOR a journalist unwilling to interview Tennessee Williams, who wrote the latest hit show, "The Glass Menagerie," the only alternative is giving up his press card. Fortunately, Williams is an amiable and adaptable young man, unruffled even by such experiences as being asked to pose for three news photographers in a single morning. He told us, as he has told other interviewers, that four years ago he was an usher at the Strand Theatre. It turns out, however, that this was merely an interlude between jobs as a Guild playwright (unsuccessful) and as a Hollywood script writer (unsuccessful). "Battle of Angels" was the name of the Williams play the Guild put on, and, though it starred Miriam Hopkins and was directed by Margaret Webster, it folded up after the tryout in Boston. "I never heard of an audience getting so infuriated," Williams told us. "They hissed so loud you couldn't hear the lines, and that made Miriam so mad that she began to scream her lines above the hissing. Then they stamped their feet, and after a while most of them got up and left, banging their seats behind them. That play was, of course, a much better play than this one. The thing is, you can't mix up sex and religion, as I did in 'Battle of Angels,' but you can always write safely about mothers."

The mother Williams wrote about in "The Glass Menagerie" is his own. The play is mainly taken from life. "We moved to St. Louis when I was about thirteen," the author informed us. "We took an old house that just had windows at the front and back. My sister, who was a year older than I was, had a sad little shadowy room that looked out on an alley, so we painted it white for her, and she collected a lot of little glass animals and put them on the white shelves to brighten things up. It's something you remember. Especially if you're a playwright." A playwright Williams certainly is, the current show being the eighth he has written, not counting his work in Hollywood. He went out there straight from his run as a Strand usher, M-G-M having topped his old salary considerably (life is that way in the arts). They put him right to work on a Lana Turner picture the name of which he cannot remember—"I always thought of it as 'The Celluloid Brassière,' " he said—and then, when this project failed to work out, tried to assign him to a Margaret O'Brien script. When he had finished telling M-G-M what he thought of child actors, they barred him from the studio. He sat out the rest of his contract on the beach at Santa Monica, drawing two hundred and fifty dollars a week. That was when he started work on "The Glass Menagerie." He finished it in Provincetown last summer. When he showed the manuscript to his agent, she said, "Well, let's get it typed, anyway."

Williams is a small, quiet man with rather close-clipped hair and a heart which is a little too unstable to allow him to be in the Army. Collectors of psychosomatic lore will be fascinated to learn that he was once paralyzed for two weeks, apparently as a gesture of protest against working in a shoe store; at any rate, when his parents told him he didn't have to go back to the shoe store, the paralysis went away. He seems to be pretty well relaxed now. "I never had a very hard time of it," he said, "so now that I'm about to have an easy time of it, it doesn't seem to make so much difference. In the last ten years I've nearly always done what I wanted, and when I needed money there were always things I could do—clerking or ushering. Sometimes it was a nuisance, taking time off from writing to make enough money to eat, but there are plenty of things about being successful that are a nuisance, too—those three photographers this morning, for instance."

1 9 4 5

LAST WORD

THIS may well be our final story on Adolf Hitler, and you may be sure we're not trying to lay the foundations for a Hitler legend—just cleaning up some odds and ends, such as the fact that two savage German shepherd dogs were the only animals he ever owned, that he had throwing flowers in his path made a penal offense (they might explode), that he was fond of cactus for interior decoration, and that he never had a checkbook in his life. He had his famous forelock cut off when he got a letter from a barber in Athens who said it was unbecoming, meat for cartoonists, and an evidence of poor barbering. Mussolini told a confidant, "Hitler is just a bad imitation of me."

Hitler did not by any means receive a unanimously bad press outside the Reich. George Bernard Shaw hailed his first actions as Chancellor as "perfectly right." Bishop Wade of the Methodist Episcopal Church said that he was not wholly bad but did have some bad advisers. He was a teetotaler, and this won him some admirers, too, though his oldest brother, Alois Hitler, a bartender in Berlin, was probably not among them. Hitler's father, by the way, died while drinking in a tavern in the village of Leonding, near Linz. Over the doorway of the tavern was the motto "Whether Christian, Pagan, Jew, we've a drink that waits for you." Hitler's habit of making important moves or announcements on Saturday resulted in a decision to keep the Paris Bourse closed Saturdays during some of those tense moments of 1937. Among the evils he introduced into our society was a revival of astrology. He was said to have chosen for the Munich coup of 1938 the moment when the sun, moon, and planets were in good configuration with his chart. Hearing of this, certain Washington believers began lobbying for the appointment of a federal astrologer. Presumably in a spirit of pure irony, Hitler was once voted the world's greatest man by the Princeton freshmen and proposed for the Nobel Peace Prize by the Swedish senate. He was not formally called *Der Führer* until 1939. Before that he was *Reichsführer, Reichskanzler, und Höchstkommandierende der Armee.*

The official fiction was that Hitler drew no salary or other emoluments, and lived on the royalties from "Mein Kampf." His black Mercedes-Benz car held the record for the run between Stuttgart and Munich. It was specifically forbidden for members of the master race to name babies after him. A Hungarian factory owner once forbade his workers to wear mustaches cut like Hitler's, declaring that they were beneath the dignity of a Hungarian, and a Czech court once ruled that to call a man a Hitler was slander. In death notices printed within the Reich, Hitler was invoked instead of God. A German linotyper once got a stiff jail sentence for accidentally or intentionally making "*Heil Hitler*" read "*Heilt Hitler*"—"Cure Hitler."

Before the war, Hitler could recite from memory the name of every warship of the British and American navies and the cast of every German movie comedy. The night after the 1934 "blood purge," he made his friend Putzi Hanfstaengl play bits of "Die Meistersinger" to him over and over. Of his library of six thousand volumes, the only one he ever gave any evidence of having read was Houston Stewart Chamberlain's "Foundations of the Nineteenth Century." He used to say he could get the gist of a book by running his hands over it. One piece of Hitler art that was extant in Germany as recently as ten years ago was a poster he painted in 1909 for the manufacturers of Teddy's Perspiration Powder; he did this after twice flunking his entrance tests to the Vienna Academy of Art. He had a dozen pairs of spectacles at each of his desks, various pairs for various hours of the day and night. In 1937, he prophesied that Berlin would be completely rebuilt within twenty years.

1945

ONE MAN'S FAMILY

HERE is a brief report on the recent visit to town of the Saudi Arabian delegation to the United Nations Conference in San Francisco. The party was headed by His Royal Highness Prince Faisal ibn-Abdul-Aziz al-Saud, Viceroy of the Hejaz and Minister of Foreign Affairs of Saudi Arabia, who is the second son of King Ibn-Saud. He was accompanied by eight official advisers, all sheiks, and two physicians, three bodyguards, and four other princes—his son, Prince Abdullah ibn-Faisal al-Saud, who is twenty-three, and Prince Fahad ibn-Abdul-Aziz al-Saud, Prince Muhammad ibn-Abdul-Aziz al-Saud, and Prince Nawaf ibn-Abdul-Aziz al-Saud, three of his twenty-four brothers. Prince Nawaf, who is twelve, is one of the youngest of the King's sons, and is (we've worked it out for you) Prince Abdullah ibn-Faisal al-Saud's uncle.

The delegation put up at the Waldorf, where we got in touch with one of the advisers, Ahmad-Abdul Jabbar, a short, chubby sheik of twenty-four. He was dressed in a white igal, white kufaya, white aba, white balto, maroon socks, and thick-soled maroon oxfords. You can take our word for this. He informed us that he is secretary of the Political Section of the royal court and a graduate, class of '43, of the American University of Beirut, in Lebanon, where he learned to speak English. He was humming "I'm the Sheik of Araby" as we arrived and a moment afterward broke into "Alexander's Ragtime Band." He was soon interrupted by music from another room. He smiled patiently. "Small Prince Nawaf is playing his records again," he said. "His Royal Highness discovered a music shop in Brooklyn that sells Arabic records. He has purchased a large collection. He plays them until three in the morning. Some of us cannot sleep. Personally, I would prefer to listen to hot jazz, but he is the Prince."

The party's visit to New York was unofficial, and Prince Faisal didn't drop in at City Hall. He attended only three formal dinners, one given by the Texas Oil Company, one by the Saudi Arabian Mining Syndicate, and one by the Near East College Association. He also had lunch with the Waves at Hunter College. Sheik Jabbar went to none of these affairs. "We go our separate ways," he told us. "You can understand that we are weary of looking at each other and of hearing speeches. In Detroit, on the way here from the Conference, we attended a dinner where twenty-eight speeches were given. Twenty-eight! In your city we have but one aim—to build up resistance."

Shopping was the most popular activity among the princes and sheiks. They all bought pin-striped business suits as soon as they got here. As Sheik Jabbar explained to us, "We were very uncomfortable when we wore the igal and aba in public. We would immediately be surrounded by several strange ladies. At least one of them was bound to tell us that we reminded her of Rudolph Valentino. As you may know, it is not our custom to speak to strange ladies. Once I went for three years without speaking to a single lady. A man usually speaks only to his wife. And a man usually has only one wife these days. The harem is a thing of the past." Sheik Jabbar told us that he had limited his shopping to inexpensive earrings, bracelets, and necklaces for his four sisters (it's all right to speak to them; he ran up that three-year record away from home) and shaving sets for his friends. "I'm no prince," he said. "I'd rather spend what money I have on cheeseburgers."

We asked if we could meet the small Prince Nawaf. He was still in the next room, under the guardian eye of a city detective. The Prince is thin, dark, and very active. He wears long pants and knows four words of English—"hello," "goodbye," "O.K.," and "cinema." Through an interpreter, he informed us that he is in the fourth grade at the School for Princes back home and that he studies geography, history, geometry, and religion. In his spare time, he goes riding and hunting birds in desert oases. While he was at the Waldorf, he spent a couple of hours every morning on his schoolwork, and then, accompanied by the detective, got into a livery Cadillac and explored the city. Among the places he and the detective visited were Palisades Park, Jones Beach, Rockaway Beach, and Coney Island. At Coney Island the Prince bought cotton candy, corn on the cob, whistles, dolls, and comic hats, and enjoyed eighteen consecutive rides on the Dodgem. Prince Nawaf went back to Coney Island so many times that his big brother, Prince Faisal, got curious about it and went out there too.

1945

ABSURDISTE

ALBERT CAMUS, the young French author, is over here for a few
lectures and the appearance of his novel, "The Stranger." He has an
idea for a daily newspaper that would take a lot of the fun out of newspapering.
"It would be a critical newspaper, to be published one hour after the first edi-
tions of the other papers, twice a day, morning and evening," he told us when
we called on him in a hotel on West Seventieth Street, where he had spent his
first five days in America. "It would evaluate the probable element of truth in
the other papers' main stories, with due regard to editorial policies and the past
performances of the correspondents. Once equipped with card-indexed
dossiers on the correspondents, a critical newspaper could work very fast. After
a few weeks the whole tone of the press would conform more closely to reality.
An international service." M. Camus, who is thirty-two and dresses like a character in "Harold Teen," retired six months ago as editor-in-chief of *Combat*, a
Paris daily he directed during the German occupation, when it was extralegal.
In the first year following the Liberation, he made *Combat* the most interesting
independent journal in France. *Combat* now, he thinks, has passed from independence to a simple habit of negation, which isn't the same thing.

For the time being, Camus is more interested in further novels, his play
"Caligula," which has been bought for New York production, and his philosophy of the absurd than he is in journalism. He is often called an Existentialist,
like his friend Jean-Paul Sartre, but he says he is not. His philosophy is not the
same thing at all as Sartre's, whose disciples, he says, are impressed with the
consciousness of existence, which is to them at times a mystic pleasure and
rather more often a pain in the neck. What burns Camus is the necessity to stop

existing. He believes man's relation to the universe is absurd because man must die. But he also believes that acceptance of this relation is the mark of maturity. Sisyphus, who was condemned to push a rock up a hill in Hades and then see it roll down again, is Camus's symbol: he knew what he was up against, but he kept on pushing. For a man arrived at such a grim conclusion, M. Camus seemed unduly cheerful, as did, in fact, M. Sartre when he was here some weeks ago. "Just because you have pessimistic thoughts, you don't have to *act* pessimistic," Camus said. "One has to pass the time somehow. Look at Don Juan." He detests the kind of "realism" that confounds greatness with strength and material success; the dangerous part he took in the Resistance was an assertion of his disagreement with this concept. When we saw him, he was looking at the translation of "The Stranger" for the first time. "There are too many quotation marks in it," he said. "I am sure that there weren't that many quotation marks in the original."

Camus has a snub-nosed face that looks more Spanish than French. His mother, who was born in Algeria, was of Spanish blood. His father, also born in Algeria, belonged to one of the Alsatian families that moved there after the war of 1870–71 rather than become German. Camus was born in Algiers himself, and is, we got him to admit without too much trouble, the first top-notch French writer born in North Africa. His birth there gave him a distinctive chemistry, because the European cities in French North Africa are as new and ruthlessly commercial as Birmingham or Detroit. They have their color problem, with accompanying overtones of guilt; their competing immigrant strains (Camus's parentage combines two); and their savage and explicit anti-Semitism (the proportion of Jews to Christians is much higher than in Continental France). They also have their crude and desperate first- or second-generation millionaires who have never learned that it sometimes pays to be reasonable. The summers are extreme, like New York's. Camus graduated from the University of Algiers and moved to France only in 1940.

The thing that bothered him about France at first was the oversupply of historic and literary associations. "What the heart craves, at certain moments, is places without poetry," he once wrote. West Seventieth Street ought to suit him fine.

1946

TWELFTH NIGHT

FOR eleven years, we have stoutly resisted the temptation to attend the *Daily News'* annual Harvest Moon Ball, but last Wednesday afternoon we weakened to the extent of gliding over to Madison Square Garden and taking in a dress rehearsal held a few hours before the twelfth presentation of the spectacle, the World Series of ballroom dancing. Demure as a wallflower, we sat in awed silence while Ed Sullivan, the *News* columnist and, perhaps not quite perchance, the master of ceremonies, explained to fifty-one pairs of contestants the rules of the prom. "You must maintain bodily contact at all times," he was saying. "That means your fingertips must always be touching. Keep it clean and dignified at all times. The Eddy Duchin hop and the Westchester hop will be permitted only in the jitterbug. In the rumba, you may make moderate movements of the hips, but no trick novelties or shimmy stunts." The hundred and two dancers listening to him seemed to understand all this perfectly.

The entrants, mostly young, and every one of them a bona-fide amateur, had been divided into five categories—Fox Trot, Rumba, Viennese Waltz, Jitterbug Jive, and Tango—and when Mr. Sullivan began to confer with the Jitterbug Jivers, we sought out the Harvest Moon editor of the *News*, a Mr. Fitzinger, whom we found settled in a loge, like a dowager chaperone. He revealed at once that he is not merely a Harvest Moon man. He is a versatile chap who also guides the destinies of such other *News* frolics as the Silver Skates and the Golden Gloves. "The way I look at it," he told us, "this ball is a public service. People have a lot of troubles—they forget them for one night. What the hell? You could sell tickets to a cat fight in an alley for a dollar-fifty these days." This year, the Garden sold twenty thousand tickets to the ball in two and a half hours. The winners in each of the classes were rewarded with contracts for a two-week appearance at Loew's State Theatre, with Ed Sullivan, of all peripatetic people, as their master of ceremonies.

The victors in the waltz division (we learned this in Thursday's *News*) were Mr. and Mrs. Angelo Pellegrino. We were delighted, because, as if by prescience, we had had a chat with them beforehand. The Pellegrinos are the only couple who have competed in all twelve Harvest Moon Balls. They were in street clothes when we saw them, so Mrs. P. assured us she would wear a feathery white gown flecked with Kelly-green sequins at the ball. "It really brings me out," she confided to us. "I"m planning to flip my skirts." Her husband is a drapery packer in Brooklyn, and he told us on the eve of their triumph that he and his wife had been dancing at the Roseland Ballroom two or three nights a week for the last fifteen years. "Teresa and I *met* at Roseland," he added, with sentiment worthy of the *News*. "She was with a party of friends, and the first three times I asked her to dance, she refused. This year, we decided to better our dancing, and we got some people at Roseland to watch us and tell us what was wrong." "It was mainly my posture," said Mrs. Pellegrino gallantly. Next year, Mr. and Mrs. Pellegrino will be ineligible for the ball, having automatically become professionals by accepting their Loew's State engagement. And next year, we may attend the ball itself.

1 9 4 6

WILLIAM SHAWN,
NICCOLÒ TUCCI, AND
GEOFFREY HELLMAN

AFTER TEN YEARS

ALDOUS HUXLEY is in New York for the first time in ten years, and we have had a talk with him in a Central Park South apartment he sublet for a month from a friend of a friend who is in California for that period. Along with his wife and their twenty-seven-year-old son, Michael, he drove here from California, where he lives in Wrightwood, a mountain village fifty miles from Los Angeles. Wrightwood enjoys an elevation of six thousand feet, and Huxley, who enjoys an elevation of six feet four, bought a forest ranger's house there and converted a nearby stable into a study. "The place has the quality of silence," he said. "The desert is five miles down. It exerts an enormous fascination. The light is extraordinary, too." Mornings, Huxley writes, using a portable and the touch system, which he learned as a boy, when he was almost blind for two years. His sight is still poor, but he continues to eschew glasses and goes in for the optical exercises he thinks have helped him. Afternoons, he walks in the neighboring pinewoods. He writes again for a couple of hours before dinner, and after dinner he and his wife play phonograph records or she reads to him—generally novels like "War and Peace" and "The Brothers Karamazov," which he likes to reread, or relisten to, every few years. He has a small Hollywood apartment, where of late he has been staying a few days every few days while working on "The Gioconda Smile," a film based on an old story of his that Universal will release in January. "It's my only murder story," he said. "I was very fortunate, because Zoltan Korda, its director, bought it on his own. We worked on it and then sold it to Universal. We didn't suffer from the extraordinary Hollywood assumption that twelve incompetent writers equal one competent one. I remember working on 'Pride and Prejudice' and finding

forty or fifty scripts on the story piled up in my office. It gave one the most peculiar feeling—all this wasted energy, this huge pile of pulp that no one looked
at."

Huxley has started a new novel, with grave misgivings. "It's a sort of fantasy
about the future," he said. "I'm feeling my way toward the right form. There's
been a lot of hit and miss at the beginning, mostly miss. It postulates a situation
in California after an atomic war. People are living in ruins. A scientific expedi-
tion comes from New Zealand, one of the few places not touched by the war,
and gets captured by the strange savages who are living as parasites on what
has been left—getting iron out of trolley lines, and so forth. It's extraordinarily
difficult to write a novel today. There's such a sense of general precariousness.
Novelists used to assume a stable background for their characters; you could
assume that their fortunes would go on. Even during the war, during the blitz,
you could hope that things were going to be O.K. Now the whole social order is
running down in the most hopeless way, with no prospect of amelioration in
the immediate future. There's a general deterioration of the European econ-
omy, caused by the pressure of population on resources. It's Malthus's nightmare come true. What novels can the Germans write in their troglodyte
existence? As for India, what one hears is horrible. Even in this country, the
whole thing is fantastic. You've had eight wonderful harvests. You did better
than Joseph; you had eight years instead of seven. And now a bad one comes
along. Suppose you get six bad ones—what happens then? We're obviously
running on a margin incredibly narrow now. The touching assumption that
man has conquered nature is absolute bosh. Two months of cold last winter,
and the whole of Europe falls flat." Huxley believes the widespread sense of in-
security may be responsible for what he calls the extraordinary efflorescence of
historical novels. "What sense can you make of life when you don't know you
and your children won't be living in caves?" he asked.

The sound of a pneumatic drill came through an open window, and Huxley
turned, briefly, to local conditions. "The music of New York!" he said. "A Grand
Canyon in every street! It's unnecessary to go to Arizona." We asked what impressed him most about the city after ten years away, and he said, "The striking
thing now is that you can get *into* the city. It used to be a nightmare getting
back from Long Island—we visit my wife's sister in Islip every weekend when
we're in town—and now you just whiz in." The Huxleys whizzed here from California in a Ford, Mrs. H. at the wheel, and are whizzing back next week. He is
grateful for the absence of travel prohibitions on this continent. "The awful
thing in so many parts of the world," he said, "is that a human being cannot
cross a frontier. Only a paper can cross it."

LUGUBRIOUS MAMA

ONE of our men, who used to admire Edith Piaf, the tiny French singer, in Paris in 1939, was afraid that she might have brightened up her repertory for her engagement at the Playhouse here, on the theory that Americans demand optimism. He was so concerned that he went over to the Hotel Ambassador to see her before he took a chance on going to the show to hear her—said he wanted to remember her in all her pristine gloom, and not be disillusioned. In Paris, he said, she used to stand up straight and plain in front of a night-club audience—no makeup, a drab dress—and delight it with a long series of songs ending in a drowning, an arrest, an assassination, or death on a pallet. At the finish of each, the listeners would gulp a couple of quick drinks before the next began. "She was a doleful little soulful," our man remarked sentimentally. He made an engagement with her for one o'clock, and when he called on the hotel phone at that hour, she thanked him in French for being so punctual. "I forgot to set the alarm clock," she explained, "and if you hadn't come, I'd have gone on sleeping." Our man went up to the chanteuse's living room to wait while she dressed, and while waiting there saw some pencilled notes lying on a coffee table beside a book titled "L'Anglais sans Peine," open to a chapter called "Pronunciation of the English Th," which began, "Some people who lisp pronounce without wishing to do so the two sounds of the th as in English perfectly." The notes were in English and were obviously for introductory speeches for songs that Mlle. Piaf was going to sing in French. Knowing that she had never appeared before an English-speaking audience, prior to her current engagement, he concluded that she had been memorizing the speeches with "L'Anglais sans Peine" as a reference.

"A woman is waiting for a suitor who promised to return to her when he becomes a captain," the first note read. "In the corner a phonograph is playing a popular record it is cold as long as there is life there is hope. She waits for 20 years but he does not come back and the record keeps on playing until it is worn out." The second said, "Perrine—and now the sad story of Perrine, a pretty girl who worked for a priest, but had a secret lover. One night the priest surprises them together and Perrine hides her lover in a large box, but alas forgets about him and leaves him to the mercies of the rats. When he is found a candlestick is made from his leg and a basin for the church from his head, and so ends the sad story of a young man who liked girls too well." Heartened by what he had read, our man greeted Mlle. Piaf, when she appeared, like an old friend upon whom he could depend. She wore gold mules with platform soles about six inches thick, which increased her height to approximately five feet. Her mop of rusty-red hair, a stage trademark, was imprisoned under a tight turban. She looked sleeker offstage than on, our man said. Mlle. Piaf was born in Belleville, a quarter of Paris not generally considered chic, and made her first public appearance at seven, in a circus in which her father was an acrobat. She made her adult début in 1935, and was a hit almost from the start. When our man asked her—disingenuously, it would seem—whether she had any more of those wonderful sad songs she used to sing, she said, "No, I don't feel the old songs any more. I have evolved. I was never really a pessimist. I believe that there is always a little corner of blue sky, nevertheless, somewhere. In those old songs, there arrived invariably, at the end, a catastrophe. But now I have one called 'Mariage,' which is quite different. It begins in the cell of a woman who has *already* murdered her husband. She reviews her life, she hears the wedding bells, she sees herself in the arms of this man whom she has killed, an innocent young bride. It's very beautiful." As for herself, Mlle. Piaf said, she has never married and never killed anybody. "For me, love always goes badly," she said. "It is perhaps because I have a mania of choosing. I don't wait to be chosen. That places me in a position of inferiority. And I always choose badly. So the relationships turn out badly. Sometimes only two or three days. But I'm always optimistic." She is studying English hard, with the assistance of an associate professor at Columbia and of the night clubs of the city. She thinks Ray Bolger is *formidable* and had been to see him three times up to the day our man called.

Reassured, our man went to hear Mlle. Piaf a couple of nights later, and turned up at the office the next morning radiant. "The best number she did," he said, "was where an accordionist goes off to the war and gets killed. His sweetheart listens to the music of another accordion and goes nuts. Then there is one about a woman tourist who has one big night with a sailor in a port where the ship stops, and the sailor goes off on another ship and gets drowned. For an encore, she sang that old honey about the woman who falls in love with a Foreign Legion soldier—she hasn't even had time to learn his name—and he gets killed and they bury him under the warm sand. I haven't had such a good time in years."

1 9 4 7

HERBERT WARREN WIND AND
SPENCER KLAW

LIVE MERCHANDISE

PLAIN old reliable Gimbel's is now selling live ponies, and we've been down and looked over the stock and had a talk with Gimbel's plain old reliable pet-buyer, Mr. Henry Fried, whom we found vigilantly at his post in the pet shop, on the eighth floor, fondly eying a sleepy-looking little black-and-white pony named Cinderella. With negligible prompting, Mr. Fried told us that Gimbel's has the largest pet shop in the country and that it was the first department store to sell pedigreed dogs, back in 1935. "Practically speaking," said Mr. Fried, "we're the first department store to sell ponies, too." He lowered his voice, and continued, "I think Macy's did have one or two ponies in its Barnyard Shop during the war, but, pshaw, they didn't amount to anything. This is a major merchandising operation."

Gimbel's, Fried said, got the idea of selling ponies from a man named Clark Garvey, who made the rounds of the pony farms early this fall taking options on ponies until he figured he'd cornered eighty-five per cent of this year's output, or approximately six thousand ponies. Gimbel's made a deal with Garvey for an option on twenty-five hundred ponies, with the understanding that for the time being he wouldn't let any other local store, including Macy's, put his ponies on sale. The ponies are mostly shipped, in good-sized crates, straight from the farm to the customer, but Gimbel's keeps fifteen or so on hand in a Brooklyn stable for quick suburban delivery, and one will always be on display at the store. For $349, F.O.B. New York, a customer gets a Shetland or Welsh pony (the Welsh ponies run a trifle larger than the Shetlands), a halter, a prefabricated wooden stable that seemed to us about the size of an upright piano, a health certificate signed by a veterinarian, and a money-back guarantee that the pony won't get the staggers or drop dead for at least thirty days.

The first pony to be installed in the pet shop was a red Shetland named Pinto, who arrived shortly before Thanksgiving and was placed in the charge of an elderly groom who had been specially hired to keep a high gloss on the merchandise. Gimbel's hadn't yet got around to advertising ponies when a man who had come into the store for a Schick razor saw Pinto and bought him on the spot. Cinderella was moved in from Brooklyn to take Pinto's place, an ad appeared in the papers, and the next day a hundred people turned up to get further details. Most prospective metropolitan purchasers aren't sure whether they can legally keep a pony on their premises. As a rule, Fried told us, anyone with an acre or more is in the clear, but people who live on small lots in the suburbs are likely to find that zoning regulations forbid the keeping of livestock. Some buyers are taking ponies without stables ($249), with the intention of boarding them out. Twenty-seven ponies were sold during the first week, along with several pony carts ($249 per cart), which was regarded as an auspicious start.

Cinderella attracted considerable attention at the store, and, as a matter of fact, moved out of stock the day after we were down to see her; Mr. Fried called us up to tell us about it. Meanwhile, one man had dropped by every day at lunchtime with a couple of red apples for her, and children had to be forcibly prevented from feeding her bubble gum. A buyer may specify the breed, color, and size of pony he wants, and if he wishes to look at some in addition to the sample on hand, he may go over to the stable in Brooklyn. The questions most frequently asked about ponies at Gimbel's are: What do you feed a pony? (Ans.: Hay, salt, and, if he's worked hard, some oats and some bran.) How much does his food cost? (Ans.: Ten to thirty cents a day, according to how active he is.) Will he be uncomfortably cold in an unheated stable? (Ans.: No. The colder the better for a pony.) Is he gentle and well trained? (Ans.: Yes, for both riding and driving.) How much of a load can a pony pull? (Ans.: Four or five children, if they're not too large.) How do you clean his teeth? (Ans.: With a sponge.)

1 9 4 7

RUGGED TIMES

WE had a talk the other day with Norman Mailer, whose novel "The Naked and the Dead" has been at the top of the best-seller lists for several months now. We met him at Rinehart & Co., his publishers, in a conference room that had, along with other handy editorial equipment, a well-stocked bar. We'd heard rumors that Mailer was a rough-and-ready young man with a strong antipathy to literary gatherings and neckties, but on the occasion of our encounter he was neatly turned out in gray tweeds, with a striped red-and-white necktie and shined shoes, and he assured us that he doesn't really have any deep-seated prejudices concerning dress. "Actually," he said, "I've got all the average middle-class fears." He thinks the assumption that he hasn't got them grew out of his meeting some of the literati last summer when he was wearing sneakers and an old T shirt. He'd just come from a ball game, and it was a very hot day. "I figured anybody with brains would be trying to keep cool," he said.

Mailer is a good-looking fellow of twenty-five, with blue eyes, big ears, a soft voice, and a forthright manner. Locating a bottle of Scotch in the bar, he poured a couple of drinks. "If I'm ever going to be an alcoholic," he said, "I'll be one by November 2nd, thanks to the rigors of the political campaign. I've been making speeches for Wallace. I've made eighteen so far and have another dozen ahead of me. I'm not doing this because I like it. All last year, I kept saying that the intellectuals had to immerse themselves in political movements or else they were only shooting their mouths off. Now I am in this spot as a result of shooting my mouth off." In general, Mailer told us, the success of his novel has caused him to feel uncomfortably like a movie queen. "Whenever I make an appearance," he said, "I have thirty little girls crowding around asking for my autograph. I think it's much better when people who read your book don't know anything about you, even what you look like. I have refused to let *Life* photograph me. Getting your mug in the papers is one of the shameful ways of making a living, but there aren't many ways of making a living that aren't shameful. Everyone keeps asking me if I've ever been psychoanalyzed. The answer is no, but maybe I'll have to be by the end of another five years. These are rough times for little Normie."

Mailer's royalties will net him around thirty thousand this year, after taxes, and he plans to bank most of it. He finds apartments depressing and has a suspicion of possessions, so he and his wife live in a thirty-dollar-a-month furnished room in Brooklyn Heights. He figures that his thirty thousand will last at least five years, giving him plenty of time in which to write another book. He was born in Long Branch, New Jersey, but his family moved to Brooklyn when he was one, and that has since been his home. He attended P.S. 161 and Boys High, and entered Harvard at sixteen, intending to study aeronautical engineering. He took only one course in engineering, however, and spent most of his time reading or in bull sessions. In his sophomore year, he won first prize in *Story*'s college contest with a story entitled "The Greatest Thing in the World." "About a bum," he told us. "In the beginning, there's a whole *tzimes* about how he's very hungry and all he's eating is ketchup. It will probably make a wonderful movie someday." In the Army, Mailer served as a surveyor in the field artillery, an Intelligence clerk in the cavalry, a wireman in a communications platoon, a cook, and a baker, and volunteered, successfully, for action with a reconnaissance platoon on Luzon. He started writing "The Naked and the Dead" in the summer of 1946, in a cottage outside Provincetown, and took sixteen months to finish it. "I'm slowing down," he said. "When I was eighteen, I wrote a novel in two or three months. At twenty-one, I wrote another novel, in seven months. Neither of them ever got published." After turning in the manuscript of "The Naked and the Dead," he and his wife went off to Paris. "It was wonderful there," he said. "In Paris, you can just lay down your load and look out at the gray sky. Back here, the crowd is always yelling. It's like a Roman arena. You have a headache, and you scurry around like a rat, like a character in a Kafka nightmare, eating scallops with last year's grease on them."

Mailer has an uneasy feeling that Dostoevski and Tolstoy, between them, have written everything worth writing, but he nevertheless means to go on turning out novels. He thinks "The Naked and the Dead" must be a failure, because of the number of misinterpretations of it that he has read. "People say it is a novel without hope," he told us. "Actually, it offers a good deal of hope. I intended it to be a parable about the movement of man through history. I tried to explore the outrageous propositions of cause and effect, of effort and recompense, in a sick society. The book finds man corrupted, confused to the point of helplessness, but it also finds that there are limits beyond which he cannot be pushed, and it finds that even in his corruption and sickness there are yearnings for a better world."

1 9 4 8

GEOFFREY HELLMAN

COCTEAU

JEAN COCTEAU, the French poet, novelist, artist, playwright, actor, critic, scenario writer, and motion-picture director, flew here recently to attend the Manhattan première of "The Eagle with Two Heads," the latest of his films to be released in this country. Advised that his English is limited, and knowing what our French is, we kept an appointment with him, in his hotel suite, with misgiving. Our anxiety was needless. A shapely lady in a green sweater greeted us in English and ushered us into Cocteau's sitting room, where he stood, poised in a gray flannel suit and beige moccasins, as tense as a man on a tightrope. Another lady, pretty, protective, and wearing a stylish black-plumed hat, sat on a sofa, and a young man with a pad and pencil sat on a chair; both of these responded in English when we were introduced. "Working conditions in France are bad," Cocteau said, in French. "Film is old, sound equipment is old. We admire Hollywood's mass-production methods, but we can't adopt them. We have few specialists—I work like a laborer myself." The young man with the pad and pencil translated this. "Mr. Cocteau has to do everything with his own hands," amplified the lady with the hat. "He is his own stage manager," said the sweatered lady. "It's like a family," said the hatted one. "Everyone pitches in." "He personally fiddles with the lights," said the interpreter. "Sometimes I sweep the studio out myself," said Cocteau. "He repairs eyelashes," said the Sweater. "He goes up and down ladders," said the Hat. "He supervises all details of costume," said the Sweater. "He's like a painter," said the Hat. "He uses the movies as a vehicle for the soul." The Sweater gave the Hat a searching look and departed for an adjoining room.

With some valuable help from the interpreter, Cocteau went on to tell us that

France is like a large village and that he feels like a peasant bringing his films to New York. "America has always given me courage," he said, in reference to this country's reception of such past pictures of his as "Blood of a Poet" and "Beauty and the Beast." "Hollywood needs a laboratory. An experimenter is hampered there today, because it's closed to risk. But it's the risk that pays off." "His films never lose money," said the Hat. Cocteau made "The Eagle with Two Heads" and "Les Parents Terribles," another picture (based on a play he wrote in 1938) that he has just finished, for a French company. He has formed his own company for his next film, which will deal with Orpheus and Eurydice. He lives alone in a small house in the country, near Fontainebleau. "All the young creative people in Paris are interested in the cinema," he told us. "Here I don't think they are. The cinema is a great art, but in America they have made an industry out of it." "It is the *modern* art," declared the Hat. "It is very young," said Cocteau. "What is fifty years in the life of a Muse?" This Muse's name, he said, is Cinema.

The lady in the sweater returned to the room. Cocteau observed that Cinema often keeps him busy from six in the morning till midnight, that forty of his drawings are being shown at the Hugo Gallery here, and that he lately completed a ten-by-twelve-foot sketch for a Gobelin tapestry of the same size. His subject was Judith bearing the head of Holofernes. It will take three years to weave the tapestry, and it will go to the Louvre. "I deliberately chose an old-fashioned, Beaux-Arts–Prix de Rome theme," he said, "but my execution was not academic." "Mr. Cocteau is exceptional," said the Sweater. The object of her admiration and ours, a delicately featured man of fifty-seven with long, thin fingers, paced about the room as he talked, gesturing with his hands and occasionally coming to rest on a chair, over one arm of which he threw a leg. He wore a brown silk tie with his initials woven on it in cream-colored letters. "Everyone in America seems so youthful," he said. "They all drink milk, as though they were still near their mothers. No Frenchman drinks milk."

1949

COLE PORTER

W E called on Cole Porter at his air-conditioned Waldorf Towers suite the other afternoon and found him spruce in a lightweight, vestless gray sharkskin suit, a black silk tie, a giant red carnation, and white cotton socks. "I go through life in paper clothes, in icy rooms," he said. "I never wear an overcoat. My wife, who has an apartment across the corridor, puts on a fur coat when she comes in here." Mr. Porter advised us that his white socks, habitual daytime accessories with him, are worn in memory of his grandfather, J. O. Cole, a West Virginia mining-and-timber bigwig, who always wore white socks, and that he and Mrs. Porter have separate apartments not only because of different tastes in temperatures but because of different hours. He works best after midnight, and often auditions people and plays the piano until early in the morning. Of late, a couple of nights a week, he has been on hand at the Columbia Records studio while the cast (other than the dancers) of "Kiss Me, Kate" has been recording an album of the show's songs (other than the first-act finale). This will require both sides of six twelve-inch records. The recordings start at twelve-fifteen and often run till four, the Columbia people providing sandwiches and hot chocolate. "I watch the lyrics for occasional lapses," Mr. Porter said, "and supervise cuts that have to be made so as to combine two numbers on one side, and so forth." The lyrics, some of which have been bowdlerized on the air, will be presented in their pristine shape in the album, except that "her goddamned nose" has been modified to "her doggone nose." One night, the recording was held up for nearly an hour because of a strange, adventitious sound, detectable only on the records, which was finally traced to a harp pedal in want of oiling.

Porter, a small man, sat like Humpty Dumpty on a big green sofa during our talk. Although he walks with a cane, he has recovered astonishingly well from the shattering accident he had in 1937, when a horse he was riding on Long Island fell on him. He has had more than thirty operations on his legs. "Dr. John J. Moorhead saved my life," he said. "He made me go back to work when I was still under drugs, and he encouraged me to take cruises to the Caribbean— I love travelling—when I had to be landed in ports in a lifeboat and then pushed around in a wheelchair." Porter wrote the lyrics for "Leave It to Me" in 1938, when he was still practically bedridden. He gets some of his best ideas while shaving, dressing, or being driven in a car. "I've never known such a nice company as that of 'Kiss Me, Kate,' " he said. "No troubles, no fights." He is going to California next week to start auditioning for a second "Kiss Me, Kate" company, which—if all goes well—will open in San Francisco in July, move to Los Angeles in August and to Dallas in September, and settle down in Chicago in October. "They're having that mysterious thing they call the Texas Centennial in Dallas," he said. "They have it every year."

Mr. Porter's living room is animated by a well-mannered black dog named Pépin le Bref—a schipperke, presented to him by Merle Oberon—and is hung with paintings by artists ranging from Dali to Grandma Moses. Grandma Moses lives not far from a place Porter owns near Williamstown, Massachusetts, where he has a library of several thousand classical records. The Porters go there many weekends and have been friends of Grandma Moses since the time, a decade ago, when they bought some of her paintings for five dollars each. Porter is a Yale man, and the author of "Bingo" and "Bulldog," as all who witnessed a 1946 movie based (roughly) on his life know, but he regards most Yale graduates as colossal bores, exempting from this indictment only his brothers in Scroll and Key, a fashionable senior society. "We used to meet two evenings a week," he said, "and, according to tradition, were supposed to march straight home, in formation, afterward. We changed all that the year I joined. Instead of going home, we marched to the Taft Hotel, where we listened to the dance orchestra."

1 9 4 9

ON FIRE

JOSHUA LOGAN, co-author, co-producer, and director of "South Pacific," was busy last week, but we contrived to get a double handful of superficial data on him by wangling an invitation to sit in one of his two aisle seats during the first act of Wednesday evening's preview, the audience for which seemed to be made up mostly of war veterans and friends of the cast. He's a big man, with big, sad eyes and a ragged mustache, and when we sat down, he said despondently, "I never saw Dick Rodgers so happy. I hope I remember to breathe tonight. I'm always forgetting to breathe on a night like this. Other times, too. Oscar Hammerstein had to keep reminding me to breathe when we were writing the show. I took a Dictaphone to his place in Bucks County, and with that we were able to replay the lines and act them out. A great help. But every so often Oscar would see me going purple from lack of breath and have to drag me back to life." Logan jumped up from his seat, stared wildly behind him, punched himself in the small of his back, and told us that he had suddenly developed a crick there. He then sat down, holding his head in his hands. "Fifteen minutes to go," he said, and drew a really deep breath.

We managed to take Logan's mind off the show by posing a few questions, beginning with a query as to where he was born. "In Texarkana," he said, slowly and reluctantly exhaling. "On the Texas, or paved, side of the street. In 1908, that was. My father died when I was three." In 1917, Logan's mother married an Army colonel. "A Yankee," Logan said, raising his head, frowning at the stage, and sinking low in his seat. "He taught at Culver Military Academy, so I went to Culver for five years. I was a fat little kid, but I marched, boxed, played football, wrote for the magazine, and got into dramatics. I hated Culver

while I was there—all that discipline. But I liked Culver the moment I left it."
Logan entered Princeton in 1927. In his senior year there, he was elected pres-
ident of the Triangle Club. Two other members of the Triangle that year were
James Stewart and Myron McCormick, who is in the "South Pacific" cast.
Logan won a scholarship entitling him to broaden his outlook by travel, and
chose to go to Russia and study at the Moscow Art Theatre. He arranged with
Princeton to leave before commencement and come back and graduate later.
He never has gone through that formality. "In Moscow," Logan said, "I listened
to Stanislavski—for my benefit, he repeated everything in French—for six
months. I owe a good deal of what I've done in 'South Pacific' to Stanislavski. I
saw him make singers sing as actors, and I saw him use the orchestra to suggest the emotion of a scene. Until then, all I'd ever seen in opera were dull,
flabby people whose dramatic expression signified only that they thought their
own voices were beautiful. I watched a man in 'Boris Godunov' sing while
jumping backward over a bed. I was twenty-one then. My God! It set me on
fire!"

On returning from Russia, Logan joined the University Players, a group that
hoped to be the Moscow Art Theatre of America. "We went broke and disbanded in '33," he told us. "After that, I tried a lot of things, including summer
theatre and directing a couple of Triangle shows." He went to Hollywood for a
term, formed a close friendship with Charles Boyer, developed a powerful
physique, came back East, and in 1938 directed his first hit, "On Borrowed
Time." Two weeks after it opened, Dwight Wiman commissioned him to direct
"I Married an Angel," and that, too, was successful. "Things had changed very
fast for me," he said. "I suddenly had two hits. So I got on a boat and went down
to South America for nine months, sailed all around the continent, and learned
Spanish." He had just finished directing "By Jupiter," in 1942, when he was
drafted into the Army. A week later, he was assigned to help direct "This Is the
Army." After that, he tried to get into combat photography. In this, as in practically everything else, Logan and the Army failed to see eye to eye. At one point,
finding himself about to become an A.A.F. mechanic, he applied for Officer
Candidate School and was rejected, on the ground that his I.Q. was too low.
When he took his intelligence test, he didn't realize that a time limit was involved. He managed to get tested again and got a high score. By V-E Day, he was
a captain in the A.A.F., assigned to the 405th Fighter Group as public-relations
and intelligence officer. "I like to think that 'Mister Roberts' and 'South Pacific'
are my way of getting even with the Army," Logan said. "High Army, I mean. I
liked those crazy kids. I kept my ears open all the time and they gave me some
wonderful lines."

Throughout the act, we jumped up when Logan jumped up, and we reminded him to breathe from time to time. "I always try to feel like the audience," he told us in a loud whisper, "but I'm so conscious of the audience that
I distract it. I make everyone within fifteen feet of me conscious only of me."

After the first-act curtain, we followed Logan into the lobby, where he tapped a man on the shoulder. The man leaped straight into the air.

"Leland Hayward," Logan said. "He's nervous."

"I thought you were Jake Shubert," Hayward said.

We were joined by Richard Rodgers, who was carrying a small notebook. "Josh," he said, "Jake Shubert says it's bringing tears to his eyes."

"Tell Oscar," said Logan.

"Oscar told me," Rodgers said. "Listen, Josh, I'm worried about the way our ocean looks."

"Dick," Logan said, "have you noticed that the audience is suppressing coughs?"

"They're hypnotized," Hayward said, "truly hypnotized."

"We've got to get the wrinkles out of that ocean," Rodgers said, studying his notebook.

Oscar Hammerstein appeared and said, "Jake Shubert's laughing."

"I don't dare trust my own senses," Logan said. He took a deep breath and held it, his face slowly darkening.

1 9 4 9

1950s

SUCCESS

O N learning that Jackie Robinson, the Brooklyn Dodgers' second base-man, is spending Monday, Wednesday, and Friday evenings each week as a television-set salesman in the Sunset Appliance Store in Rego Park, Queens, we hurried over to the place to see how he is making out. From a talk we had with Joseph Rudnick, president of Sunset, just before Robinson ap-peared, we learned that he is making out fine. Rudnick, a small, alert-looking man, graying at the temples, whom we found in an office on a balcony at the rear of the store, informed us that the accomplished young man had been working there, on a salary-and-commission basis, for five weeks, and that if he liked, he could work there forever, the year around. "Business booming like wildfire since Jackie came," Rudnick told us, looking down at a throng milling about among television sets, washing machines, and refrigerators. "Sports fans flocking in here," he said with satisfaction. "Young persons, curious about the National League's Most Valuable Player and one of the best base-stealers since Max Carey. Jackie signs baseballs for them and explains about the double steal. Since he's been here, he's sold sets to Joe Louis and Sugar Ray Robinson, among others. The newsreel people shot him selling a set to a customer. He's a natural salesman, with a natural modesty that appeals to buyers. The sales-man wrapped up in himself makes a very small package. Campanella, Hodges, and Barney dropped by to wish him luck. Campanella's his roomy. There's Jackie now! With his business agent." Robinson and a bigger, more strapping man with a florid face were making their way along the floor, the big man in the lead. "He'll be right up," Rudnick said. "Hangs his coat here. One other thing we do," he went on, "when a bar buys a television set, we send Gene Stanlee over to the bar—the wrestler. Mr. America."

Robinson and his manager for radio and television appearances came up, and we were introduced, learning that the latter's name is Harry Solow. "Jackie don't have to lay awake nights worrying about his condition, bucking that mob three times a week," Solow said. Rudnick told us that Solow also manages Joe Franklin and Symphony Sid, and Solow explained that they are radio personalities. "Jackie's all lined up for his own radio program," he continued. "He's mostly interested in boys' work, though. Spends all his spare time at the Harlem Y.M.C.A." "How I keep in shape is playing games with kids," Robinson said in a well-modulated voice. "When I quit baseball, I intend to give it full time." We learned that the Robinsons have a television set with a sixteen-inch screen and that their only child, three-year-old Jackie, Jr., likes Howdy Doody, Mr. I. Magination, and Farmer Gray better than anything else on video. As Robinson was about to go down to the main floor, it occurred to us to ask him if he'd developed any special sales technique. He looked surprised and replied that he didn't think so. "If a customer is going to buy a set, he's going to buy it," he said philosophically. "You can't twist his arm." "On the other hand," Rudnick observed, "the right angle for a salesman is the try-angle."

We bade Rudnick and Solow good-bye and followed Robinson downstairs. A short man in a heavy overcoat got him first. He wanted to see a twelve-inch set. "There's a bunch of them in the basement," Robinson told him. "All playing at once." He led the man down to the basement. We followed. It was quite dark there, but we could make out rows and rows of sets and see customers being herded from one model to another by spirited salesmen. Robinson conducted his man to a twelve-inch set, turned it on, adjusted the picture, and in rather a shout, to get his voice above the hubbub of the amplifiers, named the price and outlined the guarantee. "I like it!" the man hollered. "Could my wife work it—all those knobs?" "A child could work it," said Robinson, and it was a deal.

1950

ELIOT AND GUINNESS

W E'VE had a talk with. Alec Guinness, the mystical psychiatrist in "The Cocktail Party," and, being one of those who had an occasional feeling during the performance of the play that they couldn't exactly put their finger on what T. S. Eliot was getting at, asked him for enlightenment. "I'm only an actor, for God's sake," said Mr. Guinness, "and hardly up to interpreting a man like Eliot, but I can tell you what *he* said. He said those scenes mean whatever they mean to you." So that's that.

We switched topics, taking up Mr. Guinness himself, who is in the opinion of more than one critic on each side of the Atlantic the greatest actor on earth. Mr. Guinness is thirty-five, middle-sized, bald, slightly prognathic, rather shy, completely ingratiating, completely unrelated to the brewers of stout, and much impressed by Mr. Eliot's approach to the theatre. "After all," he said, "Eliot had done only two other plays, but he had a tremendously professional attitude. If one suggested that two or three lines might help things along here and there, he set to writing them straightway. No niggling, in the fashion of a lesser man. And he was equally helpful in blue-penciling passages that appeared repetitious. Aside from reading a few lines from my part to indicate how his verse should be read, he didn't obtrude on the production at all. The play, as you know, is written in verses that contain three stresses and one caesura, the accent falling naturally on the words that are to be emphasized." Mr. Guinness went on to inform us that poetic drama has been his meat for years, ever since he took on his first big role, a modern-dress Hamlet, when he was twenty-four. Educated at Roborough School, in Eastbourne, where, he assured us, he learned nothing whatever, he went into the advertising business at eighteen, preparing copy in behalf of lime juice, radios, valves, and clocks. "I am singularly knowledgeable about lime juice," he said. "Used to put together booklets for housewives, giving them all the medical facts about the stuff. My career in advertising ended when I mistakenly ordered a four-foot halftone engraving instead of a four-inch one, as I was supposed to." Mr. Guinness had shown a flair for amateur theatricals when he was a boy, and after abandoning advertising, he attended the Fay Compton Dramatic School, in which he won a scholarship. He presently turned up in a play called "Libel!," in which, for twelve shillings a week, he understudied an actor who had a five-line part, and also did a walk-on as a lawyer. In 1934, he played Osric in Gielgud's "Hamlet," and in 1936, after a few other engagements, he joined the Old Vic company, with whom he did, notably, Hamlet in modern dress a couple of years later.

In addition to acting in numerous plays and movies in England, Mr. Guinness has made dramatizations of two famous novels. The first of these was "Great Expectations," in which he appeared with Martita Hunt in 1939, and the second was "The Brothers Karamazov," which he worked on toward the end of the war and appeared in in 1946. "I thought a good deal about Dostoevski after the war started," he told us, "and the result was this play, which was what might be called an artistic success, although it was nothing much commercially." Mr. Guinness was in the Royal Navy from 1941 until 1946, starting in as an ordinary seaman and winding up as a lieutenant. "I was in charge of transforming the Berkeley-Carteret Hotel, in Asbury Park, into barracks for British personnel—hardly an outstanding contribution to the war effort—and then I knocked about the Mediterranean for quite a spell," he said. "My nautical methods were by guess and by God, and I was certainly glad to return to the theatre."

Mr. Guinness is married to a former actress named Merula Salaman, who took to writing and illustrating children's books a few years ago and has turned out a couple of best-sellers. "I suppose I wasn't as enthusiastic about my wife's career in the theatre as I might have been," said Mr. Guinness, "but if she were in a play and I were doing a film, we shouldn't see each other at all. Fortunately, she is happy with her writing and her painting." We asked him why "The Cocktail Party" was brought over here before being staged in London. "That was because of the Christmas season in England," he said. "All the small, smart theatres, the kind this play requires, were occupied. We did try out in Brighton and Edinburgh, though, and at the time I thought I should never play again to such an appreciative audience. The American audience, however, has been even more remarkable. I think Mr. Eliot regrets now that he didn't come over with his play. He's a director of a publishing house, you know, and he's headed for a holiday in South Africa, after ten years without a vacation. I very much doubt that South Africa will give him the pleasure he might have had here."

1950

UNFRAMED SPACE

W E improved a shining weekend on eastern Long Island by paying a call on Jackson Pollock—an uncommonly abstract abstractionist and one of seven American painters whose work was tapped for inclusion in the Twenty-fifth International Biennial Exhibition of Figurative Arts, now triumphantly under way in Venice—at his home, a big, gaunt, white clapboard, Ulysses S. Grant–period structure in the fishing hamlet of The Springs. Pollock, a bald, rugged, somewhat puzzled-looking man of thirty-eight, received us in the kitchen, where he was breakfasting on a cigarette and a cup of coffee and drowsily watching his wife, the former Lee Krasner, a slim, auburn-haired young woman who also is an artist, as she bent over a hot stove, making currant jelly. Waving us to a chair in the shade of a huge potted palm, he remarked with satisfaction that he had been up and about for almost half an hour. It was then around 11:30 A.M. "I've got the old Eighth Street habit of sleeping all day and working all night pretty well licked," he said. "So has Lee. We had to, or lose the respect of the neighbors. I can't deny, though, that it's taken a little while. When'd we come out here, Lee?" Mrs. Pollock laughed merrily. "Just a little while ago," she replied. "In the fall of 1945."

"It's marvellous the way Lee's adjusted herself," Pollock said. "She's a native New Yorker, but she's turned into a hell of a good gardener, and she's always up by nine. Ten at the latest. I'm way behind her in orientation. And the funny thing is I grew up in the country. Real country—Wyoming, Arizona, northern and southern California. I was born in Wyoming. My father had a farm near Cody. By the time I was fourteen, I was milking a dozen cows twice a day." "Jackson's work is full of the West," Mrs. Pollock said. "That's what gives it that feeling of spaciousness. It's what makes it so American." Pollock confirmed this with a reflective scowl, and went on to say that at seventeen, an aptitude for painting having suddenly revealed itself to him in a Los Angeles high school, he at once wound up his academic affairs there and headed East. "I spent two years at the Art Students League," he said. "Tom Benton was teaching there then, and he did a lot for me. He gave me the only formal instruction I ever had, he introduced me to Renaissance art, and he got me a job in the League cafeteria. I'm damn grateful to Tom. He drove his kind of realism at me so hard I bounced right into non-objective painting. I'm also grateful to the W.P.A., for keeping me alive during the thirties, and to Peggy Guggenheim. Peggy gave me my first show, in 1943. She gave me two more, and then she took off for Europe, and Lee and I came out here. We wanted to get away from the wear and tear. Besides, I had an underneath confidence that I could begin to live on my painting. I'd had some wonderful notices. Also, somebody had bought one of my pictures. We lived a year on that picture, and a few clams I dug out of the bay with my toes. Since then things have been a little easier." Mrs. Pollock smiled. "Quite a little," she said. "Jackson showed thirty pictures last fall and sold all but five. And his collectors are nibbling at those." Pollock grunted. "Be nice if it lasts," he said.

We asked Pollock for a peep at his work. He shrugged, rose, and led us into a twenty-five-by-fifty-foot living room furnished with massive Italianate tables and chairs and hung with spacious pictures, all of which bore an offhand resemblance to tangles of multicolored ribbon. "Help yourself," he said, halting at a safe distance from an abstraction that occupied most of an end wall. It was a handsome, arresting job—a rust-red background laced with skeins of white, black, and yellow—and we said so. "What's it called?" we asked. "I've forgotten," he said, and glanced inquiringly at his wife, who had followed us in. " 'Number Two, 1949,' I think," she said. "Jackson used to give his pictures conventional titles—'Eyes in the Heat' and 'The Blue Unconscious' and so on—but now he simply numbers them. Numbers are neutral. They make people look at a picture for what it is—pure painting." "I decided to stop adding to the confusion," Pollock said. "Abstract painting is abstract. It confronts you. There was a reviewer a while back who wrote that my pictures didn't have any beginning or any end. He didn't mean it as a compliment, but it was. It was a fine compliment. Only he didn't know it." "That's exactly what Jackson's work is," Mrs. Pollock said. "Sort of unframed space."

1950

SLOW

LEROY PAIGE, or Satchel Paige, a tall, slender man with a thin face, impassive features, and a relaxed manner, who has been called Joe Louis's favorite pitcher and whom Joe DiMaggio once characterized as the best pitcher he ever batted against, is far and away the oldest person ever to play major-league baseball. His age has been estimated, in the press, at anything up to fifty-two, and he himself gives it as forty-four. After being hired by the Cleveland Indians in 1948, Mr. Paige, the first Negro pitcher to enter the American League and a man whose suppleness, guile, and vast repertory of pitches are almost mythical, was extremely successful his first year and not so successful his second. He stayed away from organized baseball in 1950. When William Veeck, the former Cleveland owner, assumed control of the St. Louis Browns in 1951, he engaged Mr. Paige for a second time. In 1951, Mr. Paige's record was only fair, but in this season, his twenty-eighth year of pitching, he is coming into his own. Up to now, he has won as many games for the Browns—ten—as any other pitcher; his repertory was never larger. We finally caught up with the august gentleman one recent afternoon just before game time at Yankee Stadium, in the visiting team's locker room. It was an area full of preoccupied movement and noise. A young man in a St. Louis uniform was hurling a baseball at the wall and fielding it on one hop. Another player was whacking the lid of a trash can with a large mitt. A tall man with light hair was practicing a slow, deliberate windup. Around the room, several other players, seated on trunks, were pounding their fists into their gloves. A stocky player was asking the locker-room attendant, a large man wearing a white suit and called Tiny, where his glove was. "What kind of a ball was that you hit yesterday?" one player asked his neighbor. "A high ball," replied the other. "High and outside." A huge, cheerful man directed us to Mr. Paige, who was seated quietly in one corner, putting on his spikes. The cheerful man, whose name turned out to be Bill Durney and who is road secretary for the Browns, informed us, over the slamming and banging of the trash-can lid, that Mr. Paige had pitched in twenty-five hundred games in his career—more than anybody else in the world. "Satchel can throw a ball at least twelve different ways and he has at least four ways of winding up," Mr. Durney added, in a hearty voice.

Mr. Paige straightened, stood up, stamped on his spikes, shook hands with us, and sat down again.

"He is the slowest pitcher in the major leagues," Mr. Durney went on spiritedly. "A man with a stopwatch timed him recently on one pitch, and it took him a minute and nineteen seconds to deliver it. The major-league rule says all a pitcher is allowed is twenty seconds, but you can't hurry Satchel."

"Too many pitchers got the hurry-ups," Satchel observed with dignity. "When I talk to the young pitchers, I tell them to slow down. You last longer."

"Satchel's fast ball has been compared with Walter Johnson's, but now he depends mostly on his curve and control," Durney said. "Control! The batters dig in against Satchel; they know he won't bean them. 'Let them dig in,' says Satchel. He doesn't approve of the duster. 'I'll outfox them,' he says. Foxy! Sometimes he winds up fast and throws slow and sometimes he winds up slow and throws fast. Sidearm, underhand, overhand. His hesitation pitch is the most unusual pitch in baseball; he winds up with agonizing deliberation and then, as he nears the end of his throwing motion, stops the forward movement of his arm so that the ball just trickles toward the plate. It's the only pitch with sound accompaniment. He slaps his left foot down hard just before unclasping the ball." Durney strode away to talk with the manager, Marty Marion.

Mr. Paige's long, wiry fingers wrapped themselves around the seams of a baseball. "This is how I throw a jump ball," he told us pleasantly.

We thanked him for letting us in on it, and pressed him for details about his career. He said that he started pitching in 1924, for a semi-professional team in Birmingham, after a short trick as a redcap in Mobile, where he was born, and has since pitched for over thirty different teams. These included the Chattanooga Black Lookouts, the New Orleans Black Pelicans, the Pittsburgh Crawfords, the Kansas City Monarchs, and numerous barnstorming teams that played, mostly during the winter, in Central and South American countries and in Cuba, Puerto Rico, and Trinidad, as well as in rural sections of this country. Mr. Paige, whose father was a landscape gardener and who was the third-youngest of eight children, informed us he used to be billed as "Satchel Paige—Guaranteed to Strike Out the First Nine Men," which he generally did, and that when he was with the Monarchs, he was given an airplane as part of his salary, and the owner's son, an ex–Army pilot, used to fly him to games and, before landing, buzz the team's opponents during infield practice. "It gave us a psychological advantage," Mr. Paige remarked. "Like an eagle. When I was with the House of David team, which was managed by Grover Cleveland Alexander, we won a hundred and four out of a hundred and five games one year. For the House of David, I grew a mustache."

Durney, returning, told us that Paige had once beaten Dizzy Dean, 1–0, in a thirteen-inning exhibition game; that when he was with a team in Bismarck, North Dakota, he had pitched twenty-nine games in thirty days; that in 1935, during a baseball tournament in Wichita, he had struck out sixty men while winning four games; that he had struck out Rogers Hornsby five times in one afternoon; that Joe DiMaggio had got only one hit off him in five games; and that Satchel had pitched a no-hit game in Pittsburgh, had driven that night to Chicago, and had there pitched a twelve-inning shutout. He thrives, Durney said, on long bus rides and quick meals. A poor hitter, he is a great fielding pitcher, and a great strategist.

"I developed control from throwing rocks at cans on tree stumps," said Mr. Paige, who owns a farm in Kansas City, and has three daughters, and a wife named LaHoma. "My hobbies are photography, collecting antique silverware, and, you might say, hunting. I have five shotguns and twenty hunting dogs. When barnstorming is over, I like to hunt—in North Dakota, mostly."

We asked him if he is a good shot. "I get better all the time," he said.

1952

NO BULLIES OR TOADIES

HEARING of the existence of a local group called the Friends of Frank Merriwell, whose members have banded together out of nostalgic devotion to that famous apostle of Fair Play, we looked up its president, a man named Joseph M. Graham, who works for Equitable Life. The other night, Mr. Graham invited us to attend one of the Friends' monthly meetings, which are held in a private dining room of the Press Box Restaurant, on East Forty-fifth Street, and before the proceedings got under way, he told us a bit about the outfit. It began slightly over a year ago, when he and a handful of other Merriwell addicts got to reminiscing about their boyhood idol. "It surprised us that no one had ever become a Friend of Merriwell before," Graham said. "Frank Merriwell, I mean. We hate his brother Dick. Anyway, we've been an awfully informal outfit. We chugged along very quietly and nicely until someone said, 'Let's have membership cards.' So we got cards, and now we have fifty members, and I don't even know them all. I'm afraid we're going to get even more organized tonight. Somebody's bringing a lawyer."

Mr. Graham showed us a sampling of the mail the Friends had lately received—largely as a result of a mention of the organization in the *Times*, there being several *Times* men among the members. A man in Springfield, Massachusetts, expressing the hope that Burt L. Standish's Frank Merriwell books—out of print since 1934—would soon make a comeback, said, "It would be a great thing for our country. Maybe decency and honor would once again count for something in American life." A lady in Winchester, Virginia, wanted the Friends to know that she had learned to read by borrowing her brother's Frank Merriwells, and, having mastered them, had swiftly gone on to Shakespeare.

Presently, the meeting began, with fourteen Friends on hand, all of them well past boyhood. Mr. Graham, seated beside us, rapped for attention. "We meet in the name of Frank Merriwell," he intoned solemnly. "Hear! Hear!" murmured the assemblage. A waiter brought a round of drinks. We asked Mr. Graham, in a whisper, if Frank himself ever touched the stuff. "He gambled," said Graham. "His hands trembled with excitement just at the thought of poker. He *must* have drunk." The Friend on our other side, a *Times* man, confided to us that as a youth he often had lumps on his head, inflicted by his mother in an effort, obviously vain, to wean him away from Frank Merriwell. "Frank had a friend who could suspend the law of gravity," he told us gravely. Mr. Graham asked for a report from the book-finding committee, which turned out to be another *Times* man. The committee observed glumly that the Friends possessed not a single copy of a Merriwell book. (Over a hundred million copies have been published.) "Yale University is lousy with Merriwells," the committee said. "I understand somebody left Yale a set of two hundred and seventy in his will. Maybe we could get those, because I don't think Yale much likes the idea of being associated with Frank." "Snobs!" cried a voice downtable. Mr. Graham was instructed to write a polite letter of inquiry to Yale.

"Now, about the question of being properly organized," broke in a man at the end of the table, who we quickly gathered was the lawyer. "First of all, we'll need a person of permanent address to give summonses to."

"If we could get people to return to Frank Merriwell," said Graham nervously, "maybe we could lick the comic books."

"I'm a bachelor. I don't give a hoot what the kids read," said the lawyer. "Now, it will cost you sixty dollars to incorporate. Unless maybe you'd prefer something along the lines of a joint-venture setup."

"Let's have a quiz," said Graham hastily. He read off ten questions from a paper, including "As a baseball pitcher, what puzzling delivery did Frank have?" (Ans.: Double shoot), and "Who was old Joe Crowfoot?" (Ans.: Indian who reared Frank). The replies were hurled back confidently from all sides.

"I would suggest that there have to be certain provisions made whether you incorporate or not," the lawyer was saying. "You have to protect yourselves. There are a lot of ramifications."

"I sure would like to get us some turtleneck sweaters and bulldogs," said Graham.

"It would be advisable, all things considered, for the incorporation papers to be sent at the earliest possible opportunity to the Secretary of State of New York," said the lawyer. "It occurs to me that if no stock issue is involved, perhaps it could be done for forty dollars."

"I would like to have a letterhead with 'No Bullies or Toadies Allowed' on it," said Graham.

"Now, if any of you gentlemen happens to know a Supreme Court justice who is a Frank Merriwell fan . . ." said the lawyer.

"Gee, we're getting organized," said Graham. "I feel terrible."

1953

ANNA IN HARLEM

W E happened to be backstage at the Ziegfeld one evening last week when Anna Magnani, the Italian actress, happened along to give her regards to Leontyne Price and Cab Calloway, who figure conspicuously in "Porgy and Bess." These happenings of Miss Magnani's and ours had been arranged by a gnome called Irving Drutman, who is serving as shepherd for the eminent lady during her stay in this country. While Miss Magnani and Mr. Calloway were beaming at each other, with as fine a display of ivories as we've seen in our time, Mr. Drutman advised us that a couple of limousines were available to take Miss Magnani, an assortment of Italian moviemakers, and us to Harlem. "She's mad for this jitterbug stuff," said Mr. Drutman.

Presently, we found ourself installed in a car with the actress (she was done up funereally in black), a duenna named Mrs. Natalia Murray, and a pair of Italian gentlemen, who kept exclaiming "Ha, Harlem!" and slapping themselves on the knees. It developed that Miss Magnani's English is even sparser than our Italian, but on our ride northward that didn't matter much, since her only remark was "Madre mia!"

"Anna would like to see this 'Porgy and Bess' company in La Scala," Mrs. Murray informed us.

"Harlem—bene!" said the two Italian gentlemen, whose minds were evidently in tune.

"Your first stop," announced the driver of the limousine, "will be Sugar Ray Robinson's."

Miss Magnani rocked back and forth and hummed a mournful song.

"Anna has been tired by New York," said Mrs. Murray.

"I have been in Harlem five years ago," one of the Italian gentlemen announced to us. "Three days I have spent jitterbugging."

The limousine pulled up at Sugar Ray's, a saloon on Seventh Avenue decorated for the most part with photographic murals of the proprietor knocking people's brains out. On arrival, we were joined by Mr. Drutman and another parcel of Italians, and welcomed to the place by Mr. Robinson himself, who was arrayed in a gray-and-beige outfit of extremely sharp cut.

After Mr. Robinson had had enough tables pulled together to get the party established, he sat down beside Miss Magnani. "I go for you," he said simply.

Miss Magnani gazed at him thoughtfully.

"She don't talk no English, I guess," said Mr. Robinson. He put some gum in his mouth and began to chew vigorously.

"Boom, boom," said Miss Magnani.

"She thinks chewing gum makes a funny noise," Mrs. Murray told us.

Mr. Robinson once again addressed himself to Miss Magnani, this time as if he were talking to somebody hard of hearing. "Who—tell—you—come—here?" he said.

"*Mangiare, mangiare,*" said Miss Magnani.

"I—will—come—to—Rome—in—July," said Mr. Robinson.

"*Mangiare,*" said Miss Magnani.

"How you say July in Italian?" Mr. Robinson inquired of one of the Italians.

"*Luglio,*" he was informed.

"I—come—Rome—in—*Nulio,*" said Mr. Robinson.

"I am first time in America," said Miss Magnani, in English.

"See!" said Mr. Robinson. "You're getting on to the language already."

Mr. Robinson then ordered a round of chicken-in-a-basket, a house specialty, and disappeared for a few minutes. He returned with several autographed photographs of himself, which he presented to Miss Magnani. "Pass them around among your friends," he suggested cordially.

After the chicken, we took off in the limousines again, this time heading for the Savoy Ballroom. As we tooled along, Miss Magnani murmured, "My God, my God."

"The second time she's spoken English since she came to this country," said Mrs. Murray.

At the Savoy, one of the Italian Harlem enthusiasts declared, "Now I shall do the jitterbug."

"Two weeks in America will kill me," said Miss Magnani, in Italian.

1 9 5 3

OUTSIDE THE PROFESSION

W E'VE just had one of our annual talks with that merry, bitter, lively, ambitious, and beguiling man, Frank Lloyd Wright, who at eighty-four has more work under construction than ever before in his life. Wright is in town to get his plans for the Guggenheim Museum of Non-Objective Painting approved by our local building department—the museum has been about to be built for many a long year now, and Wright says patiently that he hopes ground will be broken for it next spring—and to oversee the erection of a temporary pavilion of his design on the site of the museum-to-be, which is the greater part of Fifth Avenue between Eighty-eighth and Eighty-ninth Streets. The pavilion, a rakish affair of red brick, canvas, and steel poles, will hold an exhibit of sixty years of Wright's work (after several years as head draftsman for Adler & Sulli-van, in Chicago, he went into practice for himself in 1893) and is scheduled to open in a week or so, though last week it was still mostly poles, piles of hollow brick, and air. The exhibit, which has been touring Europe for three years and, after two months here, will proceed to the Orient, is called "Sixty Years of Liv-ing Architecture," and we got the impression, listening to Wright, that he wouldn't consider the insertion of "the Only" before "Living" a misstatement of historical fact.

We visited Mr. Wright in his suite high up in the Plaza. "I've stayed here on my visits for forty years," he said. "A beautiful hotel. They started to remodel it downstairs a few years back, but thank God I got here in time to stop them. The little devils had already wrecked the Palm Court, but I saved the Oak Room and the dining room." On a table between Wright and us were stout pots of tea, a plate of stout sandwiches, and a scattering of magazines and papers. As we talked, the tablecloth was slowly darkened by an assortment of Wright graffiti, ranging from floor plans and elevations of houses, churches, and factories to a sketch of his Jaguar, which is currently his favorite car and is, he said, capable of reaching ninety without a tremor. Wright himself is so plainly capable of reaching ninety without a tremor that we couldn't help asking how he had managed to outwit age. At that moment, the telephone rang, and he bounded to his feet to answer it. "Damned thing rings all day!" he said with pleasure. Over the telephone, he made an appointment for nine the next morning, and then he returned to his tea. "I have seven children and ten grandchildren and three great-grandchildren, so I must be old, but I don't feel old, I feel young," he said. "I draw and build and teach my apprentices and send them out into the world, not to be like me but to be themselves. At last count, a hundred and sixty-eight practicing architects had been trained by me at Taliesin, in Wisconsin. When can I ever have been readier to do good work? When can I ever have been fitter to be alive, to help build an American culture? Not a civilization, because we already have a civilization, but a culture. And you can't have a culture without an architecture."

The telephone rang again, and Wright, racing to it, exclaimed, "*Damn* the thing!" He made an appointment for ten the next morning, hung up, ruffled his bright-blue flowing tie, took a deep breath, and asked us please not to consider him a member of the architectural profession. "I'm not a member of any profession," he said. "I'm a one-man experiment in democracy, an experiment that worked. An individual who rose by his own merits, beholden to no one. When Sullivan and I came to architecture, it had been slumbering for five hundred years. We woke it up. We gave it a fresh start. We made it organic. We said architecture was space to be lived in, not a façade, not a box, not a monument. Wallie Harrison says the slab's the thing. I say the cemeteries are full of slabs, but who wants to be in a cemetery? Does all this sound arrogant? Let it sound arrogant, then! I defy anyone to name a single aspect of the best contemporary architecture that wasn't done first by me. Or a single aspect of the worst contemporary architecture that isn't a betrayal of what I've done. Like those awful U.N. buildings. Or that Corbusier thing in Marseille. Massacre on the waterfront, I call that. Or any of those skinny glass boxes! Why, I wouldn't dare walk on the same side of the street with them. Fool things might explode. There! That's from a fellow who knew what architecture was when all these glass-box boys were just so many diapers hanging on the line."

We could see that Wright was, if anything, freshening as he went along, but we felt our own strength ebbing, and between telephone calls for him (a date for eleven the next morning, a date for an early lunch) we hastened to ask about his latest work. "I've designed a white marble building to be built in Venice, right on the Grand Canal," he said. "The first new building to go up there since heaven knows when. It's to be a memorial to a young Italian architect who was killed in an accident in this country, and aside from the Imperial

Hotel in Tokyo, it's the only work I've designed for anywhere outside the United States. I've always felt that the rest of the world was entitled to its own kinds of culture. Then, I've designed a new bridge for San Francisco. They're holding a referendum out there to see whether they want to put it up or not. And a housing project for Madison, Wisconsin. They're holding a referendum on that, too. And a skyscraper for Bartlesville, Oklahoma. A beautiful thing, in its own park. I designed it first for New York, thirty years ago. It was going to be built down on the Bowery. By now, I'm used to waiting for my buildings to come true. Six hundred and forty of them have come true so far. I've never had a building in New York. This little pavilion is my first." He jumped up and peered out the window, to where Fifth Avenue glittered and shook with the roofs of cars. "I'm flying home to Taliesin tomorrow afternoon," he said. "We have thirty-five hundred acres out there. My family followed the Indians onto that land. The name of our town is Spring Green." He said the name twice over—"Spring Green. Spring Green"—then burst out happily, "Out there, chickens give eggs, cows give milk, and old Wright he rides his Tennessee walking horse."

1 9 5 3

MR. HULOT

THE French comedian Jacques Tati, whom we make no bones about calling one of the funniest men alive, was in town briefly for the opening of
his movie, "Mr. Hulot's Holiday." As was the case with his previous movie success, "Jour de Fête," M. Tati is not only the star of the picture but also its author
and director. We called on this great benefactor of humanity one warm afternoon recently and found him perplexed in the extreme by the air-conditioning
of his hotel suite. He had on a blue-and-white striped sports shirt and a heavy
topcoat. "My first experience of your winter-in-summer machines," he said in
admirable English, fingering his topcoat and shivering. "I do not yet understand the principle. You take off your coat when you go outside and you put on
your coat when you come inside. *Bien!* But where is the gain?" M. Tati is well
over two yards tall and looks taller. He has broad shoulders, long arms, and big
hands, and wears an expression of perpetual pleased surprise. No sooner had
we sat down than he volunteered to show us a snapshot of his two children—
Sophie, who is seven, and Pierre, who is five. "They are simple and honest," he
said with a father's pride.

While Tati and his wife were in New York, their children stayed at Tati's
father's house in Saint-Germain-en-Laye, a suburb of Paris. Tati was born a
few miles from there, in Le Pecq, in 1908. His real name is Jacques Tatischeff,
and if he liked, he could call himself a count. His grandfather, Count Dimitri
Tatischeff, an attaché of the Russian Embassy in Paris, married a French-
woman. On Tati's maternal side, his grandmother was Italian and his grandfather was Dutch. This man, van Hoof by name, ran a picture-framing shop in
Paris and numbered among his customers Toulouse-Lautrec and van Gogh. On

more than one occasion, van Gogh offered to pay his bill with some of his paintings, but canny old van Hoof held out for cash. Tati's father took over the business, and Tati, at sixteen, was sent to a college of arts and engineering to prepare him for a prosperous picture-framing future. After a year's fumbling with more mathematics than he knew what to do with, Tati gave up college, and his father bundled him off to London, to serve as an apprentice to an English framer. He boarded with a family whose son, also seventeen, had a passion for Rugby, and in six months Tati learned much English, much Rugby, and very little picture framing. "Rugby is not a gentle game," he told us. "Sometimes the players hurt each other quite badly, and afterward they wish to be friendly again, so they have dinner together and try to make one another laugh. I used to imitate the way Rugby players look during a game. Everyone would laugh at me, and I was encouraged to start imitating people playing tennis and other sports. My friends said, 'Why not go into the music halls?' I went back to Paris and told my father I wanted to quit picture framing and do imitations. You can imagine his anger. He said at last that I could do as I pleased but that he wouldn't give me a sou."

Young Tati's specialty was so peculiar that not an impresario in Paris would look at him. "For years, I was broke," Tati said. "I slept every night in a different place. I sat in cafés and talked with friends, and when I needed to eat, I would go to a certain cabaret and imitate a drunken waiter who is constantly making mistakes. For an evening of supposedly drunken waiting, I would be given my dinner and fifty francs. It was the happiest and most free time I have ever known." Tati got his big break in 1934, when a friend arranged for him to appear on a program at the Ritz with Chevalier and Mistinguett. "I was so frightened that though I was supposed to go on first, I couldn't stand or talk," Tati said. "I hid in a corner backstage and the show started without me. When it was over and the people were leaving, the manager of the show saw me hiding in the corner. He ran out on the stage and shouted that one of the entertainers had been forgotten. Then he introduced me. The people returned to their seats and I had to go on. The next thing I knew, I heard them laughing. I could not imagine that they were laughing at me. I looked around for the entertainer they were laughing at. No one else was onstage. It had to be me. Soon they were applauding and shouting, and the manager was shaking my hand. Then came the impresarios, and I was playing in music halls and circuses all over Europe."

This was Tati's first visit to the United States. He was scheduled to play at the Radio City Music Hall in 1939 but wound up in the French infantry instead. He attended several baseball games in the course of his visit and plans to add a baseball pantomime to his sports act. It took him a year and a half to make "Jour de Fête" and as long to make "Mr. Hulot's Holiday," and he is only just beginning to think about a new movie. His favorite comedian is an English music-hall performer named Little Tich, whom he saw when he was seven. The comedian who makes him laugh most is the late W. C. Fields. He admires Chaplin, but for the most part Chaplin doesn't make him laugh. "Chaplin is full of ideas," Tati said. "I am so busy watching the working out of his beautiful ideas that I never find time to laugh."

1954

NOTES AND COMMENT

THAT long-winded lady we hear from occasionally has sent us another communication, this time on the subject of modern design. "I like to have a cup of tea first thing in the morning," she writes, "and for that reason, whenever I have to spend a night or two away from home, I pack a small electric kettle and a box of Keemun. I usually get the hotel to leave a cup and saucer and a teapot in my room. Recently, when I was about to have my apartment painted, I called several of the *ordinary* hotels to reserve a room, but they were filled up with one of those conventions that you never hear about but that fill up the ordinary hotels from time to time just the same, so I found myself staying in an *odd* hotel in the West Forties that had no restaurant. As there was not a teapot or a cup and saucer to be found in the building, I took myself across the street that afternoon to a five-and-ten to get some. I realize that this procedure gives an impression of *fussiness* that is not at all a part of my *nature*. It is simply that I do like my cup of tea in the morning. Well, I got the cup and saucer—in a rather pretty thistle design—and I was delighted to find just the size teapot I wanted, and in the regular old brownware, very homey, the sort of teapot we used to call brownies, except that this teapot, instead of being round and squat, with the regular curved handle, was boat-shaped. It had been designed in one graceful line from the tip of the spout to the back of the pot—a very handsome object from every point of view. I thought to myself, Well, that's nice, they're finally getting somewhere with modern design. This little teapot I bought was boat-shaped, as I said, and was really rather amusing, the old-fashioned brownware, you understand, being in *mad* contrast with its shape. You'll get the idea of this teapot more clearly if I explain that the thing you grip to pick it up with is all in one piece with the pot, so that you are supposed to put the four fingers of your right hand into a kind of hole and grip the rim of the hole when you pour the tea, much in the way you would grip a real handle. Well, I took my new tea things back to the hotel and washed them carefully and left them in readiness for the morning, along with my kettle and my Keemun. In the morning, I got up as usual, brought the water in the kettle to a good, furious boil, and made the tea. I left it to sit for about five minutes, as I always do, while I turned on my bath and pinned up my hair. Then I went back to the window, where I had arranged my tea, sat down, glanced out, and saw that it had begun to rain and that the person in the hotel across the street had left a cardboard container of milk on the window sill and that it had toppled over a short time before. It was lying on its side on the window sill and traces of the last drops of its milk were still on the sill. I hoped no passerby had been caught when the first flood of milk came down, and it occurred to me that if anyone had been caught, and if it had been raining at the time, he must have been confused. Smiling at my little fancy, I lifted my new teapot to help myself to my first cup. Well, I dropped it in a hurry, and it broke my cup and saucer, flooded the table, and ruined the front of a brand-new challis robe I had bought only the day before at Altman's. Believe it or not, the handle of that teapot, being all of a piece with the pot itself, was *hollow,* so that when you filled the pot with boiling water, the handle filled up, too, and of course was scalding hot by the time I was ready to pour. I was extremely angry, but when the pain in my hand died away, I experienced some satisfaction, because I saw that everything I have felt, and usually kept to myself, about modern design may easily be true. I have sent an informatory note to that five-and-ten and am now waiting with a good deal of curiosity to see whether I will hear from the store directly or whether they will pass along to the manufacturers who employed the designer my warning that a lot of good people are going to get their hands burned if those *handles* on those *teapots* are not somehow plugged up so the boiling water can't get in. Having been made out of the old-fashioned brownware, my pot didn't break when I let it go, although it plumped to the floor after destroying the cup and saucer, flooding the table, and ruining my robe. I bought another cup and saucer the next day and used the pot once more, after wrapping a bath towel around it, but when I checked out of the hotel, I left it on the window sill."

1955

ROCKEFELLER CENTER HO!

FIFTH and Sixth Avenues teem these days; the thronging pedestrians maneuver under rules skimpier than those of bagataway. As a service to readers who are too frail or shy for good-natured hurly-burly, we decided to plot a course from the Empire State Building to Rockefeller Center that would involve no contact with either Fifth or Sixth Avenue. So, early one morning, armed with a box lunch our wife had insisted on packing for us, we found ourself in front of the Cantigny Printing & Stationery Corporation, on Thirty-third Street, facing the tallest structure in the world. Fifth Avenue was to the east, Sixth to the west. Indomitably, we charged into the Empire State's dimly lit and brownly marbled lobby, resisted the suave pleas of uniformed attendants to ascend with them to the Observatory, cleaved between the elevator banks, and emerged on Thirty-fourth Street, opposite the great bland façade of Ohrbach's. We threaded our way among handbags, gloves, and tailored cotton shirts ($1.99), took the escalator to the Budget Balcony, wriggled through a tight crevasse at the Customers' Accommodation Desk, and thus reached Thirty-fifth Street. There we bore west until we struck a Meyers Brothers System parking lot, feebly guarded by a sign reading, "NO WALKING OR TRESPASSING THRU THIS STATION." Crouching low between the automobiles, we attained the Thirty-sixth Street end of the lot, only to discover a tall wire fence. Would we, then, have to fall back? No; under the gate, a gap of around twenty inches permitted easy egress to anyone willing to crawl on his stomach. We did this. On Thirty-sixth Street, after futilely exploring a series of shallow luncheonettes and furriers' shops, we came to the Herald Square Garage, at whose farther end the light of

Thirty-seventh Street gleamed. As slack-mouthed young men in coveralls stared, we exploited this tunnel.

Thirty-seventh Street resisted our advances. The sole block-deep building in this backward area is owned by Franklin Simon & Co. A door with the store's name on it and a tantalizing view of the men's-clothing department, with salesmen pensively studying their reflections in three-way mirrors, promised quick triumph, but the door was painted black, the handles had been removed, and instructions to use the Fifth Avenue and Thirty-eighth Street entrances were lettered upon it. We tugged brutally at the recalcitrant portal, wedging our fingers in a crack left by the imperfection of the carpentry, until a spectator said, "There's a burglar alarm on that door, you know." Chastened and despairing, we backtracked and discovered, on Thirty-fifth Street near Sixth Avenue, a dismal cave mouth titled "Independent Subway System." We descended a crooked flight of stairs, turned right, and were appalled by the extensive cavern before us. The floor tilted Surrealistically; overhead, mammoth white beams suggested the molars of an unthinkably huge whale. A few ectoplasmic figures shuffled back and forth. At the faraway end, they could be seen dissolving in mist. Only our own footsteps made noise. Our panic mounted, and eventually we did also, at Thirty-eighth Street. We walked east to Lord & Taylor's, whereby we passed over to Thirty-ninth Street. Near Sixth Avenue, we entered the back door of Schumacher's and continued through the store. The Schumacher passage is one of the trip's pleasantest; the deep repose of stacked carpets, uncut fabrics, and middle-aged couples turning the leaves of wallpaper books provides an appropriate prelude to the two-block open-air run of Bryant Park, fragile and silent in winter.

At Forty-second Street, the footsore traveller must not be dazzled into indecision by the variety of through passageways—Stern's, Woolworth's, the Salmon Tower arcade. We chose Woolworth's. The odors of cheap candy, cashews, cosmetics, and cookies, in that order, titillated our nostrils. Forty-third Street is simple enough. Arcades exist at our own 25 West Forty-third and at No. 37, though neither is as grand a throughway as that offered by the Association of the Bar of the City of New York, at No. 43. On Forty-fourth Street, the choice lies between the Berkeley Building and the Hotel Seymour, where a narrow corridor yields to vistas of affluence as the main entrance, on Forty-fifth Street, is approached.

In our chain of passageways, the link between Forty-fifth and Forty-sixth Streets demands the most hardihood and perseverance to forge. The correct procedure is: Ask for the superintendent at 45 West Forty-fifth Street. He is benign, though burly. Accompany him as he leads you through a second-story window onto a brick-and-tar projection he terms a balcony. Listen respectfully as he explains that an easy jump of about twenty feet will land you on a parking lot that fronts on Forty-sixth Street. Indicate to him that your ankles are not firm. Follow him into the basement, where deep-throated boilers chug.

Slither through an infinitesimal window. Finding yourself in a kind of concrete well, with a ledge and rusty fence perhaps three feet above your head, leap strenuously, seize the ledge and then the fence, pull yourself up, wipe your hands, and stroll through the parking lot to Forty-sixth Street.

After this, cutting through the Hotel Wentworth to Forty-seventh Street will seem as easy as a promenade in Central Park. At Forty-seventh, we once again had recourse to the subway, and this time it cost us fifteen cents. After passing through the turnstile, we inched along the platform until we came to a sign pointing the way to the United States Rubber Building. Up silver sliding stairs, through vacant halls of pearl-pink and ash-blue marble, into the open air we moved. Where were we? There was no mistaking those momentous slabs, those quaint half streets, those flat-muscled bas-relief ladies so dear to the hearts of sculptors commissioned to body forth the concepts of Labor, Valor, and Communications. Rockefeller Center.

1 9 5 6

BON VOYAGE

ONE bright, salty day last week, we went over to Pier 86, North River, to wish Harry S. Truman Godspeed on his seven-week pleasure trip to Europe. He was sailing on the S.S. United States, and he was to be found in Cabin U-89 ("U" for Upper Deck). A solid phalanx of plainclothesmen stood duty at the cabin door. We announced ourself, and were ushered in. The cabin was a cornucopia of floral arrangements, shrimps on sticks, assorted canapés, friends, and relations, and, it being a sailing, bottles of whiskey. The former President, looking as fit and trim as a growing boy, was seated on a sofa, talking with John W. Snyder, former Secretary of the Treasury. Mr. Truman was wearing a dark-blue suit, a white shirt, and a quiet blue tie. In his lapel was the bronze Victory Medal button of the First World War.

"Hi," said Margaret Daniel, the daughter of the President. "Good of you to come down to the boat."

We spotted Mrs. Truman, at the far end of the cabin. She was wearing a blue print dress. "Hope you have a fine time," we said.

"It's going to be hectic," she said. "The schedule has been wonderfully prepared—Paris, Rome, Naples, Venice, Salzburg, Brussels, The Hague, London, and Assisi, Bonn, Munich, and Florence—but it's tight, and I don't see how any of it can be changed. It's going to be tiring, but I am certainly looking forward to the trip."

We spotted Eugene Bailey, Mr. Truman's secretary, a scholarly-looking young man. "Hi," said Bailey. "Last night, I went over with the group to Mrs. Lasker's house and I have never in my entire life seen such a magnificent collection of modern art. Everywhere you turned—"

Sam Rosenman entered the cabin and went over and wrung the President's hand. Miss Margaret Carson, formerly in charge of public relations for the Metropolitan Opera, and a close friend of Mr. Truman's daughter, told us that she wanted a cup of coffee. "The coffee on this ship," she said, "is the finest coffee in the world."

We spotted Mrs. Stanley Woodward, the wife of the former Chief of Protocol of the State Department and former United States Ambassador to Canada. The Woodwards are travelling with the Trumans throughout their trip abroad, and the Trumans will stay at the Woodwards' European house, at St. Jakob am Thurn, Puch bei Hallein, near Salzburg, from June 2nd to 6th. "Last night," said Mrs. Woodward, "we all went to see 'Inherit the Wind.' The President and Mrs. Truman and the rest of us arrived at the theatre at eight-twenty, plenty of time before the curtain. We took our seats. Hardly anybody saw us come in. At the end of the show, the entire audience stood up and applauded and cheered the President. He went backstage, and when he left, there were several hundred people standing in the street, and they cheered and applauded. The President was deeply moved."

Mrs. India Edwards, of the Democratic National Committee, entered the cabin and went over to say hello to the President. "Golly, it's good to see you," he said.

"I don't know what's happened to my husband," said Mrs. Woodward. "We took separate taxis from the hotel, and he hasn't showed up."

Mr. Woodward entered the cabin.

"There you are," said Mrs. Woodward.

"Here I am," said Mr. Woodward.

The President asked for a bourbon and branch water, and it was instantly produced by a slightly flustered waiter. Mr. Snyder said that he would like the same. The two gentlemen clinked glasses. "To the former Secretary of the Treasury," said Mr. Truman. Mr. Snyder smiled warmly, and downed his drink. He rose to leave. "Have a wonderful trip," he said to Mr. Truman.

We sat down beside the former President. "I have a bad swollen ankle," he said, pointing to a brown cane perched alongside the couch. "I was carrying some empty suitcases downstairs the other day in Independence and I turned it and I spilled, and I got caught in the banister, and I tumbled right down to the bottom of the stairs. It isn't really a sprain; it's got something to do with the ligaments. I'll be all right if I stay off it."

"Looking forward to your trip?" we asked.

"You know," he said, "last night I wanted to get right back on the train and head home for Independence, Missouri. We have a tremendous schedule. I am a former President of the United States, and people that we entertained when we were in the White House have kindly invited us to visit with them. I have had invitations from the Queen of England, and Eden, and Churchill, and the Queen of Holland, and Adenauer, and many, many others. The Pope has also graciously asked me to visit him."

There was a deep, long, all-ashore blast from the S.S. United States. We shook the President's hand and wished him a good trip.

"Terribly kind of you to come down to the boat," he said.

1 9 5 6

LOVERLEE, LOVERLEE

LIKE ranks of herald angels, a display of gramophones, Echophones, Zon-O-Phones, and just plain talking machines guarded the entrance of the 1956 New York High Fidelity Show, in the Trade Show Building. The cardboard images of Edison, Eldridge R. Johnson, and Emile Berliner glared above rows of brass trumpets ranged as if to signal Judgment Day. But they were silent, and long had been. Within, a placard announced, the Ultimate had been achieved. (Hi-fi lingo is consistently transcendental; "super" is almost a diminutive.) An amplifying system, equipped with the new Catenoid horn, cried, in time to a Hispanic tune, "Ya ya ya-ya ya *ya*, ya ya ya-ya ya YA." "Loverlee, loverlee," the Sonocell Bass System answered, "loverlee, loverlee." And from another room, though from the same Broadway musical, a third device insisted, "With a little bit, with a little bit, with a little bit . . ."

Each of the hundred and four exhibitors had one or more little white rooms, many hung with hushing draperies, and even strung with velvet rope, like a funeral parlor. In attitudes of grief and respect, a dozen souls were listening to a large walnut box describe the famous difficulties of getting a cannon boom worthy of Tchaikovsky's "1812 Overture." ". . . failed to pick up the booming reverberations to best advantage. We set a single microphone seventy-five feet in front of the cannon, loaded the cannon to the limit of safety, and now listen." Even to our uneducated tympanum, it seemed an exquisite boom— plump in sound, rather flowery in its aftertones, yet withal thoroughly masculine, even austere. Over in the Zenith suite, a demonstrator holding a small black box in one hand was surrounded by activated television sets. On the largest of them, a woman singing turned abruptly into an old Shirley Temple movie, which became a confident man in a double-breasted suit talking about bacteria. "Zenith's new remote-control tuning," said the demonstrator. A boy with a drab face and the hi-fi bug's black spectacles asked, "It doesn't work on radio waves?"

"No," the demonstrator said in a condescending way. "Sound waves."

"—our hearts will be throbbing in time," the singing woman promised, her lips shaking to prove it. She vanished, and the confident man said, "But *after* disinfection—" and held up a tumbler of water that became a moon beneath which Shirley Temple wept.

"You aim it?" the bug pressed on.

"Only vaguely."

"Sound waves?"

"Ultrasonic."

"What keeps my dog from jumping out of the window?"

"A dog whistle has a frequency of around twenty-five thousand cycles. This is above forty. A dog can't hear it. It's not generated. It's just little hammers in there. Like a piano."

"And you don't have to aim it."

"Not within forty feet," the demonstrator said curtly, and, in his irritation, destroyed Shirley Temple, just when we were picking up the thread of the plot.

The show offered listening pleasure but not *sustained* listening pleasure. In among the Grundig-Majestic radios, we were promised that Hoagy Carmichael would sing his own composition "Hong Kong Blues." Sure enough, the familiar reedy voice began to sibilate, and we were taken back fifteen years. Then, hideously, between the rising tide of a German waltz and a constant barrage from a girl who couldn't help loving that man, Hoagy began to pale, and was gone. We searched frantically among the radios. We couldn't tell which were on. We gazed into the broad, blond face of one. "Ferrite Antenna," it told us mirthlessly. "BC SWI SWII FM." It had compound knobs, multiple bands! We scoured its dial, reading:

Ceylon India
Italy Brazil

Dazed by this bopster's geography, we were washed out of the room on a great waltzing breaker of Stereophonic, 3-D, ultra-highly faithful sound.

We drifted after that. Strange adjectives—"stroboscopic," "binaural," "orthosonic"—befuddled us. "I'm just saying it's *as* ultra as yours," a man passing us claimed. Inside a replica of an 1890 recording studio, a male mannequin with painted fingernails held his hand immutably poised over a banjo while a tape-recorded voice discoursed on the scratchy, metallic, staccato tone of wax-cylinder recordings. "Is there anything *new*?" a wild-haired woman beseeched us. "I just can't find anything abso*lutely new.*" Then she disappeared into a room where "The Cartridge with the Highest Compliance and Lowest Inter-modulation Distortion" was advertised. Compliant cartridges? Catenoid horns? We were leaving. On one side, Harry James swung sweetly from octave to octave; on another, Bach calmly built his intricate stairs. Burl Ives told of the big rock-candy mountain, and, fading in the distance, a clarinet and a trombone promised to dance off both our shoes when they played (on a shock-mounted, non-resonant turntable) the Jelly Roll Blues.

1 9 5 6

GOOD-NATURED MAN

J OHN OSBORNE, the twenty-seven-year-old playwright whose "Look Back in Anger" has had the British upper-middle, middle-middle, and lower-middle classes hanging on the ropes since it opened in London, last year—and the Broadway bourgeoisie equally excited, if less hurt-feelinged, since it opened here, a couple of weeks ago—may well be, as local critics have said, "an eloquent spokesman for his irate generation," a man who "spews out . . . ferocities," and "not the man for temperate statements," but when we had a tomato juice with him at his hotel, the Algonquin, the other day, he was as mild and urbane as Sir Gladwyn Jebb, and, to our colonial eyes, every bit as upper-class. Elegantly dressed, aristocratic of feature, with curly Edwardian sideburns, he lit a slender pipe and said, "I've been here only a week. The longer I stay, the more I like it. The critics here seem more responsible, more literate, and more serious generally than in England. The audiences don't get as angry as in England. Of course, not many people here feel they're being got at. In England, some of them walked out, yelling things like 'Keep quiet!' At home, everyone got the impression that the play was very dreary and dull and turgid and boring. Here, they're inclined to laugh. They sometimes laugh in the wrong places, but they laugh."

We asked what kind of tobacco he smokes, and are happy to report it is Edgeworth. "Do you know it's only twenty cents here?" he said. "In London, it's eleven shillings—about a dollar and a half. I've been to a theatre every evening—I liked 'West Side Story' immensely, and also saw a couple of musicals I *didn't* like—and I'm writing a screenplay and rewriting an old play, but

I'm rather taking a rest at the moment. I generally work at night. I spend the daytime worrying about working and then at night I work."

A beautiful young girl joined us, and Mr. Osborne introduced her as his wife, Mary Ure, who is the leading lady of "Look Back." "I've been too busy to see much here," she said. "I want to go to Brooklyn. In London, I was in 'A View from the Bridge' for six months, with a Brooklyn accent."

Mr. Osborne said that Miss Ure, who hails from Glasgow, had also played Ophelia and had appeared in Jean Anouilh's "Time Remembered," and that they had met when both were working at the Royal Court Theatre; she was in "The Crucible" and he was rehearsing for "The Desk of Satan." He was born in London and went to Belmont College, which he described to us as an obscure public (i.e., private) boarding school in Devonshire. "I hated the place," he said. "I left after four years, at sixteen; worked on some trade papers, such as the *Gas World;* and at eighteen got a job teaching English and arithmetic to the child actors in a provincial touring company. After six months, a local educational inspector inspected me, and I had to quit. I stayed on as assistant stage manager, and then began to act. I still do. I've been in five plays in the last eighteen months. I don't act in my own plays, though; one gets enough slung at one's head without inviting it two ways. I find acting a great relief from writing. When you're with actors, you have some sense of community. When you're writing, you're on your own."

Upon our soliciting a comparison between the American and the British theatrical worlds, Mr. Osborne said, "I think that, in a very superficial way, everything is a bit more panicky here. Reputations seem more at stake, perhaps because much more money is involved. In London, things are more relaxed. Success isn't quite so important. Or, at least, failure isn't so important. Let's put it that way. There's nothing like the ghastly business of going to Sardi's and waiting for the reviews. Of course, you'd have a long wait, as the English reviews don't come in until four in the morning. Here, if you have two flops in a row it's the end of the world."

We asked about fan, or non-fan, mail, and Mr. Osborne told us that in England he had received many unenthusiastic letters from colonels and bishops. "I usually answer them," he said. "I've been getting abusive letters internationally. I had one from British Columbia that simply said, 'Why don't you shut up?' My mother liked the play. Both my grandmothers are alive. One saw it on television. I *think* she liked it."

"It was thrilling when people walked out," Miss Ure said. "Exhilarating! But there were never more than three at one performance."

1957

THE MUSHROOM'S EDGE

RENÉ CLAIR, one of our favorite moviemakers, was in town last week, and we had a pleasant lunch with him in the Pierre Grill. M. Clair, whose English twenty years ago consisted of a brisk "O.K.," has become quite voluble in the language. "Although I am French," he told us, "I am now able to think pretty well like you. You know what I am thinking?"

We told him we didn't.

"I am thinking," said M. Clair, "that there should be a pension for young people. When you are young, you should pursue the wine, women, and song, and the government should provide for this. Then, when you are old, you should be able to do your work without distraction. Right now, I am past distraction, but the idea for a picture is hard to discover."

M. Clair, a lean, handsome man of sixty who looks only a bit of it, pondered for a moment, sipped a whiskey sour, and plunged ahead. "The scientists," he said, "are putting the satirists out of business. They want to go to the moon, which has been minding its own business for years, and nobody says why. They build missiles that fall into the sea, and nobody says why. And they bring us close to annihilation, and nobody says why. It reminds me of my father, who was, in his day, a cavalry officer and an expert on mushrooms. He used to go into the forest on a fine big horse, with big bags strung across his saddle, and seek the mushrooms. When he returned, he would have the cook make a dish of his discoveries, and while we ate, he would tell us about what we were eating. He would say that most of the mushrooms were ordinary stuff, but just as your fork was going to your mouth with a pretty little fungus, he would say that if its narrow yellow edge were only slightly broader it would mean death.

I'm still afraid of mushrooms, and I don't think I have as much confidence in these scientists as I had in my father."

M. Clair paused to offer us a French cigarette, which gagged us. As we gasped, he continued his remarks. "Everybody nowadays thinks that parents are guilty of the children's crimes," he said. "All kinds of movies make this point. But if a bad child, trying to shoot somebody, misses, does anybody give the parents credit for having bad eyesight? No! It seems to me that if you pursue this line of thinking—that parents are guilty of the sins of their children—then all of us back to poor Adam have nothing on our consciences. With nothing on our consciences, we have nothing on our minds—at least, nothing you could make a good drama from."

M. Clair proceeded to inform us that he had been in Moscow a couple of years ago and had met a colleague on a sound stage. "He asked me what percentage I got on my pictures," said M. Clair. "He sounded like the director of a B picture in Hollywood. When I went to Hollywood, some years ago, I was hired as a director, but presently, since I am a writer, I collaborated on a script. When my agent suggested that I ought to be paid for this endeavor, the producer said O.K., he'd give me one-tenth of my salary as director as a fee for writing. I had to tell him it should be the other way around. I believe in the script. And yet, even with a meritorious script, you never know what will appeal to the public. I put two lines in 'À Nous la Liberté' about a belt line coming to a halt because one individual refused to be mechanized, and they turned into the funniest scene in the picture. Had I known, I would have stopped not only the belt line but the town, the province, and possibly the country. But you never can tell how people will react to comedy." M. Clair sighed heavily. "It's so hard to be funny about anything now," he observed. "Even so, it may be that, with independent productions and no bureaucratic supervision, some funny fellows will come along. In the days when I started, just after the First World War, the movie business was a pleasure. I was working on L'Intransigeant, as a writer, when I was hired to play the part of a suave Parisian with the Loïc Fuller ballet troupe, in a short film. That was when I changed my name from René Chomette to René Clair. Later on, I graduated into being the hero of a serial, still very suave. But I always thought of myself as a writer until a publisher, looking over a philosophical novel of mine, insisted that 'René Chomette' must be 'René Clair,' or otherwise the thing might just as well be signed 'Anonymous.' It was the movies for me from then on. Maybe now, at sixty, I'll have to think about television. It has its points."

"Like what?" we inquired.

"You must admit," said M. Clair defensively, "that it is not suitable to CinemaScope."

1 9 5 8

CARICATURIST

ALBERT HIRSCHFELD, the theatre caricaturist of the *Times*, forty of whose drawings and gouaches are now on exhibition at the John Heller Gallery, is a calm, friendly, brown-eyed, luxuriantly spade-bearded man of fifty-five with a magisterial air. He was born in St. Louis, where his father, on his way home to Albany after a junket to Texas, had stopped off, married a girl who had just arrived from Russia, and settled down. "Mom didn't speak a word of English at the time, and Pop didn't speak a word of Russian," Mr. Hirschfeld told us over a mushroom omelet one recent afternoon. "He got a job as a travelling salesman. Mom worked in a store. I had two brothers, and we were poor, but I was never aware of it. I studied art in St. Louis; I can't remember a time when I didn't draw, paint, or sculpt. Mom felt that I had talent, and thought that St. Louis was no place for it, so when I was twelve she packed up Pop and the rest of the family and came here. We got on an Amsterdam Avenue streetcar, went to the end of the line, started walking back, and picked out—and moved into—a house at a Hundred and Eighty-second Street, which was then farmland. We later moved to a Hundred and Seventy-seventh Street, where my parents still live. Pop is ninety-one and Mom is eighty-seven. He retired at fifty and took to the park—J. Hood Wright Park. He's been sitting in that damn park for forty years. He and some friends founded a club, the J. Hood Wright Men's Club, to keep kids off the street. He got the city to appropriate two hundred thousand dollars for a clubhouse. Robert Moses sometimes asks his advice on matters of community welfare. A month or so ago, Pop gave a lecture at Carnegie Hall in favor of increasing old-age pensions. Pretty good for a man who never knocked himself out working."

We asked Hirschfeld *fils* how about himself. "Well, I went to public school and studied at the Art Students League," he said, "and at seventeen, since I had to make a living, I got a job as an office boy with Goldwyn Pictures. Two years later, I became art director for David Selznick. I moved over to the Warner Brothers art department, and in 1924, having saved a little money, quit to spend a year in Paris, where I did painting and sculpture. That was a salutary thing. Back here, I continued to paint, began to do caricatures for the *Times*, and sued *Variety* on behalf of my beard, which I'd just grown. *Variety* ran a page-one story about people who weren't able to get any work growing beards in order to get work, elevator boys growing beards to give them stature, and so forth. My name was the only one in the whole story. My lawyer, David Schenker, advised me to sue, and after a three-year delay the case came up before Judge Peter Schmuck. Schenker tried the case as though it was murder. The jury brought in a verdict of six cents against *Variety*, plus costs. My lawyer wanted compensatory as well as punitive damages, and urged me to appeal. I had discussed the difference between humor and satire at great length on the witness stand, and found that the appeal would have cost four thousand dollars, much of it going toward printing my remarks, double-spaced, on hand-made paper. You have to do this for an appeal. It's as though you were Max Beerbohm! Well, I wouldn't do it."

Mr. H. had a one-man sculpture show at the Newhouse Gallery in 1928, and since then his work, mostly drawings, has been bought by, among others, the St. Louis Art Museum, the Cleveland Art Museum, the Fogg Museum, the Museum of the City of New York, the Museum of Modern Art, and the Metropolitan. His caricatures of new shows appear in the theatrical section of the Sunday *Times* thirty or forty times a year.

As part of his job, Hirschfeld, who has written a play himself, faithfully attends out-of-town tryouts and Broadway openings. He is married to a red-haired actress, Dolly Haas, and they have a red-haired thirteen-year-old daughter, Nina, who plays the piano with authority and hopes to become a red-haired actress herself. The Hirschfelds live in a big house, on East Ninety-fifth Street, that was once owned by Jacob Ruppert, the brewer. Nina's father works her name into all his *Times* drawings, often concealing it in curlicues of curtains and the folds of costumes. "I started that in a circus poster, on which I wrote 'Nina the Wonder Child,' when she was born," he said. "Sometimes you can't find the name without a microscope. Nina has a microscope, and she always finds it. I'm told her classmates, at Brearley, look for it every week. I worked 'Brearley' in a few weeks ago. The engraving department at the *Times* has a kind of pool on this; the first to spot 'Nina' is the winner. 'Nina' is hardest to find when it's large; sometimes I make the whole design say it. I hardly ever go out during the day. I work in my studio, on the top floor of the house, until the sun is down; then I go out and raise hell. I'm a late stayer-upper. I read from 1 to 3 A.M.—anything that's in print. I've written and illustrated a couple of books—'Manhattan Oases,' about speakeasies during prohibition, and 'Harlem,' about Harlem."

Mr. Hirschfeld finished his omelet and lit a cigar. "I believe that there's been a subtle change in my style in the last few years," he said, "and that the reason for this is that *people* are changing. They're becoming more standardized. They're getting to look more and more alike. You used to be able to immediately identify the Marx Brothers, Eddie Cantor, William Jennings Bryan, and even such leading men as John Barrymore and Lou Tellegen. Now things aren't that clear. Politicians and actors and Presidents all look like advertising men. People all over the world look alike. Americans and Frenchmen and Englishmen all look alike. Twenty years ago, Soviet statesmen looked like Soviet statesmen, but today they look like Bernard Baruch. People don't write their own books, and Presidents don't write their own speeches. What does a man leave of himself except a photograph? What would we think of Lincoln if it turned out that the Gettysburg Address was written by C. D. Jackson?"

On our way to the coatroom, Mr. Hirschfeld told us that he first met his present wife when she was with the Jitney Players, in Hershey, Pennsylvania, and he did a summer-theatre drawing of her. "I was smitten with her the minute I saw her," he said. "A year later, dining at the Samson Raphaelsons', in Hollywood, I asked Sam if he'd ever heard of Dolly Haas. 'Ask this fellow. He's her husband,' he said, indicating another guest, John Brahm. They'd separated, and I looked her up when I got back, and married her."

1 9 5 8

PLAYWRIGHT

WE had a talk recently with Lorraine Hansberry, the twenty-eight-year-old author of the hit play "A Raisin in the Sun." Miss Hansberry is a relaxed, soft-voiced young lady with an intelligent and pretty face, a particularly vertical hairdo, and large brown eyes, so dark and so deep that you get lost in them. At her request, we met her in a midtown restaurant, so that she could get away from her telephone. "The telephone has become a little strange thing with a life of its own," she told us, calmly enough. "It's just incredible! I had the number changed, and gave it to, roughly, twelve people. Then I get a call from a stranger saying 'This is So-and-So, of the B.B.C.'! It's the flush of success. Thomas Wolfe wrote a detailed description of it in 'You Can't Go Home Again.' I must say he told the truth. I enjoy it, actually, so much. I'm thrilled, and all of us associated with the play are thrilled. Meanwhile, it does keep you awfully *busy*. What sort of happens is you just hear from *everybody!*"

Miss Hansberry gave a soft, pleased laugh. "I'm going to have some scrambled eggs, medium, because, as far as I know, I haven't had my breakfast yet," she went on. "I live in the Village, and the way it's been, people sort of drop in on me and my husband. My husband is Robert Nemiroff, and he, too, is a writer. Yesterday, I got back to writing, and I wrote all day long. For the first time in weeks. It was wonderful. We have a ramshackle Village walkup apartment, *quite* ramshackle, with living room, bedroom, kitchen, bath, and a little back workroom, and I just stayed in that little old room all day and wrote. I may even get time now to do some of my housework. I don't want to have anyone else to do my housework. I've always done it myself. I believe you *should* do it yourself. I feel very strongly about that."

The medium scrambled eggs arrived, and Miss Hansberry sampled them vaguely and went on to tell us something of what life has been like since her play opened, a few weeks ago. "I now get twenty to thirty pieces of mail a day," she said. "Invitations to teas, invitations to lunches, invitations to dinners, invitations to write books, to adapt mystery stories for the movies, to adapt novels for Broadway musicals. I feel I have to answer them, because I owe the people who wrote them the courtesy of explaining that this is not my type of thing. Then, there are so many organizations that want you to come to their meetings. You don't feel silly or bothered, because, my God, they're all doing such important work, and you're just delighted to go. But you're awfully busy, because there are an awful lot of organizations. The other morning, I came downstairs to walk my dog—he's sort of a collie, and he'll be six in September—and there, downstairs, were the two most charming people, a middle-aged couple who wanted me to have dinner with the New Rochelle Urban League before it went to see the play. I just couldn't say no. Meanwhile, I'd been getting telegrams from Roosevelt University, in Chicago, which is a very wonderful institution back home, asking me to come and speak. I kept sending telegrams back saying I couldn't come, and then they got me on the phone, and they had me. Once I'm on the phone, I just can't say no. I sometimes find myself doing things for three or four organizations in one day. The other morning, I started the day by taping a television program. Then I went to the National Association of Negro Business and Professional Women's Clubs Founders' Day Tea, at the Waldorf, where they were giving out Sojourner Truth Awards— awards named for Sojourner Truth, who was a very colorful orator who went up and down New England and the South speaking against slavery. Then I went home and went to the Square with my dog. When I got back home, I fed the dog and put on a cocktail dress, and my husband and I had dinner in a new Village steak house. Then we went to a reception for a young Negro actor named Harold Scott, who had just made a record album of readings from the works of James Weldon Johnson. A very beautiful album. Then we went home and had banana cream pie and milk and watched television—a program with me on it, as a matter of fact. It was terrifying to see. I had no idea I used my face so much when I talked, and I decided that that was the end of my going on television. The next day was quiet. I had only one visitor—a young Negro writer who wanted to drop off a manuscript for me to read. We had a drink and a quick conversation, and he was off. I actually got to cook dinner—a pretty good one, with fried pork chops, broccoli *au gratin*, salad, and banana cream pie. I'm mad for banana cream pie. Fortunately, there's a place in the neighborhood that makes marvellous ones."

Miss Hansberry told us that she had written her play between her twenty-sixth and twenty-seventh birthdays, and that it had taken her eight months. "I'd been writing an awful lot of plays—about three, I guess—and this happened to be one of them," she told us. "We all know now that people like the play, including the critics. Most of what was written about the play was reasonable and fine, but I don't agree that this play, as some people have assumed, has turned out the way it has because just about everybody associated with it was a Negro. I'm pleased to say that we went to great pains to get the best director and the best actors for this particular play. And I like to think I wrote the play out of a specific intellectual point of view. I'm aware of the existence of Anouilh, Beckett, Dürrenmatt, and Brecht, but I believe, with O'Casey, that real drama has to do with audience involvement and achieving the emotional transformation of people on the stage. I believe that ideas *can* be transmitted emotionally."

"Agreed," we said, and asked Miss Hansberry for some autobiography.

"I was born May 19, 1930, in Chicago," she told us. "I have two brothers and one sister. I'm the baby of the family. My sister Mamie is thirty-five and has a three-year-old daughter, Nantille, who is divine and a character. She was named for my mother, whose name is Nannie, and her other grandmother, Tillie. My older brother, Carl, Jr., is forty, and my other brother, Perry, Sr., is thirty-eight and has an eighteen-year-old daughter, who is starting college and is very beautiful. Carl, Perry, and Mamie run my father's real-estate business, Hansberry Enterprises, in Chicago. My father, who is dead now, was born in Gloster, Mississippi, which you can't find on the map, it's so small. My mother comes from Columbia, Tennessee, which is on the map, but just about. My father left the South as a young man, and then he went back there and got himself an education. He was a wonderful and very special kind of man. He died in 1945, at the age of fifty-one—of a cerebral hemorrhage, supposedly, but American racism helped kill him. He died in Mexico, where he was making preparations to move all of us out of the United States. My brother Carl had just come back from Europe, where he fought with Patton's army. My father wanted to leave this country because, although he had tried to do everything in his power to make it otherwise, he felt he still didn't have his freedom. He was a very successful and very wealthy businessman. He had been a U.S. marshal. He had founded one of the first Negro banks in Chicago. He had fought a very famous civil-rights case on restricted covenants, which he fought all the way up to the Supreme Court, and which he won after the expenditure of a great deal of money and emotional strength. The case is studied today in the law schools. Anyway, Daddy felt that this country was hopeless in its treatment of Negroes. So he became a refugee from America. He bought a house in Polanco, a suburb of Mexico City, and we were planning to move there when he died. I was fourteen at the time. I'm afraid I have to agree with Daddy's assessment of this country. But I don't agree with the leaving part. I don't feel defensive. Daddy really belonged to a different age, a different period. He didn't feel free. One of the reasons I feel so free is that I feel I belong to a world majority, and a very assertive one. I'm not really writing about my own family in the play. We were more typical of the bourgeois Negro exemplified by the Murchison family that is referred to in the play. I'm too close to my own family to be able to write about them.

"I mostly went to Jim Crow schools, on the South Side of Chicago, which meant half-day schools, and to this day I can't count. My parents were some peculiar kind of democrats. They could afford to send us to private schools, but they didn't believe in it. I went to three grade schools—Felsenthal, Betsy Ross, and A. O. Sexton, the last of them in a white neighborhood, where Daddy bought a house when I was eight. My mother is a remarkable woman, with great courage. She sat in that house for eight months with us—while Daddy spent most of his time in Washington fighting his case—in what was, to put it mildly, a very hostile neighborhood. I was on the porch one day with my sister, swinging my legs, when a mob gathered. We went inside, and while we were in our living room, a brick came crashing through the window with such force it embedded itself in the opposite wall. I was the one the brick almost hit. I went to Englewood High School and then to the University of Wisconsin for two years. Then I just got tired of going to school and quit and came to New York, in the summer of 1950. The theatre came into my life like *k-pow!*" Miss Hansberry knocked a fist into the palm of her other hand. "In Chicago, on my early dates, I was taken to see shows like 'The Tempest,' 'Othello,' and 'Dark of the Moon,' which absolutely flipped me, with all that witch-doctor stuff, which I still adore. In college, I saw plays by Strindberg and Ibsen for the first time, and they were important to me. I was intrigued by the theatre. Mine was the same old story—sort of hanging around little acting groups, and developing the feeling that the theatre embraces everything I like all at one time. I've always assumed I had something to tell people. Now I think of myself as a playwright."

1959

1960s

VIDAL

NOTHING is easier nowadays than to get a feeling of being entirely surrounded by Gore Vidal. His political drama "The Best Man" fills the Morosco nightly. His film adaptation of Tennessee Williams' "Suddenly, Last Summer" was recently reported to be doing the best business of any movie in the country. "Ben-Hur," whose script is mainly the work of Mr. Vidal and Christopher Fry, won eleven Oscars. The movie version of his "Visit to a Small Planet"—described by him as the unauthorized version—is being offered in dozens of neighborhood houses. Stay home at night, and like as not you'll be assailed by Mr. Vidal on television. He is one of the busiest of the panelists, and a while back he appeared in his own television play "The Indestructible Mr. Gore," which dealt with the life of his grandfather, the late Senator Thomas Gore, of Oklahoma. Pick up a magazine, and if it happens to be the *Reporter,* you will see that Mr. Vidal is also a theatre critic. Pick up a newspaper, and you will find that he is a Democratic candidate for Congress in the Twenty-ninth District of New York, which is composed of the counties of Dutchess, Ulster, Columbia, Greene, and Schoharie.

It is with Candidate Vidal that we are concerned at the moment, and we recently sent a man who represented himself as a seasoned political observer up to Barrytown, in Dutchess County, where Mr. Vidal lives. His home is a resplendent masterpiece of Greek revival built by John R. Livingston in 1820 and named, inevitably, Edgewater. Unlike most of the houses along the Hudson, it sits smack on the bank of the river, no more than three or four feet above water level. One of its former owners was the essayist John Jay Chapman. Its present owner acquired it ten years ago, when he was twenty-four. He greeted our representative on the front steps, and consented then and there to an exclusive press conference, the official verbatim transcript of which follows:

Q—Why are you in politics?

A—Because I find it exhilarating and satisfying.

Q—Who is your opponent?

A—The incumbent, J. Ernest Wharton, Republican, of Schoharie County.

Q—Is he formidable?

A—A foeman worthy of my steel. A five-time winner. A leading member of the Interior and Insular Affairs Committee. A creature of infinite cunning. No sooner had I entered the race and described him as a do-nothing congressman than he put me on the defensive by sponsoring a bill—I believe his maiden effort at legislation—making it a federal offense to spread false information about bombs on airplanes, buses, and the like. What could I do but applaud? Now I'm guilty of me-tooism. First round to Wharton. But I shall return.

Q—Do you think you can win?

A—Certainly. All I have to do is overcome a two-to-one Republican lead. I must create a new voting pattern.

Q—How do you expect to do that?

A—In the main, by superior industry. Actually, I have labored in the vineyard for almost a year now. Why do you suppose I've been turning up like a bad penny on television? And I have addressed practically every Rotary, Kiwanis, Chamber of Commerce, and Young Marrieds Club in the Twenty-ninth District.

Q—Have you talked politics in those places?

A—Couldn't do that or I wouldn't have been asked. I've talked Hollywood, television, Broadway, what Liz Taylor is like, and that sort of thing. They've heard the name Vidal all over the District, and it's an easy one to remember. Now and then I have injected politics in a mild way. I have a little bit about my being asked to the White House to write a speech on integration for the President.

Q—Did that happen?

A—Oh, yes. Sherman Adams asked me to do it, and he liked the speech.

Q—Did the President deliver it?

A—No.

Q—Does any machine control you?

A—No. Next question, please.

Q—Do you have a machine of your own?

A—I'm lunching with Arthur Krock next week. At the Morosco, we're selling tickets for December performances.

Q—What are the issues hereabouts? Please be commendably brief.

A—The big one is schools. We need more of them. I stand foursquare for federal aid to education. Pollution of the lordly Hudson is another, and one dear to me. As you can see, the river is a hundred feet from my door. In summer, I swim in it every day. I shall need my health to serve my people.

Q—Can you resist lobbies?

A—With the greatest of ease. I can also resist making jokes about them.

Q—Brooks Atkinson, of Greene County, has announced in the *Times* that he will vote for you. Do you welcome his support?

A—Cordially. Though nothing that votes is alien to me, I particularly welcome the approval of Mr. Atkinson. I am hoping for that of Mrs. Atkinson, too. There is immediate seating on my bandwagon.

Q—Do you consider yourself a candidate for the Pulitzer Prize?

A—I am running in Columbia County but not at Columbia University. I have not actively sought the Prize, nor will I do so. If, however, the Prize should seek the man, I would not—repeat, not—decline so signal an honor.

Q—Do you aspire to office even higher than that of Representative from the Twenty-ninth District?

A—I have, since childhood, said that I would rather be President than write.

Q—Have you a campaign slogan?

A—Yes. A fine one. It's from Alfred North Whitehead: "No code of verbal statement can ever exhaust the shifting background of presupposed fact."

Q—What does that mean?

A—It means that questions are quite as important as answers. I lack many answers, but I think I know the right questions. For example, what kind of society do we want? Only by examining presuppositions can we approach any kind of truth. In "The Best Man," I have tried to raise important questions about politics and the Presidency. I would like to go to Washington and perhaps head a Congressional investigation of what we mean when we speak of "the free world."

Q—Have you mentioned your campaign slogan to your managers? And, if so, what do they think of it?

A—To your first question the answer is yes. To the second it is that they made no audible response.

Q—Thank you, Mr. Candidate.

1 9 6 0

NICHOLS, MAY, AND HORSES

HAVING read in the program of the show called "An Evening with Mike Nichols and Elaine May" that Mr. Nichols had represented the United States on an Olympic equestrian team, we suggested last week that the partners join us at a session of the National Horse Show, at Madison Square Garden. When we met them at the entrance to the place, Mr. Nichols was quick to inform us that he hadn't been on any equestrian team in any Olympics, and Miss May told us that whatever interest she'd once had in horses had ended when she fell off one a couple of years ago on a Central Park bridle path and twisted all kinds of ligaments in her left arm.

"The horse was just walking," Miss May said, "and I kind of slid off him, and you should have seen the hurt look he gave me."

"Nobody ever falls off a walking horse," said Mr. Nichols. "You could fall down on the floor more easily than you could fall off a walking horse."

"Look," said Miss May, "I fell off this horse, and he was embarrassed and I was embarrassed, and so there. I had my arm in a cast for a long time."

Mr. Nichols, a blond and most amiable young man of twenty-nine, conceded the fall, and Miss May, who is brunette, rosy, and ebullient, seemed pleased.

"Now, about this Olympic business," we said.

"Oh, that," Mr. Nichols observed. "You see, when the program said that Elaine is a distant cousin of Ed Sullivan—we're all cousins if you take it right back to Adam—I thought it would be only fair for me to look pretty distinguished, too. Actually, I've known quite a few horses in my day, and I've ridden in horse shows in Chicago. I don't want to put on any side, but I was an instructor at the Claremont Riding Academy, up on West Eighty-ninth Street, when I was going to high school in Manhattan."

"It was one of those Claremont horses I fell off," said Miss May.

Any further discussion of Miss May's traumatic experience in the Park was interrupted by Mr. Edward Bimberg, a horse fancier and official engaged in stimulating attendance at the Show. It soon developed that Mr. Bimberg had also, in his day, been an instructor at the Claremont. Horse riders, like horse-players, are a companionable crew, and in a jiffy we all went, arm in arm, down into the basement of the Garden to have a look at the horses stabled there. At the bottom of the ramp, we encountered a large gray horse, which was walking around, accompanied by a groom, in front of the area devoted to the beasts of the Dodge saddle-horse stables.

"Biggest in the country," said Mr. Nichols knowledgeably.

Miss May made a tentative pass at the muzzle of the big gray, and it blinked its great eyes and turned its head away.

"Imagine!" said Miss May. "I'm being rejected by a horse. This is a shattering experience."

We continued past orderly rows of box stalls until we came to one occupied by a splendid black animal that was being petted by a gentleman in a blue serge suit. The horse's lips were moving nervously, and Miss May proposed that we stick around until the gentleman was bitten.

"Horses will not bite you if you let them get the scent of you," said Mr. Bimberg. "Of course, if you exude salt in your palms, they will try to get it. They are crazy about salt."

"I think I'm exuding salt," said Miss May, backing away from the stall.

Not far from the nervous animal, we came upon a groom braiding the tail of a placid chestnut. Mr. Nichols pointed out that this would improve the horse's appearance and would help to ingratiate him with the Horse Show judges.

"Imagine!" said Miss May. "You get up in the morning, you have a nourishing breakfast, you say goodbye to the wife and kids, and then you spend the rest of the day braiding horses' tails." She was looking about reflectively when Mr. Nichols suddenly advised her that just beyond there was a man combing a tail with no horse attached, as indeed there was.

"Among the gaited horses," said Mr. Bimberg, "they are allowed to put on false tails."

Mr. Nichols and Mr. Bimberg got into a perceptive chat about gaited horses, Miss May wandered off, and we went over to watch a jumper being prepared for a contest. When the party reassembled, somewhere farther along, Miss May was trying to outstare a brown dachshund, which was snarling. "He hates me," she said.

"Never look a dog in the eye," said Mr. Bimberg.

"If I sweat, I get bitten by a horse, and if I look, I get bitten by a dog," said Miss May dolefully.

We went on to watch a handsome bay having his front feet soothed in a whirlpool bath, and then made our way to the pressroom, where Miss May challenged Mr. Nichols to do his imitation of Audrey Hepburn's first entrance in "Ondine."

"Not here," he said. "Not here."

"You wouldn't believe this," said Miss May, "but my daughter Jeannie is a super rider, and she's only eleven. I was riding with her when I slid off that horse and hurt my arm. I love the outdoor life—like walking. I was surprised," she added unexpectedly, "to find all those horses being washed. I thought they just dusted them, or something."

"Give me a horse I can ride like a man," said Mr. Nichols. "Washed or unwashed."

Mr. Bimberg said that he'd like to oblige but the schedule of the show would not permit Mr. Nichols to demonstrate his equestrian skills.

"So now you'll *have* to imitate Audrey Hepburn," said Miss May. "You know," she continued, without pause, "I had a terrible argument about Shakespeare's sonnets with a man who interviewed us the other day. Just to make conversation, I said I hated them, and it turned out he loved them. But what can you do—just sit there?"

At the behest of Mr. Bimberg, we took our chums up to see some working hunters with lady riders in the main ring.

"I keep wondering whether I ought to buy a horse," said Mr. Nichols as the ladies and their mounts went through their expert paces.

"If you do, get one that really likes your scent," said Miss May.

1960

ALBEE

WE had a talk last week with Edward Albee, the thirty-three-year-old playwright whose three one-act plays now on the boards Off Broadway have established him as the critics' current man-of-promise. "The Zoo Story" opened at the Provincetown Playhouse on January 14, 1960, and has been produced in London and in Berlin, among other places; "The American Dream" and "The Death of Bessie Smith," which opened January 24, 1961, and March 1, 1961, respectively, are both at the York Playhouse. We found Mr. Albee at home, in a ground-floor, six-room apartment in a ninety-year-old, yellow-stucco-front house on West Twelfth Street—an apartment packed to the gills with modern paintings, a stereophonic record player, fresh white pompons, books on the drama, a roommate named William Flanagan (who composed the music for "Bessie Smith" and another Albee one-acter, called "The Sandbox"), and three orphaned cats rescued by Albee: Cunégonde, three and a half; Vanessa, two and a half; and a still nameless thirteen-week-old semi-Siamese kitten. Albee, who is a handsome, lean, dark-haired young man with a crew haircut and considerable charm, and who was wearing a gray tweed sports jacket, gray flannel slacks, a button-down-collar white shirt, and a black wool tie, directed us to avoid a collapsing modern sofa and to sit in a non-collapsing modern chair, out of which he shooed his cats with a few firm, authoritative, affectionate, non-sticky words.

"I get them from the Greenwich Village Humane League," Albee told us. "The League people go out and look for abandoned cats on the street, and save them from the awful things that happen to homeless kittens in New York, like being tossed into bonfires by mean kids. That sort of thing can happen in the

Village, I'm sorry to say. Although I wouldn't live anywhere but in New York. I like to be in the center of things. There are ten thousand things you can do in half an hour in New York if you feel like it. I've lived in a lot of places—a fifteen-dollar-a-month cold-water flat on the lower East Side, a great big loft right in the middle of the garment district, for seventy a month, and a couple of other places around the Village. All the good places in the Village, all the lovely nineteenth-century houses, are being torn down now and six-story tenements are being put up instead. Do you want to see something amazing in my back yard? A real one-story little cottage, with somebody living in it." He showed us the amazing view through a rear window. "Will probably be torn down soon. But I'll try to stay in the Village. It's one of the few areas where you can be in the center of things and still feel removed."

Albee lit a cigarette and sat down carefully on the sofa, and we asked him to give us an autobiographical outline. "Born in Washington, D.C., on March 12, 1928, and came to New York when I was two weeks old," he said. "I have no idea who my natural parents were, although I'm sure my father wasn't a President, or anything like that. I was adopted by my father, Reed A. Albee, who worked for his father, Edward Franklin Albee, who started a chain of theatres with B. F. Keith and then sold out to R.K.O. My father is retired now. My mother is a remarkable woman. An excellent horsewoman and saddle-horse judge. I was riding from the time I was able to walk. My parents had a stable of horses in Larchmont or Scarsdale or Rye, or one of those places. I don't ride any more. Just sort of lost interest in it. My parents gave me a good home and a good education, none of which I appreciated. I attended Rye Country Day School until I was eleven, and then Lawrenceville, where I got thrown out after a year and a half for refusing to go to classes. It was probably that I was too young to be away from home, but instead of going home I was sent to Valley Forge Military Academy—Valley Forge Concentration Camp—where parents send their children for one of three reasons: discipline, or preparation for West Point, or in the hope that they'll get an education. You do get an education there, but it's not a purely scholastic education. You march practically all the time and wear a grayish-blue uniform like West Point's, with the hat with the patent-leather brim. I had the usual routine of discipline, institutional food, and dreary living quarters. When I finally left, after a year, I decided not to get thrown out of another school. I went to Choate next, and it was marvellous, but by then I was a few years older. I appreciated Choate after the aridity of a military school. I was very happy there. I went on to Trinity College, in Hartford, for a year and a half. I didn't have enough interest in it to stick it out for four years. I wouldn't go to chapel, and I wouldn't go to one of the math courses. It was probably a basic discontent with myself that hadn't taken a specific form yet. After a year and a half, the college suggested that I not come back, which was fine with me."

Albee gave a quick laugh and, inhaling with all the abandon of the carefree pre-filter age, continued, through the smoke, "I got my first job at Station

WNYC, where I spent a year and a half writing continuity for the music programs. After that, I had an *awful* lot of jobs: forty-dollar-a-week office boy for Warwick & Legler, the ad agency; salesman in the record department of Bloomingdale's; salesman in the book department of Schirmer's; luncheonette counterman at the Manhattan Towers Hotel. Then, starting in 1955, I was a Western Union messenger for three years, all over the city. I liked it. It wasn't a job that tired you out with mental work. I liked walking, and I met all sorts of interesting people. In 1949, I had come into a very small income, from a trust fund set up by my maternal grandmother, that was not quite enough to spoil me. In 1952, I went to Florence for four or five months and tried to write a novel. The novel was awful. I had written a lot of poetry, and had even managed to get one poem published, when I was seventeen, in a Texas magazine called *Kaleidoscope.* It had something to do with turning eighteen. Then, in the spring of 1958, when I hit thirty, a kind of explosion took place in my life. I'd been drifting, and I got fed up with myself. I decided to write a play. I was getting a little bit more money from the trust fund—thirty-five hundred dollars a year—and I quit work.

"I wrote 'The Zoo Story' on a wobbly table in the kitchen of the apartment I was living in at the time—at 238 West Fourth Street. I did a draft, made pencil revisions, and typed a second script, and that's the way I've been doing my plays since. I finished 'The Zoo Story' in three weeks and showed it to a few uptown producers, who said it was nice but they wanted a full-length play. Then Bill Flanagan sent a copy of the play to David Diamond, the American composer, who was living in Florence, and Diamond sent it to a Swiss actor, Pinkas Braun, in Zurich, who later did all the German translations of my plays. Braun made a tape recording of the play in English and sent it to Mrs. Stefani Hunzinger, in Frankfurt, who is head of the drama department of S. Fischer, one of the biggest publishing houses in Germany. From there it went on to a producer named Barlog, in Berlin, and that's where I had my first audience—on September 28, 1959. 'The Death of Bessie Smith' was produced in Berlin about a year ago, before it was put on here. Aside from the interest that German audiences take in the contemporary foreign theatre, they seem to find some application to their own lives in my plays."

We asked how things were going financially.

"Strange," he said. "My income is growing. In 1959, I made about a thousand dollars on my work. In 1960, it was ten thousand dollars. In 1961, I've made five thousand dollars in two months. The New York income is a small part of it. It means I don't have to take an outside job, and I like that. Although my tastes are inexpensive, I like to sit in good seats at the theatre, so I can see what's going on. I don't think about clothes. I don't own a suit. I have a couple of sports jackets, and what I like to wear is sweater, slacks, and sneakers."

"Any plans?" we asked. "Any special thoughts on your last birthday?"

"I'm not looking forward to getting older, but I'm not horrified by it, either," he said. "I've got about two—maybe three—years' work planned out, considering how lazy I am about what I want to be doing. I'm behind, but I'd rather be behind than be completely caught up. I have three plays in mind and I'm trying to finish two others—'Who's Afraid of Virginia Woolf?' and an adaptation of Carson McCullers' 'The Ballad of the Sad Café.' I'm doing the second because it's sort of a challenge. I've never seen an adaptation of anything that was any good. I'm curious to find out if it's possible to do one without running into what usually happens—the lessening and coarsening of the material. The other play is about a two-in-the-morning drunken party of two faculty members and their wives. These will both be what they refer to as full-length plays, 'they' being people who think the theatre has got to start at eight-forty and end at eleven-ten."

"Any special influences in your writing?" we asked.

Albee gave us a cool laugh. "There are anywhere between five hundred and a thousand good plays, and I'd have to go back to the Greeks and work my way right up," he replied. "It's been an assimilative process. Of my contemporaries, after Brecht, I admire Beckett, Jean Genet, Tennessee Williams, and Harold Pinter. In fiction, I have a special preference for Salinger and Updike. I feel happy and comfortable in what I'm doing. I've become freer and less free. One develops obligations to oneself, having had one's productions reasonably well received. I more or less play it by ear. Unless you're a man like Bernard Shaw, who knew what he was doing at all times, you get yourself in trouble trying to talk about the way you write. It makes for self-consciousness. I'd like to preserve an innocence, so that what I do can surprise me. I've been forced lately to articulate what's been happening to me, and that makes you self-conscious about trying to remain unself-conscious. I go to more parties than I used to. I find I start talking and other people shut up. And that's terrible. I've met more people this past year than I ever met in the past thirty. It's interesting and valuable to meet accomplished people. It's instructive. You can always learn from your elders and betters. When I sit down to work, four or five hours at a time are all I can manage. Then I have to go out to the San Remo and have a couple of beers with friends. Summers, I go off to the beach at Riis Park by subway and bus. I stayed with all the plays throughout casting and rehearsals. It's a pleasant agony."

FACES

I T occurred to us that there is one feature of the Manhattan landscape that we have never analytically described: the faces. So we went out and examined them. The first thing that struck us was how many, many there are. They occur, with rare exceptions, in a narrow belt of space between four and six feet above the pavement. A few glimmer darklingly from windows at an elevation higher than this, and once in a great while, usually late at night, a face may be seen on the pavement itself, but by and large the faces, with surprising conformity, restrict their ebb and flow, advance and withdrawal, as well as their more intricate cross- and counter-movements, to the narrow lateral area described above. Here they hover, like a dense pink cumulus, in a dogged flux as remarkable for its variety as for its nagging persistence.

One's first impression, in scanning the faces, is of a sameness as striking as that of pigeons, wavelets, or bricks. Attentive examination, however, yields a multitude of distinctions. Not only do the faces of Manhattan vary in color and size but they differ even in individual *expression*. Some float with eyelids lowered; some stare straight ahead while the lips move rhythmically, producing a small snapping noise, possibly of chewing-gum or sassafras bark, deep in the molars; some glance now and then nervously sidewise at a second face while the lips move spasmodically, forming words. The cheeks of the female faces jounce slightly, under their veil of powder, as the supporting column of the body strides forward on pointed spike heels. A few faces are knitted and reddened by strong emotions, whose classification lies beyond the scope of this study. There are even, among the surging, bobbing mass, a few faces that, like tracer bullets, seem to glow—whether with beauty, piety, or unthinking animal happiness there is no way of ascertaining.

Roughly fifty per cent of the faces are in some way painted, red on the lips being most common, green on the eyelids being somewhat less common, and purple on the eyebrows being a downright rarity. Perhaps fifteen per cent of the faces—invariably male—bear some more or less purposefully shaped ornament of hair, and certainly not more than five per cent are marked by duelling scars, shaving nicks, or deeply dimpled chins. One out of three faces wears twin framed panes of glass in front of its eyes, and in one out of three of *these* the panes are tinted dark. Curiously—the fact may or may not be significant—the incidence in the dark-glass-pane-wearing faces of mustaches, cigarettes, and defiant scowls is disproportionately high.

How can this disproportion be explained? How, indeed, can the daily apparition of these faces on our streets be explained? How can we rationalize their perverse preference for the rather low plane that they unanimously inhabit, when just a few feet above this jostling, obviously uncomfortable concentration there are vast volumes of empty air? Furthermore, what force or natural law is it that maintains these faces in separation—that prevents them from running indistinguishably together, like the quarts of water in a river, or from swapping identities back and forth freely, like the dabs of sunlight on a ferny forest floor? These are conundrums that it may take science years to unravel.

It remains to comment on the aesthetic effect produced by these faces. There is a peculiar sense in which these natural phenomena differ from a sunset, a spectacular stunt of geological erosion, or a migration of wild birds. Passing through this tirelessly agitated cloud of visages, we felt emanations of hostility and of a danger so subtle that our perception of it was romantically tinged with awe. At the same time, we were exhilarated—despite the fact that many of the faces were wrinkled and distorted, as if from the prolonged application of some maladjusted mask. The exhilaration, furthermore, did not center on the fairer faces in the mass but, somehow, on all of them, whether rouged, bearded, bespectacled, bleary, downcast, anxious, or ecstatic. Individual facial configurations twinkled out at us much as stars must declare themselves to the mariner emerging from a storm, and aroused in us an analogous sensation of unreasonable redemption. In sum, the faces were an extraordinary sight, and we suggest that, after taking in Grant's Tomb and The Cloisters, you go look at them sometime.

1962

THE MARCH

W E flew to Washington the day before the march and, early the next morning, walked from Pennsylvania Avenue past the side entrance of the White House and toward the lawn of the Washington Monument, where the marchers were gathering. It was eight o'clock—three and a half hours before the march was scheduled to move from the Washington Monument to the Lincoln Memorial—and around the Ellipse, the huge plot of grass between the White House grounds and the lawn of the Washington Monument, there were only about half a dozen buses. Most of them had red-white-and-blue signs saying "Erie, Pa., Branch, N.A.A.C.P.," or "Inter-Church Delegation, Sponsored by National Council of Churches of Christ in the U.S.A. Commission on Religion and Race," or "District 26, United Steelworkers of America, Greater Youngstown A.F.L.-C.I.O. Council, Youngstown, Ohio." On a baseball field on the Ellipse, three men were setting up a refreshment stand, and on the sidewalk nearby a man wearing an N.A.A.C.P. cap was arranging pennants that said "March on Washington for Jobs and Freedom. Let the World Know We Want Freedom." Most of the buses were nearly full, and many of the occupants were dozing. Sitting on a bench in front of one of the buses, some teen-agers were singing, "Everybody wants freedom—free-ee-dom."

On the lawn of the Washington Monument, a group of military police, most of them Negroes, and a group of Washington police, most of them white, were getting final instructions. Women dressed in white, with purple armbands that said "Usher" and blue sashes that said "Pledge Cards," were handing out cards to everybody who passed. "I've already contributed to this," a man near us told one of the women. But the card asked for no money; it asked instead that the signer commit himself to the civil-rights struggle, pledging his heart, mind, and body, "unequivocally and without regard to personal sacrifice, to the achievement of social peace through social justice."

Outside march headquarters—a huge tent with green sides and a green-and-white striped roof—workers were setting up a rim of tables. One table held a display of pennants, offering a large one for a dollar and a small one for fifty cents. Inside the tent, a man wearing a CORE overseas cap, a blue suit, an arm-band with the letter "M" on it, and a badge saying "Assistant Chief Marshal," was testing a walkie-talkie, and another man was issuing instructions to a group of program salesmen. "Now, everybody report back by nine-fifteen, or whenever they give out," he said. Two or three Negroes were sorting signs that said "The Southern Christian Leadership Conference of Lynchburg, Virginia." In a roped-off area near one end of the tent, the official signs for the march were stacked face down in large piles, most of them covered by black tarpau-lins. Next to the signs, in an enclave formed by a green fence, half a dozen women sat behind a long table. Two signs on the fence said "Emergency Hous-ing." Nearby, three or four television crews had set up their cameras on high platforms.

By this time, there were several thousand people on the lawn, many of them gathered around the Monument. An ice-cream truck had managed to drive to within a hundred feet of the Monument and was starting to do an early-morning business. Many of those gathered near the Monument were sitting on the grass, and some were sleeping. Three boys dressed in khaki pants and shirts with button-down collars were using their knapsacks for pillows and had cov-ered their faces with black derbies. There were, we thought, surprisingly few knapsacks and sandals in the crowd. Most of the people were neatly dressed, and as they waited for the pre-march program to start, they acted like ordinary tourists in Washington, or like city people spending a warm Sunday in the park. A man took a picture of a couple standing in front of a sign that said "New Jersey Region, American Jewish Congress"; a policeman was taking a picture of two smiling Negro couples; a woman who was selling programs bal-anced her programs and her purse in one hand and, with the other, took pic-tures of the sleepers with derbies over their faces.

By nine o'clock, a group of marchers had congregated outside a green fence surrounding a stage that had been set up several hundred yards from the Mon-ument; they were standing six or eight deep against the fence. More people were arriving constantly—some in couples and small groups, others marching in large contingents. A group of young Negroes walked behind a blue-and-gold banner that said "Newman Memorial Methodist Church School, Brooklyn, N.Y., Organized 1900." Another group of Negroes—older, and wearing yellow campaign hats that bore the letters "B.S.E.I.U."—followed four boys who were carrying a long banner that said "Local 144" and two flag-bearers, one carrying the American flag and one carrying a flag that said "Building Services Employees International Union."

In front of the headquarters tent, a group of young people in overalls and T shirts that said "CORE" were marching around in a circle, clapping and singing.

"I'm going to walk the streets of Jackson," one girl sang.

"One of these days," the others answered.

"I'm going to be the chief of police," another sang.

"One of these days," the crowd answered.

Near the singing group, a double line of Negro teen-agers came marching across the lawn. All of them were dressed in black jackets. They had no banners or pennants, and they filed by in silence.

"Where y'all from?" a Negro girl in the CORE group asked one of them.

"From Wilmington, North Carolina," one of the boys replied, and the black-jacketed group walked on silently.

We started toward the stage and happened to come across Bayard Rustin, the deputy director of the march, heading that way with Norman Thomas. Following them up to the stage, we found two other members of the march committee—Courtland Cox, of the Student Non-Violent Coördinating Committee, and Norman Hill, of the Congress of Racial Equality—looking out at the people between the stage and the Monument and talking about the crowd.

At exactly nine-thirty, Ossie Davis, serving as master of ceremonies, tried to begin the pre-march program, but it had to be postponed, because Rustin and Thomas were the only two dignitaries on the stage and many more were expected.

"Oh, freedom," said a voice over a loudspeaker a little later. The program had started, and Joan Baez began to sing in a wonderfully clear voice. "Oh, freedom," she sang. "Oh, freedom over me. Before I'll be a slave, I'll be buried in my grave . . ."

Then came folk songs by Miss Baez; Peter, Paul, and Mary; Odetta; and Bob Dylan. Davis made the introductions, occasionally turning the microphone over to a marshal for an announcement, such as "Mr. Roosevelt Johnson. If you hear me, your child, Larry Johnson, is in the headquarters tent." By ten-thirty, the expanse of grass that had been visible between the crowd around the stage and the crowd around the Monument had almost disappeared, and more people were still marching onto the lawn, carrying signs and banners. Most of the signs identified groups—such as the Alpha Phi Alpha Fraternity and the Detroit Catholics for Equality and Freedom—but some had slogans on them, and one, carried by a white woman who marched up and down the sidewalk in back of the stage, said "What We All Need Is Jesus and to Read the Bible." Another folk singer, Josh White, arrived on the stage while Odetta was singing. White didn't wait for an introduction. He merely unpacked his guitar, handed the cigarette he had been smoking to a bystander, and walked up to the microphone to join Odetta in singing "I'm on the Way to Canaan Land." In a few moments, Miss Baez was also singing, and then all the folk singers gathered at the microphone to finish the song.

At about eleven, Davis announced that the crowd was now estimated at ninety thousand. From the stage, there was no longer any grass visible between the stage and the Monument. Next, Davis introduced a representative of the Elks, who presented the organizers of the march with an Elks contribution of ten thousand dollars; a girl who was the first Negro to be hired as an airline stewardess; Lena Horne; Daisy Bates, who shepherded the nine teen-agers who integrated Central High School in Little Rock; Miguel Abreu Castillo, the head of the San Juan Bar Association, who gave a short speech in Spanish; Bobby Darin; and Rosa Parks, the woman who started the Montgomery bus boycott by refusing to move to the back of the bus.

The official march signs had been passed out, and they began to bob up and down in the crowd: "No U.S. Dough to Help Jim Crow Grow," "Civil Rights Plus Full Employment Equals Freedom."

At about eleven-forty-five, Davis told the crowd that the march to the Lincoln Memorial was going to begin, and suggested that people standing near the Monument use Independence Avenue and people standing near the stage go down Constitution Avenue. We were closer to Constitution Avenue, and as we got onto the street there was a crush of people that for a moment brought back stories of the dangers inherent in a crowd of such a size. But almost immediately the crush eased, and we walked comfortably down shady Constitution Avenue. We noticed that practically nobody was watching the march from the sidelines, and that in the march itself there was a remarkable lack of noise. Occasionally, a song would start somewhere in the crowd, but to a large extent the marchers were silent. A few hundred yards from the Monument, the march was stopped by a man who was holding a sign that said "Lexington Civil Rights Committee" and wearing an armband that said "Mass. Freedom Rider." He asked the people in the front row to link arms, and, beginning to sing "We Shall Overcome," they moved on down the street.

"Slow down, slow down!" the man from Massachusetts shouted as he walked backward in front of the crowd. "Too fast! You're going too fast! Half steps!"

A few hundred feet farther on, a policeman and an M.P. stood in the middle of the street and split the crowd down the middle. We followed the group to the left, and in a few minutes found ourself standing in a crowd, now even quieter, to the left of the reflecting pool in front of the Lincoln Memorial.

1963

ALL FRESH AND WIDE-EYED

AT an exhibition of twelve modern Irish painters now being held at the New School for Social Research, we became acquainted one day last week with Anne Yeats, daughter of William Butler Yeats, niece of Jack Yeats, and an artist of considerable standing in her own right. A buxom and beaming woman in her mid-forties, Miss Yeats, who was hobbling about on a cane, immediately apologized for seeming infirm. "Ordinarily, I leap about like a goat, but I sprained my ankle getting aboard the plane to come to America," she told us. "Ah, well, thank God it didn't happen on this side of the water!"

We asked Miss Yeats what it was like to be the daughter of such a poet as her father.

"You know, when I was young, I didn't know what it was like not to be," she said. "I rather thought that everybody was like himself. I intruded upon him and my mother, who was from Devonshire, when Father was fifty-three. I've been told that Father saluted my arrival by buying a packet of sweets for me to munch upon. It was a pretty gesture, but at the time I hadn't enough teeth to appreciate it. He was a poet who never depended upon flashes of inspiration. He kept to a rigid schedule—so much so that once, in my adolescent years, I was encouraged to ease his mind at the end of each day by letting him read some essays of my devising. I think it took more out of him to read them than it did out of me to write them, and after a period of six weeks we were both happy to abandon the project. Part of this essay work was due to the fact that I was drawing five hours a day at the Royal Hibernian Academy, in Dublin, and some of my mentors thought it might be a good idea for me to get some sort of general education. But it didn't work out that way, for I guess I take after my

Uncle Jack, who dedicated his life to painting—and was, indeed, a stimulus to anyone wielding a brush in Ireland. If Uncle Jack had been forty years younger or I had been forty years older, we could have had many a good time together."

Miss Yeats smiled reflectively, and presently we interrupted her musing to inquire if she herself had ever tried her hand at verse.

"Oh, I did, I did," she said. "It was all very dramatic and very blank, and when I reached the age of twelve, I decided to let my father handle the poetry in the family, and to concentrate on painting. I'd say it was a wise decision. I've studied in Spain and France, and I'm proud of the fact that I used to be the chief stage designer for the Abbey Theatre. But even with theatre décor, and waxes and water colors, I couldn't find what I wanted, and so I changed to oils, which give me great satisfaction. You know, I'm all fresh and wide-eyed about New York, but I'm still devoted to Dublin. The Yeatses have been there for two hundred years, and Father was a Dubliner, even though he wrote so often about the West Country. We used to have an old Norman tower in Galway, in which we were comfortable, although every spring the waters around the tower would rise, and then we'd have to spend a good deal of time sweeping out the mud and worms. It was a small tower—nothing like as primitive as the one Joyce had in Dún Laoghaire—and Father was very happy there. He died when I was nineteen, but my mother is still robust, and my brother Michael, who is forty-two, busies himself with politics. He likes the agitation, I guess, just as I like circuses and fairs and people disporting themselves around pools."

As Miss Yeats was talking, we recalled a verse from a cradle song of her father's:

> I sigh that kiss you,
> For I must own
> That I shall miss you
> When you have grown.

And that led us to think of part of a prayer Yeats wrote for his daughter:

> She can, though every face should scowl
> And every windy quarter howl
> Or every bellows burst, be happy still.

Miss Yeats was looking very happy, and we thought how right her father had been in his prognostications.

1 9 6 3

FUGUE

Mr. GLENN GOULD, the pianist, held a private showing one recent morning, for Mr. Yehudi Menuhin, the violinist, of a movie starring himself. The movie, which had been made from an hour-long video-tape recording, was entitled "The Anatomy of Fugue." It was projected on a screen the size of a pillowcase, in a room the size of an average closet, in the local office of the Canadian Broadcasting Corporation, which had broadcast the tape. Mr. Gould, unslept and unbarbered, was in town for a couple of days from his home, in Toronto. He had on his usual baggy dark-blue suit with outmoded overpadded shoulders, a raggedy brown sweater, and a worn-out bluish necktie. A yellow pencil protruded, eraser end up, from his coat pocket. He was burdened with a baggy brown overcoat, a brown wool muffler, and a navy-blue cap. Mr. Menuhin, pink-cheeked, chubby, trim, and serene, had come to town from *his* home, in London, to start on a three-month, twenty-eight-city recital tour that would include several benefit appearances and one appearance on the "Bell Telephone Hour." He was neatly encased in well-tailored pin stripes and well-laundered supplementation. Mr. Gould sat on a straight-backed office chair, with his coat, cap, and muffler on his lap, and with his arms crossed and his hands tucked under his arms. Mr. Menuhin sat on a straight-backed office chair right behind him, his fingers intertwined over his midriff.

"I'm so glad you could come, I'm so glad you could really make it," Mr. Gould said, turning around, to Mr. Menuhin. "I want you to see this one. This one is a special pet."

"Such a nice thing to do in New York," Mr. Menuhin said, in a light, warm voice, and gave Mr. Gould a gentle, warm smile. "Seeing a movie, at eleven o'clock in the morning! I'm so happy you suggested it."

"I like making these films," Mr. Gould said. "I've always felt this terrible frustration in concerts—you do it and it's gone. Why not put it on film and have it? So that it will *be* there."

"Wonderful idea. Wonderful," Mr. Menuhin said, his smile broadening and a look of appreciation coming into his eyes.

Mr. Gould grinned.

"I did a television film on Bartók, covering the musical influences in his life, and playing some of his arrangements of Hungarian folk tunes and excerpts from the solo violin sonata he wrote for me, and speaking in between, and I did another one about Yoga," Mr. Menuhin said. "I find it rather difficult when they put you in front of the camera and say '*Do* something.' "

Mr. Gould bobbed his head in agreement. "We had a very good director for this one, and we even built a set, as you'll see," he said. "We shot the whole thing in two days. After two months of conferences, of course."

"Was it dreadfully expensive?" Mr. Menuhin asked. "These things do cost so much."

"Thirty thousand dollars, about," Mr. Gould said. "But I wanted to do it right. There's no point in doing it at all if you can't get what you want." He waved a hand at the projectionist, who was peeking out of a square hole in the back wall. "We're ready any time you want to start," Mr. Gould said.

Mr. Menuhin gave a little sigh and tightened his hands around his middle. "I hope this will be made available to television in this country," he said.

Mr. Gould grinned again. "Well, *they've* got Leonard Bernstein," he said. "I don't do it the way he does it. Not that I don't admire the way he does it. He has the ability to communicate on a great many levels at once. My way is different." He bobbed his head vigorously. "I don't know if my film is for the mass public. Sometimes I think they don't know what the hell I've said, but they feel elevated."

Mr. Menuhin's eyes twinkled.

"Roll it," Mr. Gould said to the projectionist behind the wall. He turned back toward the screen, and tossed his coat, muffler, and cap on the floor. The lights went out, and the movie started, showing Mr. Gould at the piano playing an improvisation based on "Do Re Mi," from Richard Rodgers' score for "The Sound of Music." When he had finished it, he looked up, on the screen, and said to the camera, "For hundreds of years, musicians have been doing the sort of thing that I was attempting just now. They have been taking little bits of musical trivia, like that theme from 'The Sound of Music,' and trying to find complicated equations into which, like a common denominator, these tidbits will fit. In fact, there is some part of almost every musician that longs to experiment with the mathematical quantities of music and to find forms in which these quantities can function most successfully. And perhaps the long-time favorite

of such forms is that special musical mix we call the fugue. The fugue is normally conceived in a number of voices, a number of individual lines that, up to
a certain point, may lead a life of their own. But they must have in common a
responsibility to some special material that is examined in the course of the
fugue, and consequently each of the voices is first heard announcing, in its
most comfortable register, the same theme. . . ."

As Mr. Gould elaborated on the give-and-take between the voices in the
fugue—each musical voice, he said, went off on "some pretty wacky tangents
of its own"—Mr. Menuhin listened intently, and when Mr. Gould explained
that the relation of the subject of a fugue to its counter-subject would be something like that of "God Save the Queen" to "The Star-Spangled Banner," Mr.
Menuhin made a soft sound of concurrence. "They ought to combine and complement their personalities in a manner that, as Johann Sebastian Bach once
said, suggests three or four civilized gentlemen conducting a reasonable conversation," Mr. Gould continued. "And the conversation that they carry on
does not necessarily always deal with particularly imposing matters. . . . In
fact, in certain cases the more ordinary the subject the better."

"Good," Mr. Menuhin said. "Very good."

The offscreen Mr. Gould got up and went right up to the pillowcase screen,
shaking his head ruefully. "Can you get a slightly sharper focus?" he called
back to the projectionist.

Nothing changed in the focus. Mr. Gould sat down again. Onscreen, he was
saying, "When we hear a fugue like the one in E Flat from Volume II of Bach's
'The Well-Tempered Clavier,' we hear a composition that not only disciplines
four profoundly beautiful lines but makes them more compelling by having
them work within a superbly disciplined harmonic regime." He then played the
fugue on the piano.

"Lovely," Mr. Menuhin said when he had finished. "Lovely."

The offscreen Mr. Gould gave Mr. Menuhin a pleased look. Then he got up
and went back to see the projectionist. When he returned, a moment later, the
image on the screen was sharper. "Better?" he asked Mr. Menuhin.

"Much better, yes," Mr. Menuhin said.

Both men settled back more easily in their chairs. Mr. Gould crossed his legs.
He hunched forward as he heard himself say, on the screen, that he was now
going to play a much more intense fugue from Volume II of "The Well-
Tempered Clavier"—the B Flat Minor, one of the finest of Bach's fugues.

"Wonderful," Mr. Menuhin said at the end of the fugue.

"It's a great piece," Mr. Gould said.

Mr. Menuhin commented on the lightness of the piano sound, and Mr. Gould
said that this particular piano had almost no aftertouch.

At one point, when the camera zeroed in on Mr. Gould as he was playing, the
watching Mr. Gould shuddered. "God, that's a nasty shot," he said. "It's like Cor-
nel Wilde in 'A Song to Remember,' with Merle Oberon leaning over the piano."

"Oh, no, it comes over beautifully!" Mr. Menuhin said.

Every time Mr. Gould finished playing something on the screen, Mr. Menuhin would lean forward slightly, Mr. Gould would turn around to him, and Mr. Menuhin would say, "Wonderful performance, wonderful performance." Near the end of the movie, Mr. Gould said, onscreen, "Paul Hindemith is one of the few composers of our own time who can undeniably be called a fuguist to the manner born. Hindemith has developed a very special language of his own, a language that is contemporary in the best sense of the word but in its attempt to provide harmonic logic uses what you might call a substitute tonality." Then he played the fugue from Hindemith's Third Piano Sonata, which Mr. Menuhin immediately said was a wonderful piece.

"And now!" the offscreen Mr. Gould said, standing up. "We come to what we've all been waiting for!" He adjusted a knob near the screen that turned the sound up. "We have to have this louder, that's for sure," Mr. Gould said, laughing and shaking with his laughter.

Mr. Menuhin smiled.

On the screen, a quartet—a baritone, a tenor, a soprano, and a contralto—started singing a composition in fugue style by Mr. Gould:

> *"So, you want to write a fugue,*
> *You've got the urge to write a fugue,*
> *You've got the nerve to write a fugue,*
> *The only way to write one is to plunge right in and write one.*
> *So go ahead."*

"Lovely, lovely," Mr. Menuhin commented.

The movie ended. The lights came on.

"Wonderful program!" Mr. Menuhin said. "Beautifully done!"

Mr. Gould suddenly looked shy. "Thank you," he said. "It was really quite fun to do. But it took a hell of a lot of work."

"I love your approach to the music and the completely unmechanical way you play," Mr. Menuhin said, beaming at Mr. Gould with admiration. "And you spoke throughout so *smoothly.* Was it impromptu?"

"I had it on the TelePrompTer," Mr. Gould said. "I looked at it often enough to pick up all the cues, but I forced myself to invent phrases as I went along, to keep it sounding natural and not too formal."

"Yes, wonderful," Mr. Menuhin said. "Especially if the words are your own."

Mr. Gould laughed shyly.

"For the one I did on Bartók, I had quite good dialogue, but not quite as good as yours," Mr. Menuhin said. He gave a little sigh. "Most enjoyable!" he said.

"Next year, if you're going to have some time, we might do one together," Mr. Gould said. "You ever done the Schoenberg Fantasia?"

"Oh!" Mr. Menuhin gave a little gasp. "What a splendid idea! I must look at the music."

"It's a dry work—one of his last things," Mr. Gould said.

"I have the music," Mr. Menuhin said. "You're not coming to England next summer? We might do it there."

"I'd love to come and visit you," Mr. Gould said. "But I'm finished with concerts. You know my feeling about concerts. I'm bored with them."

Mr. Menuhin smiled wistfully. "On the screen, it does gain dimensions," he said.

"Some people say that every performance is an experience, but it's not that for me in concerts," Mr. Gould said. "It's animal. It's all a circus. It's immoral."

"Yes, I do know what you mean," Mr. Menuhin said mildly.

"When I'm onstage, I can shut them out, but I don't like it," Mr. Gould said. "I won't do more than six concerts a year. My view of the future is the end of the concert experience and the revitalization of the home experience. I haven't gone to a concert in months. When I'm in the audience, I'm completely distracted, I'm acutely uncomfortable. I don't feel the therapy of private listening."

"You are recording, though?" Mr. Menuhin said, beginning to look alarmed.

Mr. Gould said of course, and laughed. "I want to send you the Six Bach Partitas that just came out," he said. "I'm rather proud of that record."

Mr. Menuhin appeared relieved. "Would you come to England in July?" he asked. "To make the film?"

Mr. Gould bobbed his head and grinned. "The Schoenberg," he said. "In July."

Mr. Menuhin got up to go, smiling and looking utterly at peace. He gave Mr. Gould his hand. "It will be lovely," he said. "We will do it, and then it will *be* there."

1963

BECKETT

W E have always liked to imagine Samuel Beckett as more the inhabitant of his own wild pages than of any mundane place or time, and we were consequently a bit skeptical, the other day, when we read in a newspaper that he had materialized in our very midst and could be found that morning in a small movie studio on the upper East Side, watching over the production of his first screenplay. We headed straight uptown, and were halfway down the long, dark hall of a converted bakery on Ninetieth Street when we came upon Barney Rosset, the president of Grove Press, Beckett's American publisher. Mr. Rosset informed us that he had formed a subsidiary called Evergreen Theatre to commission and produce movies by his own authors, and that Evergreen's first film, now in production but still without a title, was being made from three short screenplays by Mr. Beckett, Harold Pinter, and Eugène Ionesco. He grinned, bounded proudly down the rest of the hall and into the studio, and added that Beckett's screen treatment, which contains no dialogue at all, had not only the author as adviser but Alan Schneider as its director, Boris Kaufman as its director of photography, and Buster Keaton playing its major character. Rosset then steered us across the studio, nimbly sidestepping coils of rope and piles of boxes on the floor, and left us at the door of the set of a small, exceedingly Beckettian room. It contained a rusty cot, a mattress smeared with dirt and sprouting chicken feathers through a large rip, a crumpled green blanket, a dingy mirror, an even dingier window hung with tattered curtains and an old air-raid shade, a picture of what looked like a carnival figure, a Chihuahua, a cat, a parrot, two goldfish, a Victorian rocker, a large camera on wheels, forty spotlights, twelve technicians, one script girl, two magazine photographers, Mr. Schneider, Mr. Kaufman, Mr. Keaton, a bearded cameraman named Joe Coffey, and Mr. Beckett, who was sitting in a corner on a Coca-Cola crate, peering intently at the scene. The playwright, materialized, turned out to be tall and quite thin, with soaring eyebrows and graying brown hair that stood straight up and swept back over his head like a wiry crest. He wore small round steel-rimmed glasses, a light-blue shirt rolled up at the sleeves and open at the neck, and tan trousers that were liberally splattered with feathers from the mattress. He was nervously smoking a strong French cigarette, and his forehead was deeply lined.

We were edging across the set to Mr. Beckett's crate when Mr. Schneider called, "O.K., let's try it!," and the technicians dispersed to various posts around the room and on the scaffolding, leaving Mr. Kaufman, his cameraman, his camera steerer, and his camera-cord carrier behind the camera and Mr. Keaton in front of it. Keaton, with all his traditional gloom intact, was wearing an eye patch, baggy black trousers, bright-red suspenders, and an old, battered, pancaked hat. With Mr. Schneider counting and Mr. Beckett shyly watching, Keaton took four slow steps toward the Chihuahua and the cat. The Chihuahua and the cat, who shared a wicker basket, stared curiously at him.

"That all right, Sam?" Schneider called.

"Exactly. Just the way I'd want it," Beckett said softly, standing up to clasp his hands behind his head and stretch.

"Would you like to take a look, Sam?" Coffey said.

Beckett, pleased, peeked into the camera. "It's fine. Good," he said.

"Here, sit down, Sam," one of the technicians said, and pulled up a new crate.

Beckett took him by the shoulders and chuckled affectionately. "Really, I promise you that when I get tired of standing up, I will sit down," he said. "I promise to sit down."

Schneider held out a Coke. "Here, have a drink, Sam," he said.

A tough-looking young technician, walking across the set with an extra spotlight, stopped next to us. He looked protectively over at Beckett, who was back on his Coke crate, absorbed in the rehearsal of the next scene. "I can't believe it," the technician whispered. "Sam's the nicest guy I've ever met. He's just so nice that he makes you nice, too." He shook his head, incredulously, and continued on his way.

We walked over to Beckett. He was quite tanned, and he explained that he had spent the weekend in East Hampton, at Rosset's house. "I met Edward Albee at his place in Montauk, but I haven't done much in New York," he said matter-of-factly and not at all regretfully. "Kay Boyle brought a writer called Kenneth Koch over to say hello, but mostly I've been here, working on the film."

Schneider strode by and off the set, and we followed. We asked him about the film.

"It's really quite a simple thing," he said. "It's a movie about the perceiving eye, about the perceived and the perceiver—two aspects of the same man. The perceiver desires like mad to perceive, and the perceived tries desperately to hide. Then, in the end, one wins."

We asked Mr. Schneider who did win, and he said that he thought the perceiver won. "You know, people come in here and ask Sam 'What do you *mean?*,' trying to make him something obscure, befuddling, inscrutable. Well, I think he's the most crystal-clear poet—notice, I say poet—writing today. 'Godot'? 'Endgame'? They're lucid. Maybe it's just that we're afraid to hear what they're trying to say."

Mr. Schneider strode on, and we turned back to Mr. Beckett, who was listening to a young woman from the studio. "Sam, the teen-agers love your novel 'Murphy,' " she said. "They laugh and laugh."

Beckett smiled. "Well, it's my easiest book, I guess," he said. He then told the woman that he was returning to Paris, where he lives, as soon as the film is finished.

"You should have been around for the exteriors," said Coffey, who had walked over to the crate. "We shot under the Manhattan end of the Brooklyn Bridge. It was perfect. The street we were on was semi-demolished and desolate. It looked as though the street was all that existed, all there was—a world blocked off."

Beckett nodded in agreement. "Pearl Street, it was," he said.

Coffey edged away from the crate and beckoned to us. "You know, Sam's incredible," he said. "He grasps his own work visually. He can think cinematically. He spotted Pearl Street as the place right away, when we were driving around."

Coffey looked admiringly over at Beckett, who was now engrossed in wordless conversation with Mr. Keaton. Keaton, with a disarming dead pan, was digging into one of his trouser pockets, looking for change. He dug deeper and deeper, through the proverbial hole in the pocket and straight down to the cuff. Upon reaching the cuff, he pulled out a quarter, held it up triumphantly, and handed it to Beckett. Beckett threw back his head and laughed.

"Sam, they released 'The General' again, you know, with foreign subtitles," Keaton said at last, in a low, gravelly voice. "It went all over Europe, and all of a sudden everybody loved it. A German lady even sent me flowers." He paused thoughtfully. "Now, why couldn't she have sent them forty years ago?"

Beckett laughed again. "You could've used them then."

"O.K., let's go, Buster!" Schneider called, as Kaufman wheeled the camera into place for another take.

Beckett left his crate. He reappeared a moment later on the scaffolding, leaning over a makeshift rail, chin in hand.

Keaton, his face averted, was groping along the wall, clutching the green blanket. When he reached the mirror, he flung the blanket over it, blocking out all reflection.

"Cut!" called Schneider. "How was that? All right, Sam?"

"Exactly," Beckett said quietly.

We left him on the scaffolding, peering shyly and profoundly, and even a little inscrutably, down.

1 9 6 4

RED MITTENS!

Z ONGGGGGGGGGGGG! Innnnnnnnnn! *Swinging!* The four-year-olds and five-year-olds are . . . *swinging!* They're hot! They're so far in that they're coming out the other side. And they're fed up to the gillies with teen-agery. The teen-agers make the wrong *kind* of noise. Wear the wrong clothes. Dance around like nuts to the wrong sounds. Use too many words. Don't have pre-school style. Are physically barfy. Almost have wrinkles and attaché cases, for godsake! *Ah-yee-igh!* It's war! *Long live King Babar!* Last week, after mashed-potatoing our way through one of Tom Wolfe's sociopop essays in the *Herald Tribune,* we took a sampling in the children's playground at Fifth Avenue and Eighty-fifth. After morning kindergarten. After lunch. After *naps.* Herewith a report on our findings, for which we have borrowed a few leaves from that eminent socio-poppist's popperei:

"Ya-hoo-hee! Ya-hoo-hee! Ya-hoo-hee!" Shrieks come from five-year-old Teddy Bowen here, wearing a wiggy brown duffel coat, no hat, no gloves. He has chapped cheeks and a messy nose. He does not even live in the *neighborhood.* But he is in *charge.* "Yee-hoo-hoo!" screams Teddy as he swings. "Pooh-pooh! I need more gas! Push me! *Push* me!" His command is obeyed by Robert Levy's nanny, who—Holy Momsies!—strains her gillies pushing the swing. Robert Levy is the friend—who *lives* in the neighborhood—that Teddy Bowen is visiting. Robert Levy is small and thin of face, and he has big, worshipful eyes, which he trains on his hero, Teddy Bowen. It is Robert Levy now who starts with the Push Me thing, stooging it like crazy, yelling, "Pooh-pooh! I need more gas! Push me! *Push* me!" And Nanny falls to, pushing her guts out to please the little chaps. And true friend, true *neighborhood* friend, Pamela Tishman sits frozen and still in *her* swing. Old visitor Teddy Bowen has today become Robert's buddy-buddy, which leaves Pamela Tishman where? Until twenty minutes ago, *she* was Robert's true-blue. So Pamela sits in her swing, in her tight powder-blue Merry Mite snowsuit, her red mittens hanging down by strings—a soggy, wet, mushy, cat-smelling red wool mitten hanging from each Merry Mite elastic wristlet. Pamela's raw-red icy fisties! She'd like to smash them in the face of old visitor Teddy here. "I need more gas! I need more gas!" screams Teddy, and he—Robert's nanny outdoes herself to please—gets pushed higher and higher. Old runny-nose Teddy—where does *he* come off? He doesn't even have on a Tidykins snowsuit, like Robert's. A duffel coat! Circa 1963. Some chic! Now Teddy is yelling, "Hey! Let's go climb on Alice in Wonderland, hey!" And buddy-buddy Robert dittoes, "Hey! Let's go climb on Alice in Wonderland, hey!" They get out of the swings. Blam! Blam! Blam! Then General Chief of Police Big Daddy Cartwright Boss Teddy yells, "Hey, let's go to the carrousel!" The *carrousel,* for godsake! Pamela hasn't been to the carrousel in over six months, and she couldn't care less. The *carrousel!* Pamela feels . . . *superior*—well, why not? Pamela announces that she wants to go home and play with her Little Miss Echo Doll, and with her Tearie Dearie Doll, and with her Betsy McCall, Fashion Designer, set. Old visitor Teddy probably still self-educates around with Playskool junk. But . . . Nanny puts in the crimp. Nanny says to cool it, home is *out.* Pamela sulks. Then Pamela comes on aggressive—"Last week, I sat on Alice in Wonderland's *head,*" Pamela tells the chaps, just to impress them. They look . . . impressed. Pamela feels . . . *on top.* Nanny asserts herself some more and says that Alice is *out.* The carrousel is *out.* Pamela—this kid really *knows* what's out—says yeah, Alice, except for the head, *is* out.

On to the sand box. An idiot-faced baby girl is kneeling in the gunk, digging at it with a teaspoon. A *teaspoon,* for godsake! Idiot-faced baby has on a red coat, a red bonnet, patent-leather Mary Janes, and white stockings—*Yichhhh!*—and she is kneeling in the gunk on her white stockings . . . *excavating* . . . while her nanny sleeps. So Pamela Tishman sidles up to old baby and grabs the spoon and passes it to Robert, who sends it along to Teddy, who . . . heaves it—well, that makes Teddy Bowen *one of them.* Such yowls! Such woe! Holy Popsies! All from one idiot-faced baby, whose nanny wakes up and sees the *white stockings!* Covered with *gunk!* Now wide-awake—on the job—Nanny hauls choking, pained baby off to latest-model Krauty Karriage. Pamela Tishman is now buddy-buddy with Robert *and* with Teddy. The tribal drums! *Oh, Dondi, you hypocrite, let us study real life together!* Synesthesia! Old unholy triumvirate are now full of the Team thing. They scavenge a Baby's Pal Original rattle. A hairpin. A Texaco Fire Chief hat. *What next? What next? What next?*

On to the shoot-the-chutes. Like a flaming, souped-up, chicken-happy Triumph onto the protective rubber padding at the landing site slides . . . Miles Robertson. And behind Miles steams . . . Henry Sutro. "Kh! Kh! Kh!" they are rasping. *Total murder!* Both Miles and Henry are wearing khaki Army uniforms, and each has on a steel battle helmet decorated with this splendid four-color-job American eagle. They land, shooting Atomic Ray pistols at a little girl in Glenconner plaid with velvet leggings, who hollers desperately—*Come off it, Queen Victoria!*—for the Royal Mounties. "You know what, Henry?" Miles says to his pally. "I just shot a Zombie!" "I just shot a Beatle!" Henry says. "Kh! Kh! Kh! I just shot two Beatles!" They stand facing each other, their $9.50 Flex shoes digging into the rubber landing pad, shooting atomic rays at each other. A park attendant, broom in hand, is sweeping. He sweeps *around* Miles and Henry—do they exist, do they *feel?* "My daddy has a real gun!" Miles tells Henry. "My daddy has *two* real guns!" Henry tells Miles. *Kill! Kill! Kill!*

Then who enters the Garden of Allah on bootsied feet? Who but the transistor-radio pack, looking for space, a site, for an . . . orgy! What a racket! What sounds! The transistors give out with "Breaking Up Is Hard to Do" and "Now We're Through" and "Somebody Else Is Taking My Place" and "You've Lost That Lovin' Feeling" and "Bye Bye Baby." Hung up on sex, for godsake! Rejection! They are dragging these cretiny *guitars*—when anybody who's right in the skull knows that the *sound* is in Play Me E-Z Xylophones and Tuney Tinkle Triangles. These nutballs are singing about "The In Crowd" and "The Out Crowd." As if they knew! And they try to do tricks on the swings, and they break the swings! And they laugh funny, like crying! Nutty teen-agers!

"I'll kick them in the face!" yells Teddy Bowen.

"You better stick your hands up!" Loyal Sir Robert howls at the nuts. "Kh! Kh! Kh!"

Such noise! What it is is nuttiness . . . is what it is. Not like "The Three Little Kittens" or "London Bridge" or the story of "The Cuckoo Who Lived in a Clock." *Long live King Babar!*

"The Rolling Stones are nuts!" Pamela yells. "It looks so hot on their millions and drillions of hair!"

"Stop dancing!" Miles Robertson yells at the interlopers. He and Henry Sutro have joined forces with Pamela, Robert, Teddy.

"They scream!" Henry Sutro says. "They scream like babies!"

But the invasion is untouched. The pimply cretins are dancing in the playground, twisting and frugging and swimming in their above-the-knee skirts—stripes!—and crazy-pattern stockings and shifts decorated with stupid cans of soup, and their high black boots and furry awning eyelashes. And the boys in these tight blue jeans and these boring sweatshirts and leather jackets.

"You know what, Henry?" Miles Robertson says. "I had this baby-sitter. She was a real nutball. She took eight hundred pictures of the Stones off the television. Kh! Kh!"

"My baby-sitter wears pink-and-purple stretch pants!" Henry Sutro says. "She's ugly! Khhhhhhh!"

They look with disgust at the fuzzy-upper-lipped invaders. And who is the most recent arrival? A decomposing, decaying, arteriosclerotic, *aging* teenager. At least twenty-three! Clogged up with cholesterol. He's wearing the hair, the tight jeans, the leather jacket—*everything.* And he's being real cute . . . *identifying!* He climbs on the teeter-totter. The *teeter-totter,* for godsake! Nobody has gone near a teeter-totter since . . . last Christmas! He's flabby in the patellas. He's soft in the hypogastric zone. He's jowly. Jowly! Next thing he knows, he'll be a fatty. But there he sits on the teeter-totter . . . as if he thinks he's dripping *charisma,* for godsake! Pamela Tishman sonic-booms it, jumping on the other end of the teeter from old *identifier,* followed by Henry and Miles and Teddy and Robert. They give old blubbery Fred Flintstone here a rough, flashy totter and teeter. When Henry and Miles and Teddy and Robert and Pamela hit ground, they all cut out! At once! And old identifier makes the big crash on his soft, flabby, jowly, decaying, blubbery, cretiny innominates. The uglies stop dancing. They shut up. They pick up their fallen nut. They split. And Pamela & Co. exchange sneaky laughs. Just wait . . . wait, wait, wait. A few more ticks and tocks, and Pamela Tishman will show Baby Jane what is *really* what and who is . . . *here.*

1 9 6 5

JANE KRAMER

THE McLUHAN METAPHOR

W HEN the Westinghouse people announced that at the end of the World's Fair they will again bury a Time Capsule filled with assorted cultural and technological mementos of twentieth-century man, a friend of ours suggested that they should replace the codes and artifacts with Dr. Marshall McLuhan, who could be counted on to explain us vividly to anybody digging around in Flushing Meadow two thousand years from now. Dr. McLuhan, a professor of English at St. Michael's College of the University of Toronto, is also the director of the university's Center for Culture and Technology and the author of three startling books on Western civilization—"The Mechanical Bride," "The Gutenberg Galaxy," and, most recently, "Understanding Media," in which he joyfully explores the tribal virtues of popular culture, casts a cynical eye on the "classification traditions" that came in with print, and sees near-mythic possibilities in our computer age. He has compared the Bomb to the doctoral dissertation; discussed the "depth-involving" qualities of sunglasses, textured stockings, discothèques, and comic books; reported on the iconic properties of Andy Warhol's signed soup cans; and predicted a happy day when everyone will have his own portable computer to cope with the dreary business of digesting information. In so doing, Dr. McLuhan has earned a reputation among the cognoscenti as the world's first Pop philosopher.

Last week, Dr. McLuhan flew to New York to deliver a lecture at Spencer Memorial Church (which has its *own* reputation, as the world's first far-out Presbyterian congregation), and we took the subway to Brooklyn Heights to hear him. At the church, an old, oak-beamed building that was bustling with young McLuhan enthusiasts, we found the Professor sitting quietly in the pulpit while a young man in a green corduroy jacket and narrow trousers propped an enormous Rauschenberg painting against it. The young man, who turned out to be Spencer's minister, William Glenesk, explained to us that the poster was "left over from my Rauschenberg sermon." He then told the audience that he had been a fan of Dr. McLuhan's ever since 1951, when he attended the Professor's course on Eliot, Joyce, and the Symbolist movement at the University of Toronto. Dr. McLuhan, a tall, steel-haired man given to twirling a pair of horn-rimmed glasses in appropriately professorial style, stood up, thanked Mr. Glenesk, and remarked that the warm May weather was certainly as depth-involving as a good Rauschenberg or a good elephant joke. The new art and the new jokes have no strict, literal content, no story line, he said, and continued, "They are the forms of an electronic age, in which fragmented, dictionary-defined data have been bypassed in favor of integral knowledge and an old tribal instinct for patterned response." Several members of the audience nodded ecstatically, and Dr. McLuhan went on to tackle practically every cultural phenomenon from the tribal encyclopedia to the shaggy-dog story, from Shakespeare to Fred Allen, from the wheel to the electromagnetic circuit. He good-naturedly blamed Plato for writing down Socrates' dialogues and thus inaugurating "codified culture," and he praised the singing commercial for reinstating the old tribal institution of memorized wisdom. Every new technology, according to the Professor, programs a new sensory human environment, and our computer technology has catapulted us right out of the specialist age and into a world of integral knowledge and synesthetic responses. "The computer is not merely an extension of our eyes, like print, but an extension of our whole central nervous system," he explained. He paused, twirled his glasses, and went on to say that every new environment uses as its content the old environment—"the way Plato used the old oral tradition of the dialogue for his books and the way television now uses the story form of the novel and the movies"—but that it is the technological nature of any new medium, and not its borrowed content, that conditions the new human response. Pop Art, he said, glancing affectionately at the Rauschenberg, is merely our old mechanical environment used as the content of our new electronic environment. "One environment seen through another becomes a metaphor," he continued. "Like Andy Warhol's 'Liz Taylor.' Our new, non-literal response to the literal content of that blown-up and endlessly repeated photograph turns Liz into an icon. It takes a new technology like ours to turn an old environment like Liz into an art form."

Dr. McLuhan next suggested the possibility of a new technology that would extend consciousness itself into the environment. "A kind of computerized ESP," he called it, envisioning "consciousness as the corporate content of the environment—and eventually maybe even a small portable computer, about the size of a hearing aid, that would process our private experience through the corporate experience, the way dreams do now." Then he said, "Well, that's enough pretentious speculation for one night," and turned to Mr. Glenesk, who suggested that the audience have "an old Socratic go" at some questions and answers.

Mr. Glenesk thereupon introduced the Professor to some of the McLuhan disciples in the audience.

The first disciple told Dr. McLuhan that he had been amplifying several sounds in one room at the same time, to get the "depth-involving" sound that is part of Dr. McLuhan's brave new world.

"Must make one hell of a racket," Dr. McLuhan said approvingly.

A second disciple, a rather nervous woman from the neighborhood, announced that she could hardly wait to have an experience-processor of her own. "The way things are now, I never can remember anything," she said, and was immediately interrupted by a third disciple, a bearded student sitting next to her.

The student expressed equal eagerness for computerized ESP. "Gee, just think!" he continued. "I could go to sleep a painter and wake up a composer!"

"Terrifying," Dr. McLuhan said.

1965

LONG-WINDED LADY

WE have received another message from our friend the long-winded lady. She writes: "During the recent heat wave, all air ceased to flow through the streets of New York City. There was no air moving between the buildings, and what air had been trapped here stood still and began to thicken. There was nothing to breathe except heavy displeasure. Every time I walked into an air-conditioned restaurant, I felt very humble and thankful and anxious to sit down and start being good. I wasn't the only one. On the afternoon of the dreadful third of July (it was a Sunday), I was in the Adano Restaurant, on West Forty-eighth Street. I was happy. It seemed a miracle that the one restaurant in New York where I really wanted to be should not only be open on a Sunday, when so many places are closed, but be open on the Sunday of the longest summer weekend, and on a weekend so uneasy with the heat that even Manhattan's towering skyline appeared to waver under the fixed abyss that shimmered up there where Heaven used to be. At the Adano, the air-conditioning machine was producing ocean breezes. In this chaotic Broadway neighborhood, the Adano has always been an oasis of order and good manners and beautiful food, but that Sunday it seemed to have drifted here from another, more silent region. The restaurant is a wide oblong, with a low ceiling, lighted by star-shaped lamps of dull-yellow glass. The walls are decorated with large, placid still-lifes and views of Italian scenery, except for the rear wall, which has mirrors that carry the room into the far distance. The tables are plain and plainly set, with well-worn silver and with white linen napkins folded to stand up in smart points. Empty as it was, and with everything polished and shining, the restaurant looked like a dining room on a small, tidy ship. I was sit-

ting at the front, in one of three half-moon-shaped booths near the street door.
I faced the bar, and in the mirror behind the shelves of bottles I saw the reflection of grapes and apples in the rich still-life on the wall behind me and above
my head. And through the glass panels of the doorway I could see the street,
where the rose-red Adano awning cast a curious shadow on the burning sidewalk. Very few people passed. Once in a while, a wilted figure in summer un-
dress climbed the sweaty steps that lead to the ticket and information bureau of
the Blue Line Sightseeing Bus Tours, which is on the first floor of a poor old
brownstone across the street. The old house is one of three that still stand together there, but the two others have had their faces flattened out. The house
where the Blue Line people are has aged as naturally and as recognizably as a
human being might do. It is the same as it always was, except that too many
years have passed and life has not improved for it. There is a bar in the basement, but it was closed that Sunday. A man walked into the Adano suddenly
and then hesitated just inside the door, looking around him. He was a very
nice-looking, pale, thin man of about fifty, with not much hair, and he was politely dressed in a dark-blue summer suit, a snowy-white shirt, and a neat dark
tie with dots on it. When he spoke, he had a pleasant, squeaky voice. I am sure
he was a stranger in the city. He had an out-of-town look about him. I think he
had rashly left his nice air-conditioned hotel in the hope of finding a real New
York place, a place with atmosphere, where he would get something of the feeling of the city, and I think he must have wandered about for a while before he
happened into the Adano. He must have been getting a bit frantic, not wanting
to continue in the heat and loneliness, and not wanting to go back to the bore-
dom of a long afternoon in the nice hotel that is almost certainly exactly like all
nice hotels in big cities. Wandering around alone like that in New York City on
a Sunday is no good at all. He stood there looking at me and looking at the bartender and looking beyond us at the calm room, and at last he called out to the
bartender, 'Are you open?' 'Yes, we are open,' the bartender said benignly. He
was polishing a glass. The stranger walked over to the bar and sat up on a stool
and put his hands on the counter. 'Could I just sit here and have a beer, please?'
he asked. He sounded just the way I felt—on his best behavior. It was a day to
smile eagerly back at Good Fortune if she happened to look your way, a day to
say please and thank you and to watch your 'p's and 'q's and to look out for ladders and to watch yourself crossing streets, and so on—the heat had roused superstitious dreams and made us careful. People began coming into the Adano.
A family party, mother and father and three young children, walked in and
went straight to a table at the back. The mother and father immediately began
reading the menu aloud, and the children all sat forward and listened as intently as though they were at a story hour. Then two women walked in—tall,
strong, opulently shaped girls of about thirty who looked as though they must
be in show business. Their walk was sedate, as it well might be, because their
dresses did all the work—slinky, skintight, slithering dresses that recalled the

body of Circe, the gestures of Salome, and the intentions of Aphrodite. One dress was of white lamé sewn all over with tiny pearls and brilliants, and the other was of shiny baby-pink cotton striped up and down in thin lines with pink glass bugle beads. Each of the girls carried a cloudy gray mink stole and long gloves and a little fat handbag, and each of them, as she sat down, swept her right hand underneath herself to make sure her dress did not wrinkle, while her eyes went swiftly about the restaurant in a wary, commanding glance that took in everything there was to see. Then, without speaking to each other, the two girls examined the menu, and they ordered at once—food only, nothing to drink—and when the food began arriving they ate steadily. They emptied big plates of hot soup, plates piled with meat and vegetables, and plates with heaps of salad, and they ate a lot of crusty Adano bread with butter, and when all that was gone they had coffee—American coffee—and a slice each of glistening rum cake. While they were eating, they talked a bit—not much—but they never smiled, and as I watched them I began to be deeply fascinated by them, because their closed faces and their positive, concentrated gestures excluded every single thing in the world except themselves. Outside herself and what contributed to her, nothing existed for either of them. They were all flesh and color and movement, and yet they were like stone monuments whose eating time had come and who would, when they had finished eating, go back to being monuments. I watched them and I wondered at them, because I thought them untroubled by every emotion except anger, and free of all sensations except the sensations of satisfaction. They made no delay over their dinner, and when they had finished they paid their check and stood up and collected their belongings and walked out with the hypnotic sedateness with which they had come in. I turned my head to watch them go, and so did the stranger at the bar, and then he went back to admiring the restaurant he had discovered, and he seemed like the man at the ship's bar just after sailing time who still cannot believe that he has made it—that he is on board, at sea, and it is all as he imagined it. As much as anybody in New York that Sunday, the man at the bar of the Adano found himself where he had dreamed of being."

1 9 6 6

JAMES STEVENSON

RUNOUTS, KICKOUTS, AND POPOUTS AT GILGO BEACH

"I'M twelve years old," said a plump, cheerful, black-haired boy, marching across the sand, lugging the front end of an orange surfboard under one arm and the front end of a white surfboard under the other.

"So am I," said a slightly thinner boy, slogging along five feet behind the first, with the rear ends of the surfboards under *his* arms. "We're from Levittown."

The boys and the boards had just come wobbling out of an underpass beneath Ocean Parkway and were now crossing Gilgo Beach—six miles east of Jones Beach—toward the ocean. It was a cool, hazy Sunday morning. "I mowed lawns in Levittown until I earned the money for my surfboard," said the plump boy, who was wearing a blue-striped T-shirt and madras trunks, and who told us his name was Steven Cummings. "My father drives us over. He borrows my board and surfs, too, but only after the Fourth of July." He smiled a big smile, and a set of braces gleamed in the sunlight.

"A lot of our friends surf," said the thinner boy, who turned out to be Kevin MacNamara, and who was wearing the top half of a wet-suit above his shorts. "There's Johnny, and there's Mark—"

"*There's* a wave!" Steven yelled, and they lurched rapidly down to the water's edge. They separated—one boy, one board—and plunged into the cold surf, battled their way through the shore break, and paddled out toward the waves, where a dozen surfers were already sitting on their boards, waiting for the right wave, looking like black insects in their wet-suits.

A lean lifeguard in dark glasses and an orange parka was sitting on a bench nearby. "This is wonderful right now, but as the season goes on it's like the Black Hole of Calcutta; it's wild," he said. "We've counted six hundred to seven hundred surfboards in the water at one time, and on a good hot Sunday you can practically walk across the boards out there." He sighed, and told us his name was Michael Twohig. "Gilgo and Cedar Beach are the only ones on Long Island that really encourage surfing," he said. "We make rescues as far as we can see in either direction. Last summer, we made around four hundred— sometimes running forty or fifty a day." At his feet was a wooden pail full of coiled new rope, and next to it, stuck in the sand, was a three-foot torpedo buoy with a loop of rope. "The big danger is kids getting hit on the head by boards," he said. "That, and runouts. A runout is where you get a break in the sandbar and, depending on the wind and the tide, the water rushes back out at maybe ten miles an hour. You can't swim against it." He sighed again.

Four teen-age boys, deeply sunburned, were lying on towels inside an impro- vised lean-to of picnic tables, fifty yards down the beach. Four surfboards were resting against one table, and a transistor radio was playing "She'd Rather Be with Me." We said hello, and the boys—who were all staring at the sea—told us they had been surfing from six in the morning till around nine and were now waiting for bigger waves. A distant surfer was riding in front of a gentle wave about a hundred yards out, and as the boys watched the wave passed under him and he went head over heels into the water. "A good surfer doesn't fall off like that," one of the boys said. "He kicks out when there's no more left to the wave." He formed a wave in the sand, patting it into shape, and then—using the flat of his hand as a surfboard—showed us a proper kickout. "You ride as close to parallel as you can, and cut back and forth, and then you kick out"— he turned his hand abruptly, rotating over the top of the wave—"and you pad- dle out again."

"We've been here every weekend since January," one of the boys said. "And before that up to December."

"When the water's above forty degrees," another said, "we go."

"You can't compare surfing to anything," one said. "There's no feeling like sliding along on the face of a wave." He stood up and started to pull on his wet- suit.

"It's free!" another said. "No regulations!"

One of the boys said, "A lot of gremmies come out just to impress girls, and all they do is sit on their popouts."

"What's a popout?" we asked.

"A crummy board," the boy said. "Machine-made. And you can see the fibres going in all different directions in the resin."

The others began putting on their wet-suits. "Some girls are good surfers, but most of them just sit on their boards," one said.

"We don't mind!" another said, happily.

A short, dark-haired boy explained, "If the waves are like average, we'd go half the time with the waves and half with the girls, because you can always get average waves but you can't always get girls. But if the waves were *really* good, we'd go with the waves." He picked up his board and the others followed, walking down the beach in their black suits, their boards held overhead.

The two twelve-year-olds were just coming out of the surf, sopping wet, as we turned back, and we asked Steven, who was shivering a bit, how the waves were.

"Too small," he said, "and too cold. I'm going to get a hot dog."

We asked him what he likes about surfing and he thought for a moment, and then flashed his braces. "It's like having the power to command the wave," he declared, and Kevin nodded. "A sense of power," Steven added, and then they trotted toward the underpass, and the hot-dog stand, carrying the big boards.

1967

1970s

BIKE TO WORK

LAST Wednesday morning, it was definitively proved that it is possible to ride a bike through darkest morning-rush-hour Manhattan—all the way from Sixtieth Street and Fifth Avenue to Battery Park—and live. This important fact was established through the efforts of a young architect, Barry Fishman, and his wife, Harriet Green, who recently started an organization called Bike for a Better City. The Fishmans believe that biking is a healthy, friendly, quiet, inexpensive, non-polluting, fast, and practical means of transportation, and apparently a lot of New Yorkers agree with them. All told, about a thousand enthusiastic cyclists, including us, turned out for the Bike to Work Ride that kicked off the Fishmans' campaign for bike lanes on major thoroughfares.

At a quarter to eight, when we arrived on our battered English racer, several dozen cyclists had already gathered at the Grand Army Plaza entrance to Central Park, across from the Plaza Hotel. One of them was David Dubinsky, the president emeritus of the International Ladies Garment Workers Union. Mr. Dubinsky is a very short, solid-looking man with white hair and a sunny disposition. He was wearing a beret, smoking a cigar, and wheeling a ten-speed Hercules. "I've been riding for seventy years," said Mr. Dubinsky, who is seventy-eight. "When I came to this country, I was crazy for motorcycles, but who had the money for that? So I rode a bike. This is a new one. They already stole on me two good bikes."

"When did you get your first bike?" we asked.

"In 1937, the Union had a convention in Atlantic City," he said. "They wanted to get some kind of gift for me, so they asked my wife. She said, 'Get him a bike.' It was a nice thing to do, because when we were courting, I used to visit her on a bike. Before that, I had to rent. Look, here's Abe." He pointed to A. H. Raskin, of the *Times*, who had just wheeled up. "I often ride with him on Sundays in the park."

By this time, hundreds more cyclists had arrived. At 8:02, there was a commotion, and, once more, Mayor Lindsay's well-groomed head came into view in the middle of a crush of cameras and reporters. The Mayor took a piece of paper from his pocket and read a proclamation designating the day as Bike for a Better City Day.

A few minutes later, the Mayor took up his position at the head of the line. He was flanked by Charles Luce, chairman of the Consolidated Edison Company, and Jerome Kretchmer, the City's Environmental Protection Administrator, who had evidently found something they could agree upon. Nearby, Sid Davidoff, the Mayor's burly troubleshooter, was shouting instructions through a bullhorn.

"You got a bicycle, Sidney?" asked Mr. Kretchmer, who makes a point of always calling Mr. Davidoff "Sidney."

"You bet I do, Jerry," said Mr. Davidoff.

"Mr. Lindsay! Mr. Lindsay!" piped a female voice from the rear. The Mayor looked around. "Can we go?" the voice asked. "I have to get to school."

"And I have to catch a nine-o'clock flight to Washington," the Mayor said, and then he took off with startling speed, as if it were the Tour de France. Mr. Lindsay, moving out ahead of the pack, pedalled furiously down Fifth Avenue to Forty-sixth Street, where his limousine was waiting to take him to the airport. His performance was the more remarkable in view of the fact that his bike was a one-speed, coaster-brake model.

"The Mayor rides fast," we managed to say to Mr. Kretchmer, who was resplendently dressed in a cream-colored suit and a chocolate-brown shirt and tie, and who was setting a more reasonable pace on a shiny wine-red Raleigh.

"I've worked out with him, and he's in fantastic condition," said Mr. Kretchmer.

At the corner of Forty-second Street, a knot of pedestrians gaped at the extraordinary procession, and Mr. Kretchmer yelled at them, "Don't just stand there! Ride bicycles!"

"Cycling is basically a solitary activity," a man on a fifteen-speed Peugeot remarked to no one in particular. "When you ride a bike, you kind of go into a trance."

At the corner of Tenth Street and Fifth Avenue, where a policeman was directing the cyclists east, we pulled over and watched for a while. Because most of the cyclists were taking the unusual step of stopping for red lights, the line stretched out over many blocks. We were struck by the variety of bikes and the variety of the people on them, and by the fact that the majority of the cyclists seemed to be over thirty. A white-haired lady in a long black dress pedalled by on a penny-farthing—the kind of bicycle with a very large front wheel and a very small rear wheel which one often sees in old prints. A black girl careered past on a unicycle. A Rasputinlike hippie took the corner on a contraption that resembled a schematic model of the atom.

The last leg of the ride was on Broadway, where the police had been less successful in clearing a lane for the cyclists, and it was sometimes necessary to weave among trucks and honking cars. Nevertheless, two hundred or so managed to complete the ride to Battery Park, where we asked Ms. Green, a pretty, dark-haired woman in a gray pants suit, if the event had exceeded her expectations.

"Well, when my husband and I first thought of this, we had in mind thirty or forty people making a quiet statement by riding together," she said. "Only lately did we realize we were going to get such a tremendous response. It makes me hopeful that we'll really be able to get some bike lanes. Everybody was so friendly and respectful. I think people will realize that bikes really can make it a better city without tearing it down and building it up again."

Someone handed Ms. Green a bullhorn, she made a little speech, and the cyclists rang their bells in appreciation. Then the cyclists went their separate ways, and once again New York was Car City.

1 9 7 0

QUESTIONS AT RADIO CITY

THE most stupendissimo non-event of the Fall Publicity Season so far was the big, big Sophia Loren press conference at Radio City Music Hall last Thursday morning. The movie business has long conceived of the public prints as a transmission belt for the efforts of its public-relations departments. Joseph E. Levine, the president of Avco Embassy Pictures, which is distributing Miss Loren's latest film, "Sunflower," perfected this view of the function of the media by actually making the press a part of the show at its opening, at the Radio City Music Hall, and then charging admission for it. The reporters—there were five hundred of them—got in free, but the fifty-five hundred Loren fans who made up the cheering section paid for the privilege at the box office. The front third of the orchestra had been reserved for newsmen, studio officials, Rockettes (in mufti), and other privileged persons. When we arrived, at half past nine, the paying customers behind the press section were beginning to grumble. They had lined up early outside the Music Hall and had snagged what they assumed would be the choicest seats, and now it was dawning on them that their view of Miss Loren would be blocked by a dozen camera crews, who were in the process of setting up their equipment. Two of the paying customers, Mrs. Anna Marinello and her sister Mrs. Lucille Egitto, marched down the aisle to confront the authorities. They started yelling at a publicity man whom the privileged persons addressed as Sheldon.

"I'm up since four-thirty, I took my husband to the Fulton Fish Market, I'm here since seven o'clock, and now I can't see," said Mrs. Marinello. "I haven't got up that early in twenty years."

"Not only that but my train, the Seventh Avenue I.R.T. express from Flatbush Avenue, was on fire," said Mrs. Egitto.

"We didn't even have breakfast," said Mrs. Marinello.

"Please, darlings, be reasonable. There are seats on the other side," said Sheldon.

"Don't give me that baloney," said Mrs. Marinello. "There aren't any seats over there."

Sheldon struck a dramatic pose. "What shall I do?" he said. "Shall I kill myself?"

A booming disembodied voice announced that Miss Loren had been delayed in traffic but would arrive momentarily. Behind us, a couple of reporters were trying to predict what questions would be asked.

"How about 'Miss Loren, how do you like American men?' " said the first.

"That's *good*," said the second. "How about 'What are your impressions of the United States?' "

"Good, good. How about 'What is the secret of an ideal marriage?' "

The disembodied voice boomed out again, to introduce "the man who made all this possible, the president of Avco Embassy Pictures, Mr. Joseph E. Levine."

Mr. Levine, a stocky, benevolent-looking man, appeared in a spotlight at one corner of the stage and said modestly, "I'm not quite sure I'm solely responsible for this event. Much of the credit goes to the great producer, Mr. Carlo Ponti." Mr. Ponti, who is Miss Loren's husband, stood up in the audience and waved. He is stocky and benevolent-looking, too, and he was wearing big glasses.

Then Mr. Levine said that it was a pleasure for him to have the privilege of introducing Miss Sophia Loren. The huge gold curtains parted slightly, the audience cheered, and Miss Loren, wearing black velvet pants and a red silk tunic, entered stage center and smiled. She walked to a gold lectern surrounded by piles of chrysanthemums and made a few opening remarks. Unfortunately, the microphone did not begin to function until she had nearly finished them. ". . . affection that it reserves to a true friend. Thank you very much indeed," she said, with a slight accent. Much applause.

The dialogue that followed included these exchanges:

"Miss Loren, would you ever appear nude in a film?"

"Do you think this is a question you should ask among six thousand people?"

"Miss Loren, are you in support of the Women's Liberation movement?" (Cries of "No! No!" from the audience.)

"We are living in a male society for centuries, so what's wrong with woman giving a little push? But she must not forget her duties and responsibilities as a woman. She must not forget the qualities that make her the complement of a man, and vice versa."

"Miss Loren, what qualities do you consider make a woman a woman?"

"You mean an ideal woman? She should take care of her personal appearance, not be boring, and not show, even if she has it, too much intelligence."

"Miss Loren, what are your views on the braless movement?"

"What?"

"Miss Loren, do you have a special message for the Italians of America?"

"Me? I'm not the President of Italy. I can't tell you anything."

"Miss Loren, do you think your role in 'Sunflower' is perhaps your best performance since 'Two Women'?"

"Very much indeed so. It is a picture I care very much about. It is a story based on the everlasting pillars of human feeling."

And, at last: "Miss Loren, what is your formula for a happy marriage?"

"I can't tell you. It's something that you have got inside. Since I met Carlo, I have felt complete as a woman."

Miss Loren waved and bowed and disappeared. The reporters headed for the exits. We asked Sheldon where Miss Loren was staying.

"She's staying privately," he said.

We pondered this. "You mean at someone's house?"

Sheldon said a word that sounded like both "yes" and "no." We smiled at him in admiration. A word that sounds like both "yes" and "no" must be a useful one for a publicity man to know.

1970

THE POSTMASTER

I N 1921, William Faulkner, then aged twenty-four, became postmaster of University, Mississippi. He remained in that job until 1924, at which time he was fired. Shortly before the Post Office Department let him go, it sent him a letter, which, in a round-about fashion, has reached our hands, and which, to our knowledge, has not been published before. We print it in full, for whatever light it throws on the literary life:

Post Office Department
Office of Inspector
Corinth, Mississippi

Mark Webster,
Inspector

Case No. 133733-C
September 2, 1924

Subject: University Mississippi:
Charges vs the postmaster; neglects official duties; indifferent to interests of patrons; mistreatment of mail, etc.

Mr. William C. Faulkner
Postmaster
University, Mississippi.

Dear Sir:

The following charges have been made against you as postmaster at University, Mississippi:

1. That you are neglectful of your duties, in that you are a habitual reader

of books and magazines, and seem reluctant to cease reading long enough to wait on the patrons; that you have a book being printed at the present time, the greater part of which was written while on duty at the postoffice; that some of the patrons will not trust you to forward their mail, because of your past carelessness and these patrons have their neighbors forward same for them while away on their vacations; that you have failed to forward and properly handle mail for various patrons of the office, some of whom follows: M. G. Pasuer, Rev. W. I. Hargis, Miss M. W. Means, W. A. Scarbrough, Jimmy Jones, Judge Heminway and many others; that you have closed up the box of John Savage and others after they had paid their box rent and you had receipted them; that you returned COD parcel No. W22705, from John Ward, Mens Shoes, New York City, addressed to H. E. Ray Jr., after he had given you an order in person and left ten cents in money to forward to him at 924 Filmore Street, Corinth, Miss., and you had notified him for postage and he sent you postage from Corinth as per your order, yet the parcel was returned to senders marked "unclaimed."

2. That in addition to the above careless handling of mail you failed to deliver a letter to Jimmy Jones until after he had gone to your father (who is Secretary of University of Mississippi), and got a note regarding the delivery of same (Jones being a well known patron of your office); that on another occasion a contractor working at the University was compelled to get your father to help him get a package out of the office, which you had held for two or three days; that you placed two or three letters in the box of Mr. R. L. Sullivan (the box next to Chancellor Hume's box), which had been written to Mrs. Hume by Dr. Hume while away from home, and since Mr. Sullivan was away on his vacation these letters remained in the box of Sullivan, until placed in the box of Chancellor Hume by Assistant Postmaster Bell, some three or four days after Dr. Hume had returned home and had made considerable inquiry concerning same.

3. That you are indifferent to interest of patrons, unsocial, and rarely ever speak to patrons of the office unless absolutely necessary; that you do not give the office the proper attention, opening and closing same at your convenience; that you can be found playing golf during office hours.

4. That you mistreat mail of all classes, including registered mail; that you have thrown mail with return postage guaranteed and all other classes in the garbage can by the side entrance, near the rear door, which was addressed to the following patrons: F. E. Farquer, Howard B. Wallace, Wm. Ross Kennedy, University Store, Dean J. H. Dorrah, University of Miss. Hospital, Gordon Hall Boarding House, Alex L. Bonduarant, Mississippian, William R. Raley, Ricks Hall, Mrs. J. W. Harris, W. G. Kirkpatrick, Ike Edwards, Mrs. R. J. Shlhran, Forrest Woods, J. W. Bergman, C. O. Harris, Traber Dobbins, T. H. Samdrelette, Mrs. P. E. Irley, Chas. C. Evans, Taswdl P. Haney, Robt. Cannon, Walter Dement, R. E. Wilson and others; that this has gotten to be such a common oc-

currence that some patrons have gone to this garbage can to get their magazines, should they not be in their boxes when they looked for them.

5. That you do not prepare return receipts when requested by senders of registered mail; that you have two registered letters of foreign origin on hand that have been held since December 1921, and February 1922, that you have lost registered letter No. 104, from Arena, Miss., addressed to Mr. E. S. Roberts, and that you have carelessly handled several other registered letters.

6. That you do not give postage due mail proper attention, one instance being when a letter addressed to Rev. W. I. Hargis by Bank of Oxford, was held several days without notice being placed in addressees box, later being called for and delivered to senders.

7. That you have permitted the following unauthorized persons to have access to the workroom of the office: Dick Bell, D. B. Holmes, Jimmy Jones, M. A. Pigford and others, and have permitted card playing in the office.

You will please advise me in writing, within five days from this date, stating whether the charges are true, in part or wholly so, and show cause, if any, why you should not be removed. Failure to receive a reply in this prescribed time, will be deemed as evidence that you have no defense to offer, and action will be taken accordingly.

> *Respectfully yours,*
> Mark Webster
> Postoffice Inspector
> Corinth, Mississippi

1 9 7 0

ELVIS! DAVID!

A LOT was wrong with Elvis Presley's first-ever New York appearance, at Madison Square Garden last weekend. Somebody in the Presley organization misjudged the desires of the crowd, and as a result Elvis was preceded by a standup comedian called Jackie Kahane. No doubt Mr. Kahane's patter knocks 'em dead in Vegas, but New York is not Vegas and the Garden is not a night club. "Kids today . . ." said Mr. Kahane gamely, and lamely, as the audience clapped in unison. "I have a kid. Everything this kid eats turns to hair." He was finally booed off the stage. There was fault to find with Elvis's own performance as well. Instead of a rhythm section to back him up, he had a twenty-three-piece orchestra, a six-man rock band, and an eight-member chorus—a bit too much insurance, even for the Garden. The program was rigidly arranged and planned, allowing for little in the way of spontaneity, and it consisted largely of romantic ballads and sugary, easy-listening songs. The classics that most of the audience had come to hear—"Heartbreak Hotel," "Don't Be Cruel," "Hound Dog"—occupied only fifteen minutes of a fifty-minute program. The blandness was conceptual as well as musical, as when Elvis sang a non-controversial medley of "Dixie," "All My Trials," and the "Battle Hymn of the Republic." The gyrations that made the man famous were seldom in evidence. Instead, he offered a repertoire of stereotyped actions and heroic poses.

Oddly, none of this made any difference. The audience was ecstatic throughout. (It would have been ecstatic even if Elvis had sung nothing but Gregorian chants.) During the intermission before Elvis's appearance, our companion, a young woman who still has her Elvis scrapbook packed away in a trunk somewhere, told us a story that made it all quite comprehensible. "When I was twelve years old," she said, "I was riding in the car with my mother and brother, and a song called 'I Want You, I Need You, I Love You' came on the radio. I immediately felt a certain twinge. My mother said, 'This is that Elvis Presley they're all talking about. I don't see what all the fuss is about.' My brother said the same thing. I just sat on the back seat and didn't say anything. You see, I *did* know what all the fuss was about."

The lights went down, the orchestra struck up what used to be called "Thus Spake Zarathustra" and is now called "The Theme from '2001,' " the audience began a full-throated scream, and Elvis appeared. He looked magnificent. His coal-black hair was fuller and drier than in days of old, and he wore a fantastical white costume studded with silver. He strolled back and forth on the stage, accepting the plaudits of the crowd like a Roman emperor. He looked like an apparition, and this was appropriate, because he has been a figure of fantasy for seventeen years. As the performance went on, it became impossible to avoid the conclusion that he is a consummate professional. He never cut loose, but he did not have to. The slightest gesture of his hand, the smallest inclination of his head set off waves of screams from the favored direction. The greatest ovation, except for the one that attended his initial appearance, came when he went into the first of his old songs, "Love Me." "Treat me like a fool," he sang. "Treat me mean an' crool, but love me."

Throughout, Elvis maintained a certain ironic distance from it all, sometimes engaging in a bit of self-parody. At the beginning of "Hound Dog," for example, he posed dramatically on one knee, said, "Oh, excuse me," and switched to the other knee. But he manifestly enjoyed the audience's enjoyment, even as he indicated with a smile here and a gesture there that it all had less to do with him than with their idea of him. On our way out, we asked our companion if she had liked the show. "It was bliss," she said. "I haven't felt so intensely *thirteen* since—well, since I was thirteen."

WHICH brings us to David Cassidy. For some time now, millions of nice little girls all over the country have had mad crushes on David Cassidy. "Little" in this context means a bell curve that starts about eight, peaks about eleven, and ends about fourteen; "nice" means tractable and above the pauper line. They collect photographs of him, dream about him, write him letters, send him presents, and scream at the sight of him. Cassidy is a promising young actor with a pleasant singing voice and a smile that is sort of somewhere between cute and dazzling. He never meant to become an idol of little girls, but these things happen. A couple of years ago, he landed a part in a new TV sitcom called "The Partridge Family," which was about a fatherless American family that was a rock group but was also really just a family. Cassidy played the teen-age son of the family and the lead singer of the rock group. The show was a hit, so the Partridge Family started cutting albums of the songs they sang on the show, and

the albums were a hit, so Cassidy began making solo appearances as a singer.
Earlier this year, he came to New York and played to a packed house at the Garden. The day after the first Presley concert, he was back here for a matinée at
the new Nassau County Coliseum. Those who know about such things say that
Cassidy is on the verge of being jilted by the little girls, but in the latest issue of
16 Magazine, which is a trade magazine for little girls, he is still the leading attraction. Full-color picture on inside cover. Lead article on page 3. Last paragraph from that article:

> Now David is beginning to grow sleepy. There's a soft glow around him and he
> feels all warm and cuddly. Somehow—through a trick of his imagination per-
> haps—he feels the girl he longs for right there in the room near him, and mov-
> ing closer. As David drifts off into dreamland, he reaches out. He can feel her
> hand in his. He gently pulls her close to him, puts both his arms around her,
> snuggles up, smiles happily—and falls asleep holding his pillow in his arms.

The whole phenomenon is rather good-natured. The little girls don't take it entirely seriously. Neither does Cassidy.

There were a lot of little girls hanging around the motel that Cassidy checked
into before his appearance at the Nassau County Coliseum. We talked to a
number of them. One group banged on his door and woke him up. They then
called him on the phone to apologize and woke him up again. Another group
denounced the behavior of the first group as "teenile." A third group waylaid
us and made us write down their names in our notebook, so that we wouldn't
forget to convey their love to Cassidy. Our notebook says:

> mary and heather and vanessa and janet and sherry and nancy and debby
> and cynthia love david

The concert was sold out. As soon as Cassidy appeared onstage, the little girls
in the audience began to scream and to take pictures. All the cameras were
equipped with flash cubes, and all the flash cubes went off one after another,
squirting tiny bursts of light in Cassidy's direction. Flash cubes are a new form
of visual applause. We admired the girls' ability to do two things at once. During one of Cassidy's songs, some of the girls rushed the stage. Most of them
were headed off by several college-football players hired to augment the Coliseum's security staff, but one of them managed to grab Cassidy around his
neck and grapple with him for fully thirty seconds.

We interviewed Cassidy after the concert. He was sitting on a bed in another
motel, wrapped in a towel. His clothes hadn't caught up with him yet. He is a
small man—short, and narrow in the shoulders. He sits with his shoulders
hunched. He had a bruise on his back, and he said that the girls who had
rushed the stage had frightened him. He said that he liked most rock music but

that the years 1963, 1964, and 1965 had been the most important ones in forming his musical tastes. He said that he admired the Rolling Stones but found their recent albums disappointing. He said that Paul McCartney was his favorite songwriter and that in his opinion McCartney outranked Cole Porter and Rodgers and Hammerstein. He said that after he'd played the Garden he and his staff had sat around trying to figure out how much G.E. and Sylvania had made on flash cubes during his concert. The figure they came up with was nine thousand dollars.

1 9 7 2

ALMANAC

IN a world that is constantly changing and sometimes chaotic, the *World Almanac and Book of Facts* is a small buoy indeed but one that, whenever we stop to read it, ties us up for several hours. No matter how many trees went into the current edition, we think it was worth it. We cannot always get out into the woods when we need to, but we can read the *Almanac:* a thousand and forty pages, and each one contains something of interest, including pages 624 ("New Zealanders Eat Most Meat Per Capita"), 385 ("The Dynasties of China"), 215 ("Midnight to Dawn Best Time to See Meteors"), and 400 ("Widely Known Americans of the Present").

We examined the list (two hundred and ninety names) of widely known present Americans, and were sixty-three per cent pleased to discover that we know—or have heard of—every single one of them, from Ralph Abernathy to Ronald Ziegler, including the slightly more narrowly known, such as Derek Bok, Ray C. Bliss, and Lewis F. Powell. We were less than fully pleased only because we had just looked through "Entertainment Personalities of the Past" and drawn so many blanks.

We enjoy reading a list of towns and cities of twenty-five hundred or more population as much as the next person, and the names of Eutaw, Paragould, West Mystic, Frostproof, Palos Verdes Estates, Toast, Sweet Home, Midlothian, Ho Ho Kus, Moosic, Snohomish, and Aiea are, as always, a pleasure. Our greatest pleasure, however, is the collation and comparison of information. It took us less than forty-five minutes, for example, to figure out that the United States military has 292,491 commissioned officers on active duty in the *Almanac;* that there are more such officers than miles of railroad tracks in the entire country, members of the Amalgamated Clothing Workers of America, or square miles of Texas; that, assuming each officer to be ten feet tall, the entire officer corps put end to end would reach for 2,924,910 feet; and that at a rate of five hundred and fifty foot-pounds per second it would require a 5,318-pound horse to raise them a dollar with a pair (against which the odds are four to three) on the second hand. With a little more time, one could also calculate the number of famous religious leaders per mountain higher than fourteen thousand feet (including Colorado's Mount Conundrum), the estimated length of all home runs hit by major-league batters in 1972 in comparison to total yards gained passing and the distance between New York and Pittsburgh, and how much water has passed over Niagara Falls since last we met in terms of the number of persons that this water would supply if they were willing to drink it.

We do not recommend that you purchase a 1973 *World Almanac*; we do not recommend that you *not* purchase one. While it is good, of course, to have "Some Major Events and Trends of 1972" (page 35) at your fingertips, your old *Almanac* may be just as useful. After all, some things simply don't change. North America continues to lead all other continents in the number of telephones; the last winner of the Triple Crown is still Citation; the easternmost point in the United States is still West Quoddy Head, Maine; the major export product of Scotland is still whiskey; the Pope is still a Catholic; and Armenia still owes us money from the First World War. On the other hand, the amount of that debt keeps rising, and one needs a new almanac each year to get the latest figures. As of June 30, 1972, the Armenian war debt was $43,536,945.30, of which $31,577,045.30 was interest. According to the Treasury Department, only seventeen dollars and forty-nine cents has been paid back to us. The capital of Armenia is Erevan. The First World War lasted from 1914 to 1918. No matter how you look at it, seventeen dollars and forty-nine cents is not a lot of money, especially if you're paying that kind of interest.

1 9 7 3

MAYS AT ST. BERNARD'S

A YOUNG friend of ours in the fifth grade at St. Bernard's School, on East Ninety-eighth Street, called us up the other day to tell us that Willie Mays was coming there that afternoon to talk to the students about baseball. Our friend offered to cover the story for us and to write it after he came home from the dentist. His report arrived, as promised, and here it is:

Willie Mays spoke to the boys in the gym, where about a hundred and twenty-five of us sat around on the floor. Willie Mays stood up, looking very individual. He has great posture. He wore a beautiful suit of blue-and-white checks and a bright-blue shirt with a tie of many colors. Our headmaster, who usually wears a tweed jacket, was standing on the sidelines, and he kept smiling at Willie Mays happily. One of our older teachers stood at the entrance to the gym, peeking in, and she looked puzzled but terribly interested. Willie Mays said he loved to talk about baseball and the best way of talking about it now would be for him to answer questions. Everybody in the place, almost, raised his hand to ask a question, so Willie Mays started with a guy on one side, and then seemed to work his way over to the other side. The first question was "How come you don't use an aluminum bat?" Willie Mays said he liked wood better. He has a surprisingly light-sounding voice. He talked so fast, and the guys asked so many questions so fast, I caught about one question in five. I'll give you the questions I caught, with the answers Willie Mays gave:

Q: "What's the greatest play you ever made?"

A: "The greatest play I ever made was in high school or kindergarten. It was my first hit."

Q: "Do you think you could beat Babe Ruth's record?"

A: "I don't think I could beat anybody's record with my shoulders and legs in the shape they're in now."

Q: "Did you ever make a triple play?"

A: "Not yet."

Q: "When did you first know you were good?"

A: "Every time the ball went up in the air, I felt I could catch it."

Q: "What was your longest home run?"

A: "Well, I always felt this way—I never worry as long as the ball goes over the fence."

Q: "Did you want to get traded?"

A: "I don't have anything to say about it. My gosh, man! Do you want to get homework? You don't have anything to say about it—right, man?"

Q: "Who is your favorite pitcher?"

A: "It never made any difference to me as long as I could hit the balls."

Q: "Who'd you hit your six-hundredth home run off of?"

A: "Mike Corkins, of San Diego. Now, you didn't think I'd remember that, did you?"

Q: "What made you become a baseball player?"

A: "I just liked baseball."

Q: "How many kids do you have?"

A: "One. He's thirteen."

Q: "How many good seasons have you had?"

A: "Eight."

Q: "Which do you like better—grass or that composition stuff they play on?"

A: "I like grass better. I know my legs and what they do according to the way the ball bounces. But on this new stuff you find the ball bounces all kinds of ways. It's not reliable. On grass, you *know.*"

Q: "Do you feel sorry about anything you ever did in baseball?"

A: "The way I feel about anything I've ever done, I feel you can't look back. Always look forward."

Q: "How do you keep yourself in such good condition?" (Our gym teacher asked this one.)

A: "I sleep a lot. I don't eat too much. I eat a big breakfast—three eggs, sausage, coffee, juice. All that kind of stuff. But I eat only two meals a day. Most guys eat three. Some eat four. I play golf. I walk a lot. But eating and sleeping, those are the main things. I sleep during the day. I don't mean you have to *sleep.* Just lie down. Rest. Relax yourself. Do you guys realize how old I am?"

"Forty-two!" (This was yelled by almost everybody in the gym.)

Q: "What do you do when you're sitting on the bench?"

A: "We talk a lot."

Q: "How long did it take before you got famous?"

A: "I never think about things like that. When you're playing a sport, you don't worry about being famous. You think about catching the ball, doing the best you can at that particular moment."

Q: "Do you think baseball is a rough sport?"

A: "It *is* a rough sport, man! That ball is coming at you at ninety miles per hour. Man, that's rough."

Willie Mays wrote a lot of autographs after he stopped answering questions. Then he drove away in his car, which is a pink limousine with a white roof.

1973

ELSEWHERE

CHRISTMAS shopping is almost a science with our friend Lola Finkelstein, who has been educating us in this and that recently.

"The most exciting way to shop, and the most fun way, is *elsewhere*," Lola told us the other day. "The whole point is to get *what* other people don't and *where* they don't. For example, where do I get a Christmas present for my kitchen?"

"What Christmas present for your kitchen, Lola?" we asked.

"Wallpaper. I don't want a wallpaper you see in all the trendy, newly done homes. So I get wallpaper at Zuber Rieder, in Paris, on the Boulevard Beaumarchais. There's no question but that American wallpapers are superior in all the practical ways. But for my kitchen I got a classic Portuguese tile, in light blue and white, on heavy glazed paper. I packed it in a suitcase and took it home with me. It weighed a lot. My children think I'm nutty, and the paperhanger said, 'Not another of those terrible French papers that fall apart when you pick them up!' But the whole point is that *I* like it when I look at it. Now, my friend Mimi, who lives in Switzerland, comes to New York to do a lot of *her* shopping. She wants Woodson wallpaper, because she wants an American wallpaper that doesn't look like traditional European walls. She gave her daughter's bedroom a present of Woodson wallpaper showing a stylized bouquet of spring flowers, with bedspread and curtains made to match. But my friend Angelica, who lives in Rome, goes to *London* for wallpaper. Colefax & Fowler. Angelica lives in a fourteenth-century palazzo, and it's believed to be the only palazzo in Rome with English wallpaper. You know—those romantic, bucolic motifs, with lots of shepherdesses and animals. Mimi goes to South America for her doorknobs, but maybe that's *too* special."

"What about presents for people?" we asked.

"Well, take panty hose," Lola said. "Mimi wears panty hose exclusively from Saks, but I get mine at Marks & Spencer in London. When I look at mine, I have the feeling that I'm wearing hose from an English institution known for the best quality at the lowest prices. Everybody in England calls it Marks & Sparks. And you can return *anything* there. Or take underwear. For our husbands. My husband used to wear Sulka cotton-mesh undershorts, which he bought in Paris, but after the dollar was devalued, Sulka stopped carrying this type of cotton undershorts. So Mimi sends my husband cotton undershorts from Zimmerli, made in Switzerland. I found cotton undershorts in Marks & Sparks, but my husband won't wear any except Zimmerli's. Mimi's husband likes wool undershirts only. There's only one place that makes them, and it's in Rome. So Angelica gets them as a present to send to Mimi's husband in Switzerland. Angelica's husband won't wear any underwear except underwear from Macy's. So I go to Macy's and get him *that* as a present and ship it to him in Rome. You get the idea?"

"Yes, Lola," we said. "But isn't that a very expensive way to shop?"

"Not when you get it all together," Lola said. "Now, my husband likes Lanvin pajamas, made in Paris. They're cut slimmer than American pajamas, and you don't get all that flapping around. I went to buy some and was absolutely appalled at the price. So I sent one pair of the Lanvin pajamas to Ascot Chang, in Hong Kong—he's a well-known shirtmaker—and he copies the Lanvin pajamas for my husband. It helps even things out. Or people in London go to Mothercare, where you get very inexpensive, high-quality things for babies, and send me underpants for my granddaughter, while I'm getting Carter's baby stuff for Angelica in Rome. The general idea is that I like European things because using them reminds me every day of pleasant experiences. But Mimi feels there's much more variety here, and she is bored by what enchants me. Mimi buys her kids jeans from Sears Roebuck and wash-and-no-iron stuff from Bloomingdale's. Angelica gets her kids cotton knits at Bloomingdale's. But I get kids' clothes at—"

"Marks & Sparks?" we asked quickly.

"You're catching on," Lola said. "I go to Kids in Gear, on Carnaby Street, once in a while, too. And I get Scotch smoked salmon in London—at the Safeway supermarket on the King's Road. There's a very nice girl named Maureen who is the fish girl, and she cuts and slices the salmon like an artist and places each slice on a separate piece of paper and wraps it up beautifully, so that it can travel in my suitcase. Mimi likes to eat stuff from California. I get her Fun in the Sun Marshmallow Candies from Palm Springs. Angelica likes Nabisco graham crackers and Ring-Dings—stuff like that. But I like to munch on McVitie's Digestive Biscuits, which a London friend sends me from Harrods. And Mimi sends me chocolates from Zurich, while I send her Mary Jane peanut-butter bars from here."

"Anything else?" we asked.

"Notebooks," Lola said immediately. "Mimi won't write in anything except those spiral things I buy for her in Woolworth's. And Angelica wants Brett notebooks. You know, those black-and-white sort of speckled composition books with the hard covers—the kind we had in school. But I use notebooks from Smythson, in London, or Prisunic, in Paris. Everyone who knows me knows I like notebooks with graph paper—even index cards of graph paper, which you get in France. People send me those every December."

"Very nice," we said.

"Very," Lola said. "It's important to keep up people's *morale*. You've got to find things that make people feel cheered up by something. I've got a friend, a writer, who won't write on anything except Blokk-Notes. From Norway. These Blokk-Notes just happen to make this writer feel cheered up. So why not?"

"Agreed," we said.

"Every Christmas, Angelica sends me some tortellini and other pasta right out of Rome, and that really cheers me up," Lola said. "I bought some Chinese tennis balls, made in Shanghai, and my problem now is to find someone who really prefers them."

1 9 7 3

"WONDER BAR"

ROLLING home from the best Christmas party of the year (at Perez Print-ing, a small print shop in SoHo), we saw a gladsome sight: "Wonder Bar," a hilarious old Jolson movie that practically never gets shown in theatres, was playing at the Bleecker Street Cinema. How could this be? We dashed inside and met Les Rubin, president and founder of Movie Musicals, Inc., at the Bleecker Street Cinema—a brand-new outfit dedicated to renting the B. St. C. on weekends for the purpose of showing superior old movies.

"I just had to do this," said Les Rubin, whose background is: social director at a bungalow colony in the mountains; assistant manager of the first Jay Goldin campaign for comptroller, in 1969 (the time he ran as "the young dynamo"); public relations. "I have a little girl. I want to show her all the great movies. But 'Meet Me in St. Louis' can only be seen at 3 A.M. on television. What should I do? Get her up? And have my wife holler, 'It's school tomorrow'? So here we are. This is our second weekend. And what has everybody said? 'Les, how *could* you? The worst two weekends in the year. First the ice storm. Then Christmas.' But, I'll tell you, we took in three hundred dollars last Sunday. People came in, and their boots and shoes were *all* salt. Eight students from Adelphi came all the way from Garden City. Look, this place is not for cinema buffs. I am only running movies I think are good enough to be just plain entertainment."

Movie talk ensued. We told Les we loved Ann Miller, and he told us she had made a Second World War movie called "Reveille with Beverly." We asked him to try to find a movie whose name we can't remember but that costars—we *think*—John Barrymore and the Ritz Brothers. He told us he had for sale the only copies of the record of the original Judy Garland sound track of "Annie Get Your Gun."

"Nostalgia!" said Les. "Unh, how I hate that word! I just want to show people things they don't know and want to know. Look at my partner, Larry."

A guy came out of the ticket booth and we looked at him. It was Larry. "Larry has an M.A. in meteorology," said Les. "It wasn't until *tonight* that he realized there was a difference between William Powell and Dick Powell. And look what it's done for him! He just had a brilliant idea. We put a big sign out front that says, '40° WARMER INSIDE.' "

Then we took in the midnight show of "Wonder Bar."

1 9 7 4

HENDRIK HERTZBERG
AND GEORGE TROW

DYLAN

WE had breakfast Thursday morning with two friends (one blond, the other dark-haired, both recently turned thirty) who had been to the Bob Dylan concert at Madison Square Garden the night before. "I'll tell you some people who were there," our blond friend said. "Yoko Ono was there. Her seat was two rows in front of Dick Cavett's. Pete Hamill and Shirley MacLaine were there and had seats four rows ahead of Yoko Ono's. That's six ahead of Dick Cavett. James Taylor and Carly Simon were in the vicinity, and I want to tell you that this is only the *back* part of the front section of the orchestra I'm talking about. I couldn't see the *front* part of the front section, where one assumes the real heavies, Yeats and so forth, were sitting. I'll tell you some people who weren't there. There were no blacks there, and no transvestites, and there were very few people in embroidered jeans. Instead, there were extraordinary numbers of people who seemed to have come directly from registration at the New School. A very earnest group. One of my problems with old Dylan has to do with humor, you see. I don't think he has any. Which is why the blacks and the transvestites stay away. I personally don't *trust* any rock-and-roll concert without a single transvestite, but never mind. The point is that Dylan has irony—I mean, he knows how to milk a juxtaposition—but no humor. He reminds me of a guy I went to school with who was very bright and very ambitious and who just missed starring in 'Zabriskie Point.' My schoolmate sang songs about Franco in the offices of our school newspaper in 1957, but luckily he was completely tone-deaf and had to go into the social sciences."

"What's *that* all about?" our dark-haired friend said. "We're talking about a *Bob Dylan concert*. Look at it from the Dylan-can-do-no-wrong angle, which is how I look at it. All through his career, Dylan has been a highly elusive figure. He always manages to free himself from the expectations of his audience. When they were expecting folk songs about the struggles of the thirties, he gave them folk songs about the struggles of the sixties. When they were expecting a revolutionary anthem with all the answers, he gave them a revolutionary anthem that was all questions. 'The answer is blowin' in the wind'—was there ever a better summing up of the intuitive, improvisatory, unreflective approach of what we used to call 'the Movement'? When people expected acoustic, he gave them electric. When they expected funk, he gave them mysticism. When they expected psychedelia, he gave them simple country love tunes. When they finally learned not to expect anything in particular except genius, he gave them mediocrity. So. The first half of the concert felt strange—a little disappointing, a little disorienting. Dylan sang too fast, in a sort of strong, high chant, and he virtually obliterated the melodies—to no purpose. Or so I thought at intermission time. But in light of what happened in the second half of the concert, I look upon the whole first half as a necessary softening-up process for both Dylan and the audience. The room was full of complicated yearnings, after all. He was singing his old songs, and he had to avoid the dangers of a 'Dylan's Greatest Hits' atmosphere, so he recast them in such a way that you had a hard time recognizing them and a rather hard time enjoying them. He was nervous but not hostile. He had to establish the right mixture of friendliness and distance. He had to make it plain that he goes his way and others, including the audience, go theirs."

"And the second half of the concert?" we asked.

"Ah," our dark-haired friend went on. "Dylan came out all alone, small and brave, with just his harmonica and his acoustic guitar. I was too far away to see the details of his face, but I could see his hair, curly and mousy, and that tense, crabbed stance. He sang 'The Times They Are A-Changin'' and 'Don't Think Twice, It's All Right' and 'Gates of Eden'—still too fast, still in that almost strangled high chant. Then, halfway through 'Just Like a Woman,' it started to get magical, and when he sang 'It's All Right, Ma (I'm Only Bleeding)' it all fell into place. He was still fooling with the melody, but with a purpose. I felt I was hearing that song for the first time instead of the thousandth. When he sang the line about 'But even the President of the United States sometimes must have to stand naked,' everyone cheered, of course, but they cheered even louder for the line 'And it's all right, Ma, I can make it.' After The Band came back on again, he sang a couple of very pretty new songs, and then 'Like a Rolling Stone.' People began streaming down the aisles, and everyone stood up—there was no particular cue; we just all stood up at once. Dylan's accompaniment for the chorus was the whole audience—twenty thousand people singing 'HOW DOES IT FEEL?' at the top of their lungs. The houselights were turned on, so we could all see each other, and four huge klieg lights went on behind Dylan, making everything—Dylan, us, the music—seem half again as big. He did two encores: a reprise of 'Most Likely You Go Your Way (and I'll Go Mine),' much more melodic and accessible this time, and 'Blowin' in the Wind.' I'd never heard him sing it quite that way before. He never does anything the same way twice. His voice was clear, strong, and true. He pulled it off—he kept the myth intact."

"Personally," our blond friend said, "when it comes to mythic figures I prefer the ones like Elvis Presley, who stay mythic in spite of themselves. Dylan was never really a successful archetype, if you know what I mean. He was only someone who seemed to be somewhere we thought we ought to be. That's why people worried so much about his changes of style. People worried about where Dylan was and what he was doing because they wanted to know where *they* should be and what *they* should be doing. The style changes prophesied— falsely, perhaps—some kind of movement, and that mercurial quality of his appealed to our generation's love of novelty. But now, you see, he has run out of ways to seem some distance *ahead,* and has fallen back on devices that will allow him to seem (at all but a few carefully chosen moments) some distance *away.* It's a little sad to fight so hard for Mythic Distance."

"But that's precisely what I like about him," said our dark-haired friend. "He lives by his wits."

1974

NEW BOY

Whatever your interest, it is catered for in these compact, fun-packed, fact-packed IMPACT pages.—*The National Star*, Volume I, No. 1.

THE word "exclusive" appears five times on the front page of the first issue of the *National Star*. The word "win" appears four times. "Super" turns up twice. Other words and phrases that occur on that same page include "top pop," "top heart throb," "top beauty," "craze sweeping the world," "Prince Charming," "tot tycoons," "personality parade," "zinging showbiz," and "a newspaper for all the family." Inside, the self-promotion is maintained at a level that calls up a mental picture of an over-stimulated newsstand operator, eyes bulging, screaming his pitch at a startled pedestrian an inch or two away: "WATCH THE SUPER SHOOTING STAR EVERY WEEK. . . . AMERICA'S LIVELIEST NEWSPAPER. . . . ALWAYS . . . IN THE STAR. THE PICK OF THE PIX. . . . LET THE STAR LOOK AFTER YOU AND YOUR FAMILY—IT'S THE PAPER THAT CARES. . . . KEEP AHEAD OF THE TRENDS WITH THE STAR. . . . CATCH THE SWINGING STAR. . . . SUPER . . . SUPER . . . SUPER . . ."

Rupert Murdoch, who publishes the *Star*, and Larry Lamb, who edits it, are very good at selling newspapers. Mr. Murdoch, who is forty-two years old, Australian, and dynamic, has spent the past nineteen years building up the third-largest newspaper-publishing business in the world. Except for the San Antonio *Express* and *News*, both of which he bought in December (and the *Star*, of course), his newspapers (seventy-nine, all told) are in Australia, New Zealand, and Great Britain. His Fleet Street Sunday paper, the legendary *News of the World*, sells over six million copies a week, giving it the largest circulation of any English-language newspaper on Earth. His greatest success, though, is the London morning tabloid the *Sun*. When Mr. Murdoch bought the *Sun*, in 1968, it was a journalistic zombie with a circulation of "only" eight hundred thousand. He installed Larry Lamb as his editor, and together they refashioned the *Sun* according to a formula that relies heavily on short sentences, a simple vocabulary, melodramatic headlines, the hard sell, and (this was the distinctive Murdoch-Lamb contribution to British daily journalism) big pictures of pretty girls wearing nothing from the waist up. The *Sun* now sells over three million copies a day and is inching up on its archrival, the *Daily Mirror*.

The *Star* is apparently an attempt to transplant the *Sun*'s style of British pop journalism to the United States. The *Star* is wordier than the *Sun*, and the topless pinups have been omitted, but the similarities are more striking than the differences. Like its British cousin, the *Star* has a flashy, busy layout, with the punchy headlines ("I'VE LET HUNDREDS DIE SAYS MERCY DOCTOR") interwoven among the blocks of text instead of perched primly above, as is the American custom. The *Star* has a column called "Liveliest Letters," consisting of banal anecdotes purportedly sent in by readers, and so does the *Sun*. Most of the *Star*'s copy editors are British, and a few examples of British English slipped into the first couple of issues. We noticed, among others, "switched on" for "turned on," "whisky and soda" for "Scotch-and-soda," "post your coupon" for "mail your coupon," "motoring" for "driving," "Willy Mays" for "Willie Mays," "sport" for "sports," "in hospital" for "in the hospital," and "slimming" for "reducing." Several years ago, someone bought London Bridge, took it apart, and reassembled it in the middle of a desert in Arizona. London Bridge is now one of Arizona's chief tourist attractions. As for the *Star*, its first issue sold more than a million copies.

Larry Lamb went home to England last week to oversee the *Sun*'s coverage of the British general election, but before he left we dropped by for a word with him in the *National Star*'s offices, at 730 Third Avenue. Mr. Lamb is a tall, rugged-looking Yorkshireman of forty-four. "Why are you putting out this paper?" we asked him.

"We are in the publishing business, so we publish," he said. "We enjoy new experiences, and this—America—is the biggest English-speaking audience in the world. We feel American publishers have got away from readers. They're going after the top-twenty-per-cent income group. They're trying to please advertisers and win Pulitzer Prizes. We're not. We're trying to please readers. Journalists and advertisers tell us the *Star* is awful, so we know we've got it right." Mr. Lamb told us that Mr. Murdoch, whom he calls "the Chairman," is prepared to spend five or six million dollars promoting the *Star* on television, and that the *Star* will make its money through circulation, not through advertising. "If one regards the promotion as a long-term investment, we are very close to the break-even point already," he said. "We have funds available. We are not accustomed to failure."

"How come there's no cheesecake in the *Star?*" we asked. "Do you think Americans are more straitlaced than the English?"

"Let's say Americans are less permissive," he said. "The *Sun*'s kind of sauciness is not appropriate to the market here. There's a market for a very hardcore, clinical kind of sex but not for the light, bubbly eroticism that's part of the *Sun.*"

"How about politics? Do you have any?"

"Yes. In the last election, our Australian papers supported the Labor opposition, because we thought it was time for a change, but that wouldn't stop us backing the other side next time. Both the Chairman and myself are, I suppose, slightly left of center. We try to judge political issues as they arise rather than in a political-party context, but we think it's cowardice to sit on the fence."

"Does that mean that the *Star* will support particular Presidential candidates?"

"Yes," Mr. Lamb said.

On our way out, we stopped off in the newsroom to say hello to Stan Mieses. Like a half-dozen others on the *Star*'s editorial staff of twenty-eight, Mr. Mieses was recruited from the New York *News,* where he wrote a Sunday column on pop music. The *Star* bills him as "the rock jock who knows where it's at." Mr. Mieses, who is twenty-one, said he was enjoying his new job.

"There's nothing negative in this paper," he said. "I've got stories back for rewrite with a little note saying 'Not sufficiently optimistic.' If you want to be bummed out, you can pick up the *Times,* the *Post,* or the *News.* I look at this paper as an AM paper. Not as opposed to P.M.—as opposed to FM. The *Star* is like Top Forty radio. It comes at you like Murray the K."

1 9 7 4

FANCY

WE breezed through the Twentieth Annual National Fancy Food and Confection Show the other day, trying a cheese here and a nut there, a cookie, a glass of wine, a pickle, a cup of soup, a candy, a chocolate, a slice of salami—all of which added up to the ruination of our summer diet. As we were going into the Coliseum, where the show was held, we ran into Peter C. Simon, Sr., the slim, high-keyed, suntanned, elegant owner of Ellens, a gourmet shop on Madison Avenue near Eighty-sixth Street. Mr. Simon told us he was appalled by the mob of noshers and grabbers he had seen at the show. "The management is letting in all kinds of outsiders, and they're eating themselves sick," he said. "With the cost of eating now, these people stay all day, making three, four, five meals of it. Last year, the show was held in Chicago, and nobody unofficial was allowed in. There was only tasting—not *eating.*"

"Have you tasted anything here that impressed you?" we asked, sampling some Hawaiian Macadamia Nut Banana Crunch and washing it down with a Hawaiian Sun Guava Drink.

"Filets of smoked rainbow trout!" Mr. Simon called out. "Divine! Succulent! Smoked turkey out of this world! Personally, I hate smoked turkey. It's always dry. But I can't stay away from *this* turkey. Juicy. Moist. Marvellous. Don't miss it! Or the trout! Booth 15. High Valley Farm, from Colorado Springs." Mr. Simon turned away as we offered him a bit of Banana Crunch. "Please! I've got to stay alive to do my ordering here. I'm getting barley-sugar reindeer and tiny, tiny gingerbread houses. For Christmas."

We made a beeline for Booth 15, sampled the turkey (Mr. Simon had not given us a bum steer), sampled the trout, and then moved along to other booths, having some Souper Noodles, shrimp-flavored (manufactured by the Sammen Shokuhin Company, Ltd., of Amagasaki, Hyogo, Japan). After that, we stayed for a long time, in a trance, munching jumbo colossal natural pistachios from Iran and colossal Brazilian cashews from Brazil. Then, all perspective in a mishmash, we ate the old triangular Toblerone chocolate in a white-chocolate version. After that, dying of thirst, we went back to the Hawaiians and gulped a few paper cupfuls of Kona coffee—black. Slowing down, we headed for the exhibits from the Netherlands and listened carefully to a very nice woman named Margot de Hartog, who explained to us the nature of Jos. Poell's pastry shells.

"They are crispy, flaky, paper-thin," she told us. "You make a filling of veal and bouillon, and you stuff it into them. Are you Dutch?"

"No," we said.

"You sound Dutch," said Miss de Hartog. "Did you know that Hollanders have the longest longevity, and the lowest death rate at childbirth? We all eat a lot of sweets. Every second shop is a sweetshop."

"How are Dutch teeth?" we asked.

"No trouble. Teeth good. Cholesterol good. We do a lot of bicycling. We are great swimmers. Great skaters. We work it off. We live long. Take this package of *chocolade hagel.* Everybody in Holland has this in the house. Put it on the children's breakfast, the way we do in Holland. It makes them eat."

"Chocolate *sprinkles?*" we asked. "On bacon? On eggs?"

"On anything," Miss de Hartog said. "Here. Try this Dutch Dandy cheese. It's new. It's different. A very mild, semisoft cheese. Something that everybody else does not have. Do you like it?"

"Delish," we said, sprinkling some *chocolade hagel* on it. "Double delish."

"That is correct," Miss de Hartog said. "Now, you skate, and you live long."

We went back to the U.S.A.—Booth 1212, the Dickinson Family, from Portland, Oregon, presided over by Bob Brown, a hearty laugher. "We've always made a very fine line of Northwestern preserves," he told us. "Every one of our preserves is hand-poured. They are made in three-and-a-half-gallon batches. Wild-mountain-blackberry preserves. Golden-peach preserves. Apricot-pineapple preserves. Boysenberry jelly. Do you know what street we're on? Wild Blackberry Square!" Mr. Brown gave us his hearty laugh. He was chewing, and we asked him what.

"Look," he said. "This is what a can of our salmon looks like." He opened a can of Dickinson Family smoked salmon. "Pacific silver salmon. Caught off the mouth of the Columbia River, *before* they start up the river, which means the meat is firm. This fish is smoked over alder wood for seventy-two hours, and then the drippings are poured back into the can. Have some. . . . Well?"

"Delish," we said.

We were joined by a tall, bony maiden wearing a folksy native Austrian costume.

"Here she is, back again! Help yourself, my dear!" Mr. Brown said, laughing heartily. "My Austrian neighbor from across the aisle!"

"I come alvays *für* snocks!" the Austrian maiden said, snacking the salmon.

"She can't stay away from our salmon!" Mr. Brown called out.

"You come to see me *für* vhite vine aftervard," she said.

"Thank you, my dear," said Mr. Brown. "Let's go right now."

We were greeted at the Weinland Österreich Booth by a tall young man, with a big, long face, who looked like the Austrian maiden's brother.

"Vhite vine," she ordered, for Mr. Brown and us.

"Aren't you joining us?" Mr. Brown asked, graciously.

"I prefer the red," she said. "But they say the fish has to svim in the vhite."

"Vhite and red both, ve have had good response," said her brother. "Austrian vines are very Austrian. Charming, light, and fresh. *Spritzig.*"

"You said it. Wow, this is good!" said Mr. Brown.

"Now ve go back for more salmon," said the Austrian maiden.

"O.K., my dear," said Mr. Brown, and he gave us a hearty wave.

We headed for the Twining Tea Booth and shook hands with the Englishman in charge.

"Anything new?" we asked.

"Our Twining tea bags are now packaged exactly like the loose tea," he said. "We're saying, 'Twining Tea Bags are twins to our tins.' "

"Who thought it up?" we asked.

"Somebody in America, I believe," he said. "More and more people in America are going in for good tea, you know. We've just come out with a new one—Indian Breakfast Tea. Made from Assam. On a hot afternoon, our Earl Grey is delicious. At night, when you're weary, the Jasmine is good. But there's nothing better in the morning than a good, strong cup of tea. It pulls you around."

We were still very thirsty, but Twining wasn't offering samples, so we moseyed about, pausing at the headquarters booth of the Twentieth Annual National Fancy Food and Confection Show. The woman in charge told us the show was a big success. She was eating a hot dog on a bun, with sauerkraut, and sipping a sugar-free cola drink.

"What's the idea?" we asked, watching her take a big bite of the hot dog.

"I got it out on the street, at the corner," she told us, without apology. "Surrounded by all this glamour, I always get a yen for something more prosaic."

We went on, and made a few mistakes. Bean jelly with Japanese citrus, which some man from Tokyo told us was a very good dessert. Mistake. Some dried cuttlefish, which another man from Tokyo told us was great with beer. Mistake. Some salami Calabrese from Italy, which was supposed to be free of garlic. Mistake. (We get a garlic-free Genoa salami from a little place in Great Neck via our friend Lola Finkelstein, and that is *perfect!*) We wound up, happily, at the booth of the Vinton Popcorn Company, of Vinton, Iowa. ("It's ALWAYS popcorn time! Enjoy VINTON popcorn. It's the popping-est.") An angry-looking fellow named Donley F. Jager was in charge, and we hung around with him and ate his popcorn, which he said was selected from his own varieties of seed.

"We do not buy open-market corn," he told us angrily. "We don't aim for the movie business, because they are constantly driving you down on price. That's point one. And point two is that our yellow popcorn pops forty-four to one and our white corn pops thirty-three to one. We recommend strictly our own co-conut oil to pop with. It's strictly clear. Colored oil burns out, has a bad smell, and it costs you extra. Now, do you want to eat something special?" he asked angrily.

"Of course."

"Our parched, or toasted, sweet corn," he said, sounding angry as hell. He handed us a sample package called Krunchy Nuggets of Sweetcorn. ("Krunchy Nuggets are a swell friend to keep company with. Especially when you're just sitting around the fireside visiting with other friends and sipping your favorite beverage. Just put all these beautiful little golden nuggets in a bowl and you can't help but reaching in to say 'Hi' to the tasty little Krunchy Nuggets.")

We ate some. "Delish," we said.

"We went through forty-eight varieties of corn to get the only three that are satisfactory, but don't ask me how we make it," he said. "We've got a secret for-mula."

"What are you sore about?" we asked.

"Who said I'm sore?" he said angrily, and he ate some of his toasted sweet corn. "I'm from Iowa."

1 9 7 4

BEING PRESENT

THE newest museum in town is the International Center of Photography, which occupies the mansion that formerly served as headquarters for the National Audubon Society, on the northeast corner of Fifth Avenue and Ninety-fourth Street. The week before its recent gala opening, we talked with Cornell Capa, its executive director, and with Karl Katz, one of the moving spirits behind it. The Center will exhibit, teach, and publish photography, and will set up archives for the preservation of photographs. It grew out of the International Fund for Concerned Photography, founded in 1966 by Mr. Capa, who was one of the most eminent photographers for *Life*. Like the Fund, the Center has been dedicated to the memory of three photojournalists who were killed in the nineteen-fifties while on picture assignments: David Seymour (Chim), Werner Bischof, and Robert Capa (Cornell's older brother). All this we learned from Mr. Katz, an ebullient man of forty-five, who is Chairman for Special Projects of the Metropolitan Museum of Art, while lunching with him in the staff dining room of the Met.

"The Center will be concentrating on photography as a means of communication rather than as art," Mr. Katz told us. "It is interested in committed photojournalism—in documentary photography, which no longer has an outlet, now that the big picture magazines have folded. Documentary photography could be said to fall into two broad categories." Mr. Katz had brought a pile of books to lunch and had put them on the chair next to him. He reached for one, "The Concerned Photographer," edited by Cornell Capa, and riffled through it. "Here. This says it better than I can. It's from Cornell's introduction." He pointed to the lines "Lewis W. Hine, an early humanitarian-with-a-camera, may have stated it best: 'There were two things I wanted to do. I wanted to show the things that had to be corrected. I wanted to show the things that had to be appreciated.' " Mr. Katz shut the book and continued, "Well, that's what it's all about. Now, at last, Cornell has a place of his own. It's been a long time coming. This brilliant, absolutely lovable man, a Hungarian who murders the English language, has never had the recognition he deserves, because he hasn't wanted it. He's always doing things for other people. He has put together exhibitions for all the great museums—for the Library of Congress, the Jewish Museum, the Metropolitan. Any time those places want a guest photography exhibit, they call Cornell and he drops everything. And he's done eleven books—some of his own pictures, and some he's edited. Those books are the best. This guy's been a friend, a father figure, a teacher to anyone who cares about photography. Some of us felt we couldn't let him go on dispersing his talent, his energy. He had to have a place where he could teach, and where he could reach more people. Somehow we got a little seed money from foundations. Cornell found this lovely house. And now—Well, you'll see."

Accompanied by Mr. Katz, we left the Metropolitan and walked up the Park side of Fifth Avenue in bright sunlight. We stopped at the corner of Ninety-fourth Street and looked across at the façade of what is still known as Audubon House, a six-story Georgian building of red brick, with shiny black shutters. Lovely it is. We crossed the street and looked at the metal plaque by the front door:

LANDMARKS OF NEW YORK AUDUBON HOUSE

DELANO AND ALDRICH WERE THE ARCHITECTS OF THIS GEORGIAN STYLE MANSION, COMPLETED ABOUT 1915 FOR WILLARD STRAIGHT. LATER OWNERS WERE JUDGE ELBERT H. GARY AND THEN MRS. HARRISON WILLIAMS FROM WHOM THE NATIONAL AUDUBON SOCIETY PURCHASED THE PROPERTY IN 1952.

PLAQUE ERECTED 1964 BY
THE NEW YORK COMMUNITY TRUST

We walked into a circular, marble-floored entrance hall. A young girl with long hair and glasses sat at a table, talking into a telephone cradled on one shoulder, and filling envelopes with both hands. As she talked, a second phone kept ringing. She greeted Mr. Katz with a smile, and we headed up a broad marble stairway. On the second floor, we emerged into a long, high-ceilinged, wood-panelled room with a fireplace at one end and a handsome parquet floor. This was once the Straights' reception room and is now called Gallery 2. There we found a young man holding a metal rod. Mr. Katz introduced him to us as Bhupendra Karia, an Indian photographer, who had been working with Cornell Capa for two years and is now the Center's associate director. As we stood talking, Mr. Capa walked in—a sturdy man of fifty-six, with bushy gray hair, bushy eyebrows, and a smiling face. "There you are," he said. "The baby is about to be born. We will make it for the opening. Come. I want to show you everything."

Mr. Capa put one arm around Mr. Katz and the other arm around us, and began to steer us through. "We have put the house back exactly as it used to be," he said. "When we moved in, there were many partitions, which we have taken down. See the panelling? We will never hurt it. We designed special boards to hang pictures from, with metal rods." He pointed to the rod that Mr. Karia was holding. "A genius who was produced by Karl Katz thought these up. But, like all geniuses, he made the rods so that they wouldn't fit the holes. Right, Bhupendra?" Mr. Karia smiled.

Gallery 2 and a large wood-panelled room adjoining it were to be used for one of the opening exhibitions—"Apropos U.S.S.R. (1954 and 1973)," made up of photographs taken by Henri Cartier-Bresson on two trips to Russia. On the opposite side, the reception room opened into a wood-panelled library, which had a large number of folding chairs stacked against the walls, and three tall windows facing Fifth Avenue. "Here we will have lectures, audiovisuals, conferences," Mr. Capa said.

Mr. Katz looked at his watch and said he had to get back to the Metropolitan. Mr. Capa clapped him on the back, said goodbye, and then led us upstairs to a large panelled room on the third floor. We both sat down in directors' chairs of red canvas, drawn up to a Formica-topped table. This room, Mr. Capa explained, was to be used for master classes. Some of the leading photographers would come here once a week and conduct seminars. He went on to say that the Center would be the only museum in the country devoted exclusively to photography, except for the International Museum of Photography at George Eastman House, in Rochester, which was established in 1947. "Modern Art and Whitney, they show photography, of course," he said. "They buy a few negatives of the great photographers, but what happens to the rest? I became concerned about that when, around the same time, my brother and Bischof and Seymour died. All their negatives, all their life's work—I could save them. But what happens with the other photographers? The family puts their photographs in the attic, and one day they get thrown out. All the history of the twentieth century will be in photographs—more than in words."

Capa stood up. "Come. I want you to meet some of the young people who are with me here," he said. "Some of them come all the way from California. The door will be open from eleven in the morning till eleven at night—maybe later. Who knows, when a lot of photographers get going? There will always be coffee."

We went back down to the reception-room gallery. Capa introduced us to a baby, held by a pretty, dark-haired young woman. "This is Colin Burroughs, three and one-half weeks," Capa said. "And his beautiful mother, Wendy. His father runs the slide machine and works in the darkroom."

Downstairs, in the entrance hall, the long-haired young girl was still simultaneously talking on the telephone and filling envelopes. A bearded young man was squatting on the floor beside her with another telephone and an open telephone book. He was introduced to us as David Kutz. He said, "Today a telephone operator, tomorrow an electrician, next day a carpenter, maybe one day a photographer."

We went back to Gallery 2. The Cartier-Bresson exhibition was being hung. On a wall between two windows was a 1954 photograph of young Russians dancing in a club under giant posters of Lenin and Stalin. Mr. Karia was staring at it. A young girl approached him with two labels for the picture. "They are chocolate-colored, with white writing," she said. "Which color do you want—milk chocolate or bittersweet?" Mr. Karia chose bittersweet. Capa stood in front of the Cartier-Bresson photograph appraisingly for a moment, and then told us that Cartier-Bresson had recently given an interview to *Le Monde* in which he stated that painting, not photography, had always been his obsession, and that he drew every day and now considered his drawings much more important than his photography. The interview had caused an uproar in France. *Le Monde* had asked several French photographers to respond, and had printed the responses of, among others, Gilles Peress and Marc Riboud. "Cartier-Bresson treated Riboud like a son," Capa went on. "He was his mentor, and now he tells him that photography doesn't mean anything. So now everybody is responding. Bresson is like that. *Psst, psst, psst*—the steam gathers, then the lid blows off." He smiled. "The whole thing is so French: love, hate, respect, misrespect, answers, re-answers. So now we have these vibrations crossing the ocean."

From the library we could hear a measured voice on a loudspeaker. It was Cartier-Bresson. "That's the Master's voice," Capa said to us, pointing through the door. "You should go and watch his audiovisual. We will have it running all through his exhibition."

We went into the library and sat down on a folding chair. The room was dark and empty. Cartier-Bresson slides flicked on and off a screen, and Cartier-Bresson spoke, in almost unaccented English: "Sometimes people ask, 'How many pictures do you take?' . . . Well, there is no rule. Sometimes, like in this picture in Greece, well, I saw the frame of the whole thing and I waited for somebody to pass. . . . That is why it develops a great anxiety in this profession . . . always waiting. What is going to happen? . . . Quick, quick, quick, quick, like an animal and a prey. . . . I'm extremely impulsive . . . a bunch of nerves, but I take advantage of it. . . . You have to be yourself and you have to forget yourself. . . . And poetry is the essence of everything. . . . The world is being created every minute and the world is falling to pieces every minute. . . . It is these tensions I am always moved by. . . . I love life. I love human beings. I hate people also. . . . I enjoy shooting a picture, being present. It's a way of saying, 'Yes! Yes! Yes!' . . . And there's no maybe."

1975

LEAVING MOTOWN

ONE minor musical motif we follow involves talented people who announce that they intend to "leave Motown," the Detroit record company that superintended the most popular black music of the sixties. So far, The Spinners have left Motown and have had a great success; Gladys Knight and The Pips have left Motown and have had a great success; Martha Reeves has left Motown and has granted interviews. Motown producers like Lamont Dozier have left Motown; the management of Motown has left Motown (that is, Detroit); and there is no longer any trace in popular music of Motown's regional idiosyncrasy or much evidence of the company's former musical hegemony. Diana Ross, The Temptations, and The Miracles (all of whom remain on the label) have for the record-buying public an interest that is at least partly reminiscent; only Stevie Wonder and The Jackson Five, the last classic Motown act to develop, have continued with undiminished vitality, and last week, in an atmosphere that was—well, businesslike, the Jackson family announced that they had signed a contract with Epic Records (a subsidiary of CBS) and would leave Motown.

The Jackson family announced their decision to leave Motown at a press conference in the Rainbow Grill. For the conference, ten high-backed black chairs were arranged behind a long, narrow table on a dais; dozens of other high-backed black chairs were arranged to face the dais. Taken one by one, the black chairs resembled the chairs found in medium-priced dinette sets; massed together, they lent the room a sober quality such as one might find at the United Nations—at meetings of, say, the Trusteeship Council. Susan Blond, who works for Epic, selected the music that played while the press assembled. "I put on three Jackson Five, three LaBelle, three Jackson Five, three Harold Melvin and The Blue Notes—like that," she told us as we sat in one of the high-backed black chairs. "I can tell this is a Jackson Five song playing now, because I know it isn't LaBelle."

Eleven members of the Jackson family entered the Rainbow Grill and mounted the dais. Ten members of the Jackson family sat in the black high-backed chairs. One member of the Jackson family, Stacy, sat in the lap of her mother, Maureen, the oldest Jackson daughter. At the end of the dais, stage right, sat Joe Jackson, father of the family and manager of the group. He was dressed in a slick black suit. Ranged down the table were Jackie (green jacket, twenty-four years old), Tito (brown jacket, twenty-one years old), Marlon (white leisure jacket, seventeen years old), and Michael (black velvet jacket, plaid vest, sixteen years old). Not present was Jermaine Jackson (twenty years old), who is married to Hazel Joy Gordy (daughter of Berry Gordy, chairman of the board of Motown Records), and who has not yet decided to leave Motown.

"There are a lot of little ones," Susan Blond remarked to us.

"But do they make up for Jermaine?" asked a young woman behind us.

A reporter asked the Jackson family why they had decided to leave Motown.

"We left Motown because we look forward to selling a lot of albums," Tito Jackson answered.

"Motown sells a lot of singles. Epic sells a lot of albums," Mr. Jackson added.

A reporter asked Michael Jackson, who is really the star of the group, how he thought the move would affect him.

"I'm sure the promotion will be stronger," Michael Jackson said.

A reporter asked Mr. Jackson how the move would affect the Jacksons' relationship with Berry Gordy.

Mr. Jackson smiled. "You take it as it comes," he said.

Tito and Jackie Jackson looked as self-confident as their father, although they didn't manage to be quite as elusive. Michael looked very shy. Stacy, in her mother's lap, put her face in a glass of ice water. Mr. Jackson said he was very happy to be at CBS, because "everything is possible" at CBS. Michael Jackson said he thought the family would be going after an older audience and might, in their Las Vegas show, do some nostalgia, "so the older people can remember their younger days." Mr. Jackson said he was confident that Jermaine would rejoin the group. "Under his conditions, it'll take a while," Mr. Jackson said. No Jackson said anything sentimental. No Jackson said anything to indicate that there had been anything in the Motown ethic which couldn't be reproduced at will at CBS. No Jackson really explained why their contract with CBS is being announced now, even though they remain under contract to Motown until March, 1976.

A reporter did ask if the Jacksons had tried to renegotiate their contract with Motown.

"Sure we tried to renegotiate with Motown," Jackie said, "but the figures were just Mickey Mouse."

"Do you know that show 'The Jeffersons'?" the young woman behind us said. "About the upperwardly mobile black man who owns some dry-cleaning stores? Well, Mr. Jackson is Mr. Jefferson, and the children are his dry-cleaning stores."

WE have a report from our correspondent Jamaica Kincaid about Michael Jackson:

Here is my favorite fan letter to Michael Jackson, from the March, 1975, issue of *Right On!:*

Dear Michael Jackson:
  You are my favorite star. You have all the right things going for yourself. You're cute, beautiful, sweet, and also kind. You'll always be my favorite star, Michael, until you get married, then I'll have to put you down. But while you're free, I want you always to remember me, because I'm in your corner! I love you!

Jeanie Wilson
Norfolk, Va.

Michael Jackson is my favorite teenage idol, because he is so pretty. True, he is not the little ebony cutie he used to be, and his Afro hairdo often shows some split ends, but nevertheless he is just plain old pretty, and as far as I am concerned, if you're pretty, you're cool. Some people think Donny Osmond is cool, some people think David Cassidy is cool, some people think Foster Sylvers is cool, but I think Michael Jackson is coolest. Michael Jackson is so cool that he was discovered by Diana Ross. How many people are ever discovered by Diana Ross? Not many, I bet. Oh, I know, she really discovered The Jackson Five, but I say she discovered Michael. The Jackson Five is just his backup band. I read everything I can get my hands on about Michael Jackson, so I know a lot of things about him. I don't mean that I know his mother's name is Katherine; his father's name is Joe; he comes from Gary, Indiana; or the song "Ben" was his biggest solo venture. I mean I know things like Michael Jackson is a Virgo; he had his first date on a TV show called "The Dating Game"; his favorite drink is Kool-Aid; he likes cameras and likes to take pictures of people when they are not looking; he keeps white mice for pets; Tito and Jackie call him Big Nose as a pet name; some of his favorite entertainers are Jim Nabors, Sammy Davis, Jr., and Diana Ross; he believes "you gotta give love to get love"; he likes being treated like the guy next door; his eyes are brown; he likes paintings and likes to paint in oils. I get most of this information from *Right On!*, a fan publication for black teen-agers. It's just the greatest. In every issue, there are at least two articles on The Jackson Five and almost always an article on Michael. Recently, I came across a quiz in one issue that said, "Can *You* Pass Michael's Love Test?" The quiz said that Michael doesn't like a girl who keeps her thoughts to herself; that he delights in being around a lot of people, even when he is on a date; that he likes comics, and his favorite characters are Spider-Man, Green Arrow, and The Incredible Hulk; that he thinks personality is more important than looks; and that he doesn't like jealous types. Do you know what? I failed the test pathetically.

1 9 7 5

MINNESOTA FATS

I N the movie "The Hustler," Jackie Gleason played Minnesota Fats as a silent pro of a pool player who was vaguely associated with the big-money barracudas and sold-out types hanging back in the pool-hall shadows while the hero, Fast Eddie Felson (Paul Newman), ran the table and spoke his plucky, beleaguered soliloquy against them all, and the only line of Fats' that people remember—his interruption of Eddie with "Shoot pool, Fast Eddie"—is remembered mainly because it is a setup for one of Paul Newman's more stylish lines in movies: "I'm shootin' pool, Fats. When I miss, you can shoot." We saw the real Minnesota Fats the other night, at a benefit performance for the Palisades General Hospital at the Palisadium, an entertainment complex connected with the Winston Towers, in Cliffside Park, New Jersey, and he was not at all like Jackie Gleason in the movie. He is not particularly fat, and he is not from Minnesota. (He has worn that name since the movie, but before the movie he was most commonly known as New York Fats, because he grew up in Washington Heights, around 167th and Amsterdam. The movie producers liked the name Minnesota Fats better for the marquee.) Also, he would never let anyone else talk that long in his presence. He is one of the most skillful and financially successful of pool players, and the reason is that he really likes to play pool, and talks all the time with great self-assurance. A few years ago, he outtalked Muhammad Ali on Irv Kupcinet's show. In a game like pool, in which all the top competitors are practically equal in skill, the things that Fats says are often distracting enough to make the difference in a close match. At the exhibition at the Palisadium, he played four matches, and he talked through them all, and here is some of what he said:

"Pool. There's never been a toy on earth to compare to a pool table. I been on one ever since I was two and I got nothin' but money. Nothin' but cash. I'm a millionaire, but I'm richer than a millionaire, because I've got cash. When I was twelve years old, I broke everybody from here to Zanzibar, and I bought me a Duesenberg a block long. I had a big, beautiful doll drivin' it, in shorts. Tell ya funny story—I was playin' in one of the largest shopping centers in the world, in California, and this kid asked me, 'Do you ever scratch?' I said, 'I ain't never scratched in my life.' Just then, I took this shot and the cue ball went right in the pocket. He said, 'Well, you've scratched now.' I said, 'Well, I'm a millionaire, so what difference does it make?' Nothin' disturbs me. I went down on two ships and fought in two revolutions and I ain't scared of nothin'. When I was a kid, I used to swim the Hudson over here to Jersey, just for kicks. I'm a brilliant man. I'm like a top scientist. I can make shots no living creature can make. I've played for princes and princesses. I've had my own TV show, one of the best shows on television, 'Celebrity Billiards,' playin' pool with the stars—Zsa Zsa Gabor, Buddy Hackett, Wilt Chamberlain, Paul Newman. I can play any card game you care to name. I beat the famous poker player Amarillo Slim at pool in New Brunswick, New Jersey. I played the North Pole twice this year. I played in Baton Rouge, Louisiana, and I outdrew the Pope of Rome. On the square, I'm tellin' it like it is. I just played twenty-two benefits in a row. I played pool for three days straight without never goin' to bed. Ladies was dancin' with me at a hundred dollars a dance. Nothin' but cash, I got nothin' but cash. See this pen? The mayor of St. Louis gave me this pen today. I just did a benefit near St. Louis for the criminal *in*-sane. I live in Dowell, Illinois, and I own the whole county. I own land everywhere. I own land in outer space. You don't believe me—I do. I just don't wanna go. Who wants to go to outer space, see some moon woman all wild-lookin'. Here we got Zsa Zsa Gabor, Charo. Let the Russians go to the moon. I'd rather go to Howard Johnson's, eat an ice-cream cone."

One of his exhibition matches Minnesota Fats lost, to George Tarpenian, the champion of the Winston Towers. "Well, kid, you beat Minnesota Fats," he said. "The only problem is, if you walk into a pool hall and say, 'I beat Minnesota Fats,' ain't nobody gonna believe you."

In his youth, Minnesota Fats was also known as Double Smart Fats, and sometimes even Triple Smart Fats.

1 9 7 7

TAXI JOKES

A FEW months ago, we thoughtlessly permitted our subscription to *Taxi Drivers Voice*, the organ of the New York City Taxi Drivers Union Local 3036, to lapse. Then, the other day, somebody left a copy next to us on the subway, and when we picked it up and began to read, we were reminded that to ignore the *Taxi Drivers Voice* is to live without one convenient method of monitoring the pulse of the megalopolis. Of particular interest was an editorial titled "Taxi Driver Humor." Here is a memorable passage:

> Since Time began, or at least since the dawn of the Taxi Age, we have been the butt of comics' jokes from coast to coast. Sometimes these jokes can be cruel and personal and they hurt very much, but most of the time they are the same jokes told by cab drivers themselves when they are together.

Taxi drivers, the editorial seemed to be saying, are just another oppressed minority. The writer went on to suggest that instead of trying to "stall the career of a Johnny Carson, a Dick Cavett, or an Alan King"—a thought that has apparently occurred to some vengeful hackmen—they should learn to laugh along with the jokes. This is an intelligent and humane sentiment, hard to quarrel with even for those of us who have negligently strolled into the Taxi Age without a single taxi-driver joke in our arsenal of slurs. To be able in the future to laugh along with cabbies when they magnanimously laugh at themselves, we went to visit Ben Goldberg, the president of Local 3036 and the managing editor of *Taxi Drivers Voice*, at the union headquarters, on Park Avenue South, to ask if he would recite a few selections from his private canon of taxi-driver humor. We were received in Mr. Goldberg's office—which, in addition to a desk, a couch, and filing cabinets, contained a large portrait of Harry Van Arsdale, Jr., the founder and president emeritus of Local 3036, and photographs of various union officials and mayors and governors—but before we were introduced to Mr. Goldberg, we spoke with his son Larry, a reporter for *Taxi Drivers Voice* and co-author of the editorial. Occasionally—when he isn't busy reporting or driving a cab—Larry Goldberg, a heavyset young man, performs a stand-up comedy routine. As a rule, his repertoire includes a lot of jokes about dieting and television commercials, but it has nothing to do with taxis. His last public appearance, he told us, had taken place a couple of weeks before at the Pan American Motor Inn, on Queens Boulevard. Then Larry Goldberg explained the motive behind the editorial reflections upon taxi-driver humor. "In that column, we were telling the driver that the comedian doesn't dislike him, as a driver, personally, so the driver shouldn't attack him personally," he said. "You'll often find, especially among some of the independent taxi owners and the mini-fleet operators, that if someone on television says something derogatory about a taxi driver, they will react by saying negative things about that comic's personality."

We asked Larry Goldberg to give us an example of the sort of joke that taxi drivers might tell among themselves.

"Well, you might hear a guy around the garage tell the other drivers about a passenger getting in the cab and asking the driver if he would please refrain from smoking," he said. "And the driver might say, 'So I put out the cigarette, but I used the guy's hand as an ashtray.' " He paused, and then said, "No, that's not really a joke, that's just a crack. Oh, yeah, I know one. Here. 'What's yellow and goes up Third Avenue sixty miles an hour at one o'clock in the morning?' Now, most people will naturally say 'A taxi,' but the correct answer is 'A tow truck.' "

"That's not really a taxi joke," we said. "That's a tow-truck riddle."

"O.K., then, I've got one," said Ben Goldberg, who had come in and taken a seat on the couch. "I don't know if you'd call this a joke, but it's a true story that once happened to me in Brooklyn. I picked up a guy at the corner of Marcy Avenue and Broadway, and I heard him say, 'Keep on Broadway.' So I'm driving and driving, and all the way he's saying what sounds like 'Keep on Broadway. Keep on Broadway.' Finally, we get to the end of Broadway, where it runs into Fulton Street, and I turn to him and say, 'Now which way?' And the passenger says he wants out at Keap on Broadway—so I realized that all along he really meant Keap Street *at* Broadway, but I thought he'd been telling me to *keep going* on Broadway. Get it?"

As Mr. Goldberg finished recounting this incident, a retired driver named Howard Richman appeared in the office with a question about some union matter. "Hey, Howie," said Mr. Goldberg, "you know any taxi-driver jokes?"

Mr. Richman did not. However, he did summon up a story in the Keap-on-

Broadway vein, about a young couple who wanted to be driven to a Manhattan night club but were taken instead to a garbage dump in Astoria, Queens. "What they wanted was some joint called The City Dump, but I gave 'em the *city dump*. See, I take everything literally. Ya got that?" Mr. Richman was literally convulsed with laughter.

Next, the Goldbergs, junior and senior, gave us a guided tour of the union offices, and along the way we met another retired driver, a man named Harry Hoffman.

"I got one," said Mr. Hoffman. "A guy gets into a taxi on Park Avenue and says to the driver he wants to go to London. The driver says, 'Are you kidding?' The passenger says, 'No. Just drive over to the pier. We'll get on the Queen Mary. You keep the meter running the whole time. I'll pay you.' So they get on the boat and cross the Atlantic and they land in England and get off the boat and drive to London, and the driver lets the passenger off at Trafalgar Square, or wherever, and the passenger pays him and leaves a big tip. Now the driver realizes that he's got to get back to New York the same way he came over. So he's driving through London on his way to catch a boat, and a guy flags him down and asks for a lift. The driver says he's going to the United States. The guy says, 'Terrific, that's where I wanna go. Do you happen to know where Flatbush Avenue is?' And the cabby says, 'Sorry, Mister, but I can't take you. I don't go to Brooklyn.' "

We thanked Harry Hoffman and walked toward the elevator with Larry Goldberg. While we waited for the car to arrive, he introduced us to Mike Rosenthal, the recording secretary of the union, and Edward Zarr, a vice-president.

"Taxi jokes," Mr. Goldberg said. "Let's hear some taxi jokes."

There was a moment of silence, and then Mr. Zarr said, "Oh, yeah, I got one. You hear the one about the guy who wanted to go to London?"

1977

TWENTY-FIVE THOUSANDTHS
OF A SECOND

NEW JERSEY could be called the carpet-sample state. From the window of a Transport of New Jersey bus, you see a lot of carpet samples in store windows and in the back seats of people's cars. You also see a lot of stores like Rickel Home Center, Pergament, Syms, Pathmark, Frankart Furniture, Allen Carpet, and Two Guys. New Jersey is like late-night TV commercials, only there's no movie. Actually, that's not true. Something big happened in New Jersey earlier this month. For four days, the National Hot Rod Association's Summernationals, the biggest drag-racing event on the East Coast, caused more than sixty thousand people—gas shortage or no gas shortage—to drive to Raceway Park, near Englishtown, from all over the country. Of those sixty thousand people, about forty thousand were overweight. (Drag-racing fans tend to be overweight.) Some of them were so fat that they made up for the twenty thousand who weren't fat. Some of them were so fat that they were spread like a hand of cards; they walked around with their stomachs out and their elbows nearly touching behind their backs. Everything at Raceway Park seemed covered with trademarks—mostly of the companies that sponsored race cars and provided parts. Even some of the spectators had trademarks on them. We saw one guy with the lion that is the symbol of Löwenbräu beer tattooed on his biceps. Other people had the traditional tattoos, only all over their bodies. They were so tattooed that it looked as if someone had doodled on them while on the phone.

Acres and acres of campgrounds are part of the race-track grounds. The main thing about the campgrounds was the broken blue-and-white Styrofoam coolers. They were everywhere. People had made shelters with orange nylon wound up in the car windows and staked to the ground, lean-to style. The rescue orange stood out against the wads of dark-green trees, as did the light-gray smoke from firecrackers and the white billows from a burning-out dragster. The highest thing on the horizon was wires, probably for the public-address system, which ran the length of the track—a quarter mile. At one point, the announcer said, "Will the owner of a silver-flecked 1978 Corvette please come to the pit area and move your car, or we'll dismantle it and hide the parts in the grass."

All the biggest names in drag racing—Don (The Snake) Prudhomme, Tom (The Mongoose) McEwen, Shirley (used to be Cha Cha but now she doesn't want to be called that anymore) Muldowney, Big Daddy Don Garlits, and many more—were there. The cars were so loud you could hear them with your forehead. The nitromethane-burning dragsters, in particular, were so loud the sound went right down the center of your spinal column like a wire test-tube brush. Speeds were around two hundred and forty-seven miles an hour. Races were won by twenty-five thousandths of a second. Most of the spectators, once they were in the stands, did not feel like moving much, and anyway standing up was about the most they could do. But at one end of the stands maybe a hundred black guys were betting on every race, waving bills in the air and saying "This side!" or "Other side!" to indicate which lane they thought the winning car would be in. The cars took off, and every face followed them down the track, and at the end of each race the black guys assumed postures of joy or disappointment so extreme that it looked as if payroll safes were falling on them.

1 9 7 9

FILM

A WOMAN had the eminent international journalist Lowell Thomas on the ropes at a low-proof (white wine, Coke, Fresca) cocktail party in the Schermerhorn Room of the Union Club while people waited for the Dalai Lama, the Tibetan spiritual leader, to arrive and receive a film, made in Tibet in 1942 and 1943 by two members of the Office of Strategic Services, that the Veterans of the O.S.S. wanted to give the holy man as a gesture of friendship on his first visit to America. "As a newscaster, you visited Tibet, didn't you?" the woman was saying. "Well, when they show the film, you'll be one of the few people in the room who will know what Tibet actually looks like. You visited China, too, didn't you? Which did you like better—China or Tibet? Did you find there was freedom of speech in China? Were you able to say what you wanted, or did you have to watch yourself? I bet China was fascinating—"

Then, suddenly, a round photographer standing near the door hopped to, and the TV cameramen turned on their lights, and Lowell Thomas headed toward the door, and the people in the room came to attention in a rank, and in walked Tenzin Gyatso, His Holiness the Fourteenth Dalai Lama, who has been recognized as the reincarnation of his predecessor, the Thirteenth Dalai Lama, since he was two years old in the small village of Taktser, in northeastern Tibet, who is called *yeshe norbu* ("the wish-fulfilling gem") and *kundun* ("the presence") by the Tibetan people, and who has been living in exile since the Chinese crushed a rebellion in Tibet in 1959. As he came through the door, he was giving someone an autograph.

Lowell Thomas brought along a man in a brown suit from the crowd. "Your Holiness, I would like to present the famous Dr. Jonas Salk," he said.

The Dalai Lama sat down and watched the film, which was made for strategic purposes by Captain Brooke Dolan, of the O.S.S. Colonel Ilia Tolstoy, grandson of the writer, was the other O.S.S. officer on the Tibetan trek.

"Tibet is a land of mystery and mysticism." Shot of mountains, clouds. "Religion is the dominant influence that controls the people of this vast land. . . . The very existence of the Tibetan depends upon the yak." Shot of yaks. "Tibetans are inherently sociable." Shot of smiling Tibetans. "They have a happy disposition and make friends quickly. . . . Nature presented Tibet with the ideal focal point for Buddhism." Shot of face of Dalai Lama, aged eight. End.

The lights came on, and the Dalai Lama stood up. His head was shaved so that it looked as if his hair had been drawn on his head. He was wearing rectangular metal-rimmed glasses. His red robes reached below his knees. He was wearing red ankle socks and brown oxfords. He said something in Tibetan. "Thank you very much. It was an excellent film," his interpreter said. The Dalai Lama then threw back his robe, looked at a gold watch on his left wrist, and said something else in Tibetan. "Since there's not much time, I think I will excuse myself," his interpreter said.

1979

TURNOUT

W E happen to know that what most pleases Diana Vreeland, Special Consultant to the Costume Institute of the Metropolitan Museum, about her new show, "Fashions of the Hapsburg Era," is the saddlery. She has said it to us more than once. Mrs. Vreeland has a special way of looking at horses. She told us about it. It has to do with the horse itself, but only as a powerful source of simple energy. What Mrs. Vreeland likes is a source of simple energy so powerful that something rather excessive can be elaborated from what rises to the surface. In the case of horses, this is what Mrs. Vreeland calls the turnout. She talked to us about it in her office at the Metropolitan a few days before the opening of the Hapsburg show. "It's the *point*," she said. "It's important to make the point; it's important to *get* the point. The point is the *gleam*. It's what the nineteenth century knew. The gleam, the positiveness, the *turnout*." Mrs. Vreeland said that in search of the right gleam she had cabled to Vienna for permission to polish the twenty-two boots and shoes she has in the show and to polish the brass. The permission had been granted, she said, and the boots had been polished to a very high gleam and the brass polished with a soft cloth. Mrs. Vreeland said that she had found a friend in Dr. George Kugler, a curator of the Austrian Museum of Fine Arts and the director of its library. "He handles all of Elizabeth's clothes, but his heart is in saddlery," Mrs. Vreeland said. By Elizabeth, Mrs. Vreeland meant, of course, the Empress Elizabeth, wife of the Emperor Franz Josef. It is an opinion of Mrs. Vreeland's (and a worry to her) that the Empress is not as well known to the American public as she deserves to be. Mrs. Vreeland said, "People come, I talk about Elizabeth. I talk about her waist. They get that part. That it was a very thin waist. But I explain that we all did have very thin waists. It's another generation I'm talking about, naturally. I'm not in that generation. But thin waists were something I knew about. You get the waist you want, in the end. People understand that. But their eyes glaze, if you know what I mean. You talk for a while and then they say, 'But who was she, this Elizabeth?' There is no history known in this country. I have been shocked. Totally shocked. I am not an educated woman. You understand that. But I am shocked. I talk about Elizabeth, and people say, 'Who is she?' I talk about Elizabeth, and a woman looks at me, straight at me, and says, 'How did you make up that face?' She means *my* face. Nothing to do with Elizabeth. Someone asked me that: 'How did you make up that face?' I looked at her, straight at her, the way she was looking straight at me, because I believe in that, and I said, 'Why, I chose my *nose,* and then my *eyes.* I wanted them totally *closed,* my eyes.' You remember the story of Daisy Fellowes, who was supposed to have had her eyes opened at the ends."

"What do you mean?" we asked. "Surgically?"

"Of course, surgically. We're living in a totally scientific age."

"What is the effect?"

"Much longer eyes. Longer and almost *closed.*"

Mrs. Vreeland took us through the galleries where her show was being prepared. She pointed out an extravagant mourning dress that is thought to have belonged to the Empress Elizabeth, and she also pointed out very many uniforms. Mrs. Vreeland said she particularly liked the Hungarian uniforms. "Whenever you see the stone-marten fur and the braiding, you know you are in Hungary," she said. "Don't forget about Hungary. Never forget Hungary." Then, without any talk whatever, she led us to see a saddle. The label said, "Hungarian Horse Furniture, 17th Century." The saddle was small and not deeply shaped. It would sit rather high off a horse. The seat was of a pale-rose-colored velvet. The ends of the saddle, under the pommel and the cantle, were of silver set with semiprecious stones. Mrs. Vreeland said, "*There.*"

1979

1980s

STILL WONDERFUL

FRANK CAPRA, the gentleman and filmmaker, came to New York the other day, from his home in Southern California, to see a movie. The movie was "It's a Wonderful Life." Because Frank Capra directed this film in 1946, he had already seen it quite a few times. Never before, however, had he seen it during one of Christopher Little's and David White's "It's a Wonderful Life" celebrations. In 1970, when Little, a photographer, and White, a writer, were still college students, they discovered "I.A.W.L." (Jimmy Stewart, Donna Reed, Lionel Barrymore, Henry Travers, comic climax) on the late show. Every year since then, around Christmastime, they have invited over a couple of dozen friends who believe that there is nothing wrong with unbridled sentimentality, and that "I.A.W.L.," therefore, is a wonderful movie. The most recent party was the tenth-anniversary showing, and, because Little and White had decided that this should be the final "I.A.W.L." party, they wrote a letter to Frank Capra inviting him to attend. He wrote back, "Nothing would make me happier than to be with you guys on the night when you will be running our favorite film. I will be there."

The party took place a couple of nights before Christmas in a loft in Chelsea, where Little lives with his wife, Betsy Kittredge. A large movie screen had been set up in one area of the apartment, and a sixteen-millimetre projector was threaded with the first reel of Capra's own print of the film. A few inches of leader broke off the reel while it was being threaded, and Little and White seized this for their "I.A.W.L." memorabilia collection. These archives contain, among other things, two autographed copies of Frank Capra's autobiography; two autographed copies of "The Greatest Gift," the short story, by Philip Van

Doren Stern, upon which "I.A.W.L." was based; testimonial letters from "I.A.W.L." aficionados; and surface-to-air photographs from Ralph Wolfe's wedding. Ralph Wolfe, an architect who lives in Cambridge, Massachusetts, is a veteran of eight "I.A.W.L." celebrations. When he and Betty Gilbreath got married, in Connecticut, in 1979, Patrick Curley and Jane Bayard (nine "I.A.W.L." parties each) arranged for a chartered airplane to fly over the wedding site trailing a banner that said "RALPH AND BETTY: IT'S A WONDERFUL LIFE."

Frank Capra arrived ahead of most of the guests, accompanied by his son Tom, a film producer who lives in New York. The elder Capra settled into a chair in the Littles' living room and immediately relaxed. He wore a white sports coat, a white V-neck sweater, a white turtleneck, and coffee-brown slacks. He is eighty-three years old now and has a thick white mustache, thick white eyebrows, and what appears to be a permanent suntan. In person, Frank Capra seems like most of his movies—soulful and optimistic—and he looked as if he were prepared to withstand two hours at the head of a receiving line. Christopher Little explained, however, that an effort had been made to keep the guest list down. "We have to limit this to the dependable hard-core," Little said. "You've got to be a little ruthless. You need people you can rely on. This afternoon, when we were setting up the projector, it was giving us all sorts of trouble. We need to feel confident that in the worst possible case—total mechanical failure—we have on hand a crowd of spectators who can act out the entire movie line for line."

Soon after nine o'clock, by which time twenty-five guests had arrived, everyone took a seat in the screening area of the loft, and David White made a brief speech. He ran through a capsule biography of Frank Capra (born in Palermo, Sicily, in 1897; grew up in Los Angeles; three Oscars, in 1934, 1936, and 1938, for "It Happened One Night," "Mr. Deeds Goes to Town," and "You Can't Take It with You," respectively), and then he said, "Frank Capra is a piece of American culture and therefore a piece of each one of us—a part of why we laugh when we laugh and why we weep when we weep. Personally, although I have just met him, he's a man who is very dear to me, because he's made some wonderful movies. And, on an even more personal note, I'd like to say that this party is proof that miracles do occur, because I've wanted to meet Frank Capra for a long time, and tonight I've said hello and shaken his hand—and that's a miracle."

Frank Capra rose from his chair and said, "I'm just delighted to be here, just delighted. This is one of the proudest moments of my life. I can't tell you how pleased I am that you want to see something that I made. I won't say more than that."

The lights were turned out, and Tom Capra started the film projector. There is always quite a bit of crying during an "I.A.W.L." party; it's that sort of story. Because this evening was pitched in a particularly high emotional key, the sounds of muffled nose-blowing—originating in the vicinity of Ralph Wolfe—

began during the first of the film's four reels. After each reel, the lights went on and Frank Capra graciously conducted an impromptu seminar. People wanted to know "How did you cast this?" and "Did you know when you were making it that you had something very special?" and "Was anyone else considered for the Lionel Barrymore role?" and "Did Jimmy Stewart and Donna Reed actually fall in love during the filming?" and "How many takes did you need to get the telephone scene?"

When the last reel ended, by which time the sounds of weeping had become choruslike, there was applause, more sincerely grateful remarks by Frank Capra, and more questions from the floor. Once, to illustrate a point, Frank Capra said, "I must tell you one story about Lionel Barrymore. Have I got time?"

Christopher Little said, "You've got all night long."

1 9 8 1

FILMMAKER

JOHN SAYLES is the thirty-year-old moviemaker who wrote, edited, and directed "Return of the Secaucus Seven," a free-form comedy of manners about the reunion of seven young political activists, which opened here last summer and is now back for a brief run at the Quad. He made the movie in twenty-five days, for sixty thousand dollars—which he had earned from writing fiction (two novels, titled "Pride of the Bimbos" and "Union Dues," and a book of stories, "The Anarchists' Convention") and from writing horror-movie scripts. To help pay the editing and laboratory costs of "Secaucus Seven," he rewrote the script for "The Howling," a werewolf movie that opened last week. The other day, he came into town from Hoboken, where he lives, and, in a restaurant near the Port Authority bus terminal, he answered some of our questions about independent filmmaking and horror:

I made the seven characters in "Secaucus Seven" people who went on those peace marches and are now trying to be a little more practical, because there isn't a major political movement for them to plug into with that much energy anymore. Once I'd decided who they were, I didn't want to contrive a story around them. I said, "O.K., we've got these people together for a weekend— they're not going to end up waving guns at each other or committing suicide." If I'd done it for a studio, that's what I probably would have ended up with.

I had directed plays in summer stock—I'd directed a couple in North Conway, New Hampshire, where we shot the movie—and I had acted a lot, but I had never looked through a movie camera before. The crew had never worked on a feature before, so they weren't intimidating. They were interested in the characters as well as in the technical part of it, and I was able to tell them vir-

tually, "This is what I want to see and hear," and they were able to get it. The
sound in "Secaucus Seven" is better than the sound you'll hear in a five-
million-dollar movie. Wayne Wadhams did the sound. The guy's real good—
he's also a record producer. We were almost never able to move the camera the
way I would have liked and we weren't always able to light as well as we might
have, because that takes time, but I did take the time for the actors and for the
sound, because if it was tinny or sounded as if they were in another room you'd
lose the immediacy of the people. New Hampshire is supposed to be bucolic and
quiet, but planes were passing overhead, and there was construction everywhere, so we had to sneak takes in between jackhammers going.

I had no pressure but from myself, and a responsibility to the actors—that
they look good. If you're an actor in a film, you don't have an audience to tell
you whether it's working; you only have a bunch of technicians—who are
worrying about focus and stuff—and the director. I'm the only net they have.
So I told them, "Any time you feel you have a better take in you, tell me. I will always use the best acting take when I start editing. If it's not the best technical
take, that doesn't matter." Because the important thing about this film—it isn't
true of horror movies, necessarily—is that you believe in the people. It helped
that we were living together in a ski lodge and that they had to cook together
and play volleyball together. I was paying them about eighty dollars a week and
room and board, which is about what they had been getting in summer stock.
I said, "If this movie makes any money, which I doubt, you'll get up to Screen
Actors Guild minimum for the year." The same with the technicians.

Editing is the best part. You are just there with the film, making the story out
of the film. You learn what you covered wrong. You learn things about writing,
because you realize that a scene plays without all this dialogue or that you need
more dialogue here or some sound in the background. I rented a flatbed editing
machine and spent a night going through this damn manual—it was like
Christmas Eve and trying to figure out how to put a bicycle together. I cut for one
or two hours a day; I was doing all this screenwriting to pay for the editing machine—five hundred dollars a month. With a couple of sequences that are pure
editing   a basketball sequence and some diving   I was able to play around.
Most of it was salvaging. The time transitions are in the lines, because I knew I
wasn't going to be able to shoot a lot of footage and carve a movie out of it. Film
stock—on most budgets it's a tiny fraction of the budget, on ours it was a third.
In Poland and India, they shoot about four to one—they just don't have much
Kodak film. In Poland, they're on the state, so there's no overtime; they just re-
hearse the hell out of things, with the camera but without pulling the trigger
and exposing the film, and when they're ready to go they shoot it. So very often
they get great stuff in one take. But it would cost a fortune to do that here.

The main thing I don't like about the film business is that you do too much
work that doesn't have anything to do with filmmaking. It's like Karl Wallenda
saying that when he's on the wire he's alive and the rest is waiting. When

you're writing or directing a film, you're alive, and the rest is advertising. "Secaucus Seven" is going to make its money back, and then if we sell it to cable it'll make a profit. Not enough to make another movie on, though. We have to figure that we get from twenty-five to thirty cents out of every dollar. Prints and advertising come off the top. Prints cost fifteen hundred dollars apiece. It can cost you fifteen thousand dollars to open in Washington, D.C., thirty thousand in New York. Then the exhibitors take theirs, and we split fifty-fifty with the distributor. Independent filmmaking is not a way to get rich quick, even if the movie gets seen by a lot of people.

The first screenplay I ever wrote was about the Black Sox scandal of 1919. That's the kind of thing I couldn't make independently, because it has so many people in it. I tend to have a lot of characters. I'm interested in the way people work on each other—how that shows the inner workings of the mind more than getting inside somebody's head. These guys who make horror movies are always saying, "What is this? You've got sixty-five speaking parts here; give us a break, we've got to cast this."

Horror movies are a lot of fun to write. At least, the ones that I've written were, because you were given the premise and could do what you wanted—make the people what you want to make them. I wrote "Piranha," which Joe Dante directed. He started out being a writer for those little horror-movie magazines. When he was thirteen or fourteen, he wrote an article called "Dante's Inferno," about the fifty worst horror movies of all time. He became an editor at Roger Corman's New World Pictures, and then Roger let him direct. You work for Roger until he can't afford you anymore. Joe got "The Howling" after turning down "Motel Hell" and a couple of other chain-saw-massacre comedies. The main problem with the story they had for "The Howling" was that there wasn't any consistency in what the werewolves could and couldn't do, so in one afternoon Joe and I wrote down the rules for werewolves. We found that they had nothing to do with the full moon. Werewolves were like witches—they were shape-changers. And they usually did it to get people and eat them up and blame it on wolves. They were pretty decadent characters, so we decided to use that instead of making them be these people who couldn't help themselves. There was some responsibility involved in it.

The effects are pretty good—you haven't seen them before. It's tough for Dee Wallace to stay pinned against a wall for five minutes while a guy turns into a werewolf. It's very tough, when you've been in makeup for three hours so you'll look as if your throat's been torn away, to come out with everyone laughing at you and do a scene, even if it's just screaming. Dee Wallace does some nice things where she doesn't scream. People don't always scream when they see something horrible. That's when the Tingler grows. Did you ever see "The Tingler"? It's about a big, long worm thing that comes alive in your spine until you scream or get your fear out. But I don't like going to scary movies much, and I don't wake up in the morning saying I have to write about piranhas.

1981

MELNIKOFF'S

MELNIKOFF'S is a general-type store at Eighty-fourth Street and York Avenue. This time of year, it caters to the summer-camp crowd. You don't really belong there on a spring afternoon unless your name is Jared, Jamie, Jennifer, Jeffrey, Jonathan, Lauren, Dana, Courtney, Brian, Benjamin, Eric, Stacy, or something like that—the sort of name that's likely to be sewn into two pair white gym shorts, two pair green gym shorts, twelve pair athletic socks, one poncho, one terry-cloth robe, three nylon swimsuits, one duffelbag, etc.—or unless you are one of those happy but sad adults who have decided to spend two thousand dollars to send Jared/Jamie/Jennifer away for eight weeks so that he/she can receive individualized attention and sensitive, experienced personal instruction while learning everything it is possible to know about art, dance, drama, music (jazz, rock, folk, chamber, opera), archery, riflery, water-skiing, tennis, night tennis, soccer, horseback riding, golf, painting, sculpting, graphics, white-water rafting, canoeing, backpacking, fishing, conservation of natural resources, go-carts, minibikes, rocketry, campcraft, ham radio, video, batiking, silver-smithing, weaving, photography, lacrosse, and kayaking, with stress on citizenship and high personal values. If you happen to be such a happy but sad adult, go to Melnikoff's and take along about a thousand bucks.

"What's your name?"

"Ethan."

"Where are you going to camp?"

"Wildwood."

"I heard your mother mention that you go to school at Ethical Culture. So you're a philosopher as well as a camper, huh?"

"Dumb."

"Is it true that at the camp you're going to they make you eat your vegetables?"

"Yucch."

"Is it true that they serve *only* vegetables?"

"Yucch."

"How do you feel about insects?"

"Yucch."

"Wildlife in general?"

"Yucch."

"Ethan, when this man asks you a question can't you give more than a one-word answer?"

"Yucch-yucch."

No one named Melnikoff really has anything to do with Melnikoff's. The owner now is a Felenstein—Marshall Felenstein. Marshall Felenstein also runs a chain of retail clothing stores in the Midwest, called Marwen Stores. His wife, Diane, runs her own P.R. firm. She has just returned from Cuba. The children in Cuba lead different lives. In summer, they have activities and they learn crafts, but they have no minibikes, no video, and no lighted tennis courts. In Cuba, there is no Camp Winadu, no Camp Winaukee, no Camp Lakota, no Camp Towanda, no Camp Tegawitha. The children in Cuba are not nearly as fortunate as the children who shop at Melnikoff's.

"This size feels big."

"He's ready for a men's medium. He's just used to everything being so tight. He's going to a weight-watchers' camp next summer. The list says eight pair of socks. You want tube socks, Andrew? You want these with the colored stripes?"

"Look at those socks. You wouldn't wear those socks, Mom. Damn, you're cheap. I'm not wearing those socks. Everybody at camp's gonna think I'm gay if I wear those socks."

"That's enough of that! Try these shorts on."

"Maybe I got nice legs, but I ain't gonna wear shorts."

"Yeah, you have nice legs. Too bad they have to go with that big stomach."

"Shut up, Jill."

"Try this on. I don't have all day."

"What is this—a dressing contest? Don't *rush* me."

"Andrew, come on out now. I want to see how those fit."

"You're embarrassing me."

"I'm not embarrassing you. *You're* embarrassing *me.* Now, open the door."

"O.K. How does this look?"

"You gonna wear those with the waist all the way up around your chest, Andrew?"

"Yeah."

"You look like a dingdong."

"Shut up, Jill."

"Stop it!"

"Why?"

If you place your order before a certain date, Melnikoff's will sew in the name tapes free of charge. The name-tapers are Boris and Alex. Boris owns a tailor shop down the block from the store. Alex is his son. No question about it, free name-taping attracts a lot of customers. Marshall Felenstein supports free name-taping. Marshall Felenstein says, "Free name-taping's the hook. *That* plus personal service."

"I ordered these two extra shirts for my son, and they came late. Could you please sew name tapes in them?"

"Mr. Marcus, we already shipped your order and we mailed you extra name tapes."

"If I bring you the name tapes, could you just sew them in these shirts?"

"Mr. Marcus, it's only two shirts. Can't your wife just sew those in?"

"If she could sew them in, I'd still be married to her."

When you've put down your deposit for everything at Melnikoff's, the people there pack it in a cardboard box and put it downstairs in the storage room. If there are special-order items yet to come in, they wait for those, and when everything is ready they send the entire box to Boris and Alex for name-taping. When that job is done, it all comes back to Melnikoff's for final folding, packing, and shipping. You should plan ahead, but even if you don't, don't worry. They'll ship the stuff to you or ship it directly to the camp. They'll ship anything on your list of Necessary Articles and Optional Articles, but they will *not* ship the following items: live animals, expensive jewelry, stereo equipment, knives and axes, explosives. So don't even bother asking. They won't do it.

"I see you're here with your brother. Are you going to camp, too?"

"No."

"In a couple of years?"

"No."

"Have you already been to camp?"

"No."

"You're going to spend the summer in the park?"

"No."

"You're going somewhere, right?"

"Yes."

"Well, where else is there?"

"Italy."

1 9 8 2

BOJANGLES'

CHICKEN. Biscuits. Chicken 'n Biscuits. Bojangles' Famous Chicken 'n Biscuits. The building—three stories of crossing-guard orange—beckoned. The sign—"OPENING WEDNESDAY, 6 A.M."—tantalized. We launched an immediate investigation. Our report is as follows.

MONDAY: "It's the first Bojangles' in the North—there are a hundred-some down South," William Levitz told us. "The kicker," he continued, "is the biscuits. They are Southern biscuits—the best I've ever tasted. I'm a New Yorker, and six months ago I didn't know a biscuit from a bag of beans. But this city has seen bagels and it's seen croissants. Now it's going to see biscuits. And let me tell you—these biscuits are going to take the North by storm."

Mr. Levitz is senior vice-president of Horn & Hardart, the firm that is busting biscuits across the Mason-Dixon Line. He led us down from his office—on the second floor of the Bojangles' building, situated between Forty-fifth and Forty-sixth Streets on the west side of Sixth Avenue—to the object of his boundless esteem, the soon-to-be fast-food restaurant. On its ground floor, in preparation for the Wednesday début, five young women hunched over cash registers feverishly totalling mythical orders and making pretend change. Behind them, in the kitchen, student cooks were frying chicken after chicken and, under the watchful eye of Bob Raspanti, baking tray upon tray of biscuits. Mr. Raspanti usually works in Charlotte, North Carolina, where he is director of the Master Biscuit Maker Training Center for the entire Bojangles' chain, and, if anything, he is prouder than Mr. Levitz of his products. "You can't just come in off the street and make them," Mr. Raspanti said emphatically. "You have to *understand* the dough in order to relate to it."

Mr. Levitz informed us that all Bojangles' biscuit-makers employ the same kneading techniques. "There's an exact way of pressing down on the dough, and all, but it's secret," he said.

Mr. Raspanti chimed in, "It's like an art. It's like painting. You can do it by the numbers, but it's not the same. You have to *understand* it."

TUESDAY: From across Sixth Avenue, as we approached Bojangles' for the preopening party, we could see a woman in a large chicken costume sauntering back and forth in front of the restaurant. It occurred to us that she might have something to do with the festivities, and, on inquiry, we found our hunch to be correct. "I'm an actress; sometimes I do mime for Horn & Hardart," the chicken, whose name was Bernadette Brooks, said, adding, "I think it was my legs that got me this job."

Inside, the joint was hopping. From the restaurant's basement floor, the hot Dixieland sound of a band led by the vocalist Emme Kemp blared forth, and a number of well-dressed men and women wearing name tags boogied around the room in a long line. Upstairs, the bartender poured drink after drink, and nearly everyone ignored the soda, coffee, juice, milk, and tea that will slake the thirst of Bojangles' patrons. Almost no one, though, ignored the Cajun-spiced chicken (peppery), the biscuits (all that Mr. Levitz had claimed, and more), and the "dirty rice," a Cajun specialty, cooked with ground sausage and spices. One fast-food honcho sampled the French fries, and then told his companions, "They're better than Burger King's but not as good as Arby's. Or maybe it's the other way around. If my six-year-old was here, he'd know in a second."

Emme Kemp was singing "This Could Be the Start of Something," and William Curtis, a director of Horn & Hardart, agreed. "The concept of dirty rice will make a big hit with New Yorkers—they like something a little way out," he told us, and added, " 'Dirty rice' is just a name, of course." He went on to say, "Northerners are ready for food like this. I don't necessarily call it a Southern food, though. I call it *an American food from another part of the country.*"

WEDNESDAY: At 5:48 A.M.—with Sixth Avenue still dark and pretty well deserted—the first tray of biscuits emerged from the ovens. Shortly thereafter, Salvatore Romano, the manager, spied one employee wearing bluejeans instead of the standard-issue Bojangles'-brown trousers—a problem he solved by lending her his spare pair. Then he grabbed the restaurant intercom and said, "Attention all cashier personnel! All cashiers to the front line! Stove area, are you ready?" Shouted replies in the affirmative. "Grill area, are you ready? How are my eggs? Front line, are you set? Smiling? We're opening up!"

At 6:00.22 A.M., a man walked through the door. "*There,*" Mr. Romano announced, "is our first paying customer. No, it's not. It's our first late employee." Let history record, however, that seconds later the door opened again, and through it strode the first patron of the first Bojangles' in the American North. At precisely 6:01, he ordered a sausage biscuit, for which he tendered a dollar twenty-five and received eighteen cents in change. Behind him came a string of lesser firsts:

6:05—First customer to present a twenty-dollar bill.

6:06—First sit-down customers, who experienced the first cash-register problems after ordering the first egg biscuit.

6:12—First tray of biscuits discarded. ("Know why I'm throwing these away?" Mr. Raspanti asked. "Too *dark*.")

6:16—First customer in a suit, who ordered the first steak biscuit and had the first dispute over a bill.

6:20—First batch of iced tea produced from the depths of the kitchen and poured into an enormous vat.

6:27—First customer wearing a Key West Yacht Club windbreaker.

By 6:36, as the sun rose over Sixth Avenue, Bojangles' Famous Chicken 'n Biscuits seemed to be catching on; two customers were ordering at once. Six hours later, at the height of the lunch rush, Bojangles' had become a Studio 54 of the eighties. A pretty young woman in a white miniskirt told everyone who arrived in search of fast food that there would be at least a twenty-minute wait before they even reached the cash registers. The warning deterred some; more just plunged on into the fray. "It's a smash business!" Mr. Levitz exulted. "A record two-hour business! More than any Bojangles' has ever done." Breakfast, he said, had generated seven hundred dollars cash. By 3 P.M., five thousand five hundred dollars had been traded for meals. "It's chicken, which is an acceptable product," Mr. Levitz said on being pressed for an explanation. "It's not like Hungarian goulash. *Everyone* likes chicken."

A software problem plaguing the cash registers provided Mr. Levitz's only worry, and even that was not too serious. "It's annoying me, it's irritating me, but it's not stopping me from making money," Mr. Levitz said.

"Phenomenal," "fantastic," "excellent," and "psyched" were some of the words Mr. Romano used to describe his business and his staff. Of the customers, he reported, "They're eating chicken, chicken, chicken. They're eating *everything*."

In the Horn & Hardart boardroom, above the restaurant, folks were just as enthusiastic. "We will be the leading force in chicken within two years," the company chairman, Barry Florescue, predicted. "We'll be the ones people will think about when they think about chicken and biscuits."

1982

HANDBAG

AYOUNG woman writes:
Last week, I met my friend for tea at the Mayfair Hotel. The Mayfair has good tea, so my friend didn't have to get her own tea bag out of her handbag. Actually, if we hadn't come in out of the cold to a place that offered food and drink we would still have survived; in addition to the tea bag she carries a chocolate bar at all times. The small pepper mill she carries would probably not be useful in such a situation.

I romanticize my friend—I think her handbag contains *everything*. She has what she calls first-degree, second-degree, and third-degree carriers. The handbag changes, but the carriers—the little zippered pouches inside—don't. In the first-degree pouch she carries mostly makeup: blush, lip gloss, and hand cream, together with an emery board, a mirror, and a comb. She takes this with her if she goes out for half an hour. She takes her second-degree pouch in addition (stuffed fuller than No. 1) when she will be gone more than three hours. It contains: more hand cream; perfume; lipstick; aspirin in a small bottle; toothpaste; a folding toothbrush; Stim-U-Dents and Bit O'Wax (dental floss); tweezers; eyeliner pencil; a can opener; the tea bag (Prince of Wales); the chocolate bar; the pepper mill, in its own case; a plastic spoon ("I might want to eat yogurt"); vitamins; a sewing kit; and Papier Poudre, which is blotting paper with powder on the other side. The third-degree pouch contains a desk, of sorts: a calculator with instructions for working it (she forgets); a stapler and extra staples (she says she has no trouble opening it to reload, because she uses the tweezers from Pouch No. 2); large scissors; a large eraser; automatic pencils; a regular pencil ("if I want to feel down-to-earth"); a red pencil, for special notes to herself; one large plastic paper clip; stamps for postcards and for letters; a ball-point pen; and a roller pen. She used to carry a fountain pen, in case she had to write something romantic, but it leaked one too many times. There is a special change purse with only quarters and dimes ("If you put them with your regular change, you spend them"), and a Gucci Kleenex case ("Kleenexes eviscerate themselves in your bag"). She also has: a black Gucci wallet with one credit card (lost eight times); a big change purse, which she carries receipts in; tinted glasses (three: the same frames, with interchangeable lenses, tinted dark, medium, and light); and a red Day-Timer, which includes a calendar page for lists of things to buy, exhibits to see, records to listen to, names and addresses, books to get from the library, and places to have drinks which give you free food, and also includes a pad of paper with her name and address imprinted, all her membership cards, a phone credit card, ads offering discounts, and an acrostic puzzle. There is a small folding raincoat (turquoise), a clothesbrush, a magazine. There is another can opener—can openers seem to be among her favorite things. She often uses this one in airports, to open small cans of V-8 juice. My favorite thing, I think, is the one dearest to the heart of all her friends: a Swiss Army—knife key chain, which offers two knives, a fruit peeler, a screwdriver, a nail cleaner, scissors, and a toothpick. At the Mayfair, as she held out the Swiss Army–knife key chain the gentleman sitting at the next table, who had craned his neck around as her litany of objects progressed, quickly faced forward again.

"What do people think about all this stuff you have?" I asked her.

"They're usually a little embarrassed," she said. "It escalates from 'Oh, really?' to 'You're kidding.' "

"I don't think anyone else has a handbag like that," I said. "How did you get so organized?"

She said, "Most people just let their anxieties build. You know—'I wish I had my hand cream.' "

She blamed herself, however, for not buying more notebooks with red spirals when she was in Norway. In one—her Rapportblokk—she had made notes to herself about such things as where to find the best film processors in the country, and had copied down a recipe for fried chicken. The boarding pass for American Airlines was in there by mistake.

The inventory she gave me of her handbag was like every parent's dream of a child who doesn't say "I dunno" the day after Christmas when some relative asks what he or she got but instead remembers every single thing.

"What kind of handbag did you carry in high school?" I asked.

She looked slightly surprised. "A pencil clipped to the front of my notebook," she said. "It was too bulky to go inside." She sipped her tea. She said, "In the Midwest, nice girls carried everything in full view of the world."

Behind her, in the center of the room, was a large spray of flowers: it included spider mums, other kinds of chrysanthemums, and—what seemed

miraculous to me on such a cold winter day—branches of forsythia just starting to blossom. Somehow, from somewhere, one of the first signs of spring had
been found and brought inside the hotel.

1 9 8 3

SPEED AND ROSES

WHEN last we spoke with Barbara Cartland, it was at her home outside London, the year was 1976, her years were seventy-five, and her vital statistics looked like this: two hundred and seventeen books—a hundred and seventy of them novels—with a total of seventy million copies in print. We are happy to report that Miss Cartland, whom we encountered last month in the lobby of Penn Station, where she was greeting people coming to the second annual Romantic Book-Lovers' Conference, has since our last talk set aside her idling ways and got down to some serious work. In the intervening seven years, in which she has attained the age of eighty-one, she has had something or other to do with the Princess Di side of the Royal Wedding *and* she has written a hundred and forty-five more books—an average of more than twenty a year—to bring her total to three hundred and sixty-two. Now, with something more than three hundred and fifty million copies bought and paid for, she may well be the best-selling author of all time. "I was in Honolulu recently, and I wrote 'Island of Love,' and on the way back we stopped in San Francisco, so I wrote 'Love Goes West.' No, it's 'Love Comes West,' I think," she told us. A book takes the disciplined Miss Cartland a week to complete, and she writes for only a shade over two hours each day.

And Miss Cartland, though she is the reigning speed queen, is not alone in her literary approach, we found as we wandered through the corridors of the Hotel Roosevelt, where the conference was held, and talked to some of its participants—who were almost uniformly female and were nearly all either published writers of romance fiction or unpublished writers of romance fiction. For instance, the second-best-selling romance author, Janet Dailey, who has produced seventy-eight novels, announced, "By trial and error, I've found the best ways to write—at least for me—and now I finish a book in about nine days." One reason romance writers write so quickly is that the market for their products never dries up. Rebecca Brandewyne, who was promoting her latest work, "Love, Cherish Me," at the conference, said she sometimes reads from seven to ten Harlequin romances (which stretch a hundred and eighty-odd pages) in a single evening. And apparently there are others like her. We picked up the following facts about Harlequin Books, the leading publisher in the romance industry:

Fact: Last year, Harlequin sold over two hundred million books—about six books per second.

Fact: If all the Harlequin books sold *in a single day* last year were stacked one on top of another, the pile would be sixteen times as high as the World Trade Center (or, alternatively, eight times as high as the two towers of the World Trade Center stacked one on top of the other).

Fact: If all the pages of all the Harlequin books sold over the past ten years were laid side by side in the proper places and in the proper configurations, they would completely cover Colorado and Pennsylvania.

Fact: If all the *words* in Harlequin books sold last year were placed end to end, they could stretch ninety-three times to the moon (a fact that is especially noteworthy when you consider that many Harlequin authors avoid long words).

Fact: If the Harlequin books sold last year were placed end to end, they could run along both sides of the Nile, both sides of the Amazon, and one side of the Rio Grande.

(During that last paragraph, we got up from our desk, bought a diet Coke, joked with several friends about their writing speed, and, in general, *wasted time.* All the while, the clock was ticking.)

One reason some writers can do romances with such dispatch is that thoughtful publishers provide recipes for them to follow. For example, we talked with Denise Marcil, who, with her partner Meredith Bernstein, "came up with the whole concept" for a new series of Avon paperback romances, which will appear once a month under the over-all title Finding Mr. Right. Ms. Marcil said, "In most romances, what happens is the woman falls in love with a man, there's a little conflict, and things work out. What's different in our books is that there are two heroes, not one. And the woman has to choose between them." Ms. Marcil assured us that none of the jilted heroes do anything rash, and that the breakups are always "handled in an adult way." As an example of the new genre, Ms. Marcil cited "Dancing Season," by Carla Neggers, the second title in the series, which features a young woman who runs a bakeshop in her native Saratoga Springs and must decide between a home-town boy and a dancer in a New York City ballet company. She takes the local, leaving the dancer to leap morosely, one of her reasons being that she doesn't want to give up her ambitious plans for culinary expansion.

It would be less than honest of us to report that the seas of romance fiction are altogether glassy. On the contrary, they're stormy and roiling—even tempest-tossed—when it comes to the issue of decorous behavior for female characters. Such a fog of photographers had enveloped Miss Cartland at Penn Station that we couldn't hear everything she said, but we distinctly made out the words "disgusting" and "animals." And her voice was resolute when she declared that romance fiction was "in rather a torrid period, where everyone feels they must be modern and put in some dirty bits." Miss Cartland, none of whose heroines find themselves in bed until the necessary vows have been traded in the presence of a cleric, said it was a "medical fact" that promiscuity could damage young women. "Anyway," she added as she walked off, clutching a bouquet of red roses, "the most exciting thing in the world is still to hear someone say, 'I love you.' "

1983

THE FLOAT COMMITTEE

THE piece of sidewalk on Fourteenth Street outside Woolworth's, between Fifth Avenue and University Place, belongs to the Float Committee. It'll probably be there any minute. In the meantime, here's its card:

> THE HIGH VOLTAGE DANCE ENSEMBLE
> THE ELECTRIC SHOCK DANCE ENSEMBLE
> AN ORIGINAL GROUP WHO
> CHOREOGRAPHED THEIR OWN ELECTRIC
> DASHING STYLE
> THIS CHOREOGRAPHY USHERS IN A NEW
> DANCE VOGUE, FRESH AND EXCITING

The heart of the Float Committee is two brothers, John and William Rich, eighteen and seventeen, who live on East 106th Street and dance at parties and affairs and concerts, but mostly on the street. They usually hit this spot around three, work it an hour or two, and then head for the southwest corner of Eighth Street and Sixth Avenue. If you ask them how they settled on the Float Committee name, they look at you as if you were the biggest kind of fool, and say, "It's just some words." If you say, "Tell me about dancing," they become articulate.

JOHN: At home, I always be chilling out, doing some moves, just ticking or regular popping—twitching your joints so it looks like they're popping out of the socket. William got interested, so I taught him some things, and he developed his own style.

WILLIAM: For a while, we did strictly break dancing. The break is a dance where you bend your knees and keep one hand on the floor and spin around or kick your legs out or do handstands or flips and whatnot.

JOHN: After breaking, we started jamming—just dancing, doing some routines during the summer in a park on our street. It be falling night, and we start jamming, and everybody'd be coming around, and they'd all want to battle us.

WILLIAM: To start a battle, you challenge somebody by doing a move in front of them—any move to catch their attention—and the crowd will see it, and back up and form a circle, and sometimes we have to get people to link their arms to hold back the crowd, it can be so packed.

JOHN: Then you do your move, and they do their best, and you do your best, and the crowd decides the winner by applause.

WILLIAM: If you battle around your block, you're better off. One time, I was battling this guy Kippy by his project, and I was doing extra good, and he wasn't doing a thing against me, but he had all his friends cheering him.

JOHN: The last time I battled was last summer. I was dancing along and some guy came up to me and said, "You think you're doing all right? Deal with my friend."

WILLIAM: We make routines to records. We have one routine to "Planet Rock," by the Soulsonic Force, one to "Beat Box," one to "Big Beat," and one to a rap record by Spoonie Gee.

JOHN: There's five of us for our shows, and we have uniforms. We used to wear brown-and-white striped shirt and pants and now we wear all white. We bring the other guys to the street sometimes, but they get tired and run out of moves. You have to learn how to dance without losing energy.

WILLIAM: The best crews in our neighborhood are Larry Love, the Twins—the Twins are double-jointed in their arms—Fable, and Loose Bruce.

JOHN: There's also a real good kid on a Hundred and Seventy-sixth Street called Spud.

WILLIAM: We don't battle with any of these people, because they are our friends.

The first time you see William and John, a lot of the things they do may appear random and haphazard, or even improvised. (There is some improvisation, but not much.) The names of some of the standard moves that their routines are based on are the 3-D, the roller coaster, the chain, the wave, the electroresuscitation, the worm, and the vibration, which looks like a person imitating a heat shimmer on a summer runway. John is double-jointed around his ankles, and when he performs the standard moves exploiting this ability he is able to give them a crowd-pleasing appearance. John's style is abstract; William's is more literal. William occasionally mimes certain routines; for example, the basketball, the football, the jump rope, the rain, and the bike. In addition, he performs the glide. The glide wins a lot of battles. It is a very strange maneuver, and people really appreciate it, because they have never seen a person pull off a thing like that before. What happens is, William is dancing *here* and suddenly he's *there*, and it seems he did it by shooting out a leg, like a vine, and floating just slightly above the sidewalk to catch up to it. While the glide makes some people jealous, it opens wallets really well.

So here they are on Fourteenth Street, outside Woolworth's, midafternoon. William is the one with the purple pants and the black shirt. John has the black pants and the blue plaid jacket. Those are Kangol hats. John and William don't know if Kangol refers to the brand or the style, but they say everybody wears them. John turns up the volume on the box just enough so that you can hear it at the curb. A crowd forms. John dances out from the wall. That's the vibration. William joins him, and they clasp hands and face each other. That's the roller coaster—the wave that begins at one pair of hands and travels up William's arm to his shoulder, across his back to the other shoulder, down the arm to the other hand, and across John's body in the same fashion. John dances back to the wall, and William continues alone, on his face a look of haughty aplomb. John says softly, "Do your glide, William," and the crowd, which has been only curious, is startled awake.

"Well, I am *too through*," says a woman.

"He look like he made of *rubber* and whatnot," says another.

"He look like a *Gumby*," says a third.

Many people part with coins and a few with dollar bills, and William, catching his reflection in the store window, permits himself a sly, bashful smile.

1 9 8 3

TOURIST

THIS time, we ran into Janet in a department store, stocking up on massive books at fifty per cent off ticketed price, one day only. "I've been to Greece," she said. "Now I'm doing my Christmas shopping." We stumbled over a coat on the floor at the foot of a display of reduced games. Janet was struggling with a volume the size of a small tombstone, called "Michelangelo." "I don't know if I should get more than one of these," she said. "I think I'll get a couple of Hieronymus Bosches, one of these, two Kremlins, one Picasso, and one Art Buchwald." She piled the books on the corner of a table. "What's this?" she said. " 'Christianity Through the Ages.' This ought to be for somebody. Yoo-hoo! Is there a salesman here? Can I buy eight heavy books?" She pointed out the pile of books to a passing store employee. "Eight very heavy books," she said to him, flashing a smile, and added, "Unfortunately, I've lost my coat." We disentangled our feet from the coat and joined the procession to the sales desk.

"I think I've overdone it," Janet said to the man at the cash register. "Is everything half off? Who am I giving Picasso to?" Another fifty-per-cent-off table caught her eye. "I don't think I want 'Estate Planning,' do you?" she asked us.

We pursed our lips in thought.

The salesman asked Janet for her address and phone number. "We call you if something happens," he explained.

"To the books or to me?" Janet asked.

"I want to tell you about my trip," she said to us as we stood with her on the subway platform. We looked interested. "I have a lot of things on little pieces of paper, as you know," she said. "The whole experience on little pieces of paper."

We watched a train come and go. Too crowded.

Janet went on with her story. "In Rome, I was sick," she said. "I had planned to look up some of my favorite statues, but I ended up on the beach at Ostia, and there was no sun. When I arrived in Italy, I waited for Nunzia, my secretary in World War II, to pick me up at the airport, but she had come to pick me up on Sunday and I didn't get there till Monday. Do you know the difference between direct and non-stop?"

We shook our head.

"Direct flights all stop in Paris, and the non-stop ones don't stop," she explained. "One whole day, I was looking for Mr. Antinori, where I got all my leather boxes in World War II—the bygone days. Nunzia said he might be dead. Not only was he not dead but he's the exact same age I am. And I met a wonderful, handsome couple in this ritzy restaurant on the Piazza Navona, who had been married for thirty-two years and holding hands their entire marriage. They invited me to stay with them in Sorrento the next time I go back. I just talked to strangers and bought things; I was too tired to do anything else. I didn't see the 'Moses' or the other one—the 'Pietà.' I spent a lot of time taking pictures of cats and writing postcards. I can never get over the Colosseum. You drive down the street and there it is. You forget about unrequited love or that you can't hear out of your right ear, and you realize you're just a little speck."

Another train came in. Janet got a seat and we hovered over her, trying to hear a story about a Yale man, but the train was too noisy. When it stopped at Forty-second Street, Janet was saying, "One washcloth and three pieces of soap. I had to go down to the bar to get an ashtray. Wait a minute—let me go back to Dubrovnik. I loved Dubrovnik."

Through the roar of the train heading uptown, we heard "A room that looked like a Communist cell—no mirrors, the phone didn't work, and the only room that had a tree in front of it, so there was no view."

At the Fifty-ninth Street stop, we caught "Little streets that start low and go up high. 'What's the name of this water?' 'You're swimming in the Adriatic Sea.' I went all by myself, because the tour guide left without me."

At Seventy-second, "Two Yugoslavian brothers with gorgeous bodies. The people from New Hampshire were for anybody *except* Reagan." Something about Pavarotti's wife and someone from the Dalton School.

By the time we accompanied her off the train, at Ninety-sixth Street, Janet was in a hotel in Athens, inviting herself to share a table with a man from Sweden. "I don't like to eat alone, so I asked if he minded," she said. "I was going to pay for myself. He was what you would call overdelighted. He seemed all right until he decided to tell me how to eat a baked potato. 'First salt. Then pepper. Then butter. No, more butter. Now you take a spoon.' 'A spoon?' I asked. 'Yes, a spoon.' He invited me to his hotel, because there was a pool on the roof. 'Do you realize what it's like to see the Acropolis from a pool?' Right after the potato, he explained to me why men like to have affairs with women. 'Because for that one or two minutes,' he said, 'you *own* her.' He scared the hell out of me. By the way, a baked potato with a spoon is delicious.

"I went on a cruise with this friend of mine's daughter Debbie," Janet said as we walked with her along Broadway. "We stayed in Athens for two days, and then we went off on a boat for three days and four nights. Taking a cruise is definitely the wrong way to see Greece. You get up at crazy hours, you ride a donkey, you buy trinkets. You spend three and a half hours going to Delphi, which is gorgeous, and the guide sends you up some steep hills. He stays at the bottom, because he's seen it already. The ruins in every place consist of one, two, or three pillars, which is the one thing I learned in third grade: Doric, Ionic, and the other one—the plain one, the middle one, and the fancy one that starts with 'C.' "

In a butcher shop near Ninety-ninth Street, Janet took a number and stood in line. "The guides lead you to a ruin and show you three columns and say, 'This was the queen's bedroom,' and they show you a hole and say, 'That was the slaves' bathroom.' My friends who had sent me to Greece as a birthday present wanted me to look at ruins, but I spent a lot of time talking to people and different animals. They don't have any dogs over there, and just a couple of cats." Janet ordered a chicken and two steaks. "I did see a lot of big statues and Greek vases," she said. "I liked them very much, but in the historical part my mind wanders. On these tours, you get information like this: 'The Greek population is ten million.' The guides say things like 'As you already know, the Persians beat the Athenians, or vice versa, in something B.C.,' and 'Greek Myth No. 486: Apollo was four days old, and he was either on a dolphin or in a chariot, and he killed either a python or a man called Python, and then he purified himself for eight days.' "

Our own mind started to wander. "That was the first god that was ever sorry about something," Janet added.

"I would say, 'Quick, look out the window, there're some goats!' " Janet continued. She handed us the bag of meat and a briefcase. "I made a list of the places I went and the places I didn't go," she said, reaching into her handbag. "Now I've lost the places I went, and I won't be able to remember where I was. Oh, yes, that was Delphi. I feel very bad about missing Ephesus. Instead of going up to Ephesus, I stayed at the bottom of Turkey, and I got stuck with a harem ring. The man who sold it to me said I could break it up and give it to five people for Christmas. I forgot to ask if it was worth anything. Here's a tag from the underwear I bought for the trip: 'Intimate apparel for the woman of today who wants only what tomorrow will bring.' "

Janet turned a corner, and we followed. "Nero took five hundred statues from various places, I don't know why," she said. " 'Rich as Croesus' comes from Croesus, who was very rich. Somebody told him—one of the gods, I think—'If you cross the river, you'll destroy a great kingdom.' It turned out to be his own kingdom. On the way back from Delphi, you stop for ten minutes of shopping.

I was going to buy this fur cap with a tail for my ex-husband who lives in Canada, but my friend said he wouldn't like the tail. There were three couples on the cruise who didn't go to see one ruin or one vase. When they got to Athens, they said, 'Is there any shopping around the Acropolis?' I was exhausted from all the ruins. Near the end, in one of those Athens museums, I was following a tour group around when my friend came over to me and said, 'What are you doing?' I said I was listening to the guide. My friend said, 'She's speaking German.' I was so tired I didn't notice."

Standing in the middle of her living room, Janet suddenly said, "Damn! My life is spent looking for my eyeglasses."

She went into the kitchen.

"I'm against sisterhood," she said, turning on the oven. "I was never for it in the first place; now I'm finished with it. Everywhere I went with my semi-mutilated passport, I said, 'All you have to do is pick up the Scotch Taped tag and look underneath to find my right age. Then you put it back.' Every decent person, every man, did that. Sometimes they smiled, sometimes they scowled, but they all did it. Nobody stopped me till I got to Israel, where there was this female customs person. She said, 'What does this mean?' Then she went away and came back with an armed soldier, who said, 'If this were an Israeli passport, you'd go to prison.' At which point, he ripped off the Scotch Tape and ruined my passport. I entered the country in a rotten mood. In Tel Aviv, I met a black guy named Brian who was selling granola bars on the street, and I promised him I'd send his picture to his mother in Gary, Indiana, and say he'd be home soon. He's been gone for ten years. He belongs to a group that say they're not religious, but they all went over there because that's the first place God is coming when He comes back again. If there weren't any trees in Tel Aviv, it would be as hideous as Athens. In Jerusalem, an eighty-five-year-old priest kicked me out of St. Saviour's Church. I went in there during a service, and my camera made a very loud noise. A priest rushed back and said, 'Are you a Christian? No, you're a tourist. You have to leave immediately!' I apologized, and we had a nice talk. He speaks eight languages. He guessed my age, and then he told me he was being polite. He guessed forty, but he really thought I was fifty. He blessed me in Chinese. I have his address."

After a moment, Janet said, "If I were religious, I would want to believe in reincarnation." She dumped some Brussels sprouts into a pot. "My Israeli friend Shamai said that in the Jewish religion everybody comes back newborn. I never knew that. He said, 'Even your mother will come back.' I said, 'You mean I'm going to be newborn with the same mother? What kind of religion is that?' "

Janet looked under a dish towel. "Where are my eyeglasses?"

D. OF D.

WE have been to a party held *around* Her Grace the Duchess of Devonshire. The party wasn't given by Her Grace (it was given by B. Altman), and you couldn't say that the party was given just *for* her, either, because it was surrounded by furniture and the probability is that the hosts would have been disappointed if someone had looked only at the Duchess, and not at the furniture. But the movement of the party was around her, no doubt about that.

It isn't a good idea to go to this sort of party alone, so we took two friends: one actually English, the other American but *well versed.* Our English friend told us that the Duchess has been more in evidence than she was formerly, and that there is today a brand of tea called Duchess of Devonshire's. Our well-versed friend told us that a kind of slat-backed garden seat used at Chatsworth (Chatsworth is the principal seat of the Devonshires) is available in the English marketplace. "We ought to be on time. She will be," our English friend said.

We were on time. We walked through the cool, spacious ground floor of Altman's. Cosmetics were laid out, and handbags. We walked slowly. The ground floor of Altman's is unusual in its size and in its atmosphere. After hours (the party was held after store-closing), it is mysterious. This has to do with the things' not being for sale then. They are shiny, but they are not for sale. We went to an elevator. We were taken up by an attendant who was businesslike and made the ride up feel like a ride on a train. When we arrived at the party zone, we saw first a dominating color photograph of Chatsworth hanging on a wall. Then all kinds of furniture. The angle, or hook, of this furniture was that the originals from which these pieces had been copied were still in the possession of certain aristocratic English families. Our well-versed friend made a study of the labels on these pieces. Then he moved over to a chair that was not a part of the aristocratic line. "On the other hand, this is just a chair," he said. He reached under the seat and found a label. "It says here that the covering fabric and filling material are made in accordance with the U.F.A.C.," he told us. "And that construction criteria are designed to reduce, but not necessarily eliminate, ignition by a burning cigarette."

We walked toward the place where the Duchess was standing. "The Duchess is a very kind woman," our English friend said. "It is a recorded fact that when she and her sisters were still in the schoolroom they divided up the world. Her sister Jessica set out to be a Communist; Deborah said she was going to marry a duke. Deborah is the Duchess."

The Duchess was standing near a white platform, made not of plastic foam but not of anything much better—perhaps a kind of white construction board—upon which there was a small Plexiglas box containing a printed card that read "Inveraray Castle. His Grace the Duke of Argyll." Over the Plexiglas box stood a table—an Adam inlaid and cross-banded Pembroke table. "Wouldn't it be better to say 'From Inveraray Castle'?" our English friend asked.

The Duchess was wearing a polka-dot dress. She had shiny gray hair. Her shoes had bows. Her dress was girlish, in a certain way. People were introduced to her, and floated by her. One man was misintroduced. "Kick him," the Duchess said, referring to the man who had given the faulty introduction.

We thought that we might ask the Duchess about the tea and the slat-backed chair, but we didn't. *Self-explanatory,* we thought.

We went back downstairs. We thought, Maybe our era will be known as the era of parties in stores. The ground floor of Altman's seemed completely prosperous and happy. Everything was clean and shining.

1984

WITH FELLINI

FEDERICO FELLINI, the one-of-a-kind moviemaker, came to New York the other day to be honored by the Film Society of Lincoln Center in its annual tribute to a film artist, and here with him for a few days was his one-of-a-kind gang: his wife, the actress Giulietta Masina (star of the Fellini movies "La Strada," "Nights of Cabiria," and "Giulietta of the Spirits"); Marcello Mastroianni (star of the Fellini movies "La Dolce Vita," "8½," and "Ginger and Fred," a still uncompleted one, in which he appears with Miss Masina); the actress Anouk Aimée (star of "La Dolce Vita" and "8½," and also well known for her Claude Lelouch–directed movie "A Man and a Woman"); and various advisers, helpers, and experts on things American and many other things. We hadn't seen Fellini and the gang in several years, and so we were delighted when Fellini asked us to join them as they set out, the morning after their arrival, in a cavalcade of limos heading for Darien, Connecticut, and the country home of Dorothy Cullman, chairman of the F.S. of L.C., who had invited the whole gang, including us, for a typical Sunday-afternoon visit to her remodelled eighteenth-century Colonial house with grounds and pool. The visit was scheduled to include the obligatory swim, the quintessential tour of what-was-there-before and what-is-there-now, and a good meal. Fellini, gray-haired, ageless as ever, and nattily decked out in as preppy an outfit—navy-blue blazer with gold buttons, gray slacks, black loafers, white shirt, red silk tie—as has ever appeared in Darien, directed us to sit in the limo with him, Miss Masina (she was up front with the driver), Miss Aimée, and Mastroianni. Northward we went, followed by the others, who included a full complement of tribute workers, an admirably efficient bunch: Joanna Ney, public relations; Vivian Treves, interpreter; and Wendy Keys, co-producer, with Joanne Koch, of the whole shebang, to be put on in Avery Fisher Hall the following night. There were lots of high-spirited "*Ciao!*"s and laughter and the Italian equivalents of "Get a horse!" from those in our limo to those in the one behind us, and then Fellini settled down. He called to his wife up front, asking whether she was tired, and she replied, keeping her eyes on the road ahead, that she was never tired when she was happy, and she was happy. Fellini gave affectionate pats to the rest of us.

"This is the first time we are all together in New York," he said. "And now we go to Conneckticut," he added, giving a phonetic rendition that was used comfortably by everybody thereafter.

"When we see each other, it is always the same," Miss Aimée said. More pats from Fellini, reciprocal pats from Miss Aimée, pats from Mastroianni to both of them. Mastroianni, who was wearing a cream-colored Panama hat, adjusted it to a more rakish angle. He was wearing an impeccable, creaseless cream-colored linen suit, a black-and-white striped shirt, and a black tie.

"Anouk is a good fellow," Fellini said, in his most playful manner. "She is a famous actress who makes Western pictures," he went on, to us.

"Is that Conneckticut?" Mastroianni asked, pointing out the window at New Jersey as we drove up the Henry Hudson Parkway.

Fellini pointed in the opposite direction, at Grant's Tomb, and we identified it for him.

"Cary?" Miss Aimée asked, looking stricken.

We explained Ulysses S., and everybody looked relieved.

"We go to swim, and we will have a big lunch," Fellini said. "Soon we will see Conneckticut."

We asked Mastroianni whether he had seen any of the rushes of "Ginger and Fred," which is not about Rogers and Astaire but about two dancers who call themselves Ginger and Fred.

Mastroianni said he never goes to see rushes, because they are shown at night, after shooting, at the time he likes to go out to dinner. "Anyway, is *his* problem," he said, with a Mastroianni-charming smile-cum-shrug at Fellini.

"Is *my* problem," Fellini said. "I leave 'Ginger and Fred' with four more days of shooting to shoot, and fly to New York, and is *my* problem to go back and finish 'Ginger and Fred.' But is worth it to see Conneckticut."

There was a brief discussion about getting into bathing suits in Darien, and Mastroianni referred affectionately to the fact that Miss Aimée was still thin. More pats from Mastroianni for Miss Aimée, who laughed and tossed her hair back off her face.

"Do you remember, when we made 'La Dolce Vita,' on location in that tough neighborhood, I didn't know Italian then, and I heard the young men hanging around and shouting at you?" Miss Aimée said to Mastroianni. "Then I learned later they were shouting, 'Be careful, Marcello! You will hurt yourself holding her! She has too many bones! Give her food, Marcello!' "

"That place was full of thieves," Fellini said. "We had to pretend we were leaving, and we had to sneak back in the middle of the night, but the thieves all came back, too."

"Look at the trees!" Mastroianni called out, pointing at the countryside. "Look! There's Conneckticut!"

Not yet, we said.

Miss Aimée told us that she was going to work next making a sequel to "A Man and a Woman," on its twentieth anniversary.

Mastroianni put on a mock-doleful expression. He told us that in the mid-sixties Miss Aimée had called him in Rome from Paris to say she was going to make "A Man and a Woman," and had asked him to join her, playing the part later taken by Jean-Louis Trintignant. "She say to me a young director, unknown, no money; she plays a widow; I play a widower. I say no. I made a mistake."

"Two Academy Awards," Miss Aimée said, with a laugh. "Best Foreign Movie, Best Original Screenplay."

Connecticut! Everybody looked out at the Colonial-style wooden houses, some painted yellow, most painted white. Mastroianni wanted to know why so many Colonial houses were built of wood, unlike the old houses in Italy, which were built of stone.

Everybody looked bewildered.

"We go to the house of Dorothy Cullman, and we ask Dorothy Cullman why," Fellini said decisively, and everybody looked at ease again.

Destination reached: a light-beige-painted clapboard house with white trim, built around 1720, overlooking a slope of weedless, perfect lawn, as long as a city block, that was surrounded by weeping willow, apple, ash, dogwood, and Japanese white pine trees and led down to a waterfall and a huge, pondlike swimming pool with a Japanese-style boathouse in front of it. Here and there on the lawn were wooden sculptures, some of them abstract and some in the shape of people or birds. Up a white-and-tan pebbled walk Fellini and the gang strode—like characters in Fellini movies—toward the house, and we were all greeted on the walk by the hostess, an attractive woman with a very pale face. She wore an ample peach-and-white antique Japanese kimono over a white cotton jumpsuit, and she had on flat-heeled white sandals. On her wrists she wore handsome matching wide antique Indian bracelets of ivory and silver. She extended both hands to the guests.

"An apparition!" Fellini whispered in awe.

"Welcome, Mr. Fellini, I'm Dorothy Cullman," she said. "Lewis, my husband, has just taken our cook to the hospital, because our cook was suddenly taken ill. But I promise you there will be lunch."

Fellini kissed one of Mrs. Cullman's outstretched hands, Mastroianni kissed the other, everybody relaxed, and we were off on Sunday-in-the-country. In a glassed-in addition to the old house, with a complete view of the lawn, trees, sculptures, pool, and Japanese boathouse, we munched on crabmeat on apricot halves and pâté on toast, and chose drinks. Miss Aimée said that water would be fine, but Mrs. Cullman said, "No, no, no, you don't have to drink water—we have orange juice," so Miss Aimée took orange juice. Mrs. Cullman said that it seemed to be hot and the gentlemen might want to take off their coats, but Fellini and Mastroianni said they wanted to keep their coats on. Mrs. Cullman said that she had bought her peach-colored kimono and another one, just like it, to use as covers for her living-room cushions. Glass panels on three sides of the room were sliding doors; Mrs. Cullman slid them open, and everybody exclaimed over the view. Mr. Cullman appeared, wearing bluejeans and sneakers and an Italian striped cotton shirt, and reported that the cook was now healthy, so he had brought the cook back to the kitchen.

Mrs. Cullman sat down next to Fellini and said, "I have only two Italian words—*molto bene.*"

Fellini smiled politely and lifted a crab-filled apricot half in a gesture of salute to her. "*Molto bene,*" he said.

Mr. Cullman reappeared, now wearing a cream-colored Issey Miyake sweater shirt, cream-colored slacks, and white loafers, and led everybody on a tour of the old part of the house. "This is our pizza oven," he said, with an air of amusement, indicating a large fireplace. "This was the kitchen, and that other room was the parlor, where the minister came, and there are two bedrooms upstairs."

"Pizza oven," Fellini said, looking thoughtfully at Mastroianni, who gave his charming smile and shrug. Everybody regarded the fireplace with admiration.

Gang members from the other limos arrived and joined the tour, which wound quickly back to the room with the view.

"The rooms were small," Mr. Cullman said, "With low ceilings, to keep them warm on cold nights."

"Yes, very cold in Conneckticut," Fellini said sympathetically.

Mr. Cullman looked pleased. "The farmhouse, when it was first built, had only four rooms," he said. "Now we've got eleven."

"Very cold on a farm," Miss Aimée said.

Miss Masina said that the pâté on toast was very tasty, and she smiled gratefully at the host and hostess. Mr. Cullman invited Fellini to take off his coat, but Fellini graciously again said no. Mr. Cullman pointed up to the ceiling beams. "I got those beams from this guy who buys old farmhouses," he said to Fellini. "There's this guy Weiss, in Roxbury. Collects old barns, old timbers."

Fellini nodded respectfully.

"Why all the houses made of wood, not stone, in Conneckticut?" Mastroianni asked.

"Plenty of wood in this part of the country," Mr. Cullman said.

"I thought wood because the pioneers moved all the time—away from the Indians," Mastroianni said, acting the part of an Indian shooting an arrow at Mr. Cullman.

"Yeah," Mr. Cullman said.

Led by the host and hostess, the gang then trooped down the grassy slope to the boathouse, where Mr. Cullman pointed to a narrow wooden canoe hanging under the Japanese eaves. "It's a New Guinea canoe," Mr. Cullman said as the gang stared solemnly at the canoe. "Dorothy bought it there from a native for six dollars. It cost a hundred dollars to ship it home." He laughed heartily, and the gang coöperatively joined in with mild laughter.

On the boathouse deck, Miss Masina pushed some hanging Soleri bells, and they jangled, so she pushed them harder.

"The Whitney used to sell them," Mr. Cullman said. "Who's for a swim?"

Fellini looked at Mastroianni, who looked at Miss Aimée, who looked at Miss Masina, who turned from the bells, and all shook their heads. One gang member's son, age nineteen, said all right, he'd take a swim, and he did, while everybody else, still looking solemn, silently watched him. Mr. Cullman called to the young man, asking him what he thought the temperature of the water was. About sixty-eight degrees, the young man called back. Mr. Cullman said it should be at least seventy-two degrees, and called to the young man to get the pool thermometer and take the temperature of the water. The lone swimmer took the temperature and reported that it was sixty-eight degrees. The silent gang nodded with distress at this news. Mr. Cullman remarked that the pool held a million gallons of water. Everybody looked obligingly bowled over. Then everybody trooped up the green slope toward the house as Mr. Cullman briefed us on the sculptures. "Recognize the bird?" he said. "It's a Senufo piece, from Africa. Dorothy found it somewhere."

Back in the house, the gang again got to work on the crabmeat and the pâté. Mrs. Cullman sat with Fellini and discussed travel.

"You haven't spent much time here, Mr. Fellini," Mrs. Cullman said.

"In 1957, I came for some producers, as the guest of them," he said. "They gave me people to show to me anything I want to see, and they said, 'Do what you want.' What I want was to go back to Italy, so I left. In the plane, as we flew away from New York, I looked down, and I felt very moved, very guilty that I was leaving."

"Do you find when you travel that you're too close to it, and that later you feel differently about it?" Mrs. Cullman asked.

"Language is the medium for the relationship to reality," Fellini said, looking apologetic. "If I don't know the language, I feel lost."

"Would that be true in another European country?" Mrs. Cullman asked.

"Yes," said Fellini.

"Are you sure you won't take off your jacket?" Mr. Cullman asked.

We had a bite of crabmeat. Fellini came over. "Don't eat too much," he said. "These are only the hors d'oeuvres. There will be a lot of food."

He was right. He knew the script. The meal that followed was terrific: curried chicken, seafood pasta, steamed mussels, steamed clams, green salad, white wine, three kinds of cake, ice cream, candied-ginger sauce, fresh fruit, and espresso. Everybody ate for two hours. Then everybody hugged Mrs. Cullman and shook hands with Mr. Cullman and said very enthusiastically, "Thank you very much. Goodbye."

In the limo on the way back, Wendy Keys, the director and co-producer of the tribute, explained to Fellini how the program in Avery Fisher Hall would go—with projections of clips from his movies interspersed with three-minute speeches from Mastroianni, Miss Masina, Miss Aimée, Donald Sutherland, Martin Scorsese, and others.

"It will be pictures, people, pictures, people, et cetera, and, at the end, you," Miss Keys said.

"I want the Rockettes," Fellini said.

THE next night was a black-tie occasion. Before the program started, Fellini ran into Mr. Cullman, whose bow tie, with his tuxedo, had spectacular blue polka dots the size of dimes on a bright-red background.

"It is the tie of a Conneckticut Yankee," Fellini said knowledgeably.

The tribute went off nicely. It was pictures, people, pictures, people, et cetera, and then Fellini, who read a short speech: "My dear American friends: You are truly a simpatico people, as I always suspected since I was a child. . . . In the small movie house of my village   with two hundred seats and five hundred standing room—I discovered through your films that there existed another way of life, that a country existed of wide-open spaces, of fantastic cities which were like a cross between Babylon and Mars. Perhaps, thinking about it now, the stories were simplistic. However, it was nice to think that despite the con-flicts and the pitfalls there was always a happy ending. It was especially won-derful to know that a country existed where people were free, rich, and happy, dancing on the roofs of the skyscrapers, and where even a humble tramp could become President. Perhaps even then it wasn't really like this. However, I be-lieve that I owe to those flickering shadows from America my decision to ex-press myself through film. And so I, too, made some films and gave life to some flickering shadows, and through them I told the story of my country. And tonight I am extremely touched to find myself here, together with my beloved actors, and honored by the people who inspired me in those old years."

1 9 8 5

MONSTER TRUCKS AND MUD BOG

O N the night of the sixth game of the World Series—which turned out to be one of the most exciting World Series games ever—twelve thousand people drove to the Nassau Coliseum and paid as much as $17.50 a ticket to see the United States Hot Rod Association Monster Truck and Mud Bog Fall Nationals. Outside the Coliseum, people waited in long lines. As usual, everybody was named Richie. Inside, they saw on the arena floor a long dirt ramp—known as the mud bog—and on each side of the ramp three undistinguished-looking cars parked close together. Everybody stood for the national anthem; there was a short parade; and then came the car-crushing competition, featuring the Monster Trucks.

What Monster Trucks do is drive over cars. Monster Trucks have the bodies of stock cars (usually pickups), huge, seething engines, and wheels between five and six feet tall. The first Monster Truck was built in 1979, when a man in St. Louis named Bob Chandler jacked up a Ford pickup and fitted it with tractor tires and named it Big Foot, to promote his four-wheel-drive shop. Since then, Big Foot has appeared in movies and on TV, and toy companies have reproduced it, and Bob Chandler has built more Big Foots, and a number of people have built Monster Trucks of their own. Today, it is hard to find a ten-year-old boy in this country who has never heard of Big Foot or the Monster Trucks.

The announcer said, "Ladies and gentlemen, my name's Bret Kepner, and I'd like to welcome you and introduce you to some of the best-known names in the Monster Truck world today. First, from Fayetteville, North Carolina, is twenty-seven-year-old Kevin Dabney, in his 1968 Chevy Camaro, Blue Thunder. But before you start to cheer, all you Chevy fans, I should just mention that this monster has a four-hundred-and-fifty-six-cubic-inch *Chrysler* engine under the hood. Each one of those wheels is sixty-six inches tall and weighs twenty-one hundred pounds. The tires are ten-ply steel-belted Firestone radials built for an Army amphibious personnel-carrier, and Kevin got them at a steal from Army surplus for thirty-four hundred dollars apiece. It took him seven years of paychecks to finish that truck, at a cost of approximately a hundred and twenty thousand dollars, and if you're looking for a steering wheel, don't bother. Every single control on that vehicle except the throttle and the brake runs off a helicopter joystick. Next, we have Driver Robert Moore, from Bakersfield, California, in his '69 Chevy truck, the original Cyclops. Robert's got double sets of tractor tires all around and five hundred and thirteen inches of alcohol-burning big-block Chevy engine. But it's not under the hood—that engine sits right next to Robert in the cockpit. Now it's time for the other folks to cheer. Get ready, all you Ford fans, for Mike Spiker, in his 1983 Ford F-250, the All American, the Monster Truck of the South. Mike has developed a system of neon-gas tubes to bring the charge from the coil to the spark plugs. He says it fires quicker and smoother. Raise your hood, Mike, and show how that neon looks flashing in there—like the engine's on fire. And, finally, we've got a 1985 supercharged Ford from Winchester, Virginia, built and driven by Diehl Wilson, and it's called the Virginia Giant. This machine has a hydraulically operated body that raises up five feet off the frame—that makes it one of the 'funny cars' of the crushing circuit—and it is sponsored by Virginia Galleries, crafters of fine hardwood handmade Colonial-style furniture. All right, you Ford fans, let's hear it!"

Monster Trucks make a noise that lifts you up by the roof of your mouth. One by one, the Monster Trucks elephanted toward the parked cars, and then crunched up and over. They did plenty of honking and revving and light-flashing and raising of hoods along the way. The cars a '75 Plymouth Fury, a '74 Chrysler Newport, a '77 Mercury Marquis, a '77 Ford Torino, a '72 Cadillac Coupe de Ville, a '71 Pontiac LeMans—did not cave in as fast as you might think. "Un-be*leee*-vable wheel stand by that Cyclops!" the announcer said. "Uh-oh, looks like he's got a broken axle. Tough break for the Cyclops." The winner, decided by audience vote, was the Virginia Giant. The Monster Trucks drove off. Then a twenty-five-ton and a fifteen-ton Caterpillar front-end loader began pushing the cars over to the edges of the arena, out of the way. Through the Torino's empty rear window you could see on its sagging rear dash two magazines without covers. One magazine had a full-page ad for Chivas Regal Scotch.

Then it was time for the Mud Bog Competition. The object of mud-bog driving is to see how far you can go in the bog before you get stuck. The contestants drove four-wheel-drive vehicles divided into three classes—street, modified, and open. The winner of the street class, Dean Schultz, of Lindenhurst, New York, made it seventy-one feet and one inch. He skidded, bounced, plowed, plunged, and dug in. His front bumper slowly sank out of sight as each wheel spun its own solar system of flying mud. "He's still moving," the announcer said. "Still moving. Still moving. *Still* moving!" The audience leaped to its feet and cheered like a liberated nation.

1985

WORKOUTS

DURING the past decade, Robin Williams, the thirty-four-year-old comic actor, who seems to connect with his audiences on some wild, deep level and to make them laugh in a special way, at once loud, true, and happy, has been featured in two television programs ("Mork & Mindy" and the 1977 revival of "Laugh-In"), six movies ("Popeye," "The World According to Garp," "The Survivors," "Moscow on the Hudson," "The Best of Times," and the forthcoming "Club Paradise"), two concert performances on videocassette, and two record albums ("Reality . . . What a Concept" and "Throbbing Python of Love"). One kind of performing, however, Williams has been doing non-stop—before, during, and since his television, movie, concert, and recording activities—and that is working out, in unannounced appearances, in small, late-night comedy clubs: in the Comedy Store, in Los Angeles; in Yuk-Yuk's, in Toronto; in the Second City, in Chicago; in the Holy City Zoo, in San Francisco; in Catch a Rising Star, in New York; and in others that have become established since the early nineteen-seventies in dozens of cities in the United States. Well, before flying west to be an Oscar host extraordinaire, Williams was in New York, helping to organize last week's "Comic Relief" cable-television show—a benefit to raise money for the nation's homeless—and we tagged along with him for a while as he embarked on his midnight-and-after workouts.

When we met Williams, he had been sitting for four hours at the Public Theatre watching "Hamlet," and he emerged looking wilted and done in. He is a stocky, mild-seeming man with a rubbery face and body, which we were accustomed to seeing, in performance, go in seconds from Barry Fitzgerald to William F. Buckley, Jr., and on to Jerry Falwell, to Jesse Jackson, to Nadia Comaneci, and to God knows who or what else—always, in his inimitable way, simultaneously sharp and gentle. Now, wearing baggy brown pants tight at the ankles, black hiking boots, and a yellow rain jacket, he was calm and subdued. He expressed admiration for Kevin Kline as Hamlet and for Harriet Harris as Ophelia, noting that both actors were, like him, alumni of the Juilliard Theatre Center. He said that Jeff Weiss, a first-timer in a legitimate production, who had taken the roles of the Ghost, the Player King, and Osric, the unctuous courtier, was impressive. Then, in the taxi heading for Catch a Rising Star (First Avenue near Seventy-seventh), Williams suddenly, quietly, became, successively, a Yiddish-accented Hamlet lamenting Yorick "buried in *treyf*"; an insane Hamlet in a mental institution playing all the parts in the play; a "Hamlet" featuring George Jessel as the Ghost; a Woody Allen Hamlet, sounding exactly like Woody Allen saying "I don't know whether I should avenge him or honor him"; a Jack Nicholson Hamlet, sounding exactly like Jack Nicholson saying "To be or not to bleeping be . . ."

Then Williams retreated into his own calm, and we spent the rest of the taxi ride having him give us a quick refresher course in his history: Born in Chicago, an only child, his father an automobile-company vice-president ("He looks like a British Army officer"), who retired and moved the family to Marin County, outside San Francisco, and his mother a "very funny" prankster and cutup, originally from the South, who loves to tell jokes. "I was good in languages and thought I'd go into the Foreign Service, or something like that," Williams told us. "In high school, I was heavily into cross-country running, which I loved, and wrestling, which gave me a chance to do some damage. I went to one of the Claremont Colleges, where I took courses in political science and economics and failed them. After the first year, I left Claremont and went to the College of Marin, near home, which had an amazing Drama Department, with teachers who told me about Juilliard. I auditioned for Juilliard, got a full scholarship, and stayed three years, doing Shakespeare and Strindberg. Back home, I started going nightly to a coffeehouse called the Intersection, on Union Street in San Francisco. During the day, I worked in an ice-cream parlor. One night, at the coffeehouse, for no reason at all, I got up and imitated a quarterback high on LSD. It felt great. This was fun. No one was telling me what to do. I liked the freedom."

By the time we arrived at Catch a Rising Star, it was packed: standees three deep at the bar in front; an audience of about a hundred and fifty in the back room, seated at little tables, having drinks, facing a small platform with a standing mike. On the wall behind the platform were signs saying "BREAK A LEG" and "MONOGRAM PICTURES CORP. ENTRANCE," and nearby was a montage painting of famous comedians—Eddie Cantor, Charlie Chaplin, Milton Berle, and Abbott and Costello. On the platform, a young m.c.—short, chubby, with dark curly hair, and wearing a long-sleeved sports shirt over a T-shirt—was getting ready laughs with routine questions of and comments on the audience, which consisted mostly of young singles, young couples, foursomes of young women, threesomes of young men. The m.c. left after introducing his replacement, a tall, rangy man with thinning hair who wore jeans and a red sweater. The replacement worked for about fifteen minutes, getting dutiful laughs by telling "family" jokes: "My mother had four children. I was the only vertebrate one," and "We have a dog. He's half retriever, half vulture. He's been circling Grandma."

The chubby m.c. returned and announced that Robin Williams was there, and the place went bananas. Screams, yells, whistles, shrieks, cheers, and tremendous applause. Williams took the mike. He said, speaking as an Oscar recipient, "Thank you for making this possible. [As a snobbish theatregoer] As long as I have my glasses on, the world is mine. I just went to see 'Hamlet.' I want to see Hamlet played by Sly Stallone. [As Stallone] 'To be or what?' [As himself] Maybe he and Schwarzenegger can do a movie together. [As Schwarzenegger] With subtitles in English."

Williams went, again in seconds, from being one human cell to being Central Park squirrels, New York City pigeons ("I could fly, but I like it here"), another Oscar recipient ("I'd like to thank anybody who didn't try to kill me"), himself as penitent ("I'm sorry, God, I'm sorry that I made fun of everybody"), a Japanese manufacturer ("Not my faut, Amelican-made").

People in the audience called out subjects they had heard him do before, and these set Williams off on an even more manic scale. He went from gangster to drunk and on to Gorbachev, Reagan, Charles Kuralt covering toxic waste in New Jersey. He went from Mrs. Marcos to Louis Farrakhan and on to a small child watching his father leave and crying at a window and then turning away from the window, tearless, and saying, "Let's put on that Fisher-Price music and get crazy." (Williams has a three-year-old son, Zachary.)

Williams stayed on for about half an hour and came off looking refreshed and ready for anything. The following evening, in a taxi heading for the Improvisation (Forty-fourth near Eighth), he gave us a minicourse in comedy clubs. "That audience last night was made up of the bridge-and-tunnel people. They come in from New Jersey and Connecticut. They're a challenge. You can get a big reception, but if it's not working—one time, twice—then there's nothing. Some comics have a lot of pride. They'll do the material they set out to do, no matter what. I'm more chameleonlike. I find the basic level of the audience. Last night, I felt in the groove. I felt comfortable. I like going to the clubs, because it peels away all pretensions. About a week ago, I went to the Comedy Store, in Los Angeles. I was talking about bizarre things. I got going doing this whole thing about travelling at the speed of light, losing your luggage beforehand, doing Albert Einstein as Mr. Rogers, improvising. It was fun. It was like running in an open field."

At the Improvisation, there was even louder screaming and yelling at the mention of Robin Williams. Again, he started out as an Oscar winner, sancti-

moniously: "Thank you for your kindness. Your words are so meaningful."
Then he was South Africa's Botha, and after that he became the state of Michigan and the Statue of Liberty and Frank Sinatra and Jewish hunters ("Let's go out to the country and see if anything died") and Lee Iacocca and Henry Kissinger and El Al Airlines.

After a while, someone in the audience called out "Dr. Ruth!"

"Dr. Rufe?" Williams asked, having obviously misheard the name. Then he got it, and immediately used the error to take off as a black woman preacher giving sex advice in a scolding vein. "Get yoh act together, now," he said. "Yoh look lahk a Ken doll. Don't yoh look at me wid dose mascara eyes goin' flip-flap. Get on dat highway and make sure de bridge is open." He kept it going for a good fifteen minutes. The audience was beside itself. At the end, Williams came off looking exhilarated and told us that that one had been brand-new—a breakthrough. He looked as though he had been running in an open field.

1986

EAGER

FAITH POPCORN, the woman who has called for a Frank Perdue of fish, runs a trend-analysis firm, BrainReserve, from an uncluttered, airy office eleven stories above Fifty-seventh Street—*East* Fifty-seventh. We visited Miss Popcorn, the woman who has predicted that by the year 2001 the bathroom will be "an anti-stress center or leisure area," one day last week, because we felt we had no choice. Everywhere we had turned in recent months, and especially when we had turned to *Newsweek*, there was Faith Popcorn, the woman who recognized very early—when most people saw blue sky, and blue sky only—that Tofutti was not a sure thing. As early as the end of 1984, when *Newsweek* proclaimed that year the Year of the Yuppie, she told a reporter she was having trouble persuading her clients in the processed-food industry to develop new products such as a line of fresh baby food for the boomer market. On May 6th of last year, she told *Newsweek* that New Coke was a mistake. "The giant kneels," she said. Seven weeks later, on June 24th, she told *Newsweek* that New Coke was "the marketing fiasco of the decade." On July 22nd, *Newsweek* readers learned that she thought Coke's problem lay in America's mouth. "The American palate is dead," she said. "You know that Thomas Dolby song 'She Blinded Me with Science'? Well, you could say the same thing about Coke." This spring, she returned to *Newsweek* to discuss the Fortune 500 and similar lists of the biggest businesses—lists she said had become the *Social Registers* of the nineteen-eighties. "It's like the best-dressed list for money," she said. Unaccountably, she failed to appear in the magazine's June 2nd issue on the subject of the Marriage Crunch, but she has recently moved on the Associated Press wire (praising General Mills for the big Betty Crocker makeover), and appeared in *U.S. News & World Report*, the *Wall Street Journal* (at least four times by our count), *USA Today* (twice, but once was for making the *Savvy* register of the top sixty businesses run by women), *Adweek*, *American Banker* (taking strong exception to the Metropolitan Life ads featuring Snoopy et al., on the ground that they weren't serious enough), the *Times*, and *Boardroom Reports*, a newsletter for executives (voicing her feeling that franchise restaurants would soon be offering "fast lobster").

In short, along with the wind, time and tide, the tectonic plates, the Judeo-Christian tradition, and the Byzantine tax code, Faith Popcorn had been irresistibly shaping our life. So many of the things we thought to be true she had said. Did we independently think them to be true? Or is Faith Popcorn the ur of our era? Is she the oversoul incarnate? And, if so, is she nice? We can report she is as nice as she is omniscient, and that is almost totally. "I'm trying to think of a trend I've missed—it would be more credible if I could think of one," she said. "Well, for the past couple of years I've been predicting a car specially positioned for a woman—the safest car in the world, with airbags, an SOS device, built-in baby seats. I thought that people would be willing to pay between thirty thousand and fifty thousand dollars for it—that they'd take out a mortgage, just as they would on a house. So far, it hasn't happened." But so many other things have—things that BrainReserve, which conducts two thousand in-depth interviews with consumers each year, has known about way in advance. In 1980, she said that this decade would see a big market for salt-free products, the return of flashy cars, a rise in the popularity of older TV stars, a declining divorce rate, and media rooms in homes. Success has sucked clients in the door: the roster over the last few years includes Timex watches, Vlasic pickles, Quaker Oats, Paper Mate, Anheuser-Busch, and American Cyanamid. In some cases, she helps launch new products; in others, she generates names; and, most often, she repositions old products. In every case, she relies on BrainReserve's bank of fifteen active trends.

"At the moment, there's a trend toward trends themselves," she said. "It's part of the trend toward control. A part of that trend has a name: 'cocooning.' It's very complex, but basically it involves building a shell of safety around yourself, so you're not at the mercy of the unpredictable world. That's why people like to have their VCRs, and their Barcaloungers. Barcaloungers, some of them equipped with stereo headphones, are making a comeback. And part of the idea is that companies are hiring experts like me so the companies can be in control. Control, control, control." In fact, people are so much in control that they will start drinking again soon, overwhelming the short-lived New Sobriety trend. "If you're working hard and working out hard, how do you relieve stress?" Miss Popcorn asked us. "Not in meditation. People aren't into meditation anymore. Alcohol is coming back. Not bourbon. It's hard to work out with a hangover. And we want high style. Bourbon-on-the-rocks is not style. A wine cooler is higher style. We're seeing the drinks of the thirties coming back—the

Sidecar. You may even see the Martini coming back." Also, Nouveau Italian will be the next big restaurant thing. "We're blanded out," she explained. "We're not interested in the whites anymore—white wine, veal, it's over."

Miss Popcorn said that trends are so powerful she sometimes succumbs herself. "The control thing—mean. I hired a trainer for my morning workouts. And I'm so embarrassed. You realize it's horrifying and then you realize you're doing it. You can get your exercise if you go out and cut down a tree, so why don't we? Why do we need someone telling us how? I really admire people who don't care what's going on. I really admire people who still smoke." Some things, though, are too powerful to resist. "I have such a hard time convincing manufacturers that Health and Fitness is not just a trend, it's an intrinsic change in life style," she said. "It's how people will be from now on. Because as you get closer to death life gets sweeter."

1 9 8 6

SUSAN LARDNER

POPCORN MEMOIRS

T HE local movie house in a village that lies between the Atlantic Ocean and the Great South Bay was showing Kurosawa's "Ran" last Monday night. The hurricane watch had been called off, but a sturdy east wind was blowing, and amazing clouds were moving across the sky. The sun was setting brightly, and a practically full moon was about to rise as the movie began. A fourteen-year-old boy was making his début behind the popcorn-and-candy counter. Four hours later, he had this story to tell:

I met L——, the woman who runs the movie house, on the street one night, and we had a little conversation pertaining to summer employment. She said she would keep me in mind. This afternoon, she called up and said to be there at a quarter after six. She hurriedly showed me the ropes—basically, cleaning off the counter, making sure to see that there was enough of all the sodas, and making sure I knew where the brooms were—and she also told me to see that the men's room was mildly reputable-looking. Oh, yeah, she showed me how to do the popcorn. She did the first batch to show me how, and she told me to do three more. I say "do," not "make," because I don't actually bring the popcorn into being. L—— has a good sense of how much popcorn to do—she really knows movie crowds.

You take a measuring cup, scoop the kernels out of a huge bag, lift up the top of the popper—Oh, this reflects the way I mistakenly did it. I'm supposed to put the Tastee Pop in first—that's a popcorn oil and seasoner, it says on the box—but I forget and put it in after the kernels, usually. Tastee Pop is harder and flakier than butter. Then I'm supposed to put salt in—that's one of the things she's picky about, the salt—and then I lower the top. Oh, before I do all that, before I even start, I have to turn the little knob that says "Popper," wait till it gets hot, and then turn on a separate switch for the motor and a light switch. Then I do three or four batches—have to use my judgment—and turn everything off except the infrared lamp that keeps it warm. Once each batch is popped, there's a wooden stick that's used to knock it out of the popper into the bottom of the box, which is where I scoop it out from. The stick is about two feet long with a flattish end where it's chipped—like something you'd find on the beach.

L——'s business philosophy is the hardest thing to get used to. It's "The customer is always wrong." She didn't put it to me in so many words, but I soon got the idea. One woman started out by wondering if the popcorn might be soggy, and then she complained about the Tastee Pop—she wanted to know was I using butter or imitation (we put butter on at the end, if they want it)—and then she said it wasn't salty enough, and when I handed her the cylinder she said didn't I have a saltshaker. I said to L——, "This woman seemed to think it was a wine-tasting party, or something," and L—— said, "Oh, yes, she's a ---- -- --- ---," and she told me if I had any more trouble just say, "L——, we've got a complainer over here." She told me she had once warned the very same woman, "If you ask me whether the popcorn's stale, you'll wear it." Perhaps her thought was that I should hit complainers with the stick.

Oh, God, one weird thing. During the middle of the first show, there was a loud clatter coming from the projection room, so I ran to the foot of the stairs, and I got there just in time to see a huge reel of film speeding toward me, sort of half in the air and half on the stairs, picking up speed as it fell. I managed to jump out of the way before it landed and crashed into the wall.

I got to see some of the movie when business quieted down. The part where he was saying to the daughter-in-law, "Why do you look at me with love in your eyes?" That was so sad I began to cry, so I went over to the napkins to dry my tears, and L—— said, "Don't take too many napkins." This is another feature of her philosophy. At one point, a large person appeared and bought a large popcorn. He was a rather tough-looking fellow, perhaps wearing a black leather jacket (or I may have imagined he was). He stuck his hand into the napkin box—this was before L—— replaced the napkins—and he pulled almost all of them out. L—— had told me, "If someone takes too many napkins, just say, 'Hey, don't take so many napkins,' because they'll just wind up on the floor and I'll have to sweep them up later." But in this case I decided it would be better not to say anything.

Oh, yeah. Remember those sushi people? You know, the family that runs Sushi-Ya? This is from L——. She told me they came in and that they were delighted to have a movie in their own language. So she asked them could she have a free plate of sushi the next time she went to their place, and they said yes. I think she meant to imply that they were ecstatic.

Then, later, at the second show, a woman came in and said she had allergies, did we have any water, and L—— said, "No, no water." That struck me as harsh. Then she relented and brought some water in a cup, and the woman bought a Coke. And I thought my paper-boy job last summer was weird!

You have to have an aptitude for this popcorn biz. I know it's candy and soda, too, but I think of it as popcorn. Oh, this is part of her business philosophy: "Don't bother getting them their sodas from the cooler—they can do it themselves. You have enough to do." I was only trying to be helpful before I got too busy with the popcorn. I developed a rhythm for it surprisingly quickly. You take the— You're supposed to put half a stick of Tastee Pop in for each batch, and if it isn't cut yet, in half, take the church key and cut a groove around the middle of the bar and then snap it in half. So: cut, snap, dump the Tastee Pop in, scoop up the kernels, pour the kernels into the popper, sprinkle the salt. Cut, snap, dump, scoop, pour, sprinkle. Then you ask if they want butter. Of course, that includes somewhere in there opening and closing the lid of the popper.

One annoying incident—a Yuppie couple came in and asked for popcorn, and I filled the cup about *this* much under the rim, so it wouldn't spill out, and the woman said, "Could you fill it up, please," so I filled it to the rim and some pieces fell to the as yet unswept floor.

Last night, L—— underestimated the running time of the movie, so I ended up with only about two minutes to make two bushels of popcorn before the customers started to pour in for the second show. During the second performance, the reel ran out about half an hour into the movie. I was sweeping up, and suddenly I heard people screaming—this shout arose—and I saw the mustached projectionist running up the stairs. Every now and then, he comes downstairs and scoops up some popcorn. I was quite offended at first, as I thought of the popcorn as my domain, but he probably just wanted to save me the trouble.

One more night of "Ran," then two nights of "Desert Hearts" (a *very* adult movie, I hear), then some sort of benefit for two nights, then "Ruthless People," starting Sunday. L—— said to me, "So you think you're pretty fast, huh? When the first day of 'Ruthless People' comes around, you're gonna really understand what speed means. Maybe you'd better practice at home." She values speed over perfection—you can tell. She talked a lot about speed, but when I was sweeping the floors during my period of ennui an hour after the beginning of the first show—I was sweeping all the nooks and crannies—she said, "It doesn't have to be perfect." She runs a rough operation. She's great to work for. I haven't applied her philosophy yet, because I've been too intimidated by the customers. Probably I'll be forced to, though, when the mobs pour in. "Ruthless People," I imagine, will be the true test of my abilities. I hope I pass the test.

1 9 8 6

ADOPTION

CONGRATULATIONS are probably in order. You have been selected as the adoptive parent of a Hudson River striped bass—you and thirty-one students in Michael Lugano's sixth-grade class at P.S. 105, in the Bronx. Con Edison, which is one of the utilities operating power plants that across the years have killed significant numbers of young striped bass in the Hudson River, has more recently been doing its share to replace the striped bass. Recognizing its own good deeds, Con Edison helped to arrange a gathering at Wave Hill, in Riverdale, where you can claim your adoption certificate. There is much to be seen and studied along the way, and the potential for fun exists.

Remember to dress warmly, just in case a ten-inch snowfall begins while you are away from your desk. The following is a list of suggested activities to be performed in conjunction with your field trip:

1. Call Metro-North, ascertain train schedule to Riverdale.

2. Prior to trip, familiarize yourself with target area and establish safety rules. (No rides from strangers, no intoxicants, no explosives, etc.) Bring writing utensil and notebook in which to record meaningful data. While waiting for elevator, ask yourself whether to bring along field guides, clipboards, binoculars, twine, thermometer, surgical tape, shovels, old strainers, dip nets, plastic pail, glass jars, plastic-foam box, change of clothes, enormous plastic bag for all the above—or maybe bring none of the above.

3. Go to Grand Central. Board train. Enjoy ride. Remember to get off train. Walk up long, steep, slippery streets in approximate direction of Wave Hill. Notice general condition of area (*nice* neighborhood, ripe for historic-district designation); weather (incipient snow, sleet); bird life (may have been some);

insects (too cold); light penetration (midmorning, the usual). Find something beautiful (three Hasidim carrying black umbrellas, approaching from a hundred yards away, looking like opening frames of Fellini film).

4. If you feel lost, and panic a little, ask Hasidim for directions. Walk past Wave Hill gatehouse. Close eyes. Do you hear natural sounds? Man-made sounds? Good. Follow path to main building. Inside, find John Mihaly, Wave Hill staff member, who makes welcoming sounds, plastic-name-tag-selection sounds, then points to stairwell.

5. Go downstairs, to Wave Hill Learning Center, where members of Mr. Lugano's class from P.S. 105—Victor Andujar, Pierre Arroyo, Sewdat Budhoo, José Delvalle, Sunil Mangaru, Mary Altieri, Ashanti Butler, Michelle Laureano, Alma Franco, Elvira Kraja, Tiffiney Petrisch, Fikreta Povataj, Kelly Riffle, Plushette Sullivan, Cortina Watson, et al.—make virtually no sounds. Uta Gore, instructor in Wave Hill education program, does the talking. Note meaningful datum: children take for granted Uta Gore's veracity, acknowledge that she knows much about Hudson River. She knows, in particular, that striped bass live in ocean but spawn in river; that when striped bass are spawning there is lots of splashing; that right now New York State bans the possession and sale of striped bass, but some people are undeterred. (Mike Parker, efficiency-minded P.S. 105–er, asks, "Why don't they just put up a sign that says, 'Trespassers Will Be Shot'?") As Uta Gore passes around vials containing striped-bass eggs, larvae, a small fry specimen, record observation in notebook: "Today's young people are our hope for future. Hmm."

6. Examine fine-looking aquarium in Learning Center, with particular attention to several resident striped bass, who Uta Gore says are "spoiled rotten." (She feeds them chopped oysters, chopped Boston scrod, chopped flounder; was feeding them goldfish, but they "lost interest.")

7. Gather for future reference specimens of Uta Gore's polysyllabics: "detritus," "herbicides," "estuary," "oxygenated," "optimize," "therapeutic," "turbidity."

8. Join group next door, in audiovisual room. Watch documentary videotape "Hatchery on the Hudson," produced by Con Edison, which extolls virtues of the Hudson River Striped Bass Hatchery, in Verplanck, New York, sponsored by Con Ed and four other utility companies. Time videotape with stopwatch: ten minutes.

9. If you start to feel a little sleepy, perk up when Dr. Kenneth Marcellus, senior project biologist for Con Ed, enters room carrying brown grocery bag labelled "Hudson River," and says, "Good morning. I brought with me the Hudson River, but we're not going to touch the Hudson River just yet. We're going to wonder about it." Listen as he explains how striped bass from Verplanck hatchery get "tagged" with binary-encoded one-twenty-fifth-inch wires implanted in their cheeks. Note what happens when Dr. Marcellus at last opens brown bag—it contains many white beans. Watch as he adds handful of

pink beans, then shakes bag. Note that pink beans signify tagged fish, white beans signify wild fish. Maybe note some other stuff.

10. When moment of adoption ceremony arrives—each adoptive parent to receive certificate specifying striped bass's tag number, birthplace, birth date, date and site of release, age and length at time of release—consult stopwatch again. Measure time lapse between beginning of adoption ceremony and instant at which member of class asks, "When do we get our bass?" Result: twenty-six seconds. Note that when Julissa Cabrera asks "When do we get our bass?" Uta Gore fires back "You're not getting the bass. Your bass is in the river. It's free. Right now it's in the river consuming enormous amounts of tasty morsels. It's getting to be humongous. Don't you want it to grow to become humongous?"

11. At feeding time, observe whether it's children or grownups who eat bag lunches, of ham hero sandwiches, box juices, and whether it's children or grownups who migrate upstairs for lunch provided by Con Ed—chicken salad vinaigrette, rice dish with prosciutto and fresh shrimp, broccoli and radicchio, white wine, coffee, brownies.

12. During lunch, look out window, check atmospheric conditions (severely deteriorated). If offer of ride to midtown with Dr. Marcellus materializes, grab it (in tasteful manner). Walk in gingerly fashion to Dr. M.'s car. Conduct nature experiment, brushing snow off Dr. M.'s car.

13. While listening to Dr. M.'s tires spin, catalogue volume of freebies distributed upon exit from Wave Hill: page-long news release titled "Wave Hill"; three-page document titled "Wave Hill: A Brief History"; photocopies of four newspaper articles about striped bass and the Hudson River Striped Bass Hatchery; photocopies of two Con Ed in-house magazine articles about the hatchery; 1980 press release describing provisions of Hudson River Cooling Tower Settlement Agreement; photocopies of six newspaper articles about Wave Hill; reprint of magazine article about exhibit at Wave Hill from *Garden Design*; ditto from *Garden*; two reprints of magazine article about Wave Hill from *American Horticulturist*; reprint of magazine article from *Ovation*, about Arturo Toscanini's connection with Wave Hill; two copies of Wave Hill members' calendar for winter, 1987; two subscription applications for Wave Hill horticulture-lecture series; two subscription applications for Wave Hill concert series; map and guide to Riverdale Park; map and guide to Wave Hill woods; pamphlet describing Wave Hill education programs; boxed portfolio of Hudson River photographs by Wendy Holmes, published in 1973 (a pleasure to look at and ideal for carrying back through blizzard, providing much-needed ballast); inter-office memo to guy named Herb.

1 9 8 7

JOHN McPHEE

IN VIRGIN FOREST

I N virgin forest, the ground is uneven, dimpled with pits and adjacent
mounds. Perfect trees rise, yes, with boles clear to fifty and sixty feet; but im-
perfect trees are there, too—bent twigs, centuries after the bending—not to
mention the dead standing timber, not to mention four thousand board feet
rotting as one trunk among the mayapples and the violets: a toppled hull
fruited with orange-and-cream fungi, which devour the wood, metabolize it,
cause it literally to disappear. In virgin forest, the classic symbol of virginity is
a fallen uprooted trunk decaying in a bed of herbs.

In our latitude, the primeval forest would include grapes, their free-floating
vines descending like bridge cables. Wild grapes are incapable of climbing
trees. They are lifted by trees as the trees grow, and their bunches hang from
the top of the canopy. In our latitude, there is a great scarcity of virgin forest.
Cut the grapevines, make a few stumps, let your cattle in to graze, and it's all
over till the end of time. Nonetheless, we were in such a place only a few days
ago, and did not have to travel far to see it. Never cut, never turned, it was a
piece of American deciduous forest in continuous evolution dating to the tun-
dras of mesolithic time. Some of the trees were ninety feet tall, with redtails
nesting in them, and when the hawks took off and rose above the canopy they
could see the World Trade Center.

We had made our way to Franklin Township, New Jersey, which includes
New Brunswick and is one of the less virgin milieus in America. This is where
the megalopolis came in so fast it trapped animals between motels. It missed,
though, half a mile of primeval woods. The property, a little east of East Mill-
stone, was settled in 1701 by Mynheer Cornelius VanLiew and remained in one

family for two hundred and fifty-four years. They cleared and farmed most of their land but consciously decided to leave sixty-five acres untouched. The Revolution came and went, the Civil and the World Wars, but not until the nineteen-fifties did the family seek the counsel of a sawyer. The big trees were ruled by white oaks, dating to the eighteenth and seventeenth centuries, and their value was expressible in carats. Being no less frank than Dutch, the family let its intentions be known. As often will happen in conservation crises, this brought forth a paradox of interested parties: rod-and-gun groups, the Nature Conservancy, the Adirondack Mountain Club, the United Daughters of the Confederacy. A tract of virgin forest is so rare that money was raised in thirty-eight states and seven foreign countries. But not enough. The trees were worth a good deal more. In the end, the forest was saved by, of all people, the United Brotherhood of Carpenters and Joiners of America, whose president remarked in 1955, as he handed over the property to Rutgers University, "What happens in the woodlands is close to the carpenter's heart."

Named for a Brotherhood president, the tract is called Hutcheson Memorial Forest. A brief trail makes a loop near one end. The deed limits Rutgers to that, and Rutgers is not arguing. The university's role is to protect the periphery and to study the woods. When something attacks, Rutgers makes notes. A disease that kills American beeches is on its way from Maine. "The forest deed says basically you don't do anything about it," a biologist named Edmund Stiles explained to us. "You watch what happens." In 1981, gypsy moths tore off the canopy, and sunlight sprayed the floor. The understory thickened as shrubs and saplings responded with a flush of growth. "The canopy is now closing over again," Stiles said. "This summer, there will be a lot of death." In 1950, a hurricane left huge gaps in the canopy. "Once every three hundred years you can expect a hurricane that will knock down damned near everything," Stiles went on. "There's a real patchwork nature in an old forest, in the way it is always undergoing replacement." He stopped to admire a small white ash standing alone beneath open sky. "That's going to take the canopy," he said. "It's going to go all the way. It has been released. It will fill the gap."

Forty-two years old and of middle height—wearing boots, bluejeans, a brown wool shirt—Stiles had a handsome set of muttonchops and a tumble of thick brown hair that flowed over his forehead toward inquiring blue eyes. He had been working in Hutcheson Forest for thirteen years, he told us, and had recently become director. His doctoral dissertation, at the University of Washington, was on bird communities in alder forests. More recently, he had studied the foraging strategies of insects and the symbiotic relationships of berries and migratory birds. In other words, he was a zoologist and a botanist, too. From secretive gray foxes to the last dead stick—that was what the untouched forest was about. The big oaks (red, white, and black), the shagbark hickories, sugar maples, beeches, ashes, and dogwoods—among thousands of plant and animal species—were only the trees.

As we talked, and moved about, tasting the odd spicebush leaf or a tendril of smilax, Stiles divided his attention and seemed not to miss a sound. "Spicebush and dogwood fruits are very high in lipids," he said. "They are taken on by birds getting ready for long migratory flights. Those are wood thrushes calling. A forest has to be at least a hundred years old to get a wood thrush. Actually, it takes about four centuries to grow a forest of this kind. The gap phenomenon is typical of old forest. There's a white-eyed vireo. Blue-winged warbler. There are cycles of openness and closedness in the canopies. Trees take advantage. Fill in the gaps. These are white-oak seedlings from a mast year. There's a nice red-bellied woodpecker." He was like Toscanini, just offstage, listening idly to his orchestra as it tuned itself up. He said he had developed a theory that out-of-season splotches of leaf color are messages to frugivorous birds—the scattered early orange among sassafras leaves, the springtime red of the leaves of the wild strawberry, the red of the Virginia creeper when everything else is green. When fruit is ready, the special colors turn on. He heard a great crested flycatcher. He bent down to a jack-in-the-pulpit, saying that it bears bird-disseminated fruit and is pollinated by a small black fly.

German foresters who came to visit Hutcheson Forest had been surprised by the untidiness of the place, startled by the jumble of life and death. "These Germans are unfamiliar with stuff just lying around, with the truly virginal aspect of the forest," Stiles said. Apparently, the Germans, like almost everyone else, had a misconception of forest primeval—a picture of Wotan striding through the noonday twilight, of Ludwig D. Boone shouting for *Lebensraum* among giant columns of uniform trees. "You don't find redwoods," Stiles remarked summarily. "You don't find Evangeline's forest. You find a more realistic forest."

You find a huge white ash that has grown up at an angle of forty-five degrees, and in a managed forest would have long ago been tagged for destruction. You find remarkably deep humus. You find a great rusty stump, maybe six feet high, and jagged where the trunk now beside it snapped off. More often, you find whole root structures tipped into the air and looking like radial engines. As you will nowhere else, you find the topography of pits and mounds. In its random lumpiness, it could be a model of glacial terrain. When a tree goes over and its roots come ripping from the ground, they bring with them a considerable mass of soil. When the tree has disappeared, the dirt remains as a mound, which turns kelly green with moss. Beside it is the pit that the roots came from. When no other trace remains of the tree, you can see by the pit and the mound the direction in which the tree fell, and guess its approximate size. If cattle graze in pit-and-mound topography, they trample and destroy it. The pits and mounds of centuries are evidence of virgin forest.

There is supporting evidence in human records and in tree rings. People from Columbia's Lamont-Doherty Geological Observatory have cored some trees in Hutcheson Forest and dated them, for example, to 1699, 1678. Neighboring land was settled, and cleared for farming, in 1701. Lamont-Doherty has an ongoing project called the Eastern Network Dendrochronology Series, which has sought and catalogued virgin stands at least two hundred and fifty years old. The list is short and scattered, and the tracts are small, with the notable exceptions of Joyce Kilmer Memorial Forest, in North Carolina (thirty-eight hundred virgin acres), the cove hardwoods of Great Smoky Mountains National Park, and a large stand of hemlocks and beeches in Allegheny National Forest, in western Pennsylvania. There are three hundred virgin acres on the Wabash River in Illinois, and, in eastern Ohio, a woods of white oaks some of which were seedlings when the Pilgrims reached New England. The Ohio white oaks, like the white oaks of Hutcheson Forest, are from three to four feet in diameter. Old white oaks are found in few places, because they had a tendency to become bowsprits, barrel staves, and queen-post trusses. Virgin hemlocks are comparatively common. Maine is not rich in virgin timber—some red spruce on Mt. Katahdin, some red spruce above Tunk Lake. There is a river gorge in Connecticut where trees have never been cut. Some red spruce and hemlock in the Adirondacks date to the late fifteen-hundreds, and the hemlocks of the Allegheny forest are nearly two centuries older than that. In the Shawangunk Mountains, about seventy beeline miles northwest of our office on Forty-third Street, is the oldest known stand of pitch pine (360 years), also some white pine (370), chestnut oak (330), and eastern hemlock (500). They are up on a quartzite ridge line, though, and are very slow-growing small trees. Remnant old-growth stands tend to be in mountains, in rocky, craggy places, not in flatlands. Hutcheson Forest, in the Newark Basin—in what was once a prime piedmont area—is thus exceptionally rare. In the region of New York City, there is nothing like it, no other clearly documented patch. In fact, it is the largest mixed-oak virgin forest left in the eastern United States.

Running through the forest is Spooky Brook, spawning ground of the white sucker. Rutgers would like to control the headwaters, fearing something known as herbicide drift. Continuing population drift is no less a threat, as development fills in lingering farms. The woods are closed to visitors, except for scheduled Sunday tours. Rutgers already owns some hundred and fifty acres contiguous to the forest, and hopes, with the help of the Nature Conservancy, to get two hundred more. Manipulative research is carried out on the peripheral land, while observational research goes on in the forest, which has been described by Richard Forman, a professor at Harvard, as "probably the single most studied primeval woods on the continent." People have gone in there and emerged with more than a hundred advanced degrees, including thirty-six Ph.D.s. So many articles, papers, theses, and other research publications have come out of Hutcheson Forest that countless trees have been clear-cut elsewhere just in order to print them.

TASTE OF TEXAS

DARN right we race armadillos. Got a certificate right here to prove it. Jalapeño Sam Lewis showed us how. Handed us a bristly, wriggling, pointy-faced, armor-plated little dude and said, "Go for it." The track was a strip of AstroTurf rolled out behind the Puck Building, in SoHo, and there were thirteen entries, all but ours being handled by Texans. Our armadillo got off to a slow start. "Blow on him," Sam coached. "Blow on him where his tail meets his body, and he'll run like crazy." We confined ourself to verbal encouragement, and soon our armadillo responded. One of the other racers veered off, turned back, and went *under* the AstroTurf. That gave us a chance to gain ground. Some of the other racers were spooked, frankly, with this hump in the turf darting around, but not our guy. He ended up finishing second. Jalapeño Sam, who is the president of the World Armadillo Breeding and Racing Association, and runs, he told us, "a Hertz rent-a-diller service" at races in Texas, presented us with our certificate, which features an armadillo wearing sneakers.

We noticed that the armadillo that had won the race had half its tail wrapped in silver duct tape. We asked Jalapeño Sam what had happened to it.

Jalapeño Sam did not reply. Instead, he turned to a young woman standing nearby. "Where do you live, little lady?" he asked.

"Nowhere," she said. "West Texas."

"That's about ten miles from where I live!" Sam exclaimed.

We headed on into the Puck Building, where the Taste of Texas food show was in progress. Thirty-six Texas companies were displaying their wares, and Jim Hightower, the Texas Agriculture Commissioner, was assuring the crowd, "If you taste it, you'll buy a trainload of it."

That's basically what Tom TenBrink said, too, when we stopped in front of his booth. TenBrink was scooping Mariano's Frozen Margarita Mix out of a plastic bucket and urging Margaritas on passersby. "You gotta put it in their mouth," he told us. "You put it in their mouth, you make 'em walk backward." Mariano's Frozen Margarita Mix, which, according to TenBrink, is already big in the Dallas–Fort Worth area, is an alarmingly simple invention: you pour a bottle of tequila into a bucket of mix, stir it, and put it in the freezer, and the next morning you're looking at several dozen frozen Margaritas. "Our best customer is a female, married or not, between the ages of twenty-four and forty, who entertains a lot," TenBrink said. "She immediately appreciates it." We reckoned there were many such customers in New York, and said so. "That's why we're here," he said. Then we got down to business: we tried the Margarita. It was cold, sweet, strong, and though it didn't look exactly like other Margaritas we've seen—it was a rather disturbing deep chemical green—it tasted like the genuine article. We walked backward.

And bumped into Jane Scott, the vice-president for home furnishings, Saks Fifth Avenue. Jane was perfectly polite. She told us she found the Taste of Texas show "interesting, because it focusses on a very hot segment of the market," but she declined to say whether we should start looking for pickled okra, mesquite-grilled fajitas, bluebonnet jelly, or three-alarm chili in the gift-foods section of Saks.

Nieman-Marcus, on the other hand, has already committed itself to distributing New York, Texas Cheesecake. Lyn Dunsavage, who makes New York, Texas Cheesecake at her home, explained, "Our farm overlooks the hills of New York, Texas." NY, TX, which has a population of twelve, is seventy-five miles southeast of Dallas. "There's a Baptist church, a graveyard, and a store," Mrs. Dunsavage said. "The store doesn't sell any cheesecake. It sells mainly baling wire and oil for tractors." A young man stopped to sample Mrs. Dunsavage's cake. He pronounced it better than anything available locally. "That's a bodacious statement to make in New York," said Mrs. D.

The Texas 1015, although it was one of the few products displayed that didn't all but shout "Taste me!," was a showstopper. It's a huge, flawless-looking onion, bigger than most urban grapefruits, and Paula Fouchek was on hand to extoll its virtues. "It took ten years of research, and a million dollars, to produce the 1015," she told us. "It's a super-sweet onion. Why is it called the 1015? Because you plant it on October 15th. They tried to change the name, but it was too late. Consumers already knew it. They'd say, 'I want the one with the *number*.' They didn't know the number, but they knew the onion."

We asked where we could find a 1015 in New York City.

"Nowhere right now," Paula said. "It comes out of the ground in April, and it's only available here from about mid-April to mid-May. But it's one of the few varieties of sweet onion that can be stored. Like, we knew we would be coming here, so we put six or eight cartons in the refrigerator, and they don't look too bad, do they?" They certainly didn't. "Another thing about the 1015 is that it's predominantly single-centered. If you're a food-service outlet, making onion rings, you don't want an onion with two, three, four centers, do you?" We certainly don't. If we're a food-service outlet, we want a trainload of 1015s.

But we changed the subject. We mentioned all the Texas-shaped things at the show—Texas-shaped corn chips being served on Texas-shaped trays, for example.

Paula's colleague Betty Ricks said, "That's right. It's one of the few states that are like that. I've lived in California. I've lived in Michigan. And you just can't buy things shaped like those states. I've got Texas-shaped ice-cube makers, Texas-shaped cake pans."

Phyllis Hsu didn't have any Texas-shaped egg rolls at her booth, but that doesn't mean that her line of Amy's Egg Rolls and Fried Wontons is without patriotic content. They are named after her fifteen-year-old daughter, whose name written in Chinese characters means, according to Mrs. Hsu, "I Love America." Amy's Fried Wontons are big in Houston's public schools, and Mrs. Hsu was clear about her reasons for participating in the Taste of Texas show. "I want to get into New York schools," she said. We tried a wonton, and found it bodacious.

1987

ON DISPLAY

STEVEN JENKINS' grandfather Adolph Mayer has a big beefsteak tomato named for him. "The Adolph Mayer is a really wonderful tomato," Mr. Jenkins told us the other day when we dropped in at Fairway, the busy produce market on Broadway near Seventy-fourth Street, where he is one of four junior partners. "My grandfather helps the University of Missouri test new vegetable seeds, so they honored him by naming one after him." Being immortalized anywhere, especially in association with an appetizing vegetable, would probably please almost anyone, but for Mr. Jenkins that kind of recognition has special significance. "Would I like a cheese named after me, the way my grandfather had a tomato?" he asked himself. "That sounds great. You bet I would. You *bet.*"

Mr. Jenkins' specialty at Fairway is cheese, but his real passion is writing chatty and enticing signs for all the store's products. A few of the Fairway signs just do their job—they say something simple, like "NEW CROP YAMS" or "CRISPY WESTERN ICEBERG SOLD AT COST PRICE"—but those are made by the other Fairway partners, who figure that a sign's a *sign,* especially when you're in a hurry and there are crowds stretching from the cash register to the back door. Mr. Jenkins' signs have become something like required reading among shoppers in the neighborhood—they can be informative, argumentative, comic, autobiographical, or sassy—and whatever time he finds between checking cheese orders he spends making them.

The signs are about five by seven inches and are made of white tagboard. Mr. Jenkins hand-letters them with bright-red or orange or blue or purple laundry markers. One of his signs that day said:

HOOP CHEESE: NO FAT! NO SALT!
AN INTRIGUING MARRIAGE
OF WET COTTON AND LIBRARY PASTE

"I'm very opinionated about cheese," he explained to us, and he pointed out another sign, which said:

MIMOLETTE: HARD, BLAND. DE GAULLE'S
FAVORITE,
WHICH FIGURES. I DON'T KNOW WHY,
IT JUST DOES.
WE STOCK IT BECAUSE IT LOOKS LIKE
CHEESE.

His all-time favorite sign is no longer in service, but Mr. Jenkins was so pleased with it that he saved it for display. It's stapled to the store's back wall, and says:

RAW SEX
FRESH FIGS
SAME THING. 49 CENTS

Some of Mr. Jenkins' signs acquaint shoppers with people who supply choice items or who figure in his interest in food. On signs here and there throughout the store are mentions of Ted and Sally (makers of Wieninger cheese), Laura (California chèvre), Jane and Bo (pie bakers), Nana (Mr. Jenkins' grandmother, who introduced him to kohlrabi), Dr. Scott Severns (his dentist), and Al Grimaldi (bread baker). "I think it's important to know where food is from—that's why I name some of the suppliers," he said. "I wanted to write about my grandmother because she really taught me about the value of fresh foods, and my dentist just asked me to order sorrel for him, so I thought I'd mention him, too." Some signs have won Mr. Jenkins gratitude from customers. His treatise "NEVER WASH A MUSHROOM!" was very popular, for example. Other signs, however, have been controversial. A sign on some Illinois goat cheese asserting that the cheese was exciting but Illinois was really boring offended so many shoppers that for a while he had to post a note beside it admitting that he was from Missouri and considered it even more boring than Illinois.

Mr. Jenkins, who is late-thirtyish, curly-haired, blue-eyed, and barrel-chested, told us that he moved to New York fourteen years ago to become an actor. His career went well—he played the Dean & DeLuca counterman in "Manhattan" and had a shot at a major role in the soaps—but he soon realized that his day job as a cheese man was making him happier than his acting did. He decided to get serious about food, and he discovered that the thing that

made him happiest of all was driving around Europe looking at food and finding the villages that his favorite wines and cheeses were named for. He also
liked finding towns famous for their sauces. He more or less gave up acting, and
seven years ago he joined Fairway. Today, Mr. Jenkins has credentials in
cheese—he is America's only Master Cheesemonger, which means he's an
elected member of the Guilde des Maître-Fromagers, Compagnon du Saint-
Uguzon—and he manages to satisfy his hunger for an audience by making
signs. He recently described this professional odyssey in a sign for cornichons:

> WHEN I GOT STARTED IN THIS BUSINESS
> 13 YEARS AGO, I
> THOUGHT CORNICHONS WERE LITTLE
> CORN COBS.
> AND NOW LOOK AT WHAT A GOURMET
> I'VE BECOME.
> MY GOD, LIFE IS AMAZING.

"I think the best way to show off food is to have a big, huge, untethered pile
of stuff," he said as he tidied up around his department, straightening a sign
that chided the makers of Pecorino Toscana sheep cheese for charging so
much. "Then you stick a big, funny, outrageous, eye-catching sign in the middle of it. You say everything there is to say about the product. There are several
schools of food-display signs. One is the fancy-shmancy school, where you
have a tiny little sign that says 'One-Hundred-Year-Old Quail Eggs, Eight Thousand Dollars a Dozen.' Another school, which is the one I'm in, is where you
take a garish sign and staple it to a big stick and you wedge it into the pile of
food. It's a real peasant way of life, making your living from food, and I enjoy
the peasant quality of putting a sign on a stick into the food. My partners are
always yelling at me for spending so much time on my signs, but I love to do it.
You can tell the ones I didn't make. They're rather terse."
    As he walked past a sign that said

> HANDMADE STUFFED PEPPERS: WOW!
> HOOO!
> STRANGE BUT TRUE!
> FROM RHODE ISLAND. . . . CRAZY
> AMERICANS!

he spotted a woman in the checkout line clutching a bottle of olive oil. "Hey,
you're not going to buy that, are you?" he asked her. She eyed him nervously.
"There's another brand that's better and it's seven dollars less," he explained,
pointing toward a shelf. Then, to us, he said, "I do have an urge to communicate. The truth is, my ideas about food are not necessarily commercial, but I

think they might help people know more about what they're getting. I think people should come into the store to have fun and learn something. If you're not going to learn something, why get out of bed?"

1987

PALACE

FROM the time the Loew's Kings Theatre in Flatbush opened, in 1929, until it closed for good, in 1977 (the last feature was "Exorcist II: The Heretic"), it was the grandest theatre in New York devoted exclusively to the movies—perhaps the single most ornate movie house in the country. The Kings (it is still standing and, though derelict, is in fairly good shape) has not one but two lobbies: a forty-by-seventy-five foot outer lobby, where you could just collect your thoughts, and an immense foyer beyond it, where you would wait to be seated. The orchestra is a hundred and sixty feet wide and a hundred and fifty-five feet deep; its ceiling is seventy-two feet high. The Kings has more than three thousand seats. Its decoration—the screen is the only unornamented flat area—has been described variously as "Deco-Baroque," "Louis Quelque-chose," and "M-G-M Horror Vacui."

From August 9, 1938 (when the main feature was "Holiday" and the second feature "Prison Farm"), until July 4, 1940 ("Waterloo Bridge" and "Dr. Cyclops"), Lester Binger was an usher at the Loew's Kings. On a recent Saturday afternoon, while a man named Charles Sinclair was inside the Kings leading a walking tour called "Flatbush and the Movies" (the other stops were some old houses that the Vitagraph company built for its crews and an apartment building where Fatty Arbuckle once lived), Mr. Binger, sitting a few rows from the front, talked about those years. There are almost no working lights left inside the Kings, and as the visitors let their flashlights race around the enormous, cold theatre, one improbable detail after another suddenly came into view, and then vanished as the flashlights danced off somewhere else: a pair of thirty-foot replicas of the twisted columns on the Bernini baldachino in St. Peters; a twenty-foot mural of high life at Versailles; a group of five gargoyles holding up a balcony.

"I came to the Kings Theatre not to be an usher but as a young man with a dream," Mr. Binger explained. "It was my ambition in life to own and manage a movie house in a small town somewhere on the East Coast. Although I grew up largely in this neighborhood—Flatbush and Maple, and so on—I spent the years from 1924 to 1927 in Lakewood, New Jersey. I noticed that the people who ran the movie house in Lakewood—these were the distinguished citizens in the town. They would open for a matinée at three o'clock, go home for a dinner, and then return for the seven-o'clock and nine-o'clock shows. The Strand Theatre in Lakewood—I never forgot that. It made a great impression on me.

"In 1936, I went to the Kings and applied for a job as an usher. The head usher, Jerry Sager, told me that there were no openings. He told me to go get some seasoning at Loew's Coney Island. The Coney Island and the Kings played the same material—mostly M-G-M pictures—because they were both part of the Loew's chain. The Coney Island was a living nightmare for an usher. My first afternoon, everything was going smoothly until I heard the crack of thunder outside and it started to rain. If you can visualize a two-thousand-seat theatre filling up with people in ten minutes, that is what happened. I thought, Seating two thousand people in ten minutes—this is not a skill I am going to need in a movie house in a small town. I was able to get a job at the Patio Theatre in Flatbush, and I worked there for two years. Once in a while, I would go over to the Kings and make a polite inquiry. I waited and waited, and one day, in the summer of 1938, the call finally came.

"Working in a movie house like this was like working in a palace. Really, that's the only comparison I can make. The shows played one week. There were no stage shows. It was a *movie* palace. Punctuality was continually stressed. A day's work had elegance, and it had order. There were eighteen ushers, including four captains. If you opened the house, you would arrive at eleven o'clock. First, you would change into your uniform. We had two uniforms. The winter uniform was dark gray with red trim. In summer, we were all in blue, because in summer everything was done to emphasize coolness. All through the year, you were expected to have an immaculate pair of white gloves. Elegance and order. It was a rule that an usher could never, under any circumstances, use the word 'side,' as in 'side aisle.' You never said 'Open the side aisles.' You said 'Open Aisle 7' or 'Open Aisle 1.' 'Side' had connotations. If people heard that they were being sent to a side aisle, they might protest.

"I made twenty-seven cents an hour. I used to tell people that I made twenty-five cents an hour, but I went back and checked my records recently, and it was twenty-seven cents. No tips. 'The acceptance of gratuities is strictly forbidden'—I still remember that rule. At the end of the evening, we had to raise every seat in the entire theatre. The rule, however, was that you could not for any reason disturb a patron. Inevitably, there would be some couple sitting all by themselves, the last people there, and you would have to wait until they were gone before you could even touch a seat in their general area."

Mr. Binger walked up onto the stage to look at the huge screen—still bright silver, but torn and ruined. "I suppose the high-water mark of my years as an usher occurred during the week that 'Gone With the Wind' appeared here," he said. "This was the most long-awaited movie in the history of pictures. They sprayed the screen silver again, just to make it more reflective, more perfect. The electricians had to take down the red 'Exit' signs and change them to blue ones, so that nothing would interfere with the Technicolor effect. It was one of the few reserved-seat pictures. We had to mark out the rows with stencils and paint, and so on. The evening show was O.K. But we began the shows at eight-thirty in the morning. The theatre would fill with older women, and there would be the sound of sobbing from one end of the theatre to the other.

"Then the war came, and I went overseas. The Army—well, you know the Army. Someplace I had written down that I had worked in a movie house, so I ended up handling training films for the Signal Corps. I was still working in the distribution of Army training films when I retired, in 1970. I searched for a theatre after the war—God knows I saw a lot of them—but it never worked out. No matter how good it seemed at first, how high your hopes were, somehow it never checked out. You asked yourself, 'If it's so great, why are they ready to sell it?' Or I thought, I'll buy a ticket and go see for myself, and there was always something. I was travelling once, and I went at midnight just to look at the old Mastbaum in Philadelphia—maybe the biggest movie palace of them all. It had already closed, and a cop came up behind me and said, 'Hey, don't you see that theatre's closed?' I said, 'Yes, Officer, that's why I want to see it.' He said, 'Hey, let me see some identification.' I showed him my driver's license, and he said, 'Hey, this is from *Brooklyn.*' That made him suspicious, and he told me to go back to my hotel. He pointed me back toward the hotel, just like an usher."

1 9 8 8

IN PROGRESS

W E had no idea that 1989 was the Year of the Diary until we read *Diarist's Journal*, a fourteen-issue-old monthly tabloid out of Lansford, Pennsylvania, which Ed Gildea, the founder and publisher and co-editor, believes to be the only periodical in the world devoted exclusively to diary- and journal-keeping. We like lots of things about *Diarist's Journal*, but most of all we like Ed Gildea's candor concerning the genesis of the Year of the Diary. "It's not an official designation," he told us the other day. "We declared it ourselves, because somebody had to do it and we thought it would help circulation. We have about four hundred subscribers. We're growing, but we thought that by now we'd have twice that many. We have twenty-three subscribers in Hawaii, and we've published excerpts from a diarist in Sri Lanka. We've printed entries from the diary of a ninety-two-year-old man and from the diary of a teen-ager named Julie, who confessed in her diary that she had been reading her sister's diary. We have Jane Begos writing about women's diaries and Shelley Barre writing about diaries in general, and, best of all, we have Edward Robb Ellis writing a column for us. Have you spoken to Eddie?"

We said we hadn't, and the next afternoon we dropped by Mr. Ellis's brownstone, in Chelsea. There he fed us coffee and doughnuts and talked about diaries.

Besides writing his column for *Diarist's Journal* (February's was about Henri Frederic Amiel, a nineteenth-century Swiss diarist), Mr. Ellis serves as a consultant for Letts of London (and, more recently, of Hauppauge, New York), a hundred-and-seventy-seven-year-old publisher of diaries, which will soon publish a line of diaries designed by Ellis, and as a consultant for the in-progress New-York Historical Society and Yale University Press *Encyclopedia of New York City.* He also has a work in progress on the history of mysticism, and, of course, his own diary.

Mr. Ellis's diary, squeezed into sixty-one volumes, is eighteen million words long and counting. Except for a fortnight in 1965, at the time his wife died, he told us, he has kept a daily log since December 27, 1927, when he was sixteen years old. He is a tireless crusader for an American diary repository. "In 1980, my diary was shipped to the University of Wyoming," he said. "I have dupes of everything I've written since then, but the entire original, except 1988—I haven't shipped it yet—is in Laramie. I didn't want to give the diary up, but Gene Gressley, who is the archivist at the American Heritage Center, in Laramie, asked me a simple question: 'What about fire, Eddie?' I looked around. I had fifteen thousand books in this place. I used to smoke. I said, 'Come and get it.' "

Mr. Ellis is a big, round man, with a big, round face, a full head of swept-back brown hair, and a full white beard. Around the house, he wears cowboy boots, slacks, a hooded sweatshirt, a shawl that hangs like a gym towel around his neck, and a red beret. He looks a little like Santa Claus moonlighting as a boxing trainer.

"I'm about ninety-nine per cent honest in my diary," he went on. "I've stipulated that when I die it can be opened and published, as long as the contents don't hurt any living persons or their relatives. I don't keep an eye to posterity, but I'm *aware* that my work may be reproduced and studied. I decided long ago that it   posterity—can't influence me, or the diary will be artificial. Once, a long time ago, an actress friend asked me to read out loud what I had said about her in my diary. I found the right page and realized I hadn't been kind at all. I had to ad-lib new words, just like that."

His longest entry—fourteen pages, double-spaced, no paragraphs—came after the birth of his daughter, he said. The shortest entry is "Hung Over." "That's in there a lot, but not in the last ten years," he said. "I'm an alcoholic, a bookaholic, and a workaholic. The first one is the only one I'm recovering from."

Eddie asked if we kept a diary, and we said, "Yes. Well, no. Sort of—when we're out of town. Not really."

We should, he said.

We knew that, we said. Did he have any tips?

He gave us the following:

(1) Write every day in the same place, at the same time—morning or afternoon or evening or night. The exact hour isn't important.

(2) Keep your diary locked. Don't let *anyone* read it—not even your spouse.

(3) Don't use slang unless you note the meaning. "If you write down 'I hear you, I hear you,' as I did the other day, recording a cabbie's conversation, and don't explain it, no one will be able to understand it in a hundred years."

(4) Number all your pages, and keep a wide left margin for binding.

(5) If you write in longhand, use a pen. If you type, use a good ribbon. Use only the best paper—anything less won't last.

(6) Pick a title. "Mine used to be 'Briefly I Tarry.' Now it's 'The Ellis Diary.' "

(7) Observe details. "I have notes about platform shoes. Do you remember them? That information might come in very handy one day for a historian."

(8) Note the price of everything. "I have records of dinners in New Orleans during the Depression that cost me thirty-five cents. Hard to believe, but there it is."

(9) Include the name and address of any restaurant you go to. Chances are very good it will be gone in a year, not to mention a decade.

(10) Use a person's full name. If the name appears regularly, you can shorten it after the first notation.

(11) Record all current jokes. "I have about thirty Joe McCarthy jokes in my diary, like the time he and his wife hear the National Anthem and he says to her, 'Stand up, dear, they're playing our song.' "

(12) Note the day of the week as well as the month and the year.

(13) Keep the entries strictly chronological. Forget putting the most important event of the day at the top. Forget writing an essay.

Mr. Ellis stopped us at the door to say, "Remember, a diarist is a writer who watches himself watching himself. And one last thing: I said a diary entry had best be strictly chronological, but that isn't quite true. If on a given day I come up with any philosophical thoughts—if I've learned anything during the day that I can put down in the abstract—I wait until the very end to do it. That way, the day's entry can taper off toward the heavens."

1989

1990s

MISS SUBWAYS

BROWN cake with gray icing isn't our favorite, but no one seemed to be complaining, so we were a good sport and ate three pieces. The cake was in the shape of a subway car, and the icing represented paint. The cake commemorated the fiftieth anniversary of the naming of the first Miss Subways, and the fifteenth anniversary of the naming of the last. It had been provided by Ellen Hart Sturm, who was Miss Subways in March and April of 1959, and who had invited all the former Miss Subways she could find to a reunion at her restaurant, Ellen's Stardust Diner, on Sixth Avenue. About fifty (out of a total of two hundred or so) showed up, some of them coming from as far away as Florida and California.

The most famous Miss Subways ever was the dancer Sono Osato, who wasn't a real Miss Subways but played one (as Miss Turnstiles) in the musical comedy "On the Town." The second most famous Miss Subways was Vera-Ellen, who took over in the 1949 movie version of the show. The third most famous Miss Subways was the first real one, Mona Freeman: she went on to star, with Alan Ladd, in "Branded," which was released in 1950, and she also appeared in "Dear Ruth," "Dear Wife," and "Dear Brat"—a series of comedies from the same era. For subway riders, the zenith of her celebrity occurred somewhat earlier—in May, 1941, when posters featuring her picture appeared in trains all over the city. She was fourteen years old and had a cute smile. Her poster explained that she had been selected by the "Famous Beauty Authority" John Robert Powers (who ran a modelling agency) and that her ambition was to become "a top-notch magazine illustrator." When subway riders saw her picture, they became confident that the subway was a glamorous yet wholesome form of transportation, and only rarely did they draw a mustache on her face. Mona Freeman did not attend the reunion, but she was present in the form of video-tapes of "Branded," which were playing on four old-fashioned television sets way up near the ceiling.

Quite a few Miss Subways went on to achieve renown of one sort or another. Marie Therese Thomas Ferrari, who was Miss Subways in March of 1946, ap-peared regularly on "The Jackie Gleason Show," and in 1948 she had a part in the first live television commercial, which was for the U.S. Rubber Company, and in which she wore a bathing suit made partly and a bathing cap made en-tirely of rubber. Mary Gardiner Timoney (May, 1957) eventually gave birth to both a future columnist for *Soap Opera Weekly* and a future stand-in for the actor Bruce Willis. Marie Crittenden Kettler (January and February, 1957) be-came the First Lady of Woodcliff Lake, New Jersey. (Her husband is the mayor.) Peggy Byrne (March and April, 1958) turned out to be the aunt of Peggy Noo-nan, who has written speeches for Presidents Reagan and Bush, and who would have been named Joan if at birth she hadn't looked so much like her mother's sister.

Of course, all former Miss Subways are famous to some extent, by virtue of having been Miss Subways. Most were very eager to speak to reporters and pose for photographers and camera crews. At one point, we felt a hand on our shoulder and turned around to see a man in a dark suit, ready to introduce us to Rita Rogers Gross (March and April, 1955). She told us that the man was "a very good friend, a P.R. man for me," and then caught us up on her life. "Later that year, I married the West Pointer I was engaged to, but it was fun being Miss Subways, because you would see people nudge each other on the trains," she said. "I am now executive secretary with a pulp-and-paper consulting firm in Tarrytown. It's a Finnish firm, so I won't even bother spelling the name for you." As she talked to us, her eyes combed the room. Suddenly, she saw a cam-eraman from a local television station. "Oh, he's taking pictures!" she said, and she rushed away, the P.R. man hurrying to catch up.

Most of the Miss Subways had brought copies of their posters, and they held them up when photographers told them to. Several had brought other memo-rabilia as well. Winifred McAleer Noyes (June, 1944) showed us a copy of the April 23, 1945, issue of *Life*, which contained (along with an article about the death of President Roosevelt) a two-page spread on the Miss Subways so far. It was illustrated with pictures of posters, among them hers. "The mail that came in after that was incredible," she told us. "There were love letters, marriage pro-posals—everything imaginable. There was one very flowery letter from the Ivory Coast, in Africa, and there were letters from all over the world, the South Pacific particularly. It was great fun. The letters came in for months afterward. The post office in Jackson Heights was inundated."

The easiest Miss Subways to find at the reunion was Stella Deere (November and December, 1961), because she was wearing a large white hat that said

"BRONSON PINCHOT FAN" on it in big black letters. Stella Deere's real name is Stella Malecki. When she was chosen to be Miss Subways, she picked Deere out of the phone book, she said, because she didn't want to shock her father, who had a heart condition. Since then, she has used Deere as her middle name or, occasionally, her last. "Everyone has to have a happy experience in their life that makes them feel special," she said. "I belong to no organizations of any kind. Being Miss Subways—being one of two hundred—is really my only thing that I belong to in my life. It's a very nice feeling to belong to something. It's nice to be happy for a while."

All the Miss Subways we talked to seemed to be extremely happy. We spent some time sitting in a booth with several who were looking at newspaper and magazine clippings from the forties. One of the clippings, a two-page spread from *Collier's*, showed a number of Miss Subways frolicking together on Jones Beach in bathing suits. In one of the photographs, all the Miss Subways were kneeling in the sand, and in another they were having a tug-of-war. Dorothea Mate (June, 1942) walked past the booth, glanced down at the pictures, and said, "That's me! That's me! Oh, my God! I had forgotten that! For heaven's sake!" Looking more closely at the clipping, she found herself in a second picture. She smiled broadly. "It was our moment in glory," she said. "Even after forty-nine years, you can live it again. You think back, and you know you once had it. If you have a bad day, you think, Oh, try again—you were Miss Subways."

1991

POPSIANA

W HEN it comes to stuff, we wrote the book. You probably have a copy of it sitting around somewhere—maybe in the closet with the maracas and the snowshoes and the slides of Mt. Hood. So we understand each other, right? Because if we thought you were the kind of person who would waltz into someone's apartment and make sweeping, dismissive gestures and say things like "Those souvenir pens from the Museum of Science and Industry, and that picture of you and your tentmates at Scout camp, and that rock you found on a beach in Scotland, and this shot glass from Luray Caverns, and what about that math workbook you've been saving since fourth grade—what are you going to *do* with all this stuff?" then we would just stop right here. We certainly wouldn't tell you about a trip we took to Flushing the other day to see some of Louis Armstrong's stuff, which was on display in the main library of Queens College.

In 1943, Louis Armstrong bought a house in the Corona section of Queens, and that was where he lived until his death, in 1971. As we reported a few years ago, Queens College came into possession of the house and its contents after Lucille Armstrong, his widow, died, in 1983. Among the items in the house were eight thousand photographs; hundreds of books, records, homemade tapes, and pieces of sheet music; dozens of souvenirs, trophies, letters, and scrapbooks; and hundreds of pages of Armstrong's writings. Once everything is catalogued—a job that is expected to take from two to three years—the Louis Armstrong Archive will open its doors. (The house itself is being renovated, and will someday open as a museum.) The work has finally begun, thanks to an infusion of grant money, and, as a way of celebrating the Armstrong legacy, the college invited a handful of trumpet players and several other musicians to the campus to let them have a look at the goodies and to give them an opportunity to blow Armstrong's five gold-plated horns, which are part of the archive.

We shared the ride over to Queens with Doc Cheatham, one of the designated trumpeters. Mr. Cheatham, a dapper man of eighty-six, has a pencil mustache and a wisp of beard just under his lower lip, and he wore a dark suit set off with splashes of color: a flowered tie, an enamel lapel pin of the Eiffel Tower, a red handkerchief, and purple socks. He told us he first got to know Armstrong in Chicago, in 1926, when Armstrong threw some work his way. "Louis was very good to me," he said. "A lot of musicians from New Orleans, his home town, were very jealous of him. That's why he chose me to fill in for him." Mr. Cheatham said that he was looking forward to playing one of Armstrong's instruments. "Yeah, we'll see what we can do with his trumpets. You know, you shouldn't let a horn sit and sit without being used. If you don't play those instruments, they'll freeze. Someone I know once made a lamp out of a trumpet." He shook his head. "It's just a shame to see a good instrument go to pot."

Musicians who knew Armstrong have been asked to make donations to the archive, and now Mr. Cheatham took his contribution out of a pocket and held it up. It was a tubular piece of dull, discolored brass about three inches long and flaring slightly at one end. "This was the standard mouthpiece back then for cornet and trumpet," he said. "This is about sixty-five years old. It's what Louis would have used—it's what we all used. You don't see these anymore—all the players are dead that had these things."

The Armstrong memorabilia were in a small room off the rotunda of the library, and there we spoke to Michael Cogswell, the curator of the archive. "We've brought seventy-two boxes here from the Armstrong house," he said. "The house wasn't suitable for the archive. Here everything will be kept at sixty-eight degrees and fifty per cent humidity year-round."

Next to a TV monitor showing a documentary on Armstrong stood Dizzy Gillespie, eating a plum and saying hello to various musicians who were threading through the room: the bassist Arvell Shaw and the pianist Marty Napoleon, who played with Armstrong's All Stars; the trumpeters Jon Faddis, Jimmy Owens, and Donald Byrd; the saxophonist Jimmy Heath. (Mr. Heath and Mr. Byrd also teach at the college.) While they were posing for photographs, we took a closer look at the display cases set up around the room. One held several trumpets, nestled in a beat-up leather case; one held manuscripts of "Ain't Misbehavin' " and "Struttin' with Some Barbecue"; one held two sheets of legal-pad paper filled with Armstrong's handwriting. Toward the end of his life, when he was in the hospital in New York for long stays, Armstrong wrote pages and pages of reminiscences. These particular pages, concerning his early boy-hood, held clues to the origin of the Armstrong spark:

> When I would be on the junk wagon with Alex Karnofsky I had a little tin horn, the kind the people celebrate with. I would . . . blow it, as a call for old rags, bones, bottles or anything that the people had to sell. The kids would bring bottles and receive pennies from Alex. The kids loved the sounds of my tin horn. . . . After blowing the tin horn so long I wondered how I would do blowing a real horn, a cornet was what I had in mind. Sure enough, I saw a lit-tle cornet in a pawn shop window—five dollars. My luck was just right. With the Karnofsky loan on my salary, I saved 50¢ a week and bought the horn. All dirty—but was soon pretty to me. After blowing into it awhile, I realized that I could play Home Sweet Home, then here come the blues. From then on, I was a mess and tootin' away.

Nearby, a large scrapbook filled with clippings from Armstrong's first Euro-pean tour, in 1932, was open to a page of newspaper reviews. In one of them a sourpuss calling himself Bass Clef had written, "I heard Armstrong in Glas-gow. . . . It is quite true that he produces notes beyond the legitimate range of the trumpet, but by no stretch of the imagination can these notes be classed as music. They are screeching noises." Other Europeans were more enthusiastic and more enterprising: mounted on one wall, next to Armstrong's passport, was a round blue tin of Louis Armstrong Lip Salve, manufactured by Franz Schüritz, of Mannheim.

Out in the rotunda, the musicians and college officials were assembling. Shirley Strum Kenny, the president of the college, stood on a makeshift stage and spoke with pride of the archive's importance for jazz historians. Mr. Byrd, who is in his late fifties, told of growing up in Detroit and sneaking out of school to see Armstrong and his band when they came to town. When he added, "I had to skip school to see Dizzy, too," you-know-who cried out from the sidelines, "I'm not that old!" Mr. Cheatham spoke about his early days in Chicago, before he met Armstrong. "I got a job washing dishes in a restaurant, making thirty-five dollars a week," he said. "I was thinking about taking my father's advice and going back to school to study dentistry." But then he heard Armstrong at the Vendome Theatre. "People were astounded. It was as if a war had broken out in Chicago, he was so great. When Louis came on, the people would—You never saw anything like it in your life. I decided then that I wasn't going back to school—the heck with school."

The trumpet contingent—Gillespie, Byrd, Faddis, and Owens, now joined by Wynton Marsalis and by Nabate Isles, a fourteen-year-old graduate of the Louis Armstrong Middle School, in Queens, who has been playing the trumpet for six years—collected itself on the stage. Nabate played "St. Louis Blues," and then he and four of his elders took a whack at it together (not including Mr. Gillespie, whose upper lip was suffering from wear and tear that day).

It was right about this time that we began thinking, Got to get some of those stamps. It was Mr. Gillespie's fault, really. He's the one who put the idea in our head. Earlier in the program, he mentioned that he had been trying to get the Postal Service to issue a Louis Armstrong stamp—an honor that he thought was overdue. He said, "I'm going to write a personal letter to the President and say, 'Hey, man, what's happenin'?' "

1 9 9 1

MURPHYS

ROBERT MEYERS, the founder of the Murphy Bed Center of New York, Inc., on West Seventeenth Street, spends most of his day in the field. He may be at the site of the new Flatotel, on West Fifty-second Street, supervising the installation of dozens of Murphy beds. Or he may be at Tudor City or the Parc Vendôme, both of which were built at the peak of the Murphy-bed craze, in the nineteen-twenties and early thirties, and contain lots of antique jalopies that few people besides Robert can understand. Robert wears a beeper, so that his wife, Susanne, can contact him in the event of a Murphy-related emergency. "A lot of my job is just talking clients through their beds," Robert says. "They don't understand their beds, or they're actually afraid of them, because of the stigma these things have got from Hollywood." When Robert is explaining a Murphy bed to a client, he resembles a flight instructor coaxing a novice through his first landing. He looks the client directly in the eye, enunciates carefully, as though speaking for lip-readers, and measures out instructions with his hands. Not one of Robert's customers has been trapped or clobbered by the product. In fact, he has only ever heard of one such incident—an eighty-year-old woman in England was stuck inside her bed for three days.

The Murphy Bed Center is in a small second-story loft just west of Sixth Avenue. Half the space is devoted to furniture that is not what it seems to be—dressers, desks, cabinets, and walls of shelving that turn into beds. The other half, behind a door marked "Employees Only," is where Robert and Susanne spend their spare time. Their couch is an ordinary bifold Murphy, the Model T of the industry. On Long Island, where they go on weekends, they sleep in a bookcase-type Murphy, which is more upscale. On their showroom floor are some top-of-the-line Murphys—German Murphys, which work with pistons, and Italian Murphys, which Robert greatly admires. "The Italians have mechanisms where you go, 'Whoa, I can't believe this is happening,' " Robert said the other day, showing off an Italian model. "Watch how the legs fold out. Wild, huh?" Nearby was a filing cabinet that turned into an ironing board. "I just had to have this on the floor," he explained. "Basically, anything that can pop out of something, I enjoy."

Robert is in his early thirties. He has neatly groomed shoulder-length hair and the physique of a person with a high metabolism. He likes to wear jewelry, but he has found that thrusting his hands into the guts of Murphy beds ruins watches and bracelets, and so now he wears eight three-inch rubber gaskets on his left wrist and, as a wedding band, one three-quarter-inch gasket on his left ring finger. (He wears his real wedding ring on his right hand, surrounded by more gaskets). Robert started out in the furniture-moving business. In an effort to establish a niche for himself, he began to take apart and reassemble installations—cabinetry, bookshelves, entertainment centers—and in this way he became familiar with the anatomies of Murphy beds. The ingenuity, delicacy, and precision of the mechanisms appealed to his mechanical side. "I began telling people that if they needed the Murphy beds worked on, call me," he says. "I found out which apartment buildings had the old Murphy beds, and I'd leave my card with the doorman. Pretty soon, I became Number One in the field."

Occasionally, in older apartment buildings, Robert comes across an original Murphy In-A-Dor Bed, designed by William L. Murphy himself. Murphy was a colorful northern Californian who broke horses, drove a stagecoach, served as a sheriff, and, around 1900, had the idea of making a bed that folded out of a closet. "Basically, the idea had been around since the drawbridge," Robert says. "But Murphy got the patent on it." Someone in the movie business in Los Angeles perceived its slapstick possibilities, and Murphy's beds quickly became popular props in silent comedies. In the nineteen-twenties, Murphy was selling several thousand beds a month. In the thirties, he expanded into Murphy Cabrinettes—tiny, Pullman-style kitchens. These, together with the beds, were incorporated by developers into efficiency apartments, which were then a brand-new concept. Dale Carnegie wrote articles about Murphy. In Europe, Murphy was viewed as a kind of urban visionary.

The Murphy-bed business isn't what it used to be. After the war, the popularity of the beds began to decline. People didn't want to save space—they wanted to sleep in huge beds in big suburban bedrooms. Also, the sofa bed, popularized in the late forties by Bernard Castro, eroded Murphy's market. Robert is contemptuous of sofa beds. "It's such a misconception when people say that they don't want a Murphy bed because they want to sleep on a real bed," he says. "They say that because they're coming off sofa beds. There is just no comparison between a sofa bed and a Murphy."

Two years ago, Robert made a proposal to the Murphy Bed Company, which has its headquarters in Commack, Long Island, and is still entirely owned by the Murphy family; the president, Clark Murphy, is William's grandson. "Look," Robert said to the Murphy Bed people. "I think your bed needs some of my personal attention and focus. Because if you promoted these things aggressively they'd sell like crazy—you have a fabulous product here. I am offering to be your exclusive sales representative in Manhattan." The company turned Robert down. So he decided to start the Murphy Bed Center. "My thing is, How far can I get into this without being afraid of how far I can go?" he said, and then he raised his arms and widened his eyes. "I see a bed coming down from the ceiling, with four winches, one at each corner, slowly lowering it." He let his fingers float slowly down to his waist. Business was good, he added, and he was selling mechanisms as far away as Alaska. "In Alaska, space is a big problem," he said. "You know why? Heat. You have to have small spaces to stay warm." He paused a moment, and then shouted, "Hey, Sue!" Susanne was behind the "Employees Only" sign, watching TV. "Where's the picture of the eighteenth-century Murphy I got out of a magazine?"

"I don't know."

"This picture would blow your mind," he said. "It's a piano that turns into a bed, plus it has a dresser and a washbasin inside. I mean, it's humbling."

1 9 9 2

FLOWERING

WE slipped away to the New York Flower Show last Monday, not telling anyone, so that nobody could say, "I didn't know *you* were interested in flowers," in a dry tone suggesting something prosaic and unflorescent about us—something indehiscent. "Indehiscent" is a new word we've learned. It means "not dehiscent, not opening at maturity," as in "indehiscent fruit." During the blast of freezing cold that has been rattling our windows lately, we have sometimes dehisced in the form of a sneeze, and then hisced up all the tighter. But, of course, a dry or undehisced person, an afloral person, is exactly the kind of person a flower show is there to stimulate, and that's why we went. We took a taxi to Pier 92, one of the big passenger-ship terminals on the Hudson, and paid our eight dollars and breezed in.

We saw rex begonia and asparagus ferns and a plant labelled "A String of Peas"—a plant with leaves that look like peas—and shamrocks, violets, cyclamens, azaleas, Johnny-jump-ups, and battalions of tulips. There were whole gardens, and there were ranks of plants arranged by genus or variety—competing plants, with the prize ribbons beside them, and the judge's scoring card right there for all to see.

Roaming among sections of streptocarpus and primula, we noted how terse were the judge's compliments on the winning plants:

"Magnificent!"

"Superb plant!"

"Spectacular and showy."

"Showstopper."

"Excellent specimen."

"Beautiful."

And how sharp, how barbed, were their comments on the second- and third-place plants and the honorable mentions:

"Good start." (A third-place begonia semperflorens)

"Poor color. Severe pruning is obvious."

"Unusual growth habit."

"Slightly off-center and overpotted." (A third-place *Andromischus cristatus*)

"This plant would look better with more foliage."

"Lovely plant but a little beyond its prime." (A third-place narcissus)

The withering irony of "This plant would look better with more foliage"! The faint contempt behind "Unusual growth habit"! And imagine the poor grower bringing his best begonia down from Connecticut, an affable man in bib overalls and porkpie hat leaving the tropical calm of his greenhouse for the honk and harangue of New York: his station wagon plows south on the West Side Highway, the begonia terrified and perspiring on the seat beside him, and he parks blocks away and hauls the plant to Pier 92 and sets it in its place and spritzes it with bug juice, and a judge comes by, a big, beefy man with a long waxed mustache, and peers down at it and scribbles "Good start" on a card. How would you feel?

Once in a blue moon, a judge handed out a flowery compliment, such as "Wonderful presentation with bonus of bloom" for a winning *Mammillaria plumosa,* but most of the plants came in for digs. A pot of tulips was criticized for a lack of "floriferousness" and a narcissus for "meager growth." One of the succulents was said to have had "a cultural problem in its development," and a hippeastrum was dismissed as "immature." "Lacks ornamental value," said the card attached to a sea onion. Perhaps, we thought, but couldn't the same be said about us? The remark that the narcissus was "a little beyond its prime" stung us especially.

We had come to the end of Pier 92, and were in front of a ceiling-high window that looked south to the next terminal and to the floodlit U.S.S. Intrepid beyond. The next terminal was where, one afternoon last June, we embarked for England aboard the Queen Elizabeth 2. We stood at the port rail as she slipped down the Hudson, the blocks of Manhattan drifting past like rows of tall corn, and when we got to Forty-third we snapped a picture of our companion with the Chrysler Building coming out of her head like an immense stalk of wheat. A fireboat zipped alongside and shot a fifty-foot plume into the air, the Staten Island ferry bobbed in our wake, our funnel eased under the Verrazano Bridge, and we sailed along the coast of Brooklyn and out to sea.

We normally prepare for a trip by imagining the worst and then are grateful for what doesn't happen to us, so we fully expected cold weather and fierce winds on the crossing, with sheets of salt spray lashing the deck, and the ship rolling and plunging; and we imagined ourself lying on a bunk quietly retching into a plastic bag, and then the inevitable iceberg and the rush for the boats, with us caught in a despicable act of cowardice and going down with the boat in shame and disgrace, and then our obituary ("Was fondly regarded despite insufficient flowering over the years"). But, of course, the first day out was bright and balmy, and we lay in a deck chair and dozed and slowly burst open.

From dread comes dehiscence, just as from winter comes spring. From stern judgments come better begonias. You let a flower show drift toward permissiveness, and soon they'll be exhibiting dandelions and skunk cabbage, and where will we be then? We bought a bottle of soil conditioner and an asparagus fern and went home.

1992

JUDY HEAVEN

I F you're like most people, you probably couldn't tell us right off the bat where Judy Garland was and what she was doing on, say, January 24, 1964. And the blank expression on your face would freeze solid if we went on to ask you what Judy Garland was wearing that day and who designed it. Relax. As of now, you're off the hook, and you can thank John Fricke and Michael Benson. Mr. Fricke and Mr. Benson are serious collectors of the effects and ephemera of Garland's career, and between them they've got the five "w"s covered: who, what, when, where, and wardrobe. About two years ago, they joined forces and approached the New York Public Library for the Performing Arts with the idea of putting on an exhibition to celebrate what would have been Judy Garland's seventieth birthday, on June 10th of this year. (This is a birthday that Garland herself did not come close to celebrating; when she died, in 1969, she was forty-seven years old.) The show opened a few weeks ago, in the library's Amsterdam Gallery, with a party that drew Garland admirers and collectors from all over the country—many of whom had been persuaded to part with their own Judyana for the two and a half months the show will run—and several performers who had rubbed shoulders with the legendary Miss G.

At the party, Michael Benson was zipping around the room, saying hello to friends and pointing out some of his favorite costumes. There were twenty-two costumes on display (and a couple of pairs of shoes, but no ruby slippers) from Garland's movie days and her later concert and television career, including a brown suit she wore when she rehearsed with Fred Astaire in "Easter Parade" and the off-white winter coat she had on when Tom Drake (the boy next door, whom she could not ignore) proposed to her in "Meet Me in St. Louis." Quite a few of them belonged to Mr. Benson. He told us he had bought his first Garland costume—a short-sleeved cotton dress that was made for Judy to wear in "Everybody Sing"—eight years ago, when he was twenty-five. "I'd gone to an auction at Christie's with a friend of mine who collects Hedy Lamarr, and when this dress came up I thought, You love her—why *not* buy it?" But his feeling for Garland had started long before that. "I can remember being five and glued to the TV," he said. What was he watching? "I'll tell you, it was not 'The Wizard of Oz.' A few weeks after President Kennedy was shot, she came out and closed her TV show with the 'Battle Hymn of the Republic.' She sang magnificently. She got a standing ovation, and tears were streaming down her face. That's what turned me on to Judy Garland."

Garland's birth certificate was posted just inside the entrance to the gallery, and from there Mr. Benson took us on a quick tour of the costumes, starting with the cotton dress and ending with the high-wattage outfits that Garland favored in the sixties. One display case was lit from within by three sequinned pants suits—a red one, a white one, and an orange-and-green paisley one—and another case held the beaded jacket she wore when she sang at Carnegie Hall in 1961. The bead-and-sequin industry got a further boost from Garland's 1963–64 television series. Mr. Benson showed us an elegant white cowl top embroidered with gold beads, which was designed by Ray Aghayan with the assistance of Bob Mackie, and which Garland wore during the taping of her twentieth television show, at the CBS studios in Hollywood, on—here it comes—January 24, 1964.

Across the room, a video monitor was showing film clips in which Garland was wearing the clothes on display. A dozen people stood and watched "Broadway Rhythm," which is the finale of "Presenting Lily Mars." It's a big production number that has Garland, looking lovely in an upswept hairdo and thousand-inch heels and long black gloves and a sparkling black tulle dress, dancing over every available inch of a huge Deco stage. (In the Amsterdam Gallery, the dress was being worn by a mannequin standing ten feet away.) The camera moves in for a closeup as she belts out the final note and characteristically sweeps one arm way up over her head. When the number ended, several people shook their heads in awe. Just then, a woman Mr. Benson recognized walked by, and he reached out and tapped her on the shoulder, and said, "Hi! Is this Judy heaven, or what?"

Posters from many of Garland's M-G-M movies and other memorabilia lined the walls, and they were being examined closely by the crowd. A photograph from 1937 showed Clark Gable hugging the fourteen-year-old Judy at his birthday party after she sang "Dear Mr. Gable, You Made Me Love You" to him. There was a 1938 letter signed by Judy authorizing General Foods to use her name and likeness with the words "Nothing drives away that tired, strained feeling like a cup of Maxwell House" in advertising its product. A woman standing near the Oscar that Harold Arlen won for "Over the Rainbow" was pointing to a small figure in a photo spread about "The Wizard of Oz" from a 1939 issue of *Life*. A television camera was trained on the woman, and she looked into the camera and said, "This one—this member of the Lollipop Guild is my *cousin*." The magazine had come out several months before the movie, and the captions seemed to have been written by junior State Department officials who had been sent ahead to check out the situation in Oz. Under a picture of Dorothy and her pals was this dispatch: "In poppy field near Emerald City, quartet is doped by bad witch, who later uses flying monkeys. She dislikes Wizard intensely, is a bad influence on the countryside generally."

Eddie Bracken, who was in Garland's last M-G-M film, "Summer Stock," was among the guests, and he was easy to find. He has wavy white hair, bright-blue eyes, an Eddie Bracken nose, and a crackly voice that instantly called up images from the Preston Sturges movies he made fifty years ago. It has been said that Garland loved working with him, because he made her laugh. "Yes, that's true, and I never knew why," he told us. "I guess she just thought I had a funny face. I used to play practical jokes on her—April Fool's Day was murder. I could make Judy laugh at the drop of a hat, and I never wore a hat. She was wonderful. I love her to this day."

In an auditorium near the exhibit, the guests gathered to hear reminiscences of Garland from Mr. Bracken, Carleton Carpenter (he had a bit part in "Summer Stock"), and Elaine Stritch, who told affectionate, down-to-earth stories about her friend. More movie clips were shown—each song got a round of applause—and afterward John Fricke stood outside the auditorium and talked to fellow-fans. He was bursting with enthusiasm as he said to one of them, "She knocked me sideways when I was five. I think she's the total personification of everything that's joyous, positive, and ongoing." We asked him what had triggered his interest in Judy Garland's career. "The first thing was 'The Wizard of Oz,' " he said. "And my parents were Garland fans. They loved her. Whenever there was a movie of hers on TV late at night in Milwaukee, they would put me to bed at seven-thirty and wake me up at ten-thirty to see the movie. I admired her so much that I was interested in the facts behind her career. You know, she got reviews when she was twelve—this was before M-G-M—that said things like 'This is what Bernhardt must have been like at this age.' When you find out about Judy Garland, you find out about the history of American popular music in this century, from Al Jolson and Sophie Tucker all the way up to Barbra Streisand. And when you talk to people who worked with her you find out that so many of them consider that the high point of their professional lives." Mr. Fricke, who is forty-one, said that he began saving clippings about Judy Garland when he was eight or nine, and he now has tens of thousands of documents, which amount to an archeological record of Garland's career: scripts, scores, posters, photographs, sheet music, repertoire lists, concert schedules, theatre programs, reviews. Some of them were on display in the gallery, and many more will appear this fall in a book Mr. Fricke has written, called "Judy

Garland: World's Greatest Entertainer," which will also contain four hundred previously unpublished photographs.

We talked to Mr. Fricke again a few days later, and he told us that he, too, makes his living as an entertainer, singing mostly in night clubs and on cruise ships. He had put his career on hold for several years in order to work on a big book about "The Wizard of Oz," which came out in 1989, and to put the Garland book together, and now, he said, he was "hoping to go back to being the oldest living boy singer in America." We said he sounded like one of those destined-for-show-business people you occasionally read about, who started subscribing to *Variety* when they were still in elementary school. "I didn't subscribe, but I used to look at it in the Milwaukee library," he said. "Everyone else my age was asking for 'Curious George,' and the librarians didn't quite know what to make of me. When I watched the Judy Garland–Mickey Rooney movies, I noticed that the credits would say 'Story by So-and-So.' I thought that meant that the movie was from a *book*, so I'd say to the librarian, 'I want to read books about people who get together and put on a show.' "

1 9 9 2

SPLURGE

S
O there's this husband and wife, and one day they decide to go to Saks Fifth Avenue. They walk over to the store and end up in designer handbags. Before you know it, the wife is checking out the merchandise. Right away, the husband's getting nervous. Suddenly, he notices this pleasant-looking gray-haired woman behind the counter. This woman, believe it or not, happens to be Judith Leiber, the most famous designer of designer handbags, who is making an in-store appearance with her fall collection. For those of you who just recently fell off the turnip truck, a Leiber handbag is tiny, rhinestone-encrusted, and shaped like something cute—maybe a bird, or a panda, or a butterfly, or an egg—and is also, we mean to tell you, not cheap. A Leiber panda, say, runs three thousand bucks. Anyhow, the wife falls in love with the panda and then takes a deep interest in an egg bag, too, so the husband starts hyperventilating. Maybe she's a new wife, maybe she's an old wife—what's the difference? He just knows she's getting hung up on these three-thousand-dollar little handbags and he's going to have to do something quick. Finally, the husband—he's sweating now—says to Mrs. Leiber, "Hey, look, if I buy two, would I get a special price?"

Mrs. Leiber looks him in the eye and says, "No, but we would thank you very nicely."

O.K., O.K., so there's a priest, a rabbi, and— No, seriously, there's a reporter who walks into Saks Fifth Avenue this same day and heads over to the Judith Leiber counter, jots down a few notes about the handbags, and then goes up to Mrs. Leiber and says, "Listen, I was wondering. You were born in Hungary and learned to make handbags there, and then came to this country in 1947 and went into the handbag industry in New York, and then started your own company in 1963, designing and manufacturing luxury evening bags that have become the must-have status object for certain women, and you have fans who own dozens and dozens of your designs, including a fan in New Orleans who lent fifty of her Leibers for a show at the New Orleans Museum of Art a few years ago. But what I was wondering was: What sort of handbag do you carry?"

So Mrs. Leiber looks at the reporter and says, "One of my own, of course. Either that or a paper bag. And I won't carry a paper bag, so you figure it out."

But seriously, now—another husband and wife come up to the counter. The wife is going crazy for the handbags, and the husband is doing the death grip on his wallet when he notices Mrs. Leiber. So he says to her, "Are you Mrs. Leiber? I've long been an admirer of yours."

Mrs. Leiber says to him, "Oh, really?"

The husband says, "Actually, my wife more than me."

Mrs. Leiber says, "That's good. You shouldn't be carrying handbags. You're not the type."

Could you die?

All right, it's the same afternoon, and this skinny woman in thigh-high boots and a baggy sweatshirt comes up to the counter. She's here to meet Mrs. Leiber, but also she decided when she woke up this morning that life is short and, God willing, today she's going to splurge and buy a Judith Leiber pillbox. The pillboxes are also tiny and rhinestone-encrusted and shaped like pandas and what have you. Anyhow, this hippie type is looking at the pillboxes, and she says to the saleswoman, "Do you have any pillboxes that are bigger? I mean, these are exquisite, but I need something bigger, because I take a lot of vitamins."

So the saleswoman says to her, "We do have one shaped like an egg, which holds quite a lot."

Mrs. Sweatshirt-and-Thigh-Highs looks at her and says, "Hey, maybe I should just *eat* an egg. That way I wouldn't need the vitamins *or* the pillbox!"

You cannot make this stuff up.

O.K., now, the afternoon is rolling along, and Mrs. Leiber is the center of attention—some Japanese women have their pictures taken with her, and a lot of Saks brass come to pay their respects, because, after all, she's got a lot of real estate on the first floor. Are you still with us? So two young women in those it-wasn't-enough-for-me-to-have-a-lovely-husband-and-children-I-had-to-have-a-*career* suits come up to Mrs. Leiber, and one of them says, "Mrs. Leiber, you make me so happy. I want to thank you for doing what you do."

Mrs. Leiber looks at her and says, "Please. Don't thank me. Buy."

The other young woman says, "Mrs. Leiber, I just love coming to see your bags. It's like going to a museum."

Mrs. Leiber looks at her and says, "Sweetie, you have it all wrong. Believe me. These are to own, not to be in a museum."

Did you hear, by the way, the one about the Leiber pig bag? This is one of her new designs—a fat little pig covered with pink rhinestones, hinged at the haunches, and with a grin on his face. Hey, you'd be grinning, too, if you cost three thousand dollars, right? Anyway, the pig is the big hit of the day. One woman picks it up and says, "I've got to have this, even if it's *trayf.*" Another one says, "Take a look at this, he's even got cloven hooves. Is that biologically right?" Another one finally puts her MasterCard where her mouth is. She picks up the pink pig and hands it and her card to the saleswoman standing next to Mrs. Leiber and says, "My husband's going to kill me, but I'm going to die if I don't get this, so, the way I see it, I'm going to go one way or the other, right?"

The saleswoman takes the pig and the credit card, and then she pulls Mrs. Leiber over for a private moment and says, "Mrs. Leiber, this pink pig is just a sample. Maybe we should keep it."

Mrs. Leiber looks at her, looks at the pig, looks at the customer, looks back at the saleswoman, rolls her eyes, catches her breath, and finally says, "Darling, *please.* Don't give me a heart attack. Sell the pig. There's more where that came from."

1 9 9 2

GOOD CITIZEN

LOUIS, our main dog, went to try for his Canine Good Citizen certificate the other day. Terry and Diane, Louis's owners, weren't sure that he was ready, but they sent him for private cramming sessions with a local trainer and at the last minute decided to give it a shot. We went along.

The test was held on the lawn in front of the Western Greenwich Civic Center, in Greenwich, Connecticut, on a beautiful Saturday morning. Scattered across the lawn, at a haughty distance from one another, were the aspirants. Louis was the only German shepherd. There were three boxers: Dempsey, Jezebel, and Alex. There was a poodle named Rudy and a Doberman named Rudy. There was a French bulldog named Larry, with a sun hat, and a Shih Tzu named Maccabee, who looked like a wig with legs. There was a female bichon named Riley—a classic white fluff ball with big black eyes and a powder-blue leash. Also present was Manny, a Lowchen, or Little Lion dog. "His real name is Manet, after the painter, but we call him Manny," his owner, Carole Kramer, told us. "His brother, Andante, just became a champion at nine months. We're projecting he'll be the top Lowchen in the country next year. We don't know, but we're hoping and we're thinking. Lowchens are one of the rarest breeds in the world, and one of the oldest. There are pictures of them in tapestries from the fifteenth century. No, say the sixteenth. I think it's the fifteenth, but that sounds like a lot."

Mary Ann O'Grady, the trainer in charge, called the proceedings to order. The test, she explained, involved ten acts of canine forbearance. Among other things, the dog had to let a stranger pet him and let the examiner inspect his ears, teeth, and paws the way a veterinarian would. He had to walk through a crowd on a leash. He had to confront distractions, including other dogs, without barking or going nuts. And he had to lie down and stay, on command, while his owner walked to the other side of the lawn and walked back. In other words, he had to do calmly and competently all the things that a dog might be called upon to do in the course of a normal life. More ambitious dogs could go not just for their C.G.C. but also for their T.D.I.—membership in Therapy Dogs International, an élite corps of dogs authorized to visit nursing homes and mental hospitals. Dogs going for the T.D.I. had to face additional trials, including having people come toward them in wheelchairs at high speed.

The test got under way. Maccabee, Dempsey, Larry, Jezebel, and the Rudys passed with flying colors. Manny flunked, despite his ancestry. So did Alex and Riley. Riley's disqualification was especially poignant. Among other things, she couldn't bear to let her owner, Joan Williams, walk away from her across the lawn. She tried to follow and, in the process, got all balled up in her leash. Finally, she just lay back in the clover, a tangle of white fluff and blue leash, and gazed up imploringly at her examiner, Sherry Holm, who stood over her with a clipboard. Sherry is strict. "Come on, Rile," Joan said, scooping up the dog with one hand. "We'll go home and practice."

Mary Ann let us be part of the test. A few times we got to be the Stranger Who Tries to Pet the Dog, and we always got to be the part of the Crowd That the Dog Has to Walk Through. But we never got to be the Old Person in the Wheelchair or her sidekick, the Nurse. This act was reserved for Margie English and Sue Sternberg, two trainers who were helping Mary Ann, and they went at it with a dramatic flair rarely seen, we believe, in dog trials. "That dog! I want to pet that dog!" Sue hollered as, waving a hot-water bottle, she shot across the lawn on silver wheels, her vehicle aimed directly at Maccabee. Margie, as the Nurse, ran after her, yelling, "It's time to go back to your room now, Mrs. McGillicuddy!" Undaunted, Maccabee stood his ground and won his T.D.I.

Soon it was Louis's turn, and a hush fell over the crowd, for everyone knew how hard he had studied for the test. He trotted over to the veterinarian-simulation area with a determined gleam in his eye, but already things weren't looking good. Instead of sitting and raising his paw in a sedate manner to let the tester inspect it, he flipped over onto his back and waved his legs in the air, apparently thinking that she wanted to scratch his stomach as well. Once he was induced to sit up, he began licking her face zestfully.

The suspense built as he proceeded to the stay-on-command task. Diane gave Louis the signal to lie down, but he didn't see it. The examination area had many distractions: balloons bobbing in the breeze, airplanes crossing the sky, people buying snacks at the concession stand across the street, dogs getting their nails done at the Clip-N-Care clinic, which had set up a stand at the edge of the lawn and was offering pedicures at a special test-day price of five dollars. (Normally, it's ten.) Louis was looking at these things, not at Diane. For a very long time, Diane stood in front of Louis and signalled energetically, as he craned his neck this way and that, taking in the scenery. Finally, having studied everything else, his eyes came to rest on her. He lay down, waited for her to cross the lawn and come back, performed the remaining tasks without incident, and, as a shout went up across the lawn, became a Canine Good Citizen.

Every dog who passed the C.G.C. received a certificate. A dog who also passed the T.D.I. got a picture I.D. and a badge saying "I am a therapy dog." "I think the certificate is suitable for framing," Mary Ann said. "As for the therapy dogs, they should definitely wear their badges, and their owners should carry their I.D.s." She got out her wallet and showed us the I.D. earned by her Norfolk terrier, Tyler. Tyler couldn't show us his badge. He was having his nails done.

1 9 9 2

SCOUTING

INVENTORY of the liquidation sale of the recently vacated headquarters of the Girl Scouts of the U.S.A., at Third Avenue and Fiftieth Street:

Fourteenth floor. Three dozen assorted two-drawer lateral files. Ten workstations with acoustic panels. One case of booklets entitled "The Impact of Minority Presence in Girl Scouting on White and Minority Communities." Animal footprints, acorns for special craft projects, toasting sticks whittled from fallen tree branches, packages of gorp, illustrated chart of bandanna tricks: none. Girl Scout cookies, assorted flavors: none.

Twelfth floor. Orange Herman Miller Eames chairs, straight-backed wooden desk chairs, plastic stackable shell chairs in various colors. Troop Camper activity badges embroidered with little tents and trees, which Mom always promised to sew on when she had a free minute but never did: none. Cookies: ditto.

Eleventh floor. Wall-size chalkboard bearing message "We'll Miss You, Carole! Goodbye 11th Floor at GS-USA! I'll Miss You!!! Suzy." Assorted vertical files. Those neat Brownie Girl Scout uniforms, with the little brown jumpers and the orange bow ties and the sash with membership stars, troop numbers, and trefoil Brownie pins on it, and with plenty of space for the activity badges sitting in a drawer and just waiting for someone with one minute to sew them on, the way all the other mothers managed to: negative. Cookies: zero.

Tenth floor. One package of brochures from the 1984 Girl Scout convention. Mechanicals of a Girl Scout book, opened to a section suggesting troop activities—a Saturday lunch cookout, a Halloween tea, carolling with a junior troop, a teen fashion show, a Thinking Day event, and a supper and square dance for fathers. One heavyset woman in a black plastic windbreaker "looking for something for the house." No cookies.

Ninth floor. One impatient guy from a financial company looking for credenzas and worktables. Wait a minute—a *guy?*

Eighth floor. Fifteen Steelmaster file cabinets. One gross of small bottles of Liquid Paper. Approximately ten Girl Scout–green tape dispensers. Approximately three employees of the Affordable Used Office Furniture Company, which was liquidating the items left behind by the Girl Scouts when they relocated to their new offices, on Fifth Avenue at Thirty-seventh Street. One Presto quartz heater in as-is condition. No Buddy burners, Vagabond stoves, or kindling. No cookies.

Seventh floor. More stuff, none edible.

Sixth floor. One Wilbur Curtis Model RU-300 coffee machine. One Diet Coke/Sprite/Coke dispenser. Cookies: no way.

Fifth floor. Acoustical office dividers covered in Scout-green fabric. Several boxes of green No. 2 pencils, embossed with the Girl Scout logo. No sunshine ponchos made by cutting up one of your mother's cocktail dresses. Cookies: still none, although an employee of Affordable Furniture walking by confirmed having sighted and then eaten several boxes of Thin Mints, Peanut Butter Sandwiches, and Peanut Butter Patties.

Fourth floor. A box of books entitled "Girl Scout Educational Opportunities," marked "THROW OUT." Defective telephones. Stepladders. Coffee tables. Coatracks. Typing tables. People singing the "Brownie Smile Song": none—at least, not audibly. Former members of Junior Scout Troop 453, Daffodil Patrol, performing paper-bag dramatics to an audience of seven vertical files with slide locks, two metal desks, and some commercial shelving: one.

1 9 9 2

THE SMELL

ABOUT a month ago, a terrible new smell turned up on North Moore Street, in Tribeca. It did not coexist peacefully with the other smells on the street: the coffee and cooking smells from Bubby's, a local hangout; the sweet, strong smell of olive oil stored in Hillside Imperial Foods; pepper and nutmeg smells from Atalanta, a spice warehouse; the beer smell from Walker's, the neighborhood bar; and the hay, manure, antiseptic, and horse-sweat smells coming out of the police stables on the corner of Varick. The new smell routed all those other smells. The rich olfactory texture of the street was shattered.

The smell seemed to have no center. Sometimes it stayed at the east end of the street, sometimes at the west end. Sometimes it left North Moore altogether and glided down to Franklin or up to Beach. It behaved more like a mist than like a smell, rising at odd hours of the night, clinging to cobblestones and loading docks, creeping over roofs, and settling in the breezeways behind people's lofts. No one could say just what the smell was—only that it was certainly caused by putrefaction of some kind of flesh. Blaustein & Son, plumbers, at No. 32, thought that the smell might be rotting human flesh, and called the cops.

Blaustein: "We get a lot of bad smells in this business, but I never smelled anything like that."

Son: "It was like blood."

Blaustein: "A very stale, musty smell, like something in an old closet."

James Herman, a painter who lives at No. 42: "I worked in a slaughterhouse as a kid, and this was worse than anything I ever smelled on the killing floor. I think there were actually two smells. One was a dank, very musty odor, and the other was this real pungent, acid odor. It was a very aggressive smell."

Ernie Lee, a caterer, who lives at No. 40: "At first, I thought my dog had peed in the house, so I went out and invested in a bunch of disinfectants. Then I went to see if the fire hydrant outside the building was the source of the smell. I couldn't figure out where it was coming from. It was like a phantom smell. You'd be doing something and suddenly it would just show up, like a person. You couldn't do anything once it was there—couldn't eat, couldn't sleep, couldn't do any intimate acts."

Finally, someone had the idea of asking James, North Moore's homeless person, who sleeps in the doorway of No. 37. James pointed to No. 31–33 and said, "The Chinese."

No. 31–33 is in the middle of the block and has a sign over the door that says "T. Chan Enterprises." It turned out that the owner, Mr. Charlie Chan, had been exporting food from there for about a year. Recently, he had expanded into the shark-fin business, which is a good business to be in these days. Crates full of the dorsal fins of different species of shark were being brought to 31–33, processed, and shipped to Asia for use in shark-fin soup. The classical method of processing a shark fin is to leave it out in the sun until it rots. Mr. Chan, lacking the facilities for that, was blowing hot air onto the fins in two saunalike chambers he had installed in the basement. The exhaust was being vented from a grate on the ground floor, into the air of North Moore Street.

A spell of humid August weather set in, and the smell on North Moore became unbearable. Pedestrians avoided the street. Cabdrivers wouldn't stop there. James the homeless person left. The smell got into Bouley and the Tribeca Grill, two of the fashionable restaurants in the area. By the middle of the month, Rachel Friedman, who lives on North Moore, had plastered the street with notices urging neighbors to call Kathryn Freed, their City Council member, and to call the New York State Department of Agriculture and Markets, in Brooklyn. Ms. Friedman had already spent two weeks on the phone with an array of municipal authorities, trying to figure out which one was responsible for bad smells. She had discovered that government is not constituted to cope with smells—that, of all the senses, smell is the least susceptible to regulation. "You'd think that in this city there would be some kind of Smell Complaint Bureau, but there isn't," Ms. Friedman says. "The Department of Agriculture and Markets told me that if the shark fins inside the building were spoiled it could do something. The Department of Sanitation told me that if shark fins were lying out on the sidewalk it could help. The Bureau of Consumer Affairs would be interested if someone was charging too much for shark fins. The E.P.A. wanted to know whether breathing shark fin was harmful to your health. But no one would touch smell. When I called Kathryn Freed's assistant, Stacy, and said 'Bad smell,' she wasn't too interested. When I said 'Rats,' that changed everything."

Kathryn Freed came and smelled the street. "It was like something had died. Horrible. A carrion stench," she said later. Then, a couple of weeks ago, Inspector Paul Feldman of Ag and Markets came and smelled the street, and decided to take a look at T. Chan Enterprises. (Inspector Feldman is the nearest thing this city has to an official nose.) On the way back to his office, he found that people were fleeing the subway car he was in, he smelled so bad. Soon afterward, Feldman returned, and confiscated some of the shark fins. He asked Mr. Chan to suspend his operation, and Mr. Chan did. Whether Mr. Chan will be cited for any violations depends on whether he ever had a license to process shark fins (apparently he didn't), and on whether the Ag and Markets lab determines that the shark fins are fit to eat. "If our inspectors seized the product, something probably isn't right with the fins," Mary Ann Waters, of Ag and Markets' public-affairs office, in Albany, said, explaining why the agency had the authority to shut Chan's shark-fin operation down. "We have reports that some of the fins may be insect infested. Maybe the Chinese like their shark fins this way, but in our view it isn't right."

Several days after the Ag and Markets action, we dropped in on T. Chan Enterprises and met Daniel Chan, the son of the owner. Daniel Chan said that the company was developing a new shark-fin-processing method, and hoped to resume operations soon, on the sixth floor. He took us to the basement. The smell at the top of the stairs was bad, and it became more awful with each step down. Maybe because smell is close to the center of fantasy, as we descended the stairs we had a vision of the shark-fin business from the shark's point of view—being caught, definned, and tossed overboard still alive, unable to swim, to be eaten by other sharks.

At the bottom of the stairs were two machines called ozone neutralizers, which Mr. Chan said the company had leased for two hundred dollars a month in order to improve the smell. Beyond the ozone neutralizers were the processing chambers. Mr. Chan inhaled the foul air deeply and smiled. "No smell," he said. "See? No smell."

1992

BEAUTIFUL DREAMER

FABIO was in his golden Jaguar gliding down Sunset Boulevard on his way to the Hotel Bel-Air. He's powerful when he's driving—even more powerful than he looks on the covers of over fifty million romance novels. He's out of scale, not like a real person. His huge, smooth, tanned-to-dark-apricot forearms were on the steering wheel. His robust, long thighs were covered in loose-fitting navy-blue silk-cotton trousers. One of his navy suede cowboy boots was firmly on the gas pedal. Fabio, who is Italian, from Milan, is six feet three, and his below-the-shoulder bright-blond hair, parted on the side, was perhaps not freshly washed. Two women in a car next to him bounced up and down and screamed "Fabio!"

Fabio's behemothic presence—on paperback books with titles like "The Prince of Midnight" (he's shirtless and alone on a horse)—has loomed from the shelves of supermarkets and drugstores since 1986. For this achievement, he is getting a special award this week at the *Romantic Times* Booklovers Convention, in San Diego. There will also be a Mr. Romance Paperback Cover Model Pageant. But, even if Fabio is dislodged by the winner of that contest as the most visible emblem of romantic fiction, he will not disappear altogether. He is writing three romance novels of his own, for Avon Books, and he'll be seen on the covers of those, of course.

At the hotel, Fabio sat at a table on a balcony overlooking a few waterfalls, a garden of pinkness (azaleas, hydrangeas, camellias), and three white swans. "They weigh between thirty-five and forty pounds apiece," Fabio offered. There was nothing in the sky that day except blue. Fabio drank cranberry juice. (He said you can't find it in Europe.) He ate a piece of olive bread with real olives in it. Birds chirped crazily. Fabio talked with his big hands. His fingernails were impeccably clean and the moons were perfect. He talked about his childhood in Milan.

"I had a very masculine room, very boyish room. Blue was the sheets. Turquoise was the quilt. I had in front of my bed a nice-sized aquarium. I love tropical fish. When I grew up a little bit older, I start having the saltwater fish. I had clown fish and some imperator fish. And they're like real pets, because, you know, they come and eat from your hand and you can caress them."

He caressed the fish?

"Oh, yeahhh," he said. "You know one of those fish that they're like, you know, when you touch them they blow like a ball?"

Blowfish?

"Blowfish." He said it as if all the world's problems had been solved in one word. "I used to have that fish for close to five years. And this fish, every time I was feeding in the hand, and every time I was caressing his stomach, he was turning upside down. It was amazing. Ask my father. I was lifting him this fish off the water, and he will stay in my hand for probably about, I don't know, fifteen or twenty seconds." Fabio laughed, the way Yvette Mimieux did in "The Light in the Piazza." He has smallish teeth. "And the way they look at you, they don't look like fish. They're more like a little dog's eyes."

Between the ages of one and five, Fabio was parked at his grandmother's, in a house by the sea near San Remo, two and a half hours away from his parents, in Milan. There, he said, he spent much of his time "escalating trees."

"At the end of the Second World War, my mother won a big beauty contest in Milan," he said. "She was very young at the time. My grandmother wanted her to enter. She won a refrigerator, washing machine, dishwasher. My grandmother took them back to her place and used them."

Did he look like his mother?

"Yeah, I look like her. I look like my mother."

Nowadays, he lives in a big house on a hill in Hollywood, where he has finished writing his first novel. Its title is "Pirate." "I have a deck with a swimming pool overviewing Los Angeles," he said. "I write there beside my swimming pool with my three dogs around me. Three Great Danes. Because I like a powerful dog, and they're the biggest. And at the same time they're very gentle. Most of the time they don't let me write because they keep licking me or kissing me, you know, or try to chew a pen." Fabio pushed some blond hair away from an extra-blue eye. "You know, it's like sometime when I'm by myself I love to have my dogs around me because it's just beautiful, you know? Sometimes I'm just laying on the deck looking over Los Angeles and I caress them."

Were there any movie stars he admired?

"When I was twelve, I fell in love with Candice Berger."

Bergen?

"Bergen. I remember that movie she was in, that 'Soldier Blue.' She was playing the Indian. She was my perfect girl."

INTENSIVE CARE

THESE are the questions I've been asked since I worked on Show No. 6079 of "All My Children," which will be broadcast on Tuesday, June 29th:

Q: What's Susan Lucci like?

A: Perky, sharp, thin, underappreciated—but I'm just speculating, since she wasn't in my episode.

Q: What was your part?

A: I was a nurse. I appear in Act III, in the hospital-sun-porch scene, and I say, in a mean voice, "Intensive-care patients are only allowed two visitors per hour," and then "We don't want to overtax him," and, finally, "Rules are rules." I say this to Hayley, to stop her from seeing Adam, who is in intensive care after he and Natalie are in a car wreck while speeding to someone's wedding—I forget whose—after Natalie has had a big fight with Trevor, who has recently discovered he was duped by Laurel Banning, who then mysteriously disappears, although she—Laurel—has just sent a note to Natalie's son Timmy, which he reads to An Li, Tom, Trevor, and Myrtle, who are sitting around keeping each other company and are beginning to suspect that Jack and Laurel might have eloped.

Q: Wait a minute—what were Adam and Natalie doing in a car together? They hate each other!

A: I have no idea. I'd never seen the show.

Q: What did you wear?

A: A white pinafore, a white blouse with big shoulder pads, homely white oxfords, white panty hose, tasteful jewelry, no hat. I was hoping I'd be dressed in something skimpy, but the costume department informed me that only one nurse on the show is ever allowed to wear something really tight and short, and that's Nurse Gloria.

Q: Why?

A: I have no idea. I'd never seen the show.

Q: What's going to happen to Adam and Natalie?

A: The powerful and mercurial Adam, who is married to Nurse Gloria, and is the twin of shy, gentle Stuart, discovers he can't move his legs, although in real life he went jogging between the morning camera blocking and the afternoon dress rehearsal. I get the feeling he will recover. Natalie, on the other hand, is definitely going to die. I was told this by Natalie herself while I was having my hair done and she was getting her head bruise applied. "I'm flat-lining either this Thursday or next—I can't remember which," she said. "Natalie's sweet, so she's got to die. If you're on a soap, you want to be a bitch or be miserable, because then you'll last forever."

Q: How were you?

A: Really good. In fact, Conal O'Brien, the director, told me that I was "very steady" and that the sixteen million people who watch the show will probably appreciate my work. And this is a guy who can be tough: for instance, during camera blocking, he told Christopher Lawford—Charlie—that he was giving the camera "too much tush."

Q: How did you prepare?

A: I studied my script, I practiced my lines, I got to the studio at 7 A.M. for all the rehearsals and dry blocking, and during lunch I called my doctor for some authentic insight on nursing.

Q: What did she say?

A: She recommended that I consider my character's back story; avoid wearing my hair in a bun, because nurses don't do that anymore; work on understanding my motivation; and forget about a tight uniform, because only Nurse Gloria gets to wear one.

1993

WORD PERFECT

IN **1988,** not long after they started dating, Peter Chatzky, a Manhattan computer consultant, told Jean Sherman, a writer, that if he was ever to marry not only would the woman have to do the proposing but she would have to do it in an original and creative manner. Since they were both *Times* crossword enthusiasts, Ms. Sherman wrote in November of that year to the newspaper's puzzle editor, Eugene T. Maleska, to ask if it would be possible for her to make a marriage proposal in a *Times* crossword. "I'm writing several months in advance of being totally ready to make this move (Valentine's Day would be terrific)," she added.

Mr. Maleska, who was the editor of the puzzles from 1977 until his death, last month, replied a few days later. "Dear Ms. Sherman," he wrote. "What an interesting letter! As you may have suspected, I cannot grant your request. My puzzles are syndicated to hundreds of newspapers." But then he offered a way around this difficulty. "I can disguise it in a June, 1989, daily puzzle. The entries would include JEAN PROPOSES MARRIAGE and THOU ART PETER, a quotation from Matthew 16:18. I'm sending a copy of your letter to one of my best constructors." The letter went on, "Incidentally, my first puzzle was a personal one, created for a beautiful co-ed in the same college that I attended. Her name was Jean, and I knew she liked crosswords. I sent her a puzzle. JEAN was 1 Across. The clue was 'Most beautiful girl on campus.' Later we married and had 43 happy years together until cancer took her away from me in 1983. May you and Peter have the same joy for many years to come. Pax, amor et felicitas."

Five months later, in May of 1989, Ms. Sherman wrote to Mr. Maleska to ask on what date in June the crossword would be published, but his answer indicated that he had forgotten all about his promise. She thereupon sent him copies of their previous correspondence, and was quickly rewarded with this reply: "This is really embarrassing! . . . I cannot recall what constructor was asked to create your 'proposal' puzzle. At any rate, it never arrived! I have just sent a letter to another constructor named Albert Klaus. He will probably take a few weeks to put the puzzle together. Another problem is that I have already edited puzzles through August. Hence, it looks as if publication of your cross-word will take place in September. Does this mean that my ineptitude has caused your marriage to Peter to be delayed?" Two weeks later, Mr. Maleska wrote again to say that the puzzle would run on September 11, 1989.

Early on September 11th, Ms. Sherman picked up the *Times* from the door-mat, and told Mr. Chatzky to do the puzzle. He went pale, she says, as he deci-phered the key clues: 1 Across, "Actress Arthur or Simmons"; 5 Across, the Matthew citation; 49 Across, "Tank or Civil War General"; 10 Down, "Declares intention to wed"; 39 Down, "Love and ———, 1955 Emmy-award song"; and 36 Down, "Wedding ceremony response." Mr. Chatzky says, "I put the paper down, and said, 'Uh, I don't think I'm ready to do this puzzle.' " But, ultimately, in June, 1991, they married, in the Brooklyn Botanic Garden. Although they had invited Mr. Maleska, he demurred, writing that the wedding was too far from his home, in Wareham, Massachusetts. Ms. Sherman arranged their cor-respondence and the puzzle in a frame, and the frame now hangs over the cou-ple's bed.

1993

CYBERSPACE HAS
A V.I.P. LOUNGE, TOO

STACY HORN is the founder and owner of Echo, the city's largest electronic bulletin board, and she runs it out of her home, a small, fifth-floor West Village walkup. She has two personal computers, and running into the apartment are thirty-five telephone lines that connect to thirty-five modems. Red lights on the modems blink to announce incoming calls; the modems are arranged on shelves at one end of Horn's place in the manner of an art piece. Horn is a friendly, petite woman in her mid-thirties, with thick black hair that frames her face Cleopatra style. "Echo is an electronic salon," she said one recent evening, sitting in front of the modems, and describing the mix of topics— arts, politics, New York life—that the members of Echo (there are approximately two thousand of them) talk about via computer and modem. At the moment, the most active of Echo's members, all of whom pay $19.95 a month to engage in ongoing electronic conversations called conferences, live in downtown Manhattan, but Horn is ambitious and wants to expand to other cities on the East Coast. "It's like Donald Trump puts up this building that sticks way up in the air, whereas I'm building all these little connections you can't see," she said.

As the owner of the equipment on which Echo runs, Horn has absolute power over what goes on in the Echo community; it is not unusual to see her referred to on-line as "Lord Horn." One of her achievements has been to attract women to the bulletin board—they make up nearly forty per cent of Echo's membership—and she has done so, in part, by strongly discouraging electronic sexual harassment, which is an unpleasant aspect of the vast, chaotic sprawl of bulletin boards and other on-line services that constitute cyberspace. "If someone is sending electronic messages saying 'Ooh, baby, baby, what're you wearing,' you can tell me, and I'll send that person E-mail telling him that what he's doing is uncool," Horn said. If someone persists in behaving in an offensive manner, Horn added, she can kick that person off Echo—an electronic banning known on this bulletin board as a "kevorking."

Earlier this month word spread on Echo that a self-selected group of perhaps forty members were quietly meeting (via modem) at an exclusive night club, Xenophobia, between the hours of 11 P.M. and 7:30 A.M. Xenophobia was established as a "private conference," which means it was fitted with a software "filter" designed to keep uninvited people out. But unlike other private conferences on the bulletin board—for example, the 12 Step conference for recovering addicts—membership in Xenophobia was based simply on whom you knew. Moreover, the conference was not announced on Echo's list of conferences (as, say, the 12 Step is), which made some people think that it was supposed to be a cliquish kind of secret. Clubs like Xenophobia are, of course, a fact of life in the real, concrete-and-glass world of Manhattan, but in cyberspace they are almost unknown. Many people join electronic communities like Echo precisely because they offer a refuge from the snobbery of the f2f (face-to-face) world which can make people unhappy and lonely, and some members of Echo were startled and hurt to find out that this sort of thing existed in the electronic world, too, and that once again they were left out.

At the behest of those members troubled by the opening of Xenophobia, Horn created a space on Echo (that is, on the hard drive of her computer) that enables people to discuss their feelings about Xenophobia. From there, the following messages (known as "posts") have been taken.

80:2) Yuri Prizel 03-APR-94 19:33

The concept of Echo, as I was given to understand, was to give people a forum to exchange ideas, points of view, concepts, philosophies, etc. The very existence of an "in crowd" is in direct contradiction to everything Echo allegedly stands for.

80:4) Gabriel 03-APR-94 19:37

Could someone identify this "in" crowd? You post as if it is already determined that such a crowd exists, but, frankly, I ain't convinced of it.

Some people argued that it was a mistake for people to have supposed that exclusivity wouldn't exist in cyberspace:

80:21) Jonathan Hayes 03-APR-94 21:42

I enjoy the myth that cyberspace is democratic. I think it's hilarious.

80:71) Steve B. 04-APR-94 13:17

Since Echo is a NY kind of place, then to be true to our physical surroundings we ought to have in-crowds and especially burly bouncers and haughty
maître d's. Echo subscribers would be cheated out of the NY experience if we
didn't have them.

80:74) Kevin 04-APR-94 14:10

Can I be the burly bouncer?

Others remained adamantly opposed to the principle of an exclusive night
club in cyberspace.

80:224) Aurora Borealis 09-APR-94 12:35

Exclude me from your "club." If what you're doing is talking behind my
back, do so. Believe me, I can take it. But there's no way on God's green earth
you're going to convince me that what you're doing is either right or fair.

The final decision on what to do about Xenophobia rests, of course, with
Lord Horn. For now, she said, she had no plans to close the club down. Though
she is not a Xenophobia regular, she has visited, and reports that it's a place
where some of the earliest members of Echo like to hang out and play electronic jokes on one another—computer-hacker-type things that, she said, outsiders would find hard to understand. "I know the idea of a private club is sort
of unkind, and people may be hurt by it, but there's just no way you can stop
things that happen in the physical world from being projected into the electronic world," she said.

But hadn't some people joined Echo in order to get away from exclusivity?

"People who join the electronic world expecting it to be better than the physical world will be disappointed," Horn said. "And if you expect everyone is
going to be your friend, you'll be disappointed, too. I'm sorry. Echo is not Oz."

1 9 9 4

TOU-TOU-TOUKIE, HELLO

TOUKIE SMITH, who is the owner, the maître d', and more or less the chef behind Toukie's, the new restaurant on West Houston Street, has a big voice and a big smile and big earrings and a big body, all of which, in her unbridled enthusiasm for things quintessentially Toukie—"meeting and greeting and eating, darling"—she has poured into her new venture. Toukie's menu is one of the most autobiographical we have ever seen—offerings include "My My Those Fries," "Honey That House Salad," and "Black Bottom Pie."

Operating in a manner more animated than that of the still model she was known as in the mid-seventies (when she was a muse to the artist Jean-Paul Goude *before* Grace Jones, the photographer Guy Bourdin, and the designer Issey Miyake), Toukie says, by way of greeting, "Give me some sugar, baby," followed, whether she knows you or not, by a kiss and a hug. Sometimes she says, "Give me some sugar *now*, before you try my biscuits, girlfriend," regardless of gender. At Toukie's, Toukie follows everything her patrons do (ordering a drink, finishing dinner) with applause or a hug or a kiss—a red, red kiss.

Red, which is Toukie's preferred color and is generally present on some aspect of her person at all times (nails, dress, bracelets, lips), is also the color of the leather banquettes at Toukie's—a low-ceilinged, dimly lit room with about twenty-four tables. And it is also the color of a boldly painted mural on one of the restaurant's walls, an image that includes her ninety-four-year-old grandmother Gladys, Elizabeth Taylor, and Dorothy Dandridge. They are all women whom Toukie admires, because, she says, "they were always real, giving back to the people. Which is a very real reality."

The number of very real realities Toukie has had to contend with in recent years include the death, from AIDS, of her brother, the designer Willi Smith; the end of her long-term relationship with Robert De Niro ("Oh, child, please"); the end of her modelling career ("Girlfriend, the industry is not ready for me loving my 34D-cup-size self"); the current return, in the fashion industry, to seventies glamour ("Darling, nothing is as fierce as I was back then, going to Tokyo to smile, to Paris to smile, to Milan to smile. You can't duplicate that innocent energy now; we know too much"); and the establishment, in honor of her brother, of a foundation to promote AIDS awareness in inner-city high schools and hospitals across the country. "I tell my kids to look it straight in the eye—and then *avoid* it."

The last time we had seen Toukie, she was dining out with Robert De Niro. She'd kept urging Mr. De Niro to eat, demonstrating the delectability of his food by eating half of it herself. When we recently saw her again, after what had been a long time, candlelight bounced off of her double row of enormous silver earrings, her forearms were covered in beaded bracelets, and her red lips were moist. "I'm just loving this," she told us. "I'm just loving all this *life.*"

1 9 9 4

RUSSIAN TENNIS:
ADVANTAGE YELTSIN

IN Moscow this past November, Eugene Scott, the director of the Kremlin Cup tennis tournament, had an idea for his annual Christmas card: he would mosey up to where Boris Yeltsin, a great tennis fan, was sitting in the stands of the vast Olympic arena and get a courtside photographer to snap a picture of the two of them, apparently in amiable conversation.

In fact, Scott and Yeltsin have more than a nodding acquaintance. Two years ago, Scott, a nine-letter athlete at Yale, a member of the Davis Cup teams of '63 and '65, and the editor of the magazine *Tennis Week*, was summoned from his tournament duties on the morning of the finals to play in a doubles match with the President. "What happened," Scott said the other day, "was that my partner, Gennady Burbulis, the former State Secretary, and I had won the pro-celebrity tournament, which is called the Big Hat. The winners put on this huge hat with two holes for their heads, and the photographers take pictures. Quite ridiculous—cartoonish. At any rate, we were challenged by Yeltsin and his partner, Shamil Tarpishev, a former Davis Cup player and a former captain of the U.S.S.R. team. They hadn't played in the Big Hat—Yeltsin apparently didn't want to play in public."

The match took place on an indoor court. Each player had a separate three-room suite in which to change, and while Scott was getting into his tennis clothes Tarpishev invited himself in and began talking about Yeltsin's game. The gist of it was that the President had been in an automobile accident a few months before, and his back was in bad shape. Thus he didn't like high shots to his backhand; didn't like balls hit to him with big topspin; didn't mind short lobs; but certainly did mind those that were deep and threatened to go over his

head. It was during this litany that Scott realized that what he was being asked
to do was not to hit to Yeltsin's weaknesses. Quite to the contrary, he was supposed to set him up—like serving up clay pigeons. "I've been in a number of sit-
uations like this before," Scott said. "Pro-am tournaments, or corporate
outings where you were expected to dump one to please the C.E.O. I would start
off with noble intentions, but in the end my competitive instincts would take
over. Never had I thrown a match, and I wasn't sure about this one."

The four competitors met out by the net. Yeltsin was wearing Adidas sneakers and socks, Reebok outerwear, and a Fila shirt, and was carrying a Prince
racquet. "Physically, he's very impressive," Scott recalled. "He's six four, and he
stands unbelievably erect, as if he had a steel pipe in his back. His hands are
huge and enveloped mine when we shook hands at the net. In stride he reminded me of Don Budge, who always moved in the gait of a champion, even
long after his retirement."

THE four men went out onto the court to warm up. "I felt I was inside a pinball
machine," Scott remembered. "Yeltsin's idea is to hit every ball as hard as he
can. They were careening off the walls. He was quite undaunted—big smile,
and then he'd crack another. I was reminded of the two theories about learning
golf: one of them is that you start off with a slow, easy swing, eventually in
creasing it to full power, but the problem here is that you pick up mistakes as you
increase the swing. The other theory, totally contradictory, is that you start by
belting the ball hard, the idea being that if you can groove the swing you haven't
had the opportunity to cultivate errors. This latter is the Yeltsin principle."

In the match itself, there were a lot of double faults and a number of aces, even
against as skillful a retriever as Scott. "He could really fire them," Scott said. "Hit or
miss. A number of the aces weren't really aces, though. Part of the deal was that
he had to win his serve, so that when one of those blinding second serves would
miss a line by a foot or so, the idea was to raise a hand and call out 'Khorosho,'
which means 'good,' or even 'Ochen khorosho,' which means 'very good.' Yeltsin
never seemed to complain about these odd calls. He's very competitive."

Rather as predicted, the Yeltsin-Tarpishev team prevailed.

"It was an interesting experience," Scott said. "But you won't catch me doing
anything like that again unless Yeltsin is involved. I enjoyed him. His tennis is
rather like George Bush's. Both have an exaggerated sense of how good they are,
which makes them more effective players. They'd have a really good match."

Gene Scott got his Christmas-card picture. Seated right behind Yeltsin at the
Olympic arena, he leaned forward so that the photographer courtside snapped
him in conversation.

"I was saying, 'Ochen khorosho,' " he said.

THE SHIT-KICKERS
OF MADISON AVENUE

THE tenth graders heading up Madison Avenue at 7:30 A.M. to the private high schools are freshly liberated from their dental braces, and their teeth look pearly and magnificent. They are fifteen years old. During the week, they arrive, by bus or on foot, singly or in pairs or in clusters, and they make their way up the west side of Madison—they call it the "cool" side—toward their schools: Dalton, on East Eighty-ninth; Sacred Heart and Spence, on East Ninety-first; Nightingale-Barnford, on East Ninety-second; the Lycée Français, on East Ninety-fifth. Brearley and Chapin are farther east; Collegiate, Columbia Prep, and Trinity are in the west; Browning is south; Horace Mann, Riverdale, and Fieldston are in the north. On the weekends, the tenth graders from all points will find a way to get together. Today is only Tuesday.

Boys and girls spill out of the Eighty-sixth Street crosstown buses at Madison Avenue and join the flow of their counterparts heading north. The walking tenth graders greet one another in soft, kindly rhythms, in polite, gentle tones. The boys greet one another with high fives. Girls with girls and girls with boys bestow quick, sweet kisses on one another's cheeks—some cheeks still not completely rid of hints of baby fat. No routine air kisses from these kids. Their kisses are heartfelt, making their unity, their devotion to and trust in one another, palpable. Kisses from their mouths are like the cool little first nippy smacks of a very young baby.

MOST of the tenth graders are in the habit of leaving home without eating any breakfast. Still in clusters, with fifteen minutes to get to school, they pause in doorways. One girl in a cluster of five takes out a pack of Marlboro Lights—the brand favored at the moment—and each member of the cluster participates in lighting the cigarette, striking the match, guarding the flame, offering a propane lighter. They share. The lighted cigarette is passed from mouth to mouth. They all inhale, the girls twisting their mouths like tough pros, exhaling the smoke from a tiny corner opening on one side of the lips.

One angelic-looking blond beauty with raw, red nostrils takes a puff, inhales deeply, and says wearily, "I've like got the fucking flu or something."

"Fuck the you know fucking germs," another one says smoothly, reassuringly, a positive reinforcer.

"I got home like three?" another member of the cluster says, making her statement in the form of a question. "I sweat Henry? Who you sweat? Anybody?"

The others regard her skeptically. "Nobody," one says.

"I sweat the shit out of Henry," the one who got home at three says mildly.

On the feet of all the members of this cluster are boots, not quite Timberland. The girls, some wearing black panty hose or black kneesocks, have on chic black laceups, all with Vibram soles, all with steel tips. One girl wearing laceups two feet high lifts a knee, turning the booted foot this way and that. "New shit-kickers!" she squeals, but in subdued, ladylike tones.

"Cool," the angelic-looking one with the flu says. "Cool shit-kickers."

They crush out their shared cigarette with the heels of their shit-kickers, and they go to school.

WHENEVER the tenth graders have a break in their school program, and daily at 12:35 P.M., they head for one of their hangouts. The second floor of Jackson Hole, at the southwest corner of Ninety-first and Madison, is in at the moment. On this Tuesday, at 12:36 P.M., six four-place tables and a couple of two-place tables, accommodating twenty-eight customers, are filled. Ketchup bottles absolutely full are at the ready on every table. A teen-age Al Pacino–look-alike waiter serves them their first meal of the day: lone platters of ketchup-doused French fries or fried onion rings, or combo French fries and onion rings, and Cokes. A late arrival, dark-eyed, and smaller and chubbier than the ones settled in, turns up, and a place is found for her. Tearfully, she reports that her French teacher sprang a surprise test on her class, and she thinks she did badly on it.

"Don't like get fucking stressed out," a girl says, offering that same kindly positive reinforcement.

"Fucking teachers," a companion says, chewing on a fry and simultaneously taking a drag on a cigarette and passing it on. "I'm on my way you know to lunch, and the fucking teacher asks where I'm going?" The statements continue to sound as though they were questions. "I don't want teachers being like into my you know business?"

"I miss the teacher who used to be a model and then left the school and went to Africa to be a nun?" someone says. "She would like talk you know about her experiences? She was very like open to everybody?" The others at the table and the girls at all the other tables agree that they miss the teacher who went to Africa to be a nun.

One of the girls, very pretty, with long dark hair, is "presenting" a party and hands out printed invitations. She has dark glasses pushed up on top of her hair. She wears silver loop earrings, a double in the left ear, a single in the right. At her throat hangs a large wooden cross. The invitation shows a picture of Stonehenge on one side, and the other side has a long list of names of people supporting the party, which has a title: "The Farside."

"I can't go to the party?" one of the fifteen-year-olds says. "My father grounded me? Because I was smoking?"

"My mom is trying to like ship me off to a fucking school in fucking Spain?" another girl says. "Unless I you know quit smoking?"

"I want to quit, but I can't? I don't have a choice? It's too late?" one fatalist says.

The party entrepreneur explains that she is working with six other presenters to spread the invitations around, to telephone friends at the schools to the east, west, north, and south, and to obtain the services of a really topnotch d.j. They are working with a well-to-do party producer, whose take of the proceeds will be forty per cent, the balance to be divided evenly among the seven presenters. Admission to the party will be twelve dollars per person.

"This rich, older guy is like experienced you know?" she says. "He's twenty-nine?"

The mention of the number draws forth gasps.

"Fucking twenty-nine," one of the girls says. "That's the age of those actors in that mindless '90210' or that mindless 'Melrose Place.' They're twenty-nine, and they're like playing our age."

At any rate, there are plans to be made. The party is going to start at 10 P.M. The girls will spend the afternoon before in preparations.

"Here's what we'll do," the entrepreneur says. "We need five hours. You three come to my house you know at five? You bring all your clothes? I take everything out of my closet and spread everything out on the floor? We try on all the stuff? Depending on what kind of mood we're in, we make our selection?"

"We have to be fucking blunt," one of the potential guests says. "About what like looks good on us."

"Then we take showers? Half an hour? Then we like shave our legs? Half an hour? Then we like put cream on our legs? Half an hour? Then we call up everybody who's been like grounded? We talk to them for at least an hour? Maybe we give them an hour and a half? Then we go out and buy a quart of vodka and some orange juice and cranberry juice? Then we go to somebody else's house and drink vodka with orange juice or vodka and cranberry juice? Then we get dressed? Then we get another quart of vodka and go to somebody else's house? We become like outgoing? And we make calls to friends and invite them over? By then, we'll be ready to go?"

ON the first school day after the weekend, promptly at 12:36 P.M., the tenth graders are back in place at Jackson Hole, smoking, chewing gum, eating fries and onion rings, and reviewing the party. "I like feel real ripped off?" the young Farside presenter-entrepreneur is saying. "Too many people came to the party, which was at this nice club on West Forty-seventh Street? There were hundreds pushing and shoving and clogging the street, and the police came? And they said we had to be carded, because they had a bar? And we you know didn't like have cards, so this twenty-nine-year-old rich guy said the fee for getting the club had to be raised from three thousand dollars to eight thousand dollars, because they had to close the bar and were not allowed you know to sell us drinks? And everybody had to pay twenty dollars instead of twelve dollars just to get in? So, but even so, nobody like wanted to leave? And it was so crowded you couldn't even dance? And at the end of it the twenty-nine-year-old rich guy took forty per cent, and all I got was about fifty fucking dollars, after I did all the fucking work and made a million phone calls?"

She chews on a French fry, accepts a glowing Marlboro Light from the girl beside her at the table, and takes a quick puff. The chubby, dark-eyed girl who was stressed out by her French teacher comes over from another table and gives the entrepreneur a soft, comforting kiss on the cheek, and one by one all the other tenth graders in the area come over and do the same.

1 9 9 5

AFTER MIDNIGHT

HIGH above the East River, on a dark maintenance platform under a well-known bridge, a young jeweller named Gregory crouched and, with the help of a flashlight, studied a fat rubber cord. This was long after midnight a couple of weeks ago. All around Gregory, shadowy figures climbed ladders, spread tarps, covered girders with blankets, and rigged complicated harnesses. Gregory, his jeweller's concentration fully engaged, inspected the cord—forty feet long unflexed—lying coiled on the platform. It was composed of hundreds of thin beige strands, cinched together every foot or so. There was a fair amount of fraying, particularly toward one end. Gregory fingered the busted strands thoughtfully. Did he really want to bet his life on this thing?

A few feet above his head, trains and cars roared and whined, shaking the platform. Nearby, a steel floor plate had been removed and a coffin-size hole yawned. A hundred and thirty-five feet below, the river's surface, seen through the hole, looked solid, a whorled gray slab in the yellow lights of the Brooklyn waterfront. There was a police car parked on the waterfront, near the base of the bridge. One of Gregory's confederates, a bartender and college student named Ian, was monitoring the police car through a pair of binoculars while listening to police-radio transmissions on a pair of headphones. Such, such are the rigors and peculiar precautions of guerrilla bungee-jumping.

The owner of the cord was Michael O'Mahony, a former tent rigger for the Big Apple Circus. Brooklyn-born and bred, thirty years old, he was also the evening's jumpmaster. When he had finished rigging harnesses, he addressed the group. "This will happen fast," he said. "We got eight people jumping tonight. Some of you, it's your first time, I know, and you may feel you need some extra time, but, with the cops sitting down there, I could be making a two-thousand-dollar mistake, so it's three minutes in the hole each person. If you haven't jumped after three minutes, I'll pull you out of there, right? Now, I'm going first. Who's going second?"

"I'll go second," Gregory said. The cord had apparently passed inspection.

O'Mahony set a blue night-light on a girder and demonstrated how to hook a carabiner from the jump harness to a retrieval rig that would be lowered to him. Tall and thin, with a huge head of red curls, O'Mahony made an unlikely drill sergeant, but he had plenty of commando intensity. "This life jacket has a beacon," he said, flicking on a bright light attached to his chest. "I've never had an accident on one of my jumps, but if something happens and you do hit the water, hit the beacon. You'll find razors in the pocket here. Use them to cut the cord, then kick toward shore. I'll call 911 on this cell phone. A speedboat will come."

O'Mahony moved to the hole in the platform, stepping carefully through it to stand on a pair of light crossbars a foot or two beneath the floor. The cord hung from his waist in a thick, vaguely obscene forty-foot loop. "Boat check!" he called.

Two people crawled away to scan the river. If O'Mahony was a strange-looking sergeant, he had some appropriately improbable recruits. They included Alison, a fashion model with slim hips and a dry wit; Eric, an angel-faced motorcycle racer with a long blond ponytail; Chris, a round-faced bicycle salesman who admitted to "a profound fear of heights"; and Jon, a film-prop builder with the poise of a ballet dancer, a tiny steel barbell through his left eyebrow, and a powerful physique.

O'Mahony, who has led some twenty late-night bridge expeditions, finds his jumpers where he can—"I just look for people who seem ready to get out past the outer edge of life somewhat," he says—and he claims to get an astounding positive-response rate to his invitations. (Astounding, that is, when one considers that he is proposing something illegal, dangerous, unremunerative, and terrifying.) He does it, apparently, just for the adrenaline hell of it. "And because I can," he says. The hipster individualists whom he drafts seem surprisingly ready to submit to military-type discipline. At least, they seemed so that night—stealthily climbing catwalks onto the bridge in teams of three, giving come-aheads over walkie-talkies, using code names like Mr. Red and Mr. Black without a smirk.

The lookouts came clambering back across the platform. "No boats downriver." "Nothing upriver."

O'Mahony bent his big head and seemed to disappear into himself. A tarp snapped in the wind. Nobody spoke. Finally, O'Mahony jumped up slightly, brought his feet together, and was gone. He fell swiftly toward the swirling gray slab of river, his uplifted face shrinking to dot size with alarming speed. Then the cord reached its limit—a hundred and twenty feet—and he came bouncing

back toward the bridge. The group peering through the hole gave a sharp col-
lective exhalation. A few more vast human-yo-yo bounces, and it was time to
send down the recovery rig. Under the direction of Glenn Vegezzi, an experienced jumper, who was the night's second-in-command, O'Mahony was
hauled back to the platform. When he arrived, grinning maniacally, he
seemed, if such a thing were possible, even more wired than before.

Gregory, who was making his first jump ever, did not use a large fraction of
his allotted three minutes in the hole. Talking into a tape recorder, he answered
some questions from O'Mahony about his vital statistics, plus one about
whether he was making this jump of his own free will. Then he was gone.

After he returned, he shyly reported feeling "hyper-alert."

All the jumps went smoothly. The hard part, clearly, was the waiting. Jon, the
film-prop builder, hunkered in the dark, silently chain-smoking, for at least an
hour. Then, when his turn came to jump, a party boat appeared, chugging
slowly upriver, its lights pulsating, and he had to wait, already harnessed to the
cord, for many more long minutes. After his jump, his friend Alison took him
aside and solemnly kissed him on the mouth.

Chris, when his turn came, muttered that he had "the shakes," and went
back to the end of the line.

Alison vamped while O'Mahony cinched the harness on her, fore and aft,
and when, as she stood in the hole, he asked her age, she said, "I hope to be
twenty-nine soon." To the will-and-volition question, she replied, "Utterly,
dude."

This was her second jump. She leaped with style.

Chris went last. As he stood in the hole, answering questions for the tape
recorder, O'Mahony said to him, "You are not going to die tonight." Chris
looked unconvinced. When he finally jumped, he disobeyed instructions and
grabbed the cord, mildly abrading his forearm, and when the recovery rig was
lowered he was disoriented and had trouble attaching the carabiner.

The eastern sky was whitening as Chris was hauled back up through the
platform floor. The police car was still parked on the waterfront. O'Mahony, becoming frantic about the dissipating darkness, directed a furious restoration of
the platform, replacing the floor plate, packing up his equipment, and putting
all the tarps and ladders back where the bridge workers had left them. Then the
group moved out, jogging silently down the catwalks in teams of three, recon-
vening briefly at the base of the bridge for handshakes and goodbyes, then
melting off in different directions into the dawn-crisp city.

1995

A BATTALION OF BELLAS

"THE world is suffering a global nervous breakdown," Bella Abzug barks. You may remember Abzug as the human bullhorn of the nineteen-sixties and seventies: congresswoman, feminist at the barricades, and living symbol of the brassiness and bravado of her native New York. Now, at seventy-five, she has traded in the bullhorn for a fax machine and has gone international. As co-founder of the Women's Environment & Development Organization, Abzug organizes women around such global issues as economic development and access to political power. Late last week, she left for the Fourth World Conference on Women, in Beijing, where she plans to hold the world's feet to the fire on pretty much every issue you can think of.

Though not quite the volcanic force she once was, Abzug is still a seriously blunt instrument. On a recent afternoon, she was sitting in her crowded midtown office wearing a three-piece purple silk suit, purple platform shoes, and a straw hat—the signature Abzug accessory—with a parrot-green brim and a purple crown. A purple crystal dangled from a chain around her neck. "It's supposed to have calming qualities," she said with a derisive laugh. Serenity is not in her repertoire.

At the moment, Abzug was exercised over suggestions that Hillary Clinton ought not to attend the Beijing conference, because the Administration was at odds with China over human-rights issues. (The Chinese had not yet released Harry Wu.) "It's political!" she rasped, throwing out her hands in the classic New York go-soak-your-head gesture. "She's not there on a diplomatic mission. She's there to join women and their government delegations to see what they can do to improve the conditions of women and children, which she's been working on all her life." Reminded that the President's own Secretary of State, Warren Christopher, had expressed concern about the First Lady's plans, Abzug rolled her eyes beneath a cloud of gray hair and said, "He's a fuddy-duddy. He doesn't get it."

Lining a narrow corridor outside Abzug's office were boxes of literature waiting to be shipped off to Beijing. WEDO, as her group is called, will be playing a central role for the thirty-five thousand members of nongovernmental organizations expected to converge on the conference. "We've had a lot of words on equality," Abzug says. "Now we want the music, which is action." WEDO will be coordinating strategy among the N.G.O.s and convening a daily Women's Linkage Caucus; a giant scoreboard will list the dozen planks in the momentous-sounding Plan of Action the conference is to adopt, and will chart the specific commitments made by various nations. Abzug's faith that nations will make serious efforts to eradicate poverty or restrain "corporate greed" or cut defense spending just because they've pledged to do so seems almost touching, but she insists that words publicly uttered take on a real moral force. And women, she says, "are being mobilized by these meetings like crazy, all over the world."

BELLA ABZUG has been Bella Abzug for so many years now that she has apparently become not only an icon but an international brand name. At a recent meeting, she reports, "this young woman came in and said, 'Hi, I'm the Bella Abzug of Mongolia.' " WEDO itself represents a convening of such Bellas-in-training. After she finished talking, Abzug heaved herself to her feet and proudly introduced her colleagues, who included young women from Louisiana, Tanzania, Bangladesh, India, Korea, and Turkey. They represented the future; but Abzug also carries her past with her. WEDO's other co-founder is Mim Kelber, a friend of hers from Hunter College, and one of the volunteers is Eva Lederman, who was Abzug's high-school gym teacher, and who, at seventy-nine, remains dauntingly trim. Bella, she reports, was a terrific dancer.

1995

A DICKENSIAN TASK

MANY people fear that our ever-increasing dependence on computers will have an adverse effect on traditional intellectual pursuits, but among much evidence to the contrary is the forthcoming publication of a three-volume work of literary scholarship entitled "Everyone in Dickens," which would have been impossible to accomplish in a single lifetime without the aid of a computer. In this work, published by Greenwood Press with a list price of two hundred and seventy-five dollars, a sixty-four-year-old white-bearded pianist-singer-soldier-lawyer-banker-bibliophile named George Newlin lists thirteen thousand one hundred and forty-three names of characters, fictional and nonfictional, that appear somewhere in the vast Charles Dickens œuvre, whether in his novels, magazine articles, speeches, plays, poetry, or collaborations. Twelve separate indexes identify characters by name, family relationships, and occupation, and also give a one-line description that leads elsewhere in the text to more lengthy descriptions of them in Dickens's own words. And if, as a Dickens addict, you recall a favorite beadle or undertaker who happens not to have achieved the dignity of a name, Newlin has listed over four thousand of these humble folk according to their occupations. He also finds room in his twenty-five hundred and sixty-eight pages to deal with topics like "Major Characters' Names Used Only Once," "Striking Omissions in Characters' Given Names," and "Pet and Other Animal Names."

It was Newlin's trusty computer that enabled him to organize the immense mass of Dickens material, searching out a word with the tap of a single key, shifting thousands of words in bulk from one place to another with another tap, and so by electronic manipulation avoiding the repetitious donkeywork imposed on scholars in earlier times. He undertook the task as a consequence of becoming obsessed with Dickens seven years ago, when the breakup of his marriage prompted him to seek emotional refuge in his library. Among the books he turned to was "The Old Curiosity Shop," and he found it a far better novel than he had remembered. Armed with blocks of yellow and blue Post-its, he kept marking passages that he might one day wish to return to. Before he knew it, he had launched himself on a new career. Having already taken care to accumulate what he calls "an adequate cushion" in the world of finance, he set out, as an amateur scholar, to devote himself to a project that many Dickens academic scholars had dreamed of but had assumed to be unthinkably difficult.

Specifically, what made it possible for Newlin to complete the task in six years was his now archaic Macintosh SE and an equally archaic ink-jet printer. "Every word, every punctuation mark was typed by me," he says. "I've been a concert pianist, and probably for that reason I became a rapid typist and often had to wait for my screen to show me what I'd already written. Today I am in a position to take advantage of a laser printer, and can work much faster than I used to."

Which is Newlin's way of hinting that the Dickens obsession has not yet run its course, and that the publication of a fourth volume, which Newlin tentatively calls "A Dickens Topicon," can be looked for within a year or so. The "Topicon"—the title is a Newlin neologism—will be a thematic concordance dealing with every aspect of life that Dickens happened to note and set down *except* people: places, social conditions, inventions, and the like. Once that task has been accomplished, other authors in need of Newlinian analysis hover invitingly on the horizon. Backed by the latest resources of computerization, Newlin contemplates taking on Thackeray, Trollope, and George Eliot. He flexes his fingers over an imaginary keyboard and exclaims, "I can hardly wait."

1 9 9 5

THE *TIMES* EMBARKS ON NEW WAYS TO GET OUT THE GRAY

*T*HE *New York Times* is—as many a grizzled editor has told many a cub reporter, by way of explaining why some gamy detail or barnyard epithet or double-entendre had to be blue-penciled—a family newspaper. And, in the case of the *Times*, the phrase is more than just another way of saying that the news must be fit to print. For hundreds of thousands of veteran readers, the paper is like a member of the family. You never really chose it, it's just there—always has been, always will be. You may love it or resent it, you may find its crotchets endearing or annoying, it may bore you one day and enthrall you the next, but the idea of living without it (though the two of you may occasionally take separate vacations) never comes up. The *Times* is reassuringly familiar. And you spend a lot of time with your consciousness focussed on it. Let's say, conservatively, that a typical reader gives the paper half an hour on weekdays, an hour on Sundays. That adds up to more than two hundred hours a year. Over a sixty-year lifetime of *Times* reading, the total exceeds four years' worth of eight-hour days. How many of us will ever devote tht kind of time to gazing into the eyes of a loved one?

It stands to reason, therefore, that when the appearance of the *Times* changes discombobulation results, as if one had looked in the mirror and found oneself with an unexpected nose job. That's why the newspaper of record thinks twice, and then twice more, before it administers autorhinoplasty. The modifications that are discombobulating readers the length and breadth of the metropolitan area this week may not be all that big, but their arguable modesty does not mean that it has not required considerable effort—to wit, ten years, two high-level task forces with pulp-novel names (the Futures Group and the Mohonk Team), the building of two enormous new printing factories (one, in faraway Edison, New Jersey, opened in 1992, and the other, in exotic College Point, Queens, opened eight months ago), and the spending of more than three-quarters of a billion dollars to bring them about.

Arthur O. Sulzberger, Jr., the dapper ex-reporter, ex-ad salesman, and full-time scion who has been the *Times'* publisher since 1992, explained all this and more one afternoon last week, in the course of briefing The Talk of the Town on the upheaval to come. The Edison plant, he said, has enabled the *Times* to use color in its preprinted Sunday sections, such as Travel, Arts & Leisure, and the *Book Review;* College Point enables it to do the same in the daily paper. Starting on September 15th, the *Times* will be a five-section paper on Mondays: main news, metro, arts, sports, and business. For the rest of the week, it'll have all or the above plus one of the below: Science Times; Dining In, Dining Out (a revamped Living section); House & Home (the Home section redux); and, on Fridays, a two-part Weekend section. And now that the *Times* has a separately printed Northeast edition (plus a national edition, produced in eight plants around the country from pages downloaded by satellite), the New York edition can go to press later. "By not having to truck papers to Boston and Washington, we get a huge gain in terms of deadlines," Mr. Sulzberger said. "Before, the *Times* spoke to its readers at nine o'clock in the evening. Now we can speak to them at eleven-thirty at night."

With a flourish, Mr. Sulzberger plopped a stack of prototypes on a coffee table in his cozy office. We inspected them carefully for signs of the impending collapse of Western civilization. We detected none. The color photographs and graphics on the front pages looked surprisingly ungarish. Their tones were muted and earthy, and they brought out the crispness of the paper's classy typography. It's not quite Rembrandt, but Rembrandt never had to wrap fish.

1997

KURT ANDERSEN

SON OF EST:
THE TERMINATOR OF SELF-DOUBT

I NEVER took an est seminar, but I've always thought that Werner Erhard's human-potential scheme was way ahead of the curve: by squishy seventies standards, est was unsentimental in both form (you got yelled at; you had to pay close attention) and in substance (you are responsible for making yourself happy; there is no divine secret of life). Erhard was on his way to becoming the baby boomers' Dale Carnegie, but then, during the first few months of 1991, it all went phffft: "60 Minutes" aired an exposé of Erhard and est; he sold the business to some employees; the I.R.S. came after him; and he went into exile.

But, once again, Erhardism, like disco and marijuana, is ascendant. Erhard's former associates, reconstituted as the Landmark Education Corporation, have morphed est into something called the Landmark Forum. Landmark hasn't received much press attention. This is partly because there is no high-profile charismatic leader like Erhard. There is also Landmark's three-year-old lawsuit against the Cult Awareness Network. But Landmark is evidently becoming very popular, like est before it, among the semi-stylish upper-middle class. More than a hundred thousand people a year attend the forum and the programs it is associated with, and, since graduates are strongly encouraged to recruit family and friends, the growth may be approaching some exponential tipping point.

The forum takes place over a long weekend (Friday, Saturday, and Sunday, for fifteen hours each day), plus a Tuesday-night wrap-up session. In New York, the cost is three hundred and fifty dollars, or about seven dollars an hour—pricier than a movie (with less comfortable seats), cheaper than private-school tuition (more comfortable seats), about the same as an Off-Off Broadway show (equal seat comfort).

When I called to register, I had to give a credit-card number, describe an "issue" I wanted to resolve, and listen for half an hour as the Landmark order taker recited boilerplate—medical caveats, psychological warnings, legal indemnities. I shouldn't come, she said, if I were "unwilling to encounter enthusiasm . . . fear, empathy, sadness, or regret" in myself or others, or if coming to grips "with what it means to be human" might prove too "difficult and unsettling." I had to tell her whether my wife approved of my attending the forum. I had to confess whether I had ever quit therapy against a therapist's recommendation. Finally, regarding "any issue or claim" I might subsequently wish to file against Landmark, I had to be prepared to agree to "freely giving up my right to a jury or court trial."

EACH forum consists of between a hundred and a hundred and fifty people and is conducted in New York every two weeks in a big, tatty third-floor room off Fifth Avenue. It's like a marathon version of certain first-year law- or business-school classes—a lecture course where the teachers are gregarious dictators and classroom participation is expected. Sometimes it's a matter of anonymously shouting answers to the leaders' fill-in-the-blank exegeses ("You get annoyed with your parents because you want . . . *what?*"), but people also stand, give their names, and "share" relevant personal anecdotes, "Oprah"-style. There are short breaks every two or three hours, during which the leaders are available to answer questions privately.

Jerry, the more electric of my two forum leaders—imagine Martin Short doing Stuart Smalley live—gave us a capsule history, naming Erhard as the organization's founder. Jerry also said that he had "been doing this since 1975," suggesting a certain unashamed continuity between est and Landmark. Yet when a young woman went to one of the microphones to declare her qualms about Erhard and her fear that the forum was "a con game," Jerry replied, "Who conned you when you were young? This is about that." When Jerry explained a point to the group, he habitually said "Capeesh?" He also repeatedly mentioned that he was a former professional dancer and that he had recently fathered a darling son.

A central forum idea is that people cling unnecessarily to dissatisfactions in order to make themselves feel morally superior—what the forum calls "running rackets." The leaders spoke constantly of "causing possibility" and of "being your own life's cause." A piece of paper taped to a table reminded the staff that its goal was to make us all "audacious, self-expressed leaders." The words "sharing" and "listening" were nouns. Everyone used "empower" a lot. The goal was not happiness, exactly, but something more sci-fi neutral: "the result," which involves a kind of existential "completion."

It's easy to make fun of any freeze-dried patois, but this clunky new language is the means by which Landmark purports to reëngineer its followers' lives. Landmark employs "a language structure that creates possibility," Jerry said. "You make the interpretations. Rewrite them." There is a Landmark graduate seminar that is actually called "Inventing Oneself." The basic idea is that if you accept Landmark's epistemological conventions—scrupulously distinguishing, for instance, between facts (e.g., "She didn't call") and invidious interpretations of facts (e.g., "She didn't call because she hates me")—and then start using its particular tough-love vocabulary, your life will improve. It's as if an Up with People troupe had forsaken Scripture in favor of Derrida: deconstruction as an American applied science of cheerfulness—happy and unhappy are mere linguistic constructs, and it's up to you to assert control.

But even though Jerry was slightly terrifying and ridiculous, even though I reflexively loathe almost everything about the Landmark Forum (the jargon, the big classrooms with fluorescent lights, the one-size-fits-all feel-good doctrines, the talking to strangers about my inner life), and even though I dropped out after the first day, I found that I mostly agree with its precepts: that contentment lies within oneself; that the glass is half full; that it's pointless to belabor the past; that whining is bad. "We just made this up," Jerry told us when someone wanted religious certainty. "This is not the truth." Brian, our other leader, added, with a note of irony, "There are places you can go for truth." If I were going to start my own cult (and I am in no way implying that the Landmark Education Corporation or any of its employees constitute a "cult"), it would probably be a lot like this. But I don't think I'd hire Jerry.

1 9 9 7

DO THE ROOKIES KNOW HOW
WILLIE MAYS PLAYED?

BASEBALL reopens this week, with the fresh schedule reviving hopes
everywhere—well, maybe not in Montreal—but the icon season is over.
Once again, the spring-training camps in Florida and Arizona featured the customary assortment of aching arms and bulked-up pectorals, and the reappear-
ance on the field of some of the pastime's most august figures and uniform
numbers: leathery Hall of Famers and legends, back in the sun as invitees for
a brief tour as spring coaches. Fan dads leaning on the chain-link fences at
the Cardinals' new complex, in Jupiter, Florida, could point out Lou Brock to
their kids, right over there, talking to Red Schoendienst and—is that No.
45 . . . yes!—Bob Gibson. On a back field at Port St. Lucie, coach Mookie Wilson (a thousand kittens were named Mookie in the summer of 1986, when the
Mets were driving for their pennant) smiled engagingly, pointing to his knees
and his hips as he demonstrated leadoffs from first base to a handful of Mets
rookies; one of them was his son, Preston Wilson, who might just turn into a
legend himself a few springs down the line.

Out at the Giants' Scottsdale Stadium, in Arizona, Vida Blue sat cross-legged
in his familiar camp chair, just in front of the stands, now and then extending
a hand back over his shoulder to accept an unseen fan's pen and program; and
the man indoors, sitting at the same southeast corner of the same clubhouse
table, was Willie Mays. He is sixty-six now, and his seamed, heavy face hasn't
much say hey left in it, but he is never without company. Visiting writers and
sportscasters, stopping by to pay their respects in the morning, have found that
they share a wish to grab some of the youngest and newest Giants, chattering

over there in front of their lockers, and say, "Do you have any *idea* how this man played?"

Mays, in self-protection, has developed a selective memory, and conversational openers from his visitors about his celebrated overhead catch against Vic Wertz in the 1954 World Series or the four-homer game in 1961 no longer light up the Proustian hot stove. Nor do knowing references to any of the other lifetime six hundred and sixty dingers bring much response—not the homer that beat Warren Spahn, 1–0, in the fifteenth inning (eyeroll, with incomprehensible murmur), or the monster blow against the Astros' Claude Raymond after Mays had fouled off thirteen consecutive fastballs ("Grmpf. How'd you know about that?"). This year, though, a visiting senior writer from back East got lucky when he brought up an early Maysian catch and throw against the Dodgers—the Billy Cox play.

"Damn!" Mays cried excitedly. "You saw that? You were there?"

Yes, the writer had been there—as a fan at the Polo Grounds. "August, 1951," he said. "Cox was the base runner at third. You caught the ball running full tilt toward right, turned in midair, and threw him out at the plate. You threw before you could get turned around—let the ball go with your back to the plate. The throw went to the catcher on the fly—it must have been Westrum—and he tagged Cox out, sliding."

"You got it!" Mays said. "I've been sayin' this for a long time, and nobody here believes me." He was kidding, of course, but his voice had come up at last: almost the old, high Willie piping. "Now, tell 'em how it was."

I told it again—it was easy because I'd never seen such a play, before or since—and, as I did, it seemed to me that Willie Mays and I could still see the long, curving flight of the white ball through the afternoon light, bang into the big mitt, and the slide and the amazing out, and together remember the expanding moment when the staring players on the field and those just emerging from the dugouts, and the shouting fans, and maybe even the startled twenty-year-old rookie center fielder himself, now retrieving his fallen cap from the grass, understood that something new and electric had just begun to happen to baseball.

1 9 9 8

AL HIRSCHFELD
BLOWS OUT HIS CANDLES

I REALIZE that any minute now my dear friend Al Hirschfeld will be ninety-five. I pick up the phone for a celebratory chat. Al is in his studio, on East Ninety-fifth Street, in his antique barber chair, drawing. Always drawing. "I feel wonderful," he says. "Absolutely wonderful." I suggest that work plays a part in his miraculous vitality. I hear a full-throated snort. "It isn't work, kid. It's luxury. Pure luxury. I don't call it work. I haven't a clue how one would retire." Al uses the word "retire" the way some people pronounce "Richard Nixon." "What's a man to do? Sit around some sun-soaked beach all day? Watching the waves? Or playing golf? Golf!"—same tone as "retire." "Human beings fascinate me. People," he says. "I used to love just sitting in the window of the Howard Johnson's at Forty-sixth and Broadway, drawing the constant parade of people passing by." Does he still make notes in his pocket during a show, in the dark? "Just for reminders," he says. "I'll draw a bow tie, or a cane, or jot down one word or make a sketch that brings back an entire scene."

I remind Al that he once said, "It would never occur to me to do a drawing of the Grand Canyon. It is just a decayed molar under a very dramatic light." Now Al says, "Still feel the same way. Nature is *there*. What are you going to do? It's movement that interests me. Movement in my drawing gives me total freedom. I can go where I want. I can take the line anywhere. I'm not governed by gravity." I venture that his line is stronger today than when he was a stripling of seventy-five. "It's the freedom," he says. "The exhilarating freedom." We talk a bit about kindness. In a mean world, there is never any meanness in a Hirschfeld drawing. "Nothing funny about a big nose, or a grotesque face, or making people look like an image in some Concy Island fun-house mirror," he says. "I once did a drawing of Jimmy Durante, and I left the nose out."

I remind him of the joyous weekly lunches we used to have at the old Lobster restaurant, on Forty-fifth Street, with S. J. Perelman, Joseph Mitchell, Brooks Atkinson, Harvey Orkin, Albert Hackett. "I'd like to start those all over again," he says. "Why don't we think about it?" He goes on, "Something has happened to humor. Out of fashion—I don't understand it. Jokes aren't humor. Something to do with economics and people incapable of satirizing the times in which they live." He's thinking back now. "I miss the great Miguel Covarrubias. Tremendous influence on me. I'd like to think I had some effect on him.

"But the fuss over this birthday! Hard to believe. Photographers all over the house, in every corner but the sandbox. We have a rabbi lives across the street, and I step outside the other day and there are *six* photographers on the rabbi's roof, snapping pictures of me. On the big day, Louise and I will go to her family in Larchmont for a barbecue. So long, kid. Much love to all at your place." Click.

1998

REBECCA MEAD

THE WORLD WAS INVITED TO NOAM CHOMSKY'S VIRTUAL BIRTHDAY PARTY

I N recent months, friends of Noam Chomsky, the linguist and social critic, were wondering how to mark his seventieth birthday, which fell on December 7th. The usual academic tribute, a Festschrift, didn't seem quite sufficient. "You have to think, who shall we invite to contribute," Jay Keyser, a retired M.I.T. linguist, explained a few weeks before Chomsky's big day. "With someone of Noam's stature, it would turn into the Encyclopaedia Britannica."

So Keyser and a colleague from CUNY, Janet Fodor, came up with an alternative: a tribute Web site. "You want a vehicle that is infinitely expandable, and that is what the Internet is," Keyser said. The Celebration Project, established earlier this year at http://mitpress.mit.edu/celebration, invited all comers to contribute essays and salutations. "My view was that this would be just the way Noam would like it," Keyser said. "You don't go to an élite group—you open it up to anybody who would care to say anything."

The organizers initially decided not to alert Chomsky's obvious peers and acolytes to the existence of the Web site, hoping that potential contributors would simply browse their way into its precincts. The openness of the project made for some entries that probably would not have passed muster in a more conventional academic publication. From Israel came a linguistic analysis of Robert Frost's poem "The Birches," arguing that it "extolls the virtue of enticing young virgins to sexual activity." ("The Germanic word BiRCH sounds somewhat like the Latin word ViRGin," the writer explained, helpfully.) One Chomsky fan admitted that posting a greeting "kinda made me feel like a groupie sending a card to his or her favorite rock-and-roll star," while another, from Slovenia, gushed, "It is the greatness of that man and the brightness of his brain and the baldness of his ideas and the fruitness of his domain that make us admire him."

In all, there were a hundred and ninety-five contributions to the site. Among the more well-established academic voices taking part was that of the linguist Ray Jackendoff, who contributed "Some Things I Learned from Noam." ("Colorless green ideas sleep furiously. They really do.") Steven Pinker, the author of "The Language Instinct," wrote, "As a teenager I decided to study cognitive science after reading an article about the Chomskyan revolution in the *New York Times Magazine*, and, ever since then, practically all of my research and writing has been trying to answer questions you have posed." Pinker said last month that the understated nature of the project (it was kept secret from Chomsky, and, on his birthday, a red folder bound with a gold ribbon was left quietly on his desk) suited its subject perfectly. "He doesn't go in for ceremony," Pinker said. "Though I don't want to say that he has a small ego—he is always a hundred per cent certain that he has been, is, and will be right about everything. He is not a modest man in that sense, but he is a modest man in the sense of promoting himself."

Speaking by telephone from his home two days after his birthday, Chomsky told me, "The truth of it is that my wife had to explain to me what was going on. But when I figured it out I was overwhelmed." (He has since been reading the contributions on paper, since he doesn't access the Internet.)

"When I was a kid, my mother used to arrange a surprise party every year for me, and I never figured it out," he went on. "I was always completely surprised, and it was the same in this case. It is apparently in the genes."

1 9 9 8

A POSTMODERNIST GOES SHOPPING

MICHAEL GRAVES, the architect, used to think that a gondola was one of those long black boats that tourists like to take pictures of in Venice. That was before he signed on to design a new line of home and kitchen accessories for Target, the discount department-store chain. Now he knows that a gondola is an island of back-to-back shelves sitting in an aisle between two areas of merchandise. Starting this week, Graves will have space on several gondolas to display his products in each of the eight hundred and fifty-one Target stores.

Graves was explaining all this and other fun things he's learned about discount stores one slushy day recently as he took a break to check out the Target store in Menlo Park, New Jersey, not far from his office, in Princeton. He walked the aisles in a blue Ralph Lauren baseball cap, surveying the store's vast stocks of everything from potato chips to pillowcases. Stopping at a gondola filled with pre-Graves dishes, he picked up a set of four cobalt-blue bowls packaged in an open-fronted box ($6.99). "This is not bad," he said, obviously torn between the diplomacy required of a member of the Target team and his own designing instincts. Diplomacy won the day as Graves sped up past a display of picture frames decorated with baby shoes in bas-relief ($8.99). "I think there's always going to be that nostalgic need, but I think you could do it with greater wit," he said. He turned next to a silvery frame ($9.99) in a shape that looked like a melted valentine. "Well, these things come and go," he said. "I have learned that picture frames are a form of fashion, like sheets."

Graves has been designing household objects for years—he is particularly well known for an Alessi teakettle with a whistling bird on the spout, which re-tails for a hundred and forty-five dollars—but he has never cracked the low end of the market. Now that what might be called the Gap phenomenon, the trending downward of taste, has made mass-market goods more sophisticated, the time seems to have come for an internationally acclaimed architect to design $12.99 picture frames and a $39.99 toaster.

"People ask me, 'Why are you doing this?' " Graves, who is sixty-four years old, said. "I tell them, 'If I design a library in Denver, that's for the masses, so why not this sort of stuff?' "

During the visit to Target, it was easy to gauge Graves's level of approval by his walking speed—he slowed down to examine merchandise he liked, and accelerated when he was displeased, as if to make the offensive objects disappear. He practically sprinted past a frothy glass perfume bottle that looked like sugar-coated plastic ($11.99)—"There are so many great Art Deco perfume bottles they could have used as an inspiration," he said wistfully—whereas his eye was caught by a plastic laundry basket ($5.99) with aerodynamically shaped vent holes and sleek proportions. "Now, if I apply the best test, the my-house test—do I want that object in my house?—I'd have to say yes, I want that," he said.

He moved on to a gondola piled with toasters ($9.99 to $59.99). "For me, all of these are within ten per cent of each other in looks—they're all boxes," he said. "None of them would put a smile on my face at seven-thirty in the morning." Graves's own toaster will certainly stand out. It is voluptuously rounded, with a plump blue handle, a yellow control knob, and egg-shaped gray feet—a cartoon version of a toaster.

His pace picked up again when he passed a gondola full of doormats, including a printed still-life ($8.99), a green mat that read "Welcome" and had three frogs on it ($13.99), and a mat adorned with fake cobblestones ($27.99). This is one department that the improved-taste culture does not seem to have reached yet. "I have to say that I've never seen one of these mats at anyone's door, but maybe it's just the doors I go into," Graves said. "I guess I'd better do a doormat next."

1 9 9 9

JOHN SEABROOK

ELEGY FOR A PARKING SPACE

FOR thirteen years, I was part of the nomadic community of people who "garage" a car on the streets of Manhattan. The rhythms of parking shaped my days, my nights, and my weekends. Arriving at 10:30 A.M. on Monday to insure a spot when alternate-side parking began, at eleven, I'd sit in the car reading the paper, writing letters, or sharing information on the hard-to-predict movements of traffic cops with the other people who parked on my block. (Like salmon returning to their birth rivers, people who park on the street tend to be drawn to the same blocks.) A spot secured on Monday didn't actually have to be relinquished until Thursday, but to be sure of a Friday spot you had to move the car across the street on Tuesday. Extending a weekend on Long Island until Monday meant missing the chance for a Sunday-night spot—always iffy, but doable—and that meant, almost certainly, having to pay for a parking garage or settle for a meter, which would require leaving the house every hour to put quarters in it.

Of course, one could not actually use the car, once parked, except on weekends. Some might argue that the time and energy one invests in looking for free parking is worth more than the three hundred dollars or so a month it costs to keep a car in a parking garage. But for me parking on the street was worth it. I knew the sudden joy of spying that rectangle of heaven that I could lay claim to simply by having a car, and I knew the devastation of seeing the car right in front of me grab it. Parking for free made all the other usurious New York City expenses more bearable (such as the unincorporated-business tax, which is the penalty that the city makes the self-employed pay for not being a corporation). Even a fifty-five-dollar parking ticket is a lot easier to swallow when sweetened by the thought of what a monthly garage costs.

But life is what happens to you while you're busy looking for a parking space, as John Lennon sort of said. When my wife and I had a child, I convinced myself that it was time to upgrade to a more comfortable and reliable car than the 1987 Toyota Land Cruiser that I'd bought, with eighty thousand miles on it, in 1992. I felt we needed something that wouldn't give the kid Shaken Baby Syndrome simply driving down Greenwich Street.

Parking on the street had meant not having to worry about getting a new car. In order to discourage potential thieves, I kept my car as messy as possible—old newspapers, McDonald's wrappers, clumps of pennies gummed together with spilled Coke, empty bottles that rolled out from under the front seats when you hit the brakes. Whatever temporary loss of status I might have suffered by arriving in certain driveways in Connecticut in a semi-beater, I would regain when I informed people that I parked my car on the street. Out-of-towners, especially ex–New Yorkers, love to congratulate themselves on not having to pay three hundred dollars to park their cars, and finding out that I kept a car in the city for free was usually a blow. You mean you park on the street? And nothing happens to your car? Nope—well, nothing serious. In all the years that I garaged my car on the street, I got some dings and, once, lost a radio, but it was a crummy radio.

As I drove our new car, an Audi wagon, home from Zumbach, the dealer, to the expensive garage I would be parking it in, my perspective on New York City traffic changed drastically. Cabdrivers with whom I'd once gleefully jockeyed for position now seemed to be driving like madmen. Stay away from my car, I said out loud several times. After two days of driving in the city, it was a relief when we packed up for the recent holiday weekend and headed to New England. Only on crossing the Henry Hudson Bridge did I begin to unwind, and not until I arrived in the bucolic spaces of Vermont was I able to begin to enjoy owning a new car.

On the following morning, the warm winter sun was twinkling fiercely on my car's Santorin-blue mica finish. The snow on the roof of the house began to melt. "Usually roofs around here creep," a resident of the village later told me. "But this time they shot." A week's worth of heavy snow and ice came whizzing down, projected five or six feet away from the house, and landed directly on top of the car. The weight stove in the roof, put a "bird bath," as the body-shop guy called it, in the hood, and dented the car in other places. I had insured the car against the usual urban threats, theft and vandalism, but I hadn't thought about thawing snow falling off a roof in Vermont. I had a tense two-day wait for the insurance agent to open to find out if I was covered.

So now I have no car. It's back at Zumbach, getting a new roof. It turns out that I am insured, although I'm out the deductible and I'm paying the garage for space I can't use. I see beautiful parking spots around the neighborhood, but they no longer delight me. They mock me.

1999

A LITTLE BIT OF AUDREY FOR EVERYONE

IT wasn't breakfast at Tiffany's, but one recent evening, across the street at Bergdorf Goodman, they were passing around champagne and hors d'œuvres in celebration of a new book entitled "Audrey Style." Audrey Hepburn, whose regal neck and doe eyes—not to mention twenty-inch waist—were the envy of every woman, would have turned seventy last week. The birthdays of late, lamented icons provide the perfect marketing opportunity for misty-eyed reappraisals, and Pamela Clarke Keogh, the author of "Audrey Style," seated at a table amid the department store's cosmetics counters, couldn't sign copies of her gorgeous-looking book fast enough.

Billy Wilder, who directed the actress in "Sabrina," once remarked, "This girl, single-handedly, may make bosoms a thing of the past." And, after spotting her in her first major movie, "Roman Holiday" (for which she won an Academy Award for best actress), women rushed to copy every aspect of her guileless style, from her breezy haircut to her white cotton shirts with the sleeves rolled up. Still, Hepburn was known to refer to herself—with the entrancing modesty that was as much a trademark as her ballet flats—as "just a skinny broad."

Keogh's book is short on substance and a bit muddled on the details (did Hepburn wear a size-8½ shoe? or was it a size 10?), but it is gratifyingly long on photographs, fashion sketches, and gushing print-bites. The word "grace" appears on about every third page, and we learn that the determinedly svelte actress (Hepburn, who was five feet seven, kept her weight at a firm hundred and ten pounds) liked pasta and an occasional chocolate fix. Of course, she had trained as a dancer, which gave her enviable posture in addition to a formidable will. ("She's disciplined, like all those ballet dames," Humphrey Bogart is quoted as saying.)

"Audrey Style," published by HarperCollins, contains the briefest of introductions—no more than an imprimatur, really—by the reclusive Hubert de Givenchy, the seventy-two-year-old couturier who helped create Hepburn's signature style, beginning with "Sabrina." In 1953, he agreed to see her in his Paris atelier, under the misapprehension that she was Katharine Hepburn; since he was busy preparing a collection, she whisked through his workrooms, plucking outfits off the racks. They became lifelong friends, and whether Audrey Hepburn's sophisticated-schoolgirl look owes everything to Givenchy or is a reflection of her own taste, as well, is the stuff of bitchy speculation.

At Bergdorf, the crowd dined on miniature hot dogs, Roquefort-covered walnuts on slices of Granny Smith apples, and raspberry tartlets, a menu that was supposedly inspired by Hepburn's favorite foods. It's hard to believe that the actress, who considered herself "chubby" when she ballooned to a hundred and thirty pounds, actually ate enough food to have favorites. But Keogh insists that Hepburn "ate a lot," and credits her skinniness to that most maddening of all explanations, "great metabolism."

Explaining why she decided to do a Hepburn book, Keogh said, "She is as vital and present today as she was years ago." Sure enough, the windows of Bergdorf were filled with Audrey-stylish spring fashions, and the store is selling a hundred-and-seventy-five-dollar pink satin evening clutch filled with makeup by Prescriptives—"for people who don't read," as Keogh says. (It was going to be called the "Funny Face Kit" until the people at Paramount, who own the rights to the film, got wind of it.) Surrounded by a sea of young women in sleeveless Hepburn-like sheaths, I found it hard not to wonder what the actress, who preferred her Swiss farmhouse to the swirl of show business, and who spent her last years working on behalf of UNICEF, would have made of all the glamour and greed attached to the use of her name. Picturing her here is difficult—it's much easier to see her as Holly Golightly, that soigné waif, staring in at the windows of Tiffany.

1999

BILL AND HILL, MEET ROB AND LAURA

WESTCHESTER COUNTY cocktail-party conversations, which often wind up being about how much you think your house is worth, became unexpectedly livelier this summer. Suddenly, it was possible to speculate about how much your house would be worth if Bill and Hillary Clinton moved in next door. Most reporters missed this authentically Westchester-ish aspect of the story, because they were too busy poking television cameras in local residents' faces and asking: In the event of a Clinton relocation, how will you feel about all those television cameras?

This, of course, is a very silly question, because if there is any place on earth that has historically been hospitable to the medium of television it is Westchester County. It could be argued that without the inspiration provided by the leafy suburbs of Westchester the television sitcom could never have survived to become the mature art form it is today.

Chappaqua, where the Clintons just signed a contract to buy an eleven-room Dutch Colonial priced at $1,695,000, is down the road from Peekskill, which was home to Mrs. Garrett's cheese shop in "Facts of Life." Ann Marie, the character Marlo Thomas played in "That Girl," grew up just north of the Westchester border in Brewster, a few exits away from Pound Ridge, where the First Couple looked over a seven-acre, $1.2-million property with tennis courts. Tuckahoe, where Bea Arthur trod the fine line between feminist and harpy in the Norman Lear sitcom "Maude," is right next to Edgemont, where the Clintons toured a seven-bedroom turn-of-the-century Colonial priced at $1.7 million. (Edgemont, the Clintons may have reasoned, was less likely than Tuckahoe to inspire unflattering limericks.) And New Rochelle, which the

Clintons also visited in their quest for suburban housing, was immortalized by "The Dick Van Dyke Show"—a program that may have uncannily predicted what the Westchester phase of Bill and Hillary Clinton's life together will be like.

Comparisons between Bill and Hillary Clinton and Rob and Laura Petrie may not be as striking as those famously spooky Lincoln/Kennedy parallels (Lincoln had a secretary named Kennedy, Kennedy had a secretary named Lincoln, etc.), but they are difficult to ignore. Both couples feature one hardworking careerist trying to make it in a new field (Rob/Hillary) and one housebound spouse with way too much free time and a tendency to get into fixes that require blubbering apologies (Laura/Bill). Both families have one child (Ritchie/Chelsea), who appears infrequently and says almost nothing. Both breadwinners have to contend with irrational, mercurial screamers (Alan Brady/Rudolph Giuliani). Even the details offer up eerie parallels: Morey Amsterdam/Chuck Schumer; Capri pants/golf pants; twin beds/separate bedrooms. And so on.

Commentators discussing the retirement years of our young President have invoked Fitzgerald's shopworn dictum that there are no second acts in American lives. Part of the beauty of a sitcom like "The Dick Van Dyke Show," however, was that each episode did, reassuringly, have a second act, after the commercial break, in which the mishaps and mixups of the first half of the show were satisfactorily, if somewhat speedily, resolved. Perhaps it is this sort of expeditious redemption, and not just an eleven-room Dutch Colonial, that the Clintons are really looking for in Westchester. With this idea in mind, it is possible to envision the first few episodes of "The Hillary Rodham Clinton Show":

· Hillary is excited about putting on a talent show to raise money for local Democrats but has second thoughts when Bill is cast as Mark Antony in the "Cleopatra" sketch opposite Jennifer, her gorgeous administrative assistant!
· There's heck to pay when Bill takes Hillary's new limo, provided at taxpayers' expense, to McDonald's—and puts a big scratch in the fender!
· Bill has some explaining to do when he goes on a talk show—and blabs about what Hillary really did with those billing records from the Rose Law Firm!
· In a flashback episode, Bill and Hillary reminisce about Bill's Army days—and how he avoided having any!
· When Bill and Hillary discover they were not legally married, Bill vanishes forever. Series finale.

1999

NOSTALGIA FOR THE BYGONE DAYS OF FEMINIST FAMILY FEUDING

WHEN the feminists of the nineteen-sixties coined the expression "Sisterhood is powerful," they did not have in mind one typical characteristic of the relationship between female siblings—the way that sisters fight all the time. Susan Brownmiller, in her entertaining new history of the women's-liberation movement, "In Our Time," reminds readers that the six-ties-era feminists, for all their high achievements, did their fair share of feuding.

Three decades later, a certain nostalgia has set in, and when Brownmiller appeared at a Barnes & Noble on the Upper West Side the other day and found some of her onetime adversaries in the audience, she appeared delighted to see them. She punctuated her reading—about the daylong feminist occupation of the offices of the *Ladies' Home Journal*, in 1970—and a question-and-answer session that followed with yelps of recognition. "Judith Hennessee, who wrote the biography of Betty Friedan—I picked a fight with her!" Brownmiller cried. "Alix Kates Shulman, the novelist—one of the best feminists, although we disagreed all the time!" She spotted Michela Griffo, a radical lesbian whom she'd offended back in 1970. "Michela, you want to say something divisive?" she shouted. "I never agreed with anything you said!" Griffo shouted back fondly.

"Visionaries are difficult people," Brownmiller said later, at a party given in her honor. "Put eight visionaries in a room, and you will get eight different visions." Her book does, she said, give considerable play to some of the wackier elements of the feminist movement, such as Shulamith Firestone's erratic behavior during the *Ladies' Home Journal* sit-in. Firestone tried to assault the magazine's editor, a man, yelling, "We can do it—he's small." Brownmiller maintained that she was entitled to chronicle these goofy moments, "because I am doing it in love and celebration of the movement. Movements are always like that. Think about Freud and Jung and Adler, always at each other's throats. Or Stalin, arranging to have Trotsky killed."

All that scrapping was simply the sign of a vital movement—something that Brownmiller says she sees no hint of these days. "I feel sorry for young women today," she said. "Some young women are committed feminists, but it is hard to be an activist and a militant in nonmilitant times." (Younger women wishing for a movement of their own might have been made wary by the answer Brownmiller gave at the reading when she was asked about how feminism affected her ability to negotiate relations with men. "Well, I don't know if I did negotiate those relations," she said. "I did not know that if I wrote a book on rape"—"Against Our Will," which was published in 1975—"my popularity would plummet. Once, I said to Robin Morgan"—a former editor of *Ms.*—"that I had been alone since I wrote 'Against Our Will,' and she said, 'What did you expect?' ")

Brownmiller's party was attended by only two men and a crowd of women with hair in various shades of gray and gold. The host was Marlene Sanders, a former ABC and CBS News correspondent, who is identified in "In Our Time" as the movement's only ally on television. (Sanders indicated that there were still battles to be won for women's rights when a guest asked why she no longer appeared on television. "I'm too old," she growled. "Though I'm the same age as Dan Rather.") Guests included friends of Brownmiller's from the human-rights contingent, such as Lucy Komisar, and from the feminist movement, such as Joyce Johnson and Alix Kates Shulman. "We've disagreed, but that's history," said Shulman, glowing. "One of the consolations of history is that it's history." There was also a delegation from Brownmiller's regular Saturday-night poker game, and one from the women's Ping-Pong league in which she plays every Sunday. "That's what an old feminist does to keep active," Brownmiller said. "I do all those things in lieu of a women's movement."

1 9 9 9

2000

ANTHONY LANE

THE NEW YEAR STUMBLES IN

I T was reported last week that eighty per cent of Americans stayed home to enjoy the opening of the new millennium. This was a startling figure, although it requires further analysis: we need to know how many celebrants were clasped in the bosom of their families, and how many sealed themselves into storm cellars with a candle, a .45, and enough tortilla chips to last three months. Contrast the extrovert spirit that prevailed in Australia, say, where government statistics have revealed that the only citizens who failed to leave the house on December 31st were the McGarry family of Perth. The city of Sydney, which, despite the looming Olympics, looks pretty happy about itself, laid on an extravagant party in the harbor.

Whether this made it the Greatest Show on Earth was a matter of inflamed debate. China—the place that invented fireworks, as well as noodles, the printing press, and peeling students off tank tracks—emblazoned the heavens above the Great Wall. Layers of light ascended the Washington Monument and, with geometric elegance, the Eiffel Tower. In a daring act of multiculturalism, the good people of Tonga rose at midnight to sing the "Hallelujah Chorus" from Handel's "Messiah." Then, there was New York. Estimates put the number of revellers at more than two million, of whom at least forty-six were resident New Yorkers. Nobody in his or her right mind headed for Times Square, for the simple reason that if you wanted to get out of your right mind you had to go elsewhere; Mayor Giuliani, not content with gluing shut the manholes in case anyone was reading the Koran in the sewers, had declared midtown to remain an alcohol-free zone for the entire evening. The joke is that the only visitors who would applaud such a move were the same Islamic fundamentalists he was trying to keep out. One wonders how major an event would have to be before the Mayor thought it worthy of a beer. As rogue Korean warheads plummet toward Forty-second Street, will he announce free hazelnut mocha for children under ten? One thing is certain: thanks to the Giuliani precautions, grandparents in 2080 will be able to regale the kids with tales of that amazing night when they stood shivering beneath a giant underpants billboard and sipped apple Snapple.

For once, New York could have taken a lesson from London. There, underfoot, as revellers walked across Blackfriars Bridge at two in the morning, empty champagne bottles made a lush pastoral carpet of green and gold. At the Oxo Tower, on the South Bank, where the eighth-floor Restaurant, Bar and Brasserie threw the most geographically desirable party of the night, cocktail specialists could pass seamlessly from a Y2K—basically, a gingered-up White Lady—to a One Second To . . . , the effects of which could still be felt Eight Hours After . . . Dancing took place beneath fluorescent, Warholish portraits of Faces of the Millennium. There were, on balance, few experiences more suited to a fading, farcical century than trying to moonwalk to "Blame It on the Boogie" under a picture of Bertrand Russell.

Russell, of course, blamed it on expansionist Western capitalism. He would not have relished the last hours of 1999. The rule governing fireworks, for instance, is quite simple. If x is the amount of money that it would be prudent to spend on your fireworks display, and if y is the number of people whom you expect to attend, then the actual expenditure should be $3x + y$. There is a further rule, which states that on the occasion of a new century the equation should change to $3(x + y)$. Real fireworks addicts whisper darkly of y to the power of x, but that is unrealistic. The London fireworks, launched from a string of sixteen barges along the Thames, were as intemperate as one could have wished. The last time the city took so apocalyptic a pounding was in 1940, when the Luftwaffe flattened the docks; now, as then, St. Paul's Cathedral vanished in the smoke and slowly reappeared, ghost gray. What better than harmless hellfire to presage a fresh start?

The most fitting thing about London's millennial effort was its blend of new technological hope and comforting, old-fashioned screwups. The waiting crowds were promised a wall of fire, two hundred feet high, that would flash up the Thames at eight hundred miles an hour, presumably singeing everything in its path. The mind reeled at the idea of a million British subjects beginning the new century with no eyebrows. In the end, nothing happened; the wall failed to ignite, and the London Eye, a four-hundred-and-forty-three-foot Ferris wheel near Waterloo Bridge, failed a safety inspection. Down in Greenwich, the place where time is timed, it emerged on New Year's Eve that, of the $1.2 billion dollars spent on the Millennium Dome, almost none had been set aside for postage stamps to stick on invitations; the great and the good were therefore, to the delight of the moderate and the naughty, made to wait in line with ID for up to four hours before entering what is, in effect, the world's largest diaphragm.

Once inside, the ten thousand visitors were treated to a floor show, a plastic glass of champagne, and a prayer. As the New Year broke, they launched into a mass rendition of "Auld Lang Syne." Singers crossed their arms and linked hands with those on either side, as custom demands; unfortunately, custom doesn't say what to do if the woman adjacent to you happens to be the Queen of England. Samuel Johnson was once asked why he had not wowed King George III with one-liners. "It was not for me to bandy civilities with my Sovereign," he replied. Tony Blair is nothing if not a bandy man. He took the left hand of his sovereign and pumped it proudly up and down. The Queen offered the other hand to her husband but declined to cross her arms, the result being that she was forced to stand there and flap weakly like a chicken. The set of her mouth was the highlight of the evening: as billions of viewers looked on, Her Majesty assumed the steady, thunderous expression of a nun at a Robert Mapplethorpe exhibit. No doubt she was reflecting that, had she been the first Elizabeth rather than the second, she could have had the Prime Minister's entrails broiled in front of his eyes.

But the moment passed; a good time was had by nearly all. The world chose not to end, or even to shut down; computer wonks everywhere breathed easy once again and fingered their wads of overtime. The millennium bug has thus far failed to nip; the only substantial glitch was traced to Russia, where a software error caused a pneumonic lush to hand over nuclear codes to a war-hungry spook. The new President chose to be photographed in a patterned zip-up cardigan; if Mr. Putin's foreign policy turns out to be as aggressive as his taste in knitwear, 2000 promises to be, at the very least, a colorful year. Maybe those fireworks were just an appetizer, after all.

THE WELL-HEELED AND THE WONKY
TOAST THE MILLENNIUM

"DRESS as your favorite figure of the past millennium," the silver-embossed invitation to George and Susan Soros's New Year's Eve party said, and most guests did as they were bid. Shortly before seven, Galileo, Erasmus, and St. Francis of Assisi, not to mention Amelia Earhart and several Audrey Hepburns, gathered outside the Soroses' Fifth Avenue apartment, where a fleet of minibuses was on hand to ferry them up to the speculator-cum-philanthropist's country estate in Katonah. Passing through iron gates, the distinguished guests approached a large red brick mansion, with a slate roof and a modern extension jutting out of one side—which, on closer inspection, turned out to be a fully equipped sports atrium. Once inside, they were greeted by liveried servants in white wigs. The Soroses, famously kind hosts, had a rack of extra costumes standing by for those who had overlooked, or simply forgotten, their previous instructions. Jagdish Bhagwati, an eminent professor of economics at Columbia, chose to be the Emperor of Japan. His wife, Padma Desai, another noted economist, opted for the Empress of India.

After being individually announced by a butler, the guests drank cocktails in a tented area around the swimming pool. "It was such a phantasmagoria," said Gloria Deák, who fulfilled a lifetime ambition by dressing as Gloria Swanson. (Her husband, the historian Istvan Deák, came as Noël Coward.) On the walls hung ten large oil canvases, one for every century of the second millennium, and each featuring an image of the hosts. Beneath these modest portraits, George and Susan Soros greeted their guests in person: George a trim and smiling Christopher Columbus, Susan a striking Queen Isabella of Spain. The crowd numbered about two hundred and fifty, and there were many familiar faces in unfamiliar garb: Steve Brill, the publisher of the magazine *Brill's Content*, had come as Winston Churchill, complete with top hat and cigar (in truth, the cigar was no stretch); Paul Volcker, the former chairman of the Federal Reserve Board, made an imperious Zeus (nobody dared question his grasp of the calendar); Zbigniew Brzezinski, the former national-security adviser, was a spirited Karl Marx (although he told some guests that he was Father Christmas); and the former British diplomat Sir James Murray, a sprightly octogenarian, entered in a bright-yellow jacket, delighted to be announced as Hugh Hefner.

After a lengthy cocktail hour, the revellers took a footbridge across the pool—some stopping to stare at two gold-clad hired nymphs cavorting in the water—to the high-ceilinged atrium, where dinner was served. As Genghis Khan and Henry VIII and the rest tucked into lobster risotto, a troupe of trapeze acrobats whizzed to and fro above their heads. The acrobats were young, lithe, and dressed, or partly dressed, as signs of the zodiac. Two buff young fellows made a particularly strong impression, grinding sinuously against each other in an arresting interpretation of Gemini. "There was a beautiful young woman writhing above me as I ate," Bhagwati later recalled. "My wife said, 'Watch out! She's going to fall on you.' I said, 'I hope she does.' " When the assembly could avert its eyes from the sights above, there was music, including a piece composed specially for the occasion by Lewis Flinn and performed by a small orchestra.

At midnight, the crowd counted out the old year in fine voice, and gave the new one a resounding cheer. As the guests set off back to the city, at least some of them stared at the bronze medals they had been handed on the way out and wondered if the dawning millennium could ever match such understated splendor. Their hosts, in any case, had no such doubts. Beneath etched profiles of George and Susan Soros, the medals featured the following inscription: "Enlightened by the past. Embraced by the present. Empowered by the future."

2 0 0 0

TWO MENUS

KING'S RANSOM
Paducah, Kansas
Fine dining at its best.

Fried-Butter Appetizer
Butter, cream, fat, lard,
shortening, palm oil, drawn-
butter dip.

Greaseballs
Four greaseballs served flaming
hot in your hands (grease, balls).

♥ *Cow Organs Charlton Heston*
Steaming entrails and freshly
slaughtered virgin cow brains,
marinated in lard. Find the bullet
and eat free!

Maybelle's Vegetarian Special
Ham, ham hocks, pork rinds,
butter, eggs. Ask for Bac-O-Bits!

SYNERGY
Beverly Hills, California
Phone: Yeah, right.

Air Salad
Dehumidified ocean air on a
bed of fileted basil.

Egg-White Omelette
Egg whites, pumpkin seeds,
Vitamin C, nonfat cheese buttons,
aerated yogi urine.

Spaghetti à la Nerf
Our natural eggless spaghetti,
cooked in desalted Caspian Sea
water, simmered in oliveless olive
oil, and sprinkled with parsley
skins. As light as a Nerf ball!

Filet of Sole
Sole.

Double Height Rib-Eye Steak
Cooked in its own juice while alive,
served with hot buttered metal
screws, cardboard.

Egg-Yolk Omelette à la Mitt
Yellow hearts of egg folded into an
omelette. Cooked and served inside
a boxing glove.

Our Banana Split
Fried ice cream, butter, double-
cream-infused banana, whipped
cream, cherries in red dye No. 2,
triple-fudge chocolate sauce,
pancakes, cow fat.

♥ Heartwise!

Chilean Sea Bass
The Patagonian toothfish is
overfished, so try our soya-based
lo-fat substitute, swimming in hot
water. Soy, water, gelatin added for
viscosity. Garlic vapor. A natural
face-lift dish.

Our Banana Split
One banana lying in its own skin,
covered in chocolate, on a bed of
arugula. A cheesecloth mouth
condom is supplied to enable you
to taste the chocolate without
swallowing.

Hemlock Tea
Try our depoisoned herbal infusion.

THE BOOK TO HAVE WHEN
THE KILLER BEES ARRIVE

H ERE'S the situation: Your enemies have used their car to block the road ahead of you, and a bear, a python, and a mountain lion are gaining on you from behind. To your right: quicksand. To your left: a body of shark-infested water. Meanwhile, a woman is giving birth in your back seat, and the woman is unable to breathe, and you have a bullet lodged in your leg, and a package lying on the seat beside you looks as though it might contain a bomb. What do you do?

Answering that question is much easier today than it was just a little while ago: all you have to do is open your copy of "The Worst-Case Scenario Survival Handbook," by Joshua Piven and David Borgenicht, and consult pages 34, 50, 44, 54, 18, 46, 99, 88, 109, and 94, respectively. The book, which was published late last year by Chronicle Books, has a bright-orange cover and is small enough to be tucked under the strap of a life jacket or a parachute pack. It contains straightforward, step-by-step, illustrated instructions for extricating yourself and others from all kinds of terrible predicaments. To fend off sharks, for example, you want to use "anything you have in your possession" to make "quick, sharp, repeated jabs" on or near the sharks' eyes or gills—not on the tips of the sharks' noses, as so many people erroneously assume. The book also explains how to jump from a building into a Dumpster, how to escape from killer bees (forget about swimming pools—the bees will wait for you to resurface), and how to win a sword fight.

Piven and Borgenicht ought to have been longtime friends by now—they have lived in Philadelphia much of their lives and have many acquaintances in common; they both graduated from the University of Pennsylvania in the early nineties; and they are both writers—but they didn't meet until just over a year ago, when Borgenicht, after wondering one evening how to land a pilotless airplane, went looking for a like-minded writing partner. Their book was inspired, Piven says, by "paranoia and too much television," and also by certain formative life events. Piven was once attacked by knife-wielding thugs while riding a motorcycle in Jamaica—an incident that led him to wonder about the proper technique for leaping from a moving motorcycle to a moving car. (See page 84.) Borgenicht, whose previous works include "Mom Always Said, 'Don't Play Ball in the House,' and Other Stuff We Learned from TV," first began to worry about quicksand as a child, while watching Tarzan movies and certain episodes of "Gilligan's Island." ("Tarzan was usually rescued by Cheetah," he says. "We stress self-reliance in our book—leave the chimpanzee at home.") Still, the authors' advice is drawn not from their own experiences but from the accumulated wisdom of experts in various disaster-related fields. The instructions for landing a plane, for example, come from two accomplished aviators, one of whom once wrote a book called "How to Crash a Plane (and Survive!)."

"The Worst-Case Scenario Survival Handbook" has apparently tapped a deep lode of apprehension in American society; it is now in its sixth printing. "The last time I checked Amazon," Borgenicht says, "we were ahead of 'Angela's Ashes,' "—a book that managed to become a nationwide best-seller despite its silence on the subject of how to survive if your parachute fails. (See page 137.)

A curious fact about "The Worst-Case Scenario Survival Handbook" is that it tends to increase rather than to allay a reader's irrational anxieties. Even to someone who has no contact whatsoever with stampeding bulls, the knowledge that bulls "are not like horses, and will not avoid you if you lie down" is unsettling. And the advice about "how to maneuver on top of a moving train and get inside," though thoroughly persuasive, raises a disturbing question: how did you get up there in the first place?

2 0 0 0

THE FAST-FOOD PRESIDENT
GOES HAUTE CUISINE

JULIAN NICCOLINI, a managing partner in the Four Seasons restaurant, was taken aback to read in the *Times* the other day a lengthy account of an elaborate dinner—lobster salad with caviar-cream dressing, a duo of stuffed saddle and roasted rack of lamb with tomato-spinach compote and rosemary-lemon polenta, apple tarte Tatin—prepared for President Clinton by the restaurant Daniel on a recent Thursday evening. Niccolini's surprise derived from the fact that the very same evening his restaurant had prepared a similarly elaborate dinner—tuna tartare with beluga caviar, roast filet of lamb with truffle sauce and sautéed spring vegetables, a dish of mixed berries—for the President, which had been consumed with gusto. "After the main course, he cleaned his plate with bread," Niccolini explained, speaking in the Grill Room one afternoon last week.

The President's appetites, for cream puffs as well as for comestibles, have caused him considerable embarrassment over the years, and even though he was reported to be looking svelte on the evening in question, it appears that his voraciousness remains undiminished. Clinton was at Daniel for less than an hour, and he spent twenty minutes delivering a speech to the dinner guests—sixty-six members of the Democratic National Committee. Nonetheless, according to Anthony Francis, the restaurant's banquet director, he managed to eat every scrap of his appetizer and his main course. (He ordered his tarte Tatin to go.) The President was then driven thirteen blocks south, to the Four Seasons, where he settled in for a three-hour blowout and gabfest, eventually leaving for Chappaqua—with another doggie bag, containing a slice of Key-lime pie—at twelve-forty-five in the morning.

After a physical last September, when he weighed in at two hundred and fourteen pounds, the President expressed a wish to drop ten pounds, and was reported to be trying to stick to a regimen of low-fat meals and no late-night snacking. Clinton's staff had presented the Four Seasons kitchen with a list of dietary restrictions. "They told us exactly what he likes, what he doesn't like," Niccolini said. "And he is not allowed to have chocolate or cheese." A Presidential taster was stationed in the kitchen, to insure that the food was prepared in accordance with Clinton's preferences.

Even so, an approximate nutritional analysis of the President's two dinners indicates that he had better duck next time he's in danger of running into the surgeon general, since he is far from meeting the recommended caloric intake for a man of his height and activity level, which would be about twenty-eight hundred calories a day. The meal at Daniel cost him around two thousand calories and included about a hundred and twenty grams of fat, or sixty per cent of calories from fat. (That's twice as much fat as most nutritionists recommend as a daily percentage.) The meal at the Four Seasons was slightly more spa-like and totalled about twelve hundred calories, with perhaps fifty per cent of those coming from fat. Even if the President had spent the whole day starving himself in preparation—which is as easy to imagine as him endorsing Giuliani for the Senate—he still would have consumed approximately thirty-two hundred calories. That's nearly ten hours of non-stop golfing right there.

People fearing for the First Waistline might seek comfort in the fact that the President asked for his desserts in a doggie bag, but it appears that they were not destined to make it to Buddy's bowl. Niccolini said he did not feel snubbed that the President declined the Four Seasons pie (five hundred calories, thirty fat grams) in favor of berries. "The plan was that we were supposed to bring his dessert to the limousine," Niccolini said. "I guess he wanted to eat it on the way home. It's almost an hour to Chappaqua. At least it gave him something to do in the car."

WHAT'S IN A
DOMAIN NAME?

"WHO steals my purse steals trash," Iago claims. "But he that filches from me my good name / Robs me of that which not enriches him, / And makes me poor indeed." I'm not sure it was robbery (the filcher did pay), but it was definitely my name: julianbarnes.com, not to mention julian-barnes.org and julianbarnes.net—all snaffled by a cybersquatter in the last few weeks. And not just me: the fellow has hoovered up the dot-coms of vs-naipaul, fayweldon, jungchang, germainegreer, ianmcewan, martinamis, and louisedebernieres. Some Americans, too: dondelillo, alicewalker, martincruz-smith, davasobel. A hundred and thirty-two by the final count. The fact that many such names should still be available isn't much of a surprise—the speedy joust of E-commerce is temperamentally far from the slow ragout of bookmak-ing—but the identity of the squatter was. He turned out to be Dr. Mark Ho-garth, a research fellow in the history and philosophy of science at Cambridge. Hogarth is evidently better paid than Iago: at a hundred and five dollars to reg-ister each writer, his purse has been trashed to the tune of nearly fourteen thousand dollars.

At first, I was faintly irritated (hey, that's *my* name) and faintly flattered. Per-haps the guy was an E-version of Rolland Comstock, a Springfield, Missouri, lawyer who for decades has been collecting and warehousing modern first edi-tions, plus ephemera, arcana, curiosa, and marginalia, on an obsessive, indus-trial scale. All for passion, not profit: the man even buys up hundreds of remainder copies when it offends him that an admired book should be thus downgraded. Perhaps, I thought, acquiring domain names was like collecting wine labels, a private if peculiar homage to something enjoyed.

And, if I didn't really believe that, I vaguely imagined that what we loosely call "literary values" still linger on in this new E-territory. For instance, my current Web site (www.jbarnes.com, if you're interested) is tended by a librarian in Illinois who actually forks out some of his own money to have advertising strips removed from the screen. But the British philosopher is somewhat less noble. He is now holding an on-line auction of all the names he owns; the lucky buyers will then, he judges, set up individual sites to sell each writer's books on commission. "Robs me of that which not enriches him"—uh-huh. And in the meanwhile Dr. Hogarth invites me to buy back my own name. His fee: three per cent of the cover price of all my books sold, worldwide, in any language, in 1998. Assuming that a writer's royalty, over a range of contracts, might average out at about nine per cent, he's asking me for a third of that year's income, the same amount that I handed over in taxes to the British government, which does at least mend the roads and bomb distant nations on my behalf.

But it wasn't the grotesque profit expectation that stirred my more atavistic feelings. It was a photograph of Dr. Hogarth in a British newspaper. Not his physiognomy (we know that the reading of mug shots alters entirely with the context) but the background. Behind him were four well-stocked shelves of books: all seemingly in prime condition, ordered, respected, honored. These were the books that helped him work; behind the books, their authors. No doubt there are more things dreamed of in Dr. Hogarth's philosophy than in mine. And mine, increasingly, boiled down to this: Hey, no, that's *my* name. That's what it says on my spines. Books are but words, yet those are two of the most charged and indicative. They're also the last ones I insert into my typescript. Text, dedication, title, author: that's how I do it, ritualistically. Those two words are me. They're proof that I do such things.

First you lowercase me, then you sell me. "And makes me poor indeed"—on the nose again, Shakespeare. And I don't think he would have paid up, either.

HOW TO MAKE THE MOST
OF SOME SEXY SNAPSHOTS

IS there in the English language a more cheering, endearing, hope-inducing word, pithy and punchy, a scant five letters, barely two syllables, ten Scrabble points, than "naked"? Which is also to ask, is there—hate to be crude about this, but—a word more purely ripe with commercial possibilities? ("Sex" is by no means such a word; far too complicated. Back to "naked": Would Norman Mailer be where he is today if he'd called his first novel "The Fully Clothed and the Dead'? Not that Mark Helfrich, a forty-seven-year old professional film editor and amateur photographer who lives in Los Angeles, was thinking merely mercenary thoughts one particular day seven years ago while perusing a box of old black-and-white and color prints—mostly, naked pictures of his ex-girlfriends. Mainly, he was recalling how happy he'd been when he took the photographs and how excellent his subjects looked naked. It occurred to him that a carefully chosen portfolio would make an interesting book, and about a nanosecond later the thought occurred that sales probably wouldn't suffer if its title was "Naked Pictures of My Ex-Girlfriends." (As opposed to, say, "My Life in Linoleum" or "Frog Raising for Pleasure and Profit.")

According to Mr. Helfrich, "Naked Pictures of My Ex-Girlfriends" is "not a definitive compendium," just a photo-memoir of thirty-two women he got to know during a decade of rabbity concupiscence—the book's subtitle is "Romance in the 70's"—who, when tracked down twenty or thirty years later, obligingly signed releases that said, in effect, "Sure, go right ahead. It's only me naked." Rounding up the releases took seven years, and the book is finally being published next week. The result isn't a collection of arty nudes, nor does it fit the shrink-wrapped-on-the-newsstand definition of pornography, nor is it stupid, the way the *Cosmo*-for-guys beer-and-babes-and-accessories magazines are. The accompanying text, in white hand-lettering against a black background, is neither pre-feminist nor post-feminist—just the candid testimony of a guy handy with a Nikon in the twilight of the pre-H.I.V. era, a fellow who without sounding boastful makes clear that he never flagged in his willingness to get laid. ("It was fun. It was like playing a game. It was like living Antonioni's 'Blow-Up.' Sometimes it was foreplay . . .")

"I think for the people who look at this book the pictures are voyeuristic, because you're looking at somebody else's girlfriends," Mr. Helfrich said the other day during a phone conversation. "By the same token, I feel that other men can recognize one or two of their girlfriends in the stories or shots. I wanted the photographs to look like a boyfriend took them. When editing, I looked for that twinkle in the eye that took me to a certain intimate setting. With apologies to *Playboy*, I think these really are the girls next door, I'm a fan of *Playboy*. I'm a lifetime subscriber."

And, just as orthodox *Playboy* philosophers have always insisted, it's the writing, not the pictures, that really counts:

Jill, a long-haired brunette, sitting upright, legs crossed, filing her nails, with a "Do Not Disturb" sign from a Holiday Inn suspended from her left nipple: "About once a month I'd get together with my friend from out of state, Jill. We'd meet at the airport and make a beeline for the nearest bed. Passionately, we'd rip each other's clothes off and become a couple of hyperactive love-monkeys."

Cynthia: "Cynthia was claustrophobic with a capital 'C.' She wouldn't even close the shower curtain to take a shower. She was also extremely farsighted. And she was addicted to Tang. Some people wake up and the first word out of their mouth is 'coffee'—she said 'Tang.' "

Barbara: "Barbara taught me that large tits and large brains don't always travel in pairs . . . She voted for Nixon in '72. By then it was all over."

"Ms. Minter": " 'Ms. Minter' was the youngest teacher at my high school. . . . She was a great English teacher. We spent many afternoons at her house having naked lunches, then she'd send me home with another great novel. Talk about incentive to read!"

The publisher of "Naked Pictures of My Ex-Girlfriends" is Rat Press, a subsidiary of Rat Entertainment, an eponymous entity founded by Brett Ratner, a young television and film director ("Money Talks," "Rush Hour"), who says he hopes to adapt the book for TV: "Right now we're working on the concept. Either a series or a kind of documentary-style show. We have to refine it before we go out to the networks. First of all, the title alone—if there was a show titled 'Naked Pictures of My Ex-Girlfriends'—would be huge. And there might be more books. Hopefully, we're gonna go through Mark's archives and we can do a sequel. Like, you know, naked pictures from the eighties and nineties, which would be awesome."

Mr. Helfrich, meanwhile, has settled down. He met his wife, Alexandra, four years ago, they've been married three years, and they have a two-year-old daughter. Though he's compiled quite a bit of recent material, he has no plans to publish a family photo album.

"Alexandra had never posed nude for anybody before she met me," he said. "Early on, I asked her to let me photograph her, and she said O.K., but she demanded to keep the film until we were married. So she had rolls and rolls of film, and as a wedding gift she had them developed, put them in a box, and gave me a box of naked photographs of my wife. Which I thought was a great gift— even better than scores of naked pictures of my ex-girlfriends."

2 0 0 0

THE GUY WHO MAKES THE PRESIDENT FUNNY

I T is not, perhaps, the most important event in Bill Clinton's farewell tour of Washington, but April 29th marks the President's final speech at the White House Correspondents' Dinner, and thus the last time he must deliver laughs on command. As a consequence, the occasion is a turning point for a thirty-six-year-old New Yorker named Mark Katz, who has served as Clinton's chief jokewriter for both tumultuous terms. "It's been a remarkable window on this Administration," Katz said the other day over lunch. "I can tell you the joke answer to every crisis that's come up—the haircut, gays in the military, everything. I've sat in front of a word processor and tried to handle them all."

Katz is on the short side, built close to the ground, and he is easily amused. (What, you expected Gary Cooper?) Like most humorists, he began his career by getting thrown out of class in the seventh grade, in his case in Rockland County, a place Katz remembers as "a hotbed of social rest." After college, he volunteered in the Dukakis campaign and soon found himself a sort of comedy czar for that doomed undertaking. "Yes, I'm the man who made Mike Dukakis so funny," he said. "When people say that campaign was a joke, I can't help but feel a little proud."

Katz puttered around in advertising for a few years, until, in 1993, friends from the Dukakis campaign hooked him up with Clinton for the annual round of after-dinner speeches—at the Gridiron, Radio and TV, and White House Correspondents' Dinners—where the President was expected to entertain ballrooms full of grumpy reporters in evening dress. Katz has come to see the speeches as a kind of unofficial history of the Clinton years. "He says stuff in these speeches that he never would have said anywhere else," Katz suggests.

For example, the President never admitted that he used the Lincoln Bedroom to raise campaign funds, but at the 1996 Correspondents' Dinner he said, "The bad news is, our only child is going off to college. The good news is, it opens up another bedroom." Last year, Clinton winked at his well-known distaste for the correspondents themselves, noting that if he had lost the impeachment vote in the Senate he would not be appearing before them. "I demand a recount," he intoned. There are, however, no Clinton jokes about skirt-chasing.

Katz has turned his post as shtickmaster general of the United States into a one-man humor-consulting operation that he calls the Sound Bite Institute. In addition to various corporate jobs, Katz has consulted with Hillary Clinton and has advised Al Gore on a number of recent speeches. (Gore turned down one of his more edgy offerings: "You know, the *Washington Post* just reported that I got C's and D's in my sophomore year, but they failed to report that that was also the year I invented the bong.")

Katz's fondest memory of his White House years concerns a speech that Clinton did not give. "I was all set to do the rehearsal for his White House Correspondents' speech in 1995," Katz recalled, "and at the last minute they decided that it was too close to the Oklahoma City bombing for him to do something funny. I was despondent. Then, a couple of minutes later, I got a call that the President wanted to see me. I ran back to the Oval Office, and he said, 'Let's just read it through for laughs.' And that's what he did, and it was probably my funniest speech ever. So I've been pitied at the highest levels. He felt my pain."

2 0 0 0

NAKED AND TRUTHFUL
IN THE BRONX

THE makers of the movie "Finding Forrester"—Opus No. 65 for Sean Connery, who is co-starring with a sixteen-year-old newcomer named Rob Brown—were messing with the South Bronx the other night. They were filming scenes that featured Brown, a local six-foot-tall basketball-playing eleventh grader, interacting with Connery and assorted neighborhood folks, including the rapper Busta Rhymes. A few years before Brown was cast in the film, he was relocated from an inner-city public school and placed, on scholarship, in a prestigious private school. Last February, when he was cast in "Finding Forrester," he had no manager, no agent, and had never before acted in anything. "There's an inner peace about him—he's a most unflappable fellow," one of "Finding Forrester"'s several producers said. "And we're doing everything not to shake his confidence, everything to keep him concentrated."

The movie is about the unlikely friendship between Forrester (Connery), a cranky, hard-drinking, withdrawn-by-choice, basketball-loving writer who mysteriously seems to have stopped writing, and Jamal (Brown), a high-school basketball player who has been relocated to a prestigious private school and who secretly wants to be a writer. Jamal goes to Forrester for literary help, and he tries to draw the older man out of his isolation. Busta Rhymes, who had his own trailer on the set, and his own hair stylist to do his dreadlocks, plays Jamal's older brother, Terrell.

Russell Smith, the movie's handsome twenty-five-year-old basketball consultant, said, "Rob knows how to play, but I'm teaching him some aggressive things, some moves, and elbowing, shoving, things like that. I didn't have to teach him things like the Hood. It's the handshake with three stages—clasp with thumb up, regular shake, then clasp fingers."

At the location—on the stairs of the elevated subway platform at 167th Street and River Avenue—the life of the neighborhood was going on as usual, amid screaming sirens, thundering trains overhead, yelling residents, and tantalizing aromas drifting over from a nearby Cuban deli. The director, Gus Van Sant, worked with his cinematographer on the camera's placement and with the electricians on the lighting. Neighborhood kids kept begging, "Gus, put me in the movie, please, Gus!"

Everybody on the set seemed to be supremely mindful of the danger of disturbing Rob Brown's calm. "If anybody shows panic, everybody feels it," a young production assistant whispered solemnly.

"Rob originally answered an ad for an open-audition call," said a producer, munching on a juicy Cuban sandwich. "When he walked into our office, we liked the way he said his name: 'Rob Brown.' Just like that. That was it." After casting Brown, who usually lives at his school, the producers placed him in the custody of an acting coach, with whom he is sharing an apartment while he shoots the movie.

Another producer, savoring a fried plantain from the deli, said, "On Rob's first day of shooting with Sean, Sean said to him, 'Did you have any trouble sleeping last night?' This kid just looked puzzled and said, 'No.' Can you believe? Only that—'No.' "

Connery is larger in life than 007. Waiting in his trailer to be summoned to the set, he entertained a couple of friends by recounting his visit, that day, to his four-year-old granddaughter's nursery school, in midtown. "It's like no school I ever saw—you should see this school!" he said, in an overpowering Scottish accent. "All the equipment! All the paints! Buckets of brushes! Every damn thing you could imagine! And they cook and they bake and they wear these little aprons and chef's hats!" He laughed joyously and did an excellent impersonation of four-year-old cooks and bakers.

Then he was called to duty. He put on a tan duffel coat and a matching cap— quickly all business and no nonsense—and strode with serious purpose to the set. Rob Brown, escorted by a couple of solicitous P.A.s, followed. He wore black Nike Air Jordan sneakers, fashionably baggy jeans, a hooded black sweatshirt, and an alpaca Tibetan hat with ear flaps and fake yak fur. Brown coolly propelled himself forward in a floppy lope, arms swinging. He looked around with mild interest.

Both actors—attending the routine shouts of "Stand by!" "Here we go!" "Roll sound!"—plunged into action and worked for several hours doing scenes on the train steps, on the platform, and inside Yankee Stadium. In the stadium, standing alone together on the pitcher's mound, they did what Barry Papick, Brown's acting coach, said was the "cathartic" scene of the movie.

"The scene is all about loss, so I tried to get Rob down to his own loss," he said. "I follow the Lee Strasberg method: Sense memory! Get to the bottom! Find the real emotion! The rediscovery-of-emotion thing! Like Brando! Rob is fearless. In front of the camera, he's naked and truthful."

After the shot, Gus Van Sant, who had rehearsed the actors quietly and briefly, with minimal suggestions, told them the scene was "perfect," and they looked happy. A few minutes later, he talked to some friends about what had prompted him to make "Finding Forrester."

"This is almost a sister project to 'Good Will Hunting,' " Van Sant said. "This is mainstream, but good. You can get top dollar for this. Today, it's all about overhead."

"It's tough to disguise hard work and preparation, but it pays off," Connery said.

"This movie is a mixture of the old and the new," one of the producers said. "That's what the movie is about."

At about 4:30 A.M., when the shooting was done, Brown hung around on the set with Russell Smith and Busta Rhymes and Barry Papick and some of the local kids who were playing his friends. They did a lot of gleeful elbowing and carefree shoving and, fearless and naked and truthful, they gave each other the Hood.

2 0 0 0

NUDIE PIX REDUX

AHEM. A couple of months ago, we reported the imminent publication of a book with a title that bore the earmarks of a commercial slam dunk, "Naked Pictures of My Ex-Girlfriends: Romance in the 70's." Here, it seemed was an exceptional journalistic and social document. Evidently, not only had Mark Helfrich, a Los Angeles–based film editor and photographer, enjoyed himself inordinately during that particular decade; he'd brought along a Nikon. And, remarkably, he'd managed to remain on such good terms with his old flames that, when he began tracking them down, two-plus decades later, thirty-two (!) women graciously signed releases saying it was O.K. to publish their nude photographs. Beyond its simple voyeuristic appeal, Helfrich's book delivered a mixture of ostensibly candid and posed snapshots, skillfully composed, that evoked in a novel way a familiar cultural-historical epoch. The accompanying text, hand-lettered in the manner of a family photo album, hummed along with a straightforward crudeness that somehow came across as disarmingly blunt rather than crassly macho.

End of story? Not exactly.

After reading in these pages about Helfrich's excellent adventures (reviews or features also appeared in *Time*, *Details*, and the *Times*), a painter named David Glynn picked up a copy of "Naked Pictures" in a SoHo bookstore. For his own work, Glynn has photographed dozens of nude models, and he recognized in Helfrich's book three women he knew, including two who had posed for him about three years ago, when they were in their mid-twenties. The math wasn't complicated: even toward the end of the nineteen-seventies, these "ex-girlfriends" would have been less than ten years old. "As sexually free as I remember (and want to believe) the 70's were," Glynn wrote in a letter to me, which I read with chagrin as well as a degree of relief, "this guy was making this stuff up!"

When, with Glynn's help, I spoke to four women who appear in "Naked Pictures," it was on a first-name-only basis. What they had to say made it plain that they (a) had modelled for Helfrich because they were getting paid, (b) hadn't known him in the Biblical sense, and (c) hadn't anticipated how they would be depicted in this book.

"Wanda" ("Wanda had a boyfriend who worked night-shifts. She would call me up at 2:30 A.M. and say, 'You want some company?'"): "I read about the book in *Time* and I immediately recognized Mark Helfrich's name. I didn't think any pictures of me would be in there, because they were taken seven or eight years ago and I hadn't been contacted since then. I'd have no problem if the book had been called, say, 'Pictures of Beautiful Women I've Met.' The ex-girlfriend thing I had a problem with, because it wasn't true. I knew Mark over a period of eight months and saw him maybe four times and he was single that whole time and didn't have a girlfriend. He definitely came across as a guy who did not go out with a lot of women. He seemed very lonely. I don't know what his intentions were. Maybe it was to look real studly. He says in the book that Wanda's breath always smelled of rum-and-Coke, and that implies I'm an alcoholic. And then he says, 'You know how people say, "That's the best sex I've ever had" . . . I never had that kind of sex with Wanda. But it was either sleep or Wanda at 2:30 A.M., so what the hell?' Well, I don't like that either."

"Delhi" ("What can I say about Delhi! We were in love"): "I appreciate photography and I appreciate art. But I might not do it again if I knew how it would come out. Things he wrote made him come out on top, when in fact he probably couldn't get a date. If he had really been intimate with these women, I think there would have been more tenderness in the writing. But instead it seemed sort of calloused and clichéd."

A dark-haired model who doesn't even want her alias mentioned: "I found the writing derogatory toward women. I found it really stupid. But I think the pictures are nice. I think he's a good photographer."

"Angela" ("The times I spent with Angela were pretty idyllic. We'd walk through the woods sharing a joint and end up naked together in a pile of Connecticut leaves. We were casual lovers. These pictures were taken during one of our 'Strip Ping-Pong' matches"): "The text is kind of cheesy. Am I offended? I think the world itself is so offensive, especially the way women are portrayed, it just seems a bit late in the game to be offended by that."

All this gives rise to a variety of questions: "Naked Pictures of My Ex-Girlfriends" is unmistakably art, but the meaning of art shifts with its context, so what kind of art is it? Conceptual? Can it work as conceptual art if it enlists collaborators who aren't fully clued in to the concept? In this instance, the label "pseudo-personal journalism" fits the concept. Is pseudo-journalism exempt from the ethical strictures of real journalism? In the end, what's a reader to make of the author's statement? "I've remained friends with most of my ex-es, and I asked their permission to publicly display these intimate photos. In the same spirit that the snapshots originally were taken, the women consented."

"I knew it was just a matter of time before someone asked the questions you're asking me," Helfrich said when I called him and told him what I'd learned. "The book is full of models. But the intent of the book is still intact. I do have naked pictures of all my ex-girlfriends, but when I asked whether I could publish them the overwhelming response was 'No way!' So I decided I would just re-create these photographs, which I did over a few years. Even though the photographs aren't authentic period photographs, they're re-creations of the real thing. I could show you some of the originals."

I happened to have plans to be in Los Angeles, so I arranged to take him up on this offer. One recent Saturday morning, we sat on the patio of the commissary of the Disney lot, in Burbank, where he was working on a Keenen Ivory Wayans movie. He'd brought along a copy of "Naked Pictures," bookmarked with a half-dozen loose photographs that he said had inspired his re-creations. For instance, in the book, "wild and crazy Cindi," a long-haired brunette with unshaved armpits, wore a silver mask and playfully pointed a revolver at her temple. Handing me a snapshot, also of a brunette with unshaved armpits, Helfrich said, "See? Same mask, same gun. Have I spoken with her? No, I don't remember her last name." On another page, "Jill" was shown sleeping, prone on a bed with a mirrored headboard—minus the curled-up cat in the snapshot Helfrich proffered as the original. "I had enough trouble getting women to pose—I wasn't about to work with animals, too," he said.

Scrutizining the loose photographs, I asked, "And how do I know these are original originals?"

"You have to trust me. They're real."

And I believed him, though I can't exactly say what this exercise proved.

"Just to make it fun," Helfrich said, "I'll tell you that there are some authentic pictures in the book, but I'm going to choose not to say how many"—an indication that, notwithstanding the exposure of his talent for deception, his commercial instinct hasn't dulled.

"These are real memories," he continued, referring to the text. "I embellished a couple of things here and there. But these are actual slices of life. Just because the photo opposite a particular passage of text isn't actually . . . Now, how do I want to say this? Well, let's just say I used photographs to illustrate the thoughts in the book. And the actual photographs—the ones I couldn't get permission to publish—conjured most of the stories in the book."

What about the aggrieved "Wanda"? "I'm sorry if any of the models feel distressed by the juxtaposition of the text and their photographs, but I told them what the project was. I told these models that they were like actresses playing a role. There's no way she could be mistaken for that woman in 1979. Anybody who knows her would, seeing her in the book, realize I'm obviously not talking about her."

I studied Helfrich's face—early forties, light-brown hair, blue eyes. He was pleasant-enough-looking but definitely didn't exude a lock-up-your-daughters vibe. How many women did he sleep with in the seventies? "Truthfully, I never counted. I'm not even going to venture a guess. But the late seventies and early eighties were very good to me."

The present decade has thus far been good to him in a different way. The first two printings of "Naked Pictures," a total of ten thousand copies, are almost sold out, and a third printing is in the works. "Originally, I wanted to include a little line on the copyright page that said 'Photography/Fiction.' But my publishers talked me out of it. They just said, 'Go with it. People will believe what they want to believe.' Which is true."

2 0 0 0

BALLOON DIPLOMACY FOR ELIÁN

THE Cuban psychologists and teachers who have been drafted to help Elián González readjust to life back home have doubtless discussed with him the traumatic experience of being corralled by masked men and carted off in the middle of the night with nothing but the pajamas on his back, not to mention the experience of seeing Diane Sawyer stand on her head. But one wonders what they will make of Elián's account of a less well-publicized event that took place during his American sojourn: his visit, one Saturday in June, to the home of a Washington, D.C., couple named Judy and Gary Kopff. On the strength of an E-mail account of the event which the Kopffs sent to the members of an on-line neighborhood group, the outing was just the kind of thing that, were you a hard-line Communist ideologue looking for evidence of the decadence—or the plumb insanity—of the United States, would keep you busy for weeks.

In the mass E-mail, Judy Kopff explained how she and her husband, who is a financial strategist, volunteered to throw a party for Elián and his friends, be-cause they thought he would enjoy their large collection of life-size toy animals. "Jasper the Kangaroo is about six feet tall and stands in what we call Evie's Ballet Room (where we pretend that our cat Everest practices her ballet lessons!)," Kopff writes. "In the third corner of the dining room is our collection of furry lowland and mountain gorillas." The children also met George, a brass monkey who hangs from a trapeze in the front hall; Archie, a seven-foot wooden ostrich who wears sneakers; Jock, an eight-foot papier-mâché giraffe; Susie, a three-foot cow with a hand-crocheted udder; and dozens of other inanimate livestock.

Most of the seventy-odd guests were Cubans, among them four of Elián's schoolmates from back home and Cuba's equivalent of an ambassador. Among the guests was Ruthanne Miller, the chair of the local Advisory Neighborhood Commission, who had suggested to a Cuban contact that a party at the Kopff house might amuse Elián and company. "Part of this might have been over-whelming to them," Miller said last week. "A lot of the houses they saw in Washington were very, very, very nice—a big contrast to their lives at home." Such concerns, however, don't seem to have deterred Elián and his young friends: they lined up to have their photographs taken as they sat on Dolly, the six-foot rocking llama in the Kopffs' living room, and joined in when Judy gave the children a lesson in making balloon animals. "Although they had a difficult time learning how to make a balloon in the shape of a dachshund dog, they easily understood how to make balloon hats and showed a lot of creativity in fashioning their individual versions," she writes in her E-mail.

There were other amusements of an order not to be found in Cárdenas. "The children went to Gary's second-floor office to watch (on our large plasma monitor) four DVD Walt Disney movies in Spanish (i.e., 'Lion King II,' 'Lady and the Tramp,' 'Jungle Book,' and 'Mulan'). Watching them sing the words to the songs in the 'Lion King II' movie was heartwarming," Kopff writes. It seems that the Cuban children were also capable of being just as intractable as their spoiled, materialistic American counterparts: "The kids would not leave our house until they had finished watching all four videos."

The visitors weren't just couch potatoes, though. "The children also played in our gym located in our British-style conservatory in our back yard," Kopff writes. "We had disconnected the treadmill, elliptical trainer, StairMaster, and other electrical exercise equipment. Gary supervised them in the gym and told them about his climbs up Mt. Everest, Vinson Massif in the Antarctic, Mt. Kili-manjaro in Africa, and Mt. Elbrus in Russia." Each child left with an assort-ment of party favors, including an eraser in the shape of a cat, a yo-yo in the shape of a hamburger, a medal with the word "Winner" written on it, and a balloon pump so that he or she could practice making dachshunds back at home. Elián also received "a large battery-operated clock with baseballs in-stead of numbers on its face" and a backpack in which to carry his loot home.

Kopff concludes her account by writing, "Gary and I did not make any judg-ments about whether sending Elián home to Cuba is a good idea or a bad one. We just wanted to extend some humanitarian warmth to children from an-other country. We believe that we did the right thing." And although you might think that the guest of honor would have had enough of zoos after months with the press camped outside the home of his Miami relatives, he was, appar-ently, "extremely well behaved and patient, considering how many of the Cuban people were asking to have their photos taken with him. We think that he was reluctant to grin, however, because his two front teeth recently fell out!"

AN ODE TO GOLF

I FELL in love with golf when I was twenty-five. It would have been a healthier relationship had it been an adolescent romance or, better yet, a childhood crush. Though I'd like to think we've had a lot of laughs together, and even some lyrical moments, I have never felt quite adequate to her demands, and she has secrets she keeps from me. More secrets than I can keep track of; when I've found out one, another one comes out, and then three more, and by this time I've forgotten what the first one was. They are sexy little secrets that flitter around my body—a twitch of the left hip, a pronation of the right wrist, a cock of the head one way, a turn of the shoulders the other—and they torment me like fire ants in my togs; I can't get them out of my mind, or quite wrap my mind around them. Sometimes I wish she and I had never met. She leads me on, but deep down I suspect—this is my secret—that I'm just not her type.

Who is her type? Well, go figure. Fat guys like Craig Stadler and Tim Herron, and skinny wispy guys like Corey Pavin, and lanky skinny guys like Tiger Woods, and grim intense guys like Jack Nicklaus and Ben Hogan, and laid-back jokers like Fuzzy Zoeller and Walter Hagen and Lee Trevino. Golf isn't exactly choosy, you'd have to say, but she can turn a cold shoulder to anybody on a given date. If there's one kind of suitor she consistently rejects, it's the jittery, overanxious types, worrywarts who for all their lessons and driving-range prowess whiff on the first tee and stub a crucial three-foot putt on the eighteenth green. Golf likes a bit of sang-froid, the "What, me worry?" slouch, and spurns those who care too much and try too hard. I've tried not caring, but maybe I've tried too hard. She's an intuitive old girl; she sniffs you out. Those extra ten yards you think you can squeeze out of your swing—she's onto you while the club is still approaching horizontal. She likes guys (gals, too—she's through with gender hangups) who keep things simple and don't mind repeating themselves. And that, it breaks my heart to have concluded, lets me out.

So, why do I still love her? Why do I continue to pour hours and treasure into a futile and unreciprocated courtship? Well, she's awfully pretty. All those green curves, and dewy swales, and snug little sand traps; and the way she grassily stretches here and there and then some. She makes you think big, and lifts your head up to face the sky. When you connect, it's the whistle of a quail, it's the soar of a hawk, it's the sighting of a planet hitherto unseen; it's mathematical perfection wrested from a half-buried lie; it's absolute. And golf never lets you go a round without your connecting once or twice. You think she's turned her back, but, with a little smile over her nicely mowed shoulder, she lets a long putt rattle in, or a chip settle up close, or a seven-iron take a lucky kick off a greenside mound. Another foot to the right, and . . . oh, she is quite the tease.

And quite the accountant, too. How can you not love a game where a three-hundred-yard drive and a two-inch putt count the same? I mean, that's a sport with a sense of proportion. And the shapely, rhythmic way a round dwindles down, hole after hole, far and then closer, and closer yet and in, a journey ending in a burial and—whoa!—up out of the grave again, eighteen times in all, twice a cat's number of lives. In other games, somebody else is always getting in your way, all elbows and trash talk, brushing you back from the plate, serving to your backhand, giving you aggravation. Golf lets you do the aggravation all by yourself; there is nothing between you and the hole but what you've managed to put there. She's no flatterer, but she doesn't grudge credit where it's due, either: a scuffed drive, a skulled approach, and a putt that would have rolled ten feet past still make a par 3 on the scorecard.

The tools—is it too intimate to talk about the tools, the tender way the leather grips invite the fingers to curl around them and adhere, the grainy grooved faces of the irons, the slither of a club being withdrawn from the bag, the flexing elegance of the tapered graphite shafts, even the merry dimples on the ball and the tiny sensation of give when the wooden tee penetrates the turf? Golf has the equipment to please a man, and she's not ashamed to use it. She's been around since the Scots monarchs were stymieing the English and old Tom Morris would spend a drizzly afternoon stuffing a single feathery with duck down; but you're as young as you feel, and my sweetheart still runs me ragged. And ragged, she keeps letting me know, isn't good enough. We'd break up in a flash, except we never really got together.

A RUBIN'S GUIDE TO GETTING IT ALL

FINISH your own sentences, indulge in intimidating rages, mete out arbitrary punishments, look as tall as possible, wear sunglasses, weed a flower bed, boast about how little sleep you need. These are some of the things that Gretchen Craft Rubin would have you do in the pursuit of power, money, fame, and sex. But Rubin resorted to nothing so obvious last week as she sat against the zebra-adorned wallpaper at Gino, the crusty Upper East Side cash-only relic.

Rubin, the daughter-in-law of former Treasury Secretary Robert Rubin, has just published "Power Money Fame Sex: A User's Guide." In form and tone, it is related, distantly, to the "Official Preppy Handbook," and in content, not so distantly, to primers like Michael Korda's "Power! How to Get It, How to Use It." The book lays bare the contrivances of power and gives tips on how to do things right—for example, "curry favor with someone who can protect you from your faults" (page 20) or waste something to signal your wealth: "Try ordering an expensive wine in a restaurant, then leaving it opened and untouched when you leave" (page 129).

Rubin, who is a slim, freckled thirty-four-year-old redhead, was doing a little signalling herself at Gino, however inadvertently. She did not finish her spaghetti (see "waste," page 129); she unclasped her Filofax to write down an address (how full it was!); and she wore a sleeveless cotton dress with a cool Mondrian pattern (she admitted that she'd thought it would suit the restaurant's fifties aesthetic). "People become very self-conscious when they read this book," she said. "A lot of it is pretty reprehensible. But I have definitely applied things from it that I wouldn't have thought of before, like the self-promotion checklist."

She has, without apparent embarrassment, thrown herself into the task. She used her Rubin connections to secure blurbs from Kurt Andersen, Ken Auletta, and Harold Evans. She laced her acknowledgments page with the names of powerful people, among them Steven Spielberg and Warren Buffett—though a tip on page 196 indicates that their presence there is a hoax: "Pack your acknowledgements with thanks to several stars in your field. . . . How could anyone ever know that you've never spoken to them? (See acknowledgements page.)" And she has helped arrange a book party for herself, later this month, to be hosted by Bob and Judy Rubin, at Michael's, on West Fifty-fifth Street—a perfect arena for what she calls "proximity power" (page 21).

Gretchen Rubin knows a thing or two about proximity power. Having been the editor-in-chief of the *Yale Law Journal*, she clerked for Supreme Court Justice Sandra Day O'Connor and served at the Federal Communications Commission as an adviser to its then chairman, Reed Hundt, with whom she now teaches courses at Yale and Columbia on the business and regulation of television. She met her husband, Jamie Rubin, an investment banker at Allen & Company, in the library at Yale Law School: "Our carrels were back to back, just like Bill and Hillary." Then there's her father-in-law, who has just signed a $3.3-million contract to do a book of his own.

"Bob Rubin's a great example, and I'm not just saying this because I'm his daughter-in-law," she said. "Bob has what I like to call 'the attraction of prowess.' He has this air of not having to try so hard. And 'the attraction of presence'—not having a lot of needs, not being insecure. One of the stories that was told about him in Washington was that every week he was given a certain allotment of the President's time. But when he didn't have to see the President he would cede his time and use it for something else. And everybody around him was, like, 'Oh my God, giving up your time with the President is so amazing!' " In the right circumstances, relinquishing proximity power can be the real power move.

"I think Gretchen is enormously talented, but this is her project," Bob Rubin said the other day, explaining that he didn't really want to say much about "Power Money Fame Sex." Here, he was abiding by one of the "pillars of power": "control information" (page 28). He added, "I have a feeling that her book is going to sell a lot better than mine." That's self-deprecation (page 70).

QUIZ WHIZ

YOU may be a person of vast knowledge, able to rattle off answers—Yalta, 1066, the Taft-Hartley Act, Olduvai Gorge, Rogers Hornsby—to all kinds of questions, but unless you've been on a television game show you don't know this: it's all about the pickle. Several journalists found this out a few weeks ago when they were invited to be mock contestants on "History IQ," a new quiz show that began in early October on the History Channel and is on at seven-thirty every weeknight. Standing under bright lights in a Manhattan television studio, wired for sound, and with noses and foreheads deglazed by a makeup woman, three writers from three magazines practiced with the pickle, struggled with the pickle, and eventually came to terms with the pickle—the little button on the top of the handheld plastic buzzer (its business end, if you will), the mastery of which can make all the difference between walking away with a twenty-five-thousand-dollar grand prize and walking away wishing you hadn't told everyone you know that you were going to be on TV.

Before the taping began (the proceedings weren't going to be broadcast, and no real money was to be given away that day, but the game was taped anyway, to heighten the writers' feelings of excitement, hopefulness, and nausea), an assistant gave the players a brief tutorial in pickle-handling. She stressed the importance of waiting until the host finished asking a question before applying thumb to pickle, and warned that each time it's pressed there's a three-second "lockout," during which any further pressing won't register. This forced silence discourages contestants from frantically pressing the buzzer, machine-gun style—like a kid in class going *Oh oh oh me me me me me!* when the teacher asks a question—and gives the other contestants a chance to have a fair crack at things. Then Marc Summers, the host of "History IQ," came into the studio and greeted the writers, who were lined up on three platforms set just far enough apart to make fist-fights between the competitors difficult. Summers, a youthful-looking man in his late forties with wavy blond hair, has a substantial résumé as a TV host, and is well remembered by the greatest generation's grandchildren for his nearly decade-long association with Nickelodeon's "Double Dare," a game show for kids that featured messy physical challenges and generous dumpings of green slime (an amalgam of vanilla pudding, applesauce, oatmeal, and food coloring) on the little darlings' heads when they answered questions incorrectly.

"History IQ" consists of three rounds, with one contestant being eliminated after each of the first two rounds. In order to shield the identities of the participants, the three seekers after glory shall be referred to here as A, from *Brill's Content*; B, from *Newsweek*; and Killer, from the magazine that was, as those with a high history I.Q. will know, founded in 1925 by Harold Ross. To satisfy himself that their pickle-pushing skills were up to snuff, Summers asked some warmup questions, such as "Who played the part of Fred Mertz on 'I Love Lucy'?" Killer got this one, and seemed well on her way to establishing herself as lord of the pickle, but when the pressure was on—when Summers started asking the real questions—it appeared that A had the best mind-thumb coordination, and he got to answer the first question, which was about Ford's famous fifties dud, the Edsel. In an aside to each other, B and Killer, huddling together for warmth in their cave of failure, confirmed that they, too, knew the answer, and tacitly agreed to blame the equipment. Things were all A and B for a while, and B had an impressive run with some questions related to Caesar (the emperor *and* the salad), but Killer made an unexpected surge when the subject turned to the Dust Bowl, and before B knew what had hit him he was walking away with an empty wallet and a consolatory "History IQ" T-shirt, muttering the kind of thing people in his position always mutter you know, something about how he had to get back to the office anyway, because he had a deadline.

Killer began the second round with four hundred dollars and A with three hundred and fifty, and it would be too cruel to explain in detail exactly how it was that Killer ended the round with a thousand dollars and A with two hundred and fifty. Perhaps it had to do with Killer's having some twenty years on A, or perhaps A was having a problem with his pickle; all that really needs to be said is that by the time a question about the Titanic came around— a subject whose lore Killer happens to know fore and aft—A was beginning to understand how Ernie Els must feel when he's paired up with Tiger Woods.

The third round of "History IQ" is the hardest, or so Killer has reported. After the second-round loser, smiling politely on the outside and crying like a baby on the inside, has been led away, the remaining contestant sits alone at a console with an electronic touch screen on it and attempts, in sixty seconds, to match ten headlines of a given decade with the correct year. Killer's ten head-lines covered the years 1931–40, and she got only three of them right: the years that Prohibition ended (1933), Huey Long was shot (1935), and "The Wizard of Oz" was released (1939). Still, each correct matchup was worth five hundred dollars, so the sting of Killer's ignorance was supplanted almost im-mediately by the glow of having earned twenty-five hundred theoretical dol-lars in a half hour—enough to buy some really nice theoretical clothes or go on a theoretical romantic vacation for two. And Killer, having climbed out of the dustbin of history once, has declared that she could do it again any old time. A and B, however, have not answered calls for a rematch, which, in truth, is completely understandable—they are only human, and there are few among us who could stand losing to a pickle twice.

2 0 0 0

PROVERBS ACCORDING TO
DENNIS MILLER

1. A rolling stone . . . if not acted upon by any force will keep rolling in a straight line at the same speed.

2. Every cloud has . . . water vapor that has the potential of producing ice crystals or raindrops, depending on the Bergeron or coalescence process.

3. The grass is always greener . . . if it receives an adequate supply of $C_{55}H_{70}MgN_4O_6$.

4. A penny saved . . . if doubled every day for two months would be worth more than the combined GNP of the industrialized nations of the world.

5. A bird in the hand . . . is dead or alive, depending on one's will.

6. What goes up   will stay up if it has an escape velocity of 11.3 kilometres per second.

7. When the cat's away . . . the mice will play cautiously if it's Schrödinger's cat.

8. People who live in glass houses . . . are surrounded by a strange hybrid of solid liquids or liquid solids.

9. Nothing is certain but death and . . . Heisenberg's uncertainty principle.

10. There's a time and place . . . but not before the big bang.

2 0 0 0

THE GOODEST GUYS

SOMETIME after midnight, Joe Torre walked slowly into a low-slung "media room" in the bowels of Shea Stadium carrying a flute of champagne. He held his glass with pinkie-out panache, as if he had trained all his life for a role in "Design for Living," but his face registered nothing like serenity or elation. His jowls slumped, his eyes were funereal, red-rimmed. He'd been crying for a while now, unashamed, burying his face in the crook of his arm, hugging his wife, his players, even George Streinbrenner (what a man must do!). Now he eased into his chair with an exhausted old-guy sigh. It was as if this victory—leading the Yankees to their third straight World Series title, the first team to three-peat since the Oakland A's did it, twenty-six years ago—was merely a relief, the relief of not failing.

Where was the crowing? Where was the joy? Even now, flanked by Andy Petitte, who had pitched the night through with such intelligence and gall, and Luis Sojo, the lumpy role player who'd whacked home the winning runs off Al Leiter in the top of the ninth, Torre focussed most keenly not on the highlights, the big hits, but, rather, on the game's slender margins. His hair slick with Mumm's and Bud, the shampoo of champions, he sensed the abyss. With two out in in the bottom of the ninth, the Yanks leading 4–2, and a man on base for the Mets, Mike Piazza had cracked one to center field off the most indomitable man on the Yankee payroll, Mariano Rivera.

"I screamed, 'No!' " Torre said. "It was probably the most scared I've been."

Only when Bernie Williams trotted back nearly to the warning track, looked up into the cool hazy night for the ball, and found it spinning into his glove for the last out—only then could Torre afford to think something other than the worst.

"Anytime Piazza hits a ball in the air, it's a home run in my mind," he said.

It was infinitely worse, of course, down the hall. One after another—Piazza, Leiter, Benny, Fonzie—the Mets tromped heavily through Shea's tunnels. They had that vacant, battle-weary stare you see in First World War prints. They didn't speak, didn't acknowledge their wives, their heartbroken kids. Their steel spikes clicked on the concrete floor.

Bobby Valentine, the Mets manager, answered for them all, but he blamed only himself. He'd left his pitcher in too long. Leiter, like all true starters, had promised his manager everlasting endurance, and so Valentine followed his heart and not the cold logic of the scorecard. "I was wrong," Valentine said. "It was the wrong decision, obviously. If I'd brought somebody else in, they definitely would have gotten the guy out, and we'd still be playing." And then he walked off and hugged the Mets co-owner, Fred Wilpon, hugged him hard, a terrible embrace.

They're amazing, these scenes. No one's died, everyone's rich, it's a kid's game, and yet . . . For a few minutes, for the cameras, partly out of joy, partly from a sense of ritual, the winners douse each other with champagne. They drench the mayor, toast the owner. But it breaks up pretty quickly, and even some of the players, most of them not yet as careworn as Torre, look strung-out, overtired, impatient to go home. It was as if they were beginning to realize that the smell coming up from the locker-room rug was worse than a frat house on a Sunday morning. Enough. "Can't a guy get a shower around here?" Derek Jeter said. It was time to go get lost.

ROGER Clemens tore back the plastic sheeting that covered his locker, grabbed his pants, and said to no one in particular, "This champagne is burning my eyes." And that was pretty much all he'd said in days.

Like it or not, the lasting image of this World Series will undoubtedly be that of Clemens winging that broken bat back at Piazza in the first inning of Game Two. Aesthetes and true fans everywhere will prefer to talk into the night about the more elevated moments: how two of the most brilliant pitching performances of the Series—El Duque's in Game Three and Leiter's in Game Five— were, in fact, defeats; we'll look to Paul O'Neill's triples and masterfully long at-bats, to his helmet-slamming moments of frustration even as he hit for a Series average of .474. But the broken-bat tape is forever. Baseball's Zapruder film, some of the TV guys called it. The next morning, Don Imus was on WFAN joking about the "second-bat theory" and some columnists were talking in terms of a psychotic episode. In the *News*, Mike Lupica referred to Clemens and his "Mike Tyson moment." Some beat writers and columnists for the dailies even felt that Piazza and the Mets had betrayed the imperatives of retribution and machismo in failing to rush the mound and pummel the pulp out of Clemens. "Meek the Mets" was the headline over Wallace Matthews's attack in the *Post*.

The sanest reaction, I thought, came from Piazza himself. For World Series week, Piazza had agreed to an old tabloid tradition. He would "write" a daily column for the *Post;* that is, he would let the paper run his postgame quotes in the form of a bylined article. He was angry, but mainly he was bewildered by the "bizarre" incident; most of all, he resented that the press was asking him why he had not gone after Clemens. Grow up, Piazza counselled the hysterics: "The situation happened. It's done. Argue it left and right. O.K., should I go out and bleeping kill the guy? It's the World bleeping Series and I get suspended, now I can't bleeping play in the World Series. So I go out and kill the guy, I'm bleeping selfish and I look like a hero to some guys. Meanwhile we go out and bleeping lose the World Series 'cause I'm suspended for a couple of games. Anybody else who is not in that position doesn't know what the bleep they're talking about. Sorry about the bleeps. The more I write, the more emotional I get." (Join the bleeping club, Mike.)

"Emotion" was the very word Clemens used to describe his (a) confusion, (b) transgression, (c) regression, (d) all of the above. Ever since Clemens beaned Piazza in July, the great tabloid narrative had been building to this confrontation. He was in a frazzle prior to the game and worse when the first inning ended. Before coming out for the second, Clemens was like an overwrought kid giving himself a "timeout": he went off to a special room to be alone and settle down.

Clemens is thirty-eight now, and he has been tightly wound for as long as he has been in the majors. Lupica's Tyson analogy—with its hint of gnawed-upon ears—is extreme, but Clemens does gear up for his starts like a fighter. To strengthen his hands, he fills a big bowl with uncooked rice and squeezes handfuls of it. His house is filled with exercise machines. Every time he pitches, he comes close to destroying his arm. His freezer is loaded with bags of ice that he uses to stem the inflammation. When Clemens was pitching for the Red Sox, the team's physical therapist, Rich Zawacki, said, "I've never seen a pitcher whose body breaks down the way his does in a game. . . . Basically, we wind up piecing him back together from game to game." And that was ten years ago. "If someone met me on a game day, he wouldn't like me," Clemens told *Sports Illustrated* back then, and things haven't changed at all. "The days in between, I'm the goodest guy you can find. On the day of a game? If I'm watching television with you, I'm not hearing you, and I'm not hearing the television. . . . I want to be relentless. I want to pound guys. Once you pound guys, everything is quicker. I know how it is. I know how I felt those times when I started out against Nolan Ryan or Tom Seaver or Dwight Gooden. I know how guys feel when they face me now."

THE rest of the country, or much of it, according to the TV ratings, thought of the Subway Series as the ballyard equivalent of the Iran-Iraq war: "A pox on 'em both." "At least, one New York team has to lose." That sort of thing. And, truth be told, there were moments that you didn't necessarily want aired west of the Hudson. It was not a source of great pride, for example, to see the governor, George Pataki, sitting in his box at Game One wearing a Yankee sweatshirt and taking as his ballpark refreshment . . . white wine. Nor was there any happy explanation for the way some Yankee fans discovered a rationale for booing Piazza every time he came to bat.

But there were countless true fans, crazed fans, intelligent fans everywhere, all over the city. For Game Five, at Shea, I sat up in the mezzanine near the left-field foul pole. I had on my right a friend who saw his first World Series game in 1941, the Mickey Owen dropped-third-strike game. He had the equanimity of his years, dividing his admiration between O'Neill's twilight struggles and Leiter's march to Waterloo. On my left was a Mets fan, one Joyce Mandelkern, of Port Washington, Long Island, whose comments to her husband all night were so quick and insightful, and whose emotions were so raw, that I couldn't resist getting to know her. She told me that when she watched the Mets at home, she turned off the sound to keep the tension at a manageable level, and that when things got out of control she'd go to her garage and sit in the car.

"Sometimes, it's just too unbearable," she said.

The awful moment came Thursday night at 11:42 P.M. Top of the ninth. Yankees up. Men on first and second. Luis Sojo at bat. Al Leiter readied himself on the mound. Joyce Mandelkern of Port Washington buried her face in her arm.

"I can't watch this!" she said.

Then came the pitch.

2 0 0 0

AN ANALOG TOAST TO THE DIGITAL AGE

IT was name-dropping paradise the other night in the Four Seasons Grill Room, at a party thrown by Toni Goodale—identified in impressively comprehensive publicity handouts as a big-time fund-raising and management consultant for social services, performing arts, education, and whatnot; and as a competitive tennis player, youth hockey coach, and an awful lot more. Her husband, James Goodale, was identified likewise as a big-time First Amendment lawyer, *Times* general counsel during the Pentagon Papers case, Yale grad, and host of the PBS talk show "The Digital Age." The purpose of the party was to celebrate the fifth anniversary of the show.

The ceiling of the Grill Room was covered with thousands of giant balloons, and the floor held a lot of the people who had appeared on Goodale's show discussing such "Digital Age" topics as "Is There a Place for Two Tabloids in N.Y.C.?" (Mort Zuckerman); "If I Were to Do It All Over Again in the Digital Age" (Dan Rather); and "Can an All-Newspaper Company Make It?" (Arthur Sulzberger, Jr.). Right off the bat, the "Digital Age" alumna Robin Byrd turned up, grinning to beat the band and partaking of the lobster and caviar canapés. She was wearing an Austrian-crystal-studded leather bustier, black leather pants, and black patent-leather mules with six-inch stiletto heels.

"This is a great mix," she said enthusiastically, looking around the room and spotting Dan Rather, William Bratton, Howell Raines, Charlie Rose, Peter Duchin, Carl Bernstein, and Kenneth Starr. "It looks like not many are under the age of fifty or sixty. Nobody's talking digital to me," she said. "I was one of Jim's first guests. I pioneered cable twenty-five years ago. Time Warner tried, but failed, to get me off the air. I'm not digital, but I have a Web site and I want to get a Webcam at my house on Fire Island. I could be in my apartment on Sixty-seventh Street and see the ocean waves in front of my house. Otherwise, all that digital means to me is higher electric bills."

Victor Navasky, who is the publisher and editorial director of *The Nation*, and who has an elegant, patriarchal white beard, said he wasn't digital, either: "Everything starts with print on paper." Navasky said that he had assigned one of his students at the Columbia School of Journalism to come to the party. "I asked her to find out if the media élite go to parties with each other in order to do business together," he said. "And, if so, is that a good thing or a bad thing?"

Ben Bradlee was in no mood to consider such philosophical questions. "I'm here because my wife, Sally, was Toni Goodale's roommate at Smith," he said. He opened his hands, spread his fingers, and held them up as though in surrender. "It has nothing to do with the digital age, if that's what we're in. I use my computer only as a word processor. I don't do E-mail or go on-line."

"Me, neither," said Morley Safer, the "60 Minutes" man. "I'm not giving up my typewriter."

"Me, neither," said Avery Corman, the author. "I'm here for Toni. I met her in tennis. She was a fourth in doubles. I'm working on a musical with Cy Coleman about the American Yiddish theatre. But I'm not a computer person. I don't even know anybody at this party except Toni. Who's the new media?"

"Me," answered a skinny young man. He was the youngest-looking person in the room. "Jeffrey Dachis," he said, offering his hand to anyone who would take it. He offered it to Michael Bloomberg, who took it coolly. "I'm Razorfish. C.E.O.," Dachis said.

"Razorfish?" a woman nearby asked. "What is it?"

"We design Web sites for companies," Dachis said.

"I know what you do," Bloomberg said evenly.

Dachis blossomed.

"The digital divide is closing between the haves and the have-nots," a man in a dark suit murmured to the young C.E.O.

Bloomberg turned and headed in the direction of Ben Bradlee and Harold Evans and Tina Brown and Arthur Sulzberger and Tom Brokaw.

A gentleman introduced himself as Tom Goodale, the brother of James. Tom, unlike his sibling, looked well rested, tanned, and carefree. He said that he knew hardly anybody at the party. "I go on cruise ships and dance with all the single ladies," he said. "I don't worry about the digital age. I'm out of it."

Robin Byrd approached, and Tom Goodale stared hard at her bustier.

"Somebody said I was just talking to Kofi Annan," she said. "But I wasn't. It was Carl McCall. Everybody is addressing him as 'Governor.' Is he running, or something?"

"The Goodales are taking the McCalls to St. Bart's after Thanksgiving," somebody said.

James Goodale got up to make a speech. "For a media lawyer, this is media fantasy camp," he said. "My friend Ben Bradlee has been bucking me up by saying, 'Hey, Goodale! There are more people here tonight than watch your show.' " (Much laughter.) He plowed gamely on: "We are truly in the digital age. I like to think I am in the middle of the greatest revolution since the Industrial Revolution." (Much applause.)

Victor Navasky paused at the head of the stairs leading to the exit. He said that his student had reported back to him about whether the media élite did business with one another at parties. The answer, she had told him, was yes, and when she and Navasky were back in class, somebody would decide whether this was a good thing or a bad thing.

2 0 0 0

ABOUT THE TYPE

This book was set in Photina, a typeface designed by José Mendoza in 1971. It is an elegant design with high legibility, and its close character fit has made it a popular choice for use in distinguished magazines and art gallery publications.